Russia Beyond Communism

CCRS SERIES ON
CHANGE IN CONTEMPORARY SOVIET SOCIETY
Nicolai N. Petro, Series Editor

Russia Beyond Communism: A Chronicle of National Rebirth, Vladislav Krasnov

Christianity and Russian Culture in Soviet Society, edited by Nicolai N. Petro

Self-Government and Freedom in Russia, Sergei Pushkarev, with an Introduction by Nicholas V. Riasanovsky

Christianity and Government in Russia and the Soviet Union: Reflections on the Millennium, Sergei Pushkarev, Vladimir Rusak, and Gleb Yakunin

FORTHCOMING

Reflections on Russia, Dmitrii S. Likhachev, translated by Christina Sever, with a Foreword by S. Frederick Starr

Published in cooperation with
the Center for Contemporary Russian Studies,
Monterey Institute of International Studies

Russia Beyond Communism

A Chronicle of
National Rebirth

Vladislav Krasnov

Westview Press
BOULDER • SAN FRANCISCO • OXFORD

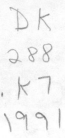
CCRS Series on Change in Contemporary Soviet Society

This Westview softcover edition is printed on acid-free paper and bound in library-quality, coated covers that carry the highest rating of the National Association of State Textbook Administrators, in consultation with the Association of American Publishers and the Book Manufacturers' Institute.

Published in 1991 in the United States of America by Westview Press, Inc., 5500 Central Avenue, Boulder, Colorado 80301, and in the United Kingdom by Westview Press, 36 Lonsdale Road, Summertown, Oxford OX2 7EW

Library of Congress Cataloging-in-Publication Data
Krasnov, Vladislav.
  Russia beyond communism : a chronicle of national rebirth / by
Vladislav Krasnov.
    p. cm. — (CCRS series on change in contemporary Soviet
society)
  ISBN 0-8133-8361-7
  1. Soviet Union—Politics and government—1985–   . 2. Nationalism—
Soviet Union. 3. Patriotism—Soviet Union. I. Title.
II. Series
DK288.K7 1991
947.085′4—dc20   91–17680
                                                                         CIP

Printed and bound in the United States of America

⊗ The paper used in this publication meets the requirements
of the American National Standard for Permanence of Paper
for Printed Library Materials Z39.48-1984.

10   9   8   7   6   5   4   3   2

To the millennium of Russian Christianity

Contents

Chapter Three: Beyond Communism: Voices of Glasnost, 1989   125

Chapter Four: Revolution and Russia   171

Foreword

Vladislav Krasnov's book comes at the right moment to give American readers help in understanding the momentous changes taking place in the Russian heartland of the Soviet Union. What do they portend? When Western eyes were fixed by the media on the Gorbachev phenomenon and the perestroika slogan, Dr. Krasnov was drawing our attention instead to the rapid coming of the "future beyond Gorbachev." His timely analysis looked past the vain attempt of this last of the Soviet Marxian princes at salvaging Communism and on to the new world being born today in the ancestral lands of Russia.

The empire that bore the name of the Union of Soviet Socialist Republics for the past seven decades is disintegrating, and the nations it subjugated are coming back to life with a vengeance. The Russians themselves are taking part in this universal reawakening, reasserting their own personality and wiping away the ideologically imposed Soviet identity. Gorbachev has lost the high ground to the popular Boris El'tsin and will be hard put to get it back. More attuned to the direction of change, the new President of the Russian Federation champions restoration of Russia's sovereignty and democracy without socialism. However, two towering figures, not politicians, but a famed Russian scientist and a Russian writer, inspired the drama of change unfolding before our eyes. Andrei Sakharov fought for more than two decades against the Soviet regime's suppression of human rights and, before his recent death, led the new democratic forces coming to life under Gorbachev's glasnost. Sakharov's death in December 1989 left a spiritual void which is now being filled by the return of Aleksandr

Solzhenitsyn to the fray. This great Russian writer, author of the monumental *Gulag Archipelago*, and, like Sakharov, a moral force to be reckoned with, sounds the trumpet of Russia's national and religious rebirth "from under the rubble" (the title of his prophetic 1974 book) of collapsed Communism.

However, the great issue before us is: Can democracy and the Russian idea together bring forth a civilized and peaceful Russia? Or, will the Russian lands suffer a return to despotism from today's turmoil? Can a midpoint between the extremes of tyranny and anarchy, the twin curses of Russia's past, be found? Can the counterpoint mirrored in a Sakharov and a Solzhenitsyn, between the causes of democracy and national revival, culminate in a felicitous synthesis? Obviously liberty cannot be secured in a political order that denies basic civil and human rights (as Sakharov argued), nor can a people long remain free if as individuals they renounce their inner freedom of moral choice in the knowledge of good and evil (as Solzhenitsyn argued).

Dr. Krasnov shows in his book that there is room for hope for just such a synthesis in this time of change and historic opportunity for the Russian nation. He punctures the false but all too widespread impression lately given currency that Russian patriotism is extremist or anti-Semitic or both. He shows in his survey of a spectrum of new voices that the Russian mainstream has so far remained politically moderate and favors neither a return of empire nor arbitrary rule. It is of utmost importance that we Americans understand this if we are to help and not hinder Russia's struggle to free itself from its totalitarian and despotic past. While the Russian revival cannot be easily effected from outside, it nonetheless lays down a challenge for Americans and their leaders. The revival of Russian national awareness and self-affirmation in its time-honored and natural form is, above all, an indwelling and pacific love of the land and its people. It is by no means inimical to the American vision of a community of nations, each free and self-determining within its sphere. Therefore, we should neither deprive Russian nationalism of our sympathy and support, nor confuse it with extremist fringes seeking to pervert it for malignant purposes. To do so would only dishearten the former and unwittingly abet the latter.

A thoughtful reading of Dr. Krasnov's timely and informative book will assist us in avoiding this pitfall.

Carl A. Linden
Institute for Sino-Soviet Studies
The George Washington University

Preface

Preface

Recent events in the USSR and other Communist countries clearly indicate that world Communism is undergoing the deepest crisis since Lenin founded the first Communist state in Russia in 1917. The crisis is far from over. The worst is yet to come. With dismay and trepidation, Communists and their numerous apologists all over the world are awaiting the resolution. The crisis may well result in the disintegration of the largest Communist empires, the USSR and the People's Republic of China. That would mean the demise of world Communism and its departure from the center stage of world history. The question that ought to be asked now is not whether Communism will depart, but rather how soon and in what manner.

At least one prominent American scholar, Zbigniew Brzezinski, has already pronounced the crisis "terminal" and has predicted the "death" of Communism before the end of this century in his book *The Grand Failure.*[1] I like to believe that his prediction is correct. However, Brzezinski has largely avoided dealing with the more important questions that must be asked: In what manner shall Communism die? Will it be a violent or natural death? A suicide? A transmogrification? Or just a retirement? And--most important of all-- who will be the successors? These are not frivolous questions. For Communism in its agony could be just as dangerous as it was at the height of its global expansion. Considering Communism's past record, these are the million-lives questions. The answers largely depend on whether the West would be able to convince the Communist rulers that they must begin sharing power.

During his tour of the United States in September 1989, Boris El'tsin, the maverick politician[2] who has discovered that opposition to the ruling elite is the best vote-getter in the USSR today, predicted that Mikhail Gorbachev has no more than a year to make perestroika work before a revolution from below will start in earnest. El'tsin may have been self-serving in saying so. But he was right in reminding the West that, contrary to our mass media who have consistently interpreted every move by Gorbachev as a victory for the reformist forces, Gorbachev has been losing control over the rapidly deteriorating economic and political situation.

El'tsin was not alone in his forecast. Since summer 1989, Soviet newspapers have been vocal in pointing out a rapid weakening of Moscow's central authority. Noting the emergence of "dual power" [*dvoevlastie*] in the form of the Politburo and the Supreme Soviet, they warned against its danger, pointing out that the last such dvoevlastie under the Provisional Government ended with its overthrow by the Bolsheviks.[3] Soviet newspapers are now filled with forecasts of apocalyptic doom--not just for the Communist regime or the Soviet Empire but also for the Russian people and their neighbors.

This book is about the demise of Communism in the USSR. It is about a new Russia emerging to succeed the ailing Communist regime. It is about a Russian national (or multinational) alternative to the virtually defunct ideology of Marxism-Leninism on which the "legitimacy" of the current regime has been founded. It is about a gradual but unstoppable withering away of the Communist state. Will it wither to the extent that it will collapse under its own weight, burying beneath it both the Communists and non-Communists, the Russians and non-Russians? Or can it be restructured and reinforced, even if temporarily, to assure safety for all? Isn't perestroika doing just that? It was supposed to, but . . .

Gorbachev may have been right in saying that there is no alternative to perestroika. But an alternative certainly must be found to the way perestroika has been carried out so far. This is a book about achieving national (and multinational) consensus for fundamental change in the system. It is about a peaceful and orderly transformation of the totalitarian regime into a normal nation-state under the rule of law. It is about how to make the succession the least painful for everybody involved, how to diminish ethnic violence and avert the possibility of civil war--in short, how to overcome the forecasts of doom with the tidings of hope.

The rapid pace of events in the USSR has dictated an unusual genre for this book. The title, "Russia Beyond Communism," suggests its futuristic and predictive quality. The subtitle, "A Chronicle of National Rebirth," suggests that some contours of a future Russia are already discernible as they emerge from within. To show the reader what I was able to discern, I had to marshal all the empirical evidence I could find, relying on a large amount of research, drawing from sources on both sides of the Iron Curtain, the remnants of which, alas, continue to obscure and distort our view of the USSR. However, this book is not a chronicle of political events. Rather, it is a "chronicle" of various articles by Soviet authors, which, in my opinion, form milestones on the way toward new Russian national thinking and toward a new Russia.

Vladislav Krasnov

1. Zbigniew Brzezinski, The Grand Failure: The Birth and Death of Communism in the Twentieth Century (New York: Scribners, 1989).

2. El'tsin quit the Party during its twenty-eighth Congress in Moscow in July 1990.

3. As of summer 1990, dvoevlastie has been transformed into mnogovlastie [multi-power], which, in the Soviet context, does not mean a division of power, but rather a collision of powers. The main conflict now seems to be shaping up between Gorbachev's Union government, on the one hand, and the sovereignty-minded republican governments, most notably that of Russia's El'tsin, on the other. For more, see Appendix 3.

Acknowledgments

I am grateful to the Hoover Institution at Stanford University for awarding me a Title VIII State Department grant for the project "Alternative Visions of the Soviet Future," from which this book has evolved. That grant enabled me to use the sabbatical year 1987-1988 for research and writing. Special thanks to Dr. Nicolai Petro, former director of the Center for Contemporary Russian Studies (CCRS) at the Monterey Institute of International Studies, for his support and encouragement. Thanks are also due to Dr. Nicholas Vaslef, former director of Radio Liberty's USSR Division, for giving me the opportunity to do research at Radio Liberty's Samizdat Archives in Munich, and to William Bowen and Tom Pauken of Dallas, Texas, for making my research trip there possible. The Earhart Foundation's research fellowship enabled me to complete the project. Donald W. Treadgold of the University of Washington, Carl Linden and Franz Michael of George Washington University, and Edward E. Ericson, Jr., of Calvin College, read my manuscript and made valuable suggestions. Many thanks to Cameron Binkley, Paul Palumbo, Peter Schultz, and Polly Wirtz for proofreading and comments. Rebecca Ritke of Westview Press was very helpful in the final preparation stages. Finally, I am indebted to CCRS research associate Christina Sever for overall editing and formatting of the book.

Final responsibility for possible errors rests, of course, with me.

V. K.

Introduction

WHY NOT AN ALTERNATIVE?

The major reason for the seeming stability, up until recently, of the present Soviet regime is the absence of a constructive alternative to Marxist-Leninist doctrine, which "legitimizes" this regime. Fully aware of that, Soviet leaders have spared no effort to prevent such an alternative from emerging. Using the enormous resources of Soviet propaganda, they have tried for generations to inculcate into every Soviet citizen the idea that there is not, and cannot be, any other future but a Communist one for the country and the world. Not only did they suppress all free discussion of alternative visions among Soviet citizens, but they largely succeeded in convincing the rest of the world that the very idea of a non-Communist future is outlandish. They were less successful with their own citizens. Undaunted by suppression at home and indifference abroad, Soviet defectors, dissidents and emigres have been searching for an alternative to the Communist doctrine for a long time.

It is understandable why Soviet leaders, until recently, were anxious to suppress all searching for an alternative to Marxism-Leninism. After all, their mandate for dictatorial rule is based largely on that ideology. But why hasn't the free world, in particular the United States and its Western allies, been searching for an alternative to Communism? Why have those free to think, to see and to dream not been thinking, looking, and dreaming beyond the system that vowed to destroy them? The reasons are many and complex, and it is

1

out of place to discuss them here. But two major reasons need to be identified.

The first has to do with the falsity of our fundamental assumptions about Communism. One such widely held assumption was that Communism was a "progressive" force for modernization, democratization and even Westernization.[1] Based on that assumption, we further assumed that, whenever the Communists took over, they somehow expressed a "popular will" without having to subject themselves to the test of popular vote. Indulging in our own self-righteousness and condescension toward others, we lulled ourselves into a wishful thinking that even though Communism might not be exactly the wave of the future for the Western nations, refined and steeped in democratic traditions, it had come to stay among the lesser breeds of mankind, such as the Russians and the Chinese, the Vietnamese and the Cubans, or even the *East* Germans (as if they were inferior to *West* Germans). Yet another assumption was that, brutal and uncouth as they might be, the Communists somehow assured stability in the countries they ruled, and consequently contributed to world peace.

The second major reason was the fallacy of our thinking--to the extent that we thought at all--about what might happen to a Communist country after the Communist "order" was gone. Take the USSR, for instance. At this point, we actually stopped thinking rationally at all. Alas, our rational thought was displaced not by a euphoria of hope, but by an Alfred Hitchcock nightmare. Among the horrors of post-Communist Russia, we imagined such scenes as the restoration of tsarist despotism and Orthodox theocracy, the triumph of Russian chauvinism, the return of the "Black Hundreds" and anti-Jewish pogroms, the bacchanalia of an anti-Communist "witchhunt" presided over by a Russian Joseph McCarthy, who would certainly put to shame not only the American senator but also the Georgian Joseph Stalin. The vision of the Russian hordes marching to India via the Persian Gulf to fulfill the "secret testament" of Tsar Peter completed the nightmare. We woke up to the "sober" realization that it was the Russians, not the Communists, who were our true enemies. After all, we knew the Communists by their Marxist scriptures, while the Russians were, are, and will remain a riddle and a mystery wrapped up inside an enigma. In short, the Communists are the enemy we love to hate. So why bother to think beyond Communism at all?

The above two reasons have effectively prevented Western strategic planning, "Beyond Communism."[2] Although they were largely of our own making, it was certainly in the interest of the KGB to perpetuate them. All the KGB's "agents of influence" had to do was to massage our "reasons" until they became deeply entrenched and virtually unassailable misconceptions.[3] The left-liberal dominance over much of the West's mass media and academic establishment assured the perpetuation of two hysterical equations: (1) of Communism with "progress," "humanism" and "striving for peace," and (2) of anti-Communism with "fascism," "anti-Semitism," "war-mongering," "religious fanaticism," and "reaction." With these two equations becoming cliches, planting a seed of poisonous disinformation here, choking a few sprouts of information there, and cultivating ignorance and paranoia (about Russia) everywhere, that was all that the KGB needed to do the trick.

Based on these fundamental misconceptions, Western leaders concluded that the only realistic goal the West could strive for was to achieve some kind of accommodation with the Communist rulers. It was envisioned that such an accommodation might include nuclear arms control, partial disarmament, and the division of the world into spheres of influence. What the West wanted most of all was to stop Communist expansion into "our" territory. (As to their expansion in the Third World, we were willing to accept it as fair play.) In our most daring moments, we insisted on their showing some progress in the area of human rights, such as increased emigration (mostly Jewish) and the release of dissidents from insane asylums. We were all too willing to accommodate Communist rulers, over the heads of their citizenry, with increased credits, trade and transfer of technology to help them to consolidate their system. We just hoped that such accommodations would buy some time for their system to evolve into Communism "with a human face."

As long as Western strategy was committed to such a minimal goal, Soviet rulers from Lenin and Stalin to Brezhnev and Andropov did not have to bother about their dictatorship being threatened from the outside. They knew how to exploit our desire for peace by extorting more and more concessions from us. With a constant threat of expansion, they blackmailed us into helping them offset an increasing pressure for change from within. They knew that, as long as Communism continued to be associated, in the prevalent Western opinion, with such virtues as "progress," "stability" and "striving for peace," they could count on being bailed out of their economic difficulties with Western credits, loans, and technology transfers. And when pressure from within made opting for reforms unavoidable, the Communist reformers, Deng Xiaoping and Gorbachev, knew that they could count on Western support.

Both Deng and Gorbachev unequivocally stated that the chief purpose of their reforms was consolidation of the Communist system. Both knew that this would not discourage Western help, as long as a "progressive" shingle, "Reform Communism" (or "market socialism"), was put out. What neither the two reformers nor the West realized was that the system they were trying to reform is both unpopular and unworkable. It is also irredeemable; it cannot be reformed, unless the reforms lead out of it and away from it. Recent events in China, Central (or Eastern) Europe and the USSR proved just that. They showed that the people in the Communist countries want not reforms of the system, but reforms out of the system. That means "Beyond Communism." They thus made a shambles of the Western strategy predicated on the assumption of Communism's popularity and longevity.

BEYOND-COMMUNISM DREAMERS

The chief obstacle to the KGB-sponsored Communism-forever propaganda was not the West, but Soviet citizens. They refused to accept the notion that their lot could be improved only under Communism. They could not stop thinking "Beyond Communism." After failing to eradicate *samizdat* and *tamizdat* publications, the most the KGB could do was to bar their authors, the Beyond-Communism dreamers, from access to Western policy-makers and the Western public. It largely succeeded in isolating the "dreamers" from Western governments. Western radio stations broadcasting in Russian certainly did not indulge in projections beyond Communism. Moreover, even though some "dreams" did appear in English translation, the KGB largely succeeded in isolating them from Western media and the academic press.

Even in the early 1980s when the stench of stagnation in the gerontocratic Politburo reeked all the way across the Atlantic, there was no Western government, nor reputable Western university, that was willing to sponsor a conference on the future "Beyond Communism." Only in August 1985, a few months after Gorbachev's ascent to power, was such a conference finally put together. Taking place in Geneva, Switzerland, it brought together, for the first time, Western sovietologists and a number of prominent Soviet emigres and defectors. For several days these futurists discussed "The Fall of the Soviet Empire: Prospects for Transition to a Post-Soviet World."

The most remarkable thing about the conference was that it took place at all. It was sponsored by the Professors' World Peace Academy (PWPA), and among its chief organizers were two prominent scholars, Dr. Alexander Shtromas, a Soviet emigre, and Dr. Morton Kaplan of the University of Chicago. However, as soon as it was discovered that the PWPA was affiliated with Rev. Sun Myung Moon's Unification Church (which affiliation was indicated only in small print in the invitational package), many scholars who had originally accepted the invitation, cancelled their plans, some under pressure created by negative publicity in the mass media. Some of them did so for fear of harming their academic careers by the association, however indirect, with a Moon-funded enterprise. Rev. Moon, it must be remembered, was commonly described in the mass media as a "rabid anti-Communist." Some felt that having their trip paid by the Moon organization would somehow jeopardize academic freedom. Still others objected to being sponsored by a "cult."

At any rate, after the speakers who withdrew were replaced by people who were not afraid of being dubbed "anti-Communist," the conference did take place. But the specter of anti-anti-Communist hysteria continued to haunt it. So unprecedented was its topic that, ignoring the fact that virtually all participants were bona fide scholars, the *Tribune de Geneve* described the conference as a "weird gathering" of the "rightist fringe" and the "extreme right of the world Jewish community." (The latter was apparently a reference to the fact that a number of organizers and participants were of Jewish origin, many of them Soviet emigres). Bad publicity notwithstanding, the conference proved to be a success. It may go down in history as the only exception to the absence of foresight and imagination that has distinguished Western attitudes toward Communism. It resulted in a series of volumes, *The Soviet Union and the Challenge of the Future*, in which some of the changes occurring now in the USSR were anticipated and predicted.[4]

I had the honor of being a participant in that conference due to the withdrawal of one of the invited speakers. I was asked to review various visions of the Soviet future offered by Soviet dissidents. The resultant paper was entitled "Images of the Soviet Future: The Emigre and Samizdat Debate."[5] The "images," or alternative visions, included in my paper ranged across a wide ideological spectrum--from Marxist, socialist, and Westernist to liberal, "capitalist," conservative and neo-Slavophile. Pointing out that Soviet defectors, dissidents and emigres have been searching for an alternative to Communism for a long time, I focused chiefly on a futurist debate that had raged since 1968. That was the year when Andrei Sakharov, in a search for socialism with a human face, released his memorandum, *Progress, Peaceful Coexistence and Intellectual Freedom*, for samizdat circulation and publication abroad. A number of well-known authors, such as Andrei Amal'rik (*Will the Soviet Union Survive Until 1984?*), Vladimir Bukovskii, Valerii Chalidze, Anatolii Fedoseev, Igor' Glagolev, Vladimir Maximov, Roy Medvedev, Iurii Orlov, Vladimir Osipov, Igor' Shafarevich, Sergei Soldatov, Aleksandr Solzhenitsyn, Lev Timofeev and Valentin Turchin took part in that debate. Defying Soviet state borders, the debate has continued for years.

In summing up my findings, I classified the visions into twelve distinct categories. In spite of considerable differences in philosophical inspiration--from Marxism, socialism and anarchism to Russian nationalism and pro-Western capitalism--there were large areas of consensus among the twelve. All of them (1) found the present totalitarian Soviet system unworkable and destined to be either completely replaced or fundamentally changed; (2) saw the need for democratization as the first step out of the impasse; (3) tended to agree that a future Russia cannot simply adopt a ready-made Western-style democracy but needs to find its own "Third Way" between capitalism and socialism, the West and the East; (4) favored a mixed economy encompassing private, cooperative, and state enterprise; (5)

affirmed the right of self-determination, including secession, for national minorities (the only exception was the "true Marxist-Leninist," Roy Medvedev); (6) advocated the cessation of the nuclear arms race and the establishment of friendly relations with the West; and (7) insisted on evolutionary and non-violent methods of attaining their goals.

I concluded that virtually all non-Communist alternatives to the present regime "are not only compatible with the interests of the free world, but promise to eliminate exactly those features of the present regime which inherently make it an enemy of peace, freedom, and human dignity. A future Russia may never become a copy of Western democracies, but it will certainly be their friend and partner in creating a better world." While praising all authors as a group, I made clear my preference for those who emphasized the need for a Russian national and religious revival. I particularly singled out Solzhenitsyn's 1973 *Letter to the Soviet Leaders*, in which a program of reforms similar to that of Gorbachev's perestroika was eloquently urged. Solzhenitsyn's proposals included *glasnost*, ideological pluralism, democratization, an enhanced role for the local Soviets, freedom of religion, economic restructuring, ecological prudence, the end of Soviet imperialism, and the right of secession for national minorities.

What especially distinguished Solzhenitsyn's proposals was their practicality. Unlike the others, he realized that totalitarianism could not be done away with at once, even if Soviet leaders wanted to do so. He did not ask Soviet leaders to relinquish their power. Instead, he suggested a compromise. As long as they were willing to start dismantling the totalitarian features of the Soviet state, they could stay in power. Solzhenitsyn's pragmatism was especially evident in that he envisioned a transitional stage, a sort of authoritarian Communism during which the Communist Party would remain in charge. Whether Gorbachev intended it or not, this is the stage in which the country actually finds itself right now. The only condition which the Soviet leaders had to meet was to make clear that they no longer were guided by the precepts of Marxist-Leninist ideology and put Russia's national interests ("patriotism") above their partisan interests. Should the Soviet leaders agree to such a condition, national compromise and reconciliation would be possible, Solzhenitsyn suggested. These in turn would guarantee the preservation of civil order and the stability of the country as a whole.

Pointing out that Solzhenitsyn's approach "has the potential to appeal to the largest possible democratic constituency, the Russian people," I concluded that not only does it constitute a constructive alternative to the Soviet regime, but it "has the best chance to succeed."

> All negative demographic trends notwithstanding, ethnic Russians will continue to be the largest bloc of potential voters for the foreseeable future. When combined with the millions of Ukrainians and Belorussians of Orthodox Christian background, that bloc would command if not a majority then an overwhelming plurality for a long time.

Emphasizing the need for the Soviet leaders to abandon their partisan interests in favor of Russia's national interests, Solzhenitsyn's *Letter* certainly contained the fundamentals of a Russian national alternative to the totalitarian Communist state.

TOWARD SOLZHENITSYN'S PATH

The development of Soviet society since 1985 fully confirms the vitality of Solzhenitsyn's approach. In fact, perestroika itself may be seen as a belated and grossly inadequate response to the contingencies that Solzhenitsyn so eloquently pinpointed in his *Letter*. The chief reason for the failure of perestroika is that Gorbachev and his associates have not yet abandoned the illusion that a national consensus can be achieved on the basis of Marxism-Leninism, to which the Party remains formally committed. Gorbachev may be right in saying that there is no alternative to perestroika. But as the Party-sponsored perestroika has obviously run its course and reached a dead end, an alternative to the way it has been carried out must be found.

Although this book was originally conceived as a critical evaluation of various alternative visions, by the end of 1987 I became convinced that no such evaluation was needed, because the Russian national alternative already had clearly shown the greatest vitality. It became obvious that the policy of glasnost would inevitably lead to a *de facto* abolition of the Marxist-Leninist ideological monopoly, the key demand of Solzhenitsyn's *Letter*. It became equally clear that the vacuum left behind would be naturally filled not by any particular political ideology, be it Western-style socialism, free-market capitalism, liberalism or "Communism with a human face," but by a revival of national-democratic and patriotic sentiments among all peoples of the USSR, especially the Russians, on whom the future of the country depends most.

The basic conception of this book was crystallized in a speech entitled "Beyond Gorbachev: A New Russia," which I gave before the Alaska World Affairs Council in Anchorage on February 12, 1988. In that speech I noted that "even though perestroika is usually associated with Gorbachev, he does not own it. The tide of change is sweeping in the USSR; it obeys its own momentum, and it may take us into a future beyond Gorbachev." The general tendency in the development of reforms was clearly "from ideological to spiritual, from 'internationalist' to national, from formal to non-formal, from rigid to spontaneous, from Marxism-Leninism to no 'isms' at all, from *Partia* to *Patria*, from things Communist to things Russian." Pointing out that Western observers have either ignored that tendency or focused on its least fortunate manifestations, such as the judophobic rhetoric of *Pamyat* (a non-formal group of Russian nationalist zealots), I called that tendency "the most hopeful development during the last three years." "The country [Gorbachev] rules seems to be irrevocably drifting toward Solzhenitsyn's path," I concluded.

THE PURPOSE

Since the Alaska speech so many important events have occurred in the USSR that they suggest a degree of intellectual unrest unprecedented in Soviet history. In fact, they have snowballed so fast that even the most prodigious Western sovietologists cannot keep track of them, much less analyze or respond to them. Three things are clear, however. First, the USSR, the matrix of the world Communist movement, is facing today an extremely grave and all-pervading crisis. It is not just an economic crisis, but also a political, ideological, inter-ethnic, and moral one. Second, unless a way is found soon for a fundamental and peaceful change of the system beyond Communism, the current crisis will inevitably lead to a catastrophe of apocalyptic proportions. Third, there already exists in the USSR an intellectual climate for fundamental change far beyond what most sovietologists ever predicted or expected: beyond the one-party system. That means moving beyond Communism as we have known it since 1917. This book is motivated by the urgency of finding a solution for the current Soviet crisis before it degenerates into such an apocalyptic catastrophe.

Gorbachev and his associates did not cause this crisis. Rather they recognized it and made it public by proclaiming the necessity of reforms. However, their belated, sometimes half-hearted, and always timid efforts have only increased both the expectations and the frustrations across the width and breadth of the Soviet Empire. This twin combination is explosive indeed. It is a recipe for revolution. A time is approaching when the twin emotional charges, of expectations and frustrations, might reach a critical mass sufficient to start a chain reaction and a revolutionary explosion, the consequences of which for the peoples of the USSR and the rest of the world are inestimable. It is in the interests of all to avert such an explosion. It is in the interests of all to prevent the "building of socialism," which, Soviet leaders now admit, needs a fundamental restructuring, from suddenly collapsing on the rulers and the ruled, Communists and non-Communists, Russians and non-Russians.

It is in the interests of both the rulers and the ruled to find an alternative to the present Soviet system, which has proved to be both unworkable and unreformable, and which now threatens stability in that part of the world. The time of mere dissidence aimed at greater respect for human rights within the existing system is over. The time of open opposition to the existing regime has just begun. And the question is: Will the government and the opposition find a common language for preventing the breakdown of civil order and the collapse of the building of the state? Will a formula for a national consensus in solving the country's crisis be found? Will the opposition be loyal to the government and play a constructive role? Or will the two be set on a collision course?

In the latter case the chances for a peaceful solution of the crisis will greatly diminish. Therefore, the creation of a positive alternative to the one-party system and to the unitary structure of the "Union" should have the highest priority on the national agenda. There are signs that some members of the Party establishment and, perhaps, Gorbachev himself realize the urgency of finding such an alternative. Unfortunately, despite considerable progress achieved under the policy of glasnost, conditions of a totalitarian society--which the USSR still is-- are such that opportunities for an open discussion of alternatives to Communism remain rather limited. Yet, there is no dearth of Beyond-Communism thinkers among leading Soviet intellectuals, including Party members. An increasing number of them express ideas similar to those of Solzhenitsyn and other protagonists of a Russian national alternative.[6]

The purpose of this book is then two-fold: first, to acquaint Western readers with the depth and range of Soviet thinking "Beyond Communism" and, second, to introduce them to thinking along the lines of a Russian national alternative. It is my hope that the book will correct the Western misconceptions about both Communism and Russia which I discussed earlier. Further, I hope that the book will prompt Soviet authors to freely express their views, without having to look back at the restraints and limitations implicit in the policy of glasnost.

The articles I have selected form milestones on the way of emancipation of Soviet society from the yoke of Marxism-Leninism. Collectively they represent a genuine new thinking, in contradistinction to that largely phony "new thinking" which Gorbachev pushes on the West and which basically is old Marxist-Leninist wine in new bottles. I shall try to demonstrate a growing acceptance in the USSR of the idea that, for the sake of saving the country from the worst, the present system, based on utopian Marxist-Leninist dogmas, must be allowed to evolve beyond Communism. I shall argue that such an evolution cannot proceed without a rebirth of Russia's national heritage. Insofar as the intellectual emancipation from Communism is often paralleled by a rediscovery of Russia's pre-Communist heritage, the book may be read then as a chronicle of Russian national rebirth.

A POLYPHONIC CHOIR

The book's organization reflects this dual process of intellectual emancipation and national rebirth. As a rule, Soviet authors are presented in chronological order, with the more recent ones taking an increasingly radical stance.

The book consists of five chapters. Chapter 1, "Beyond Gorbachev," will set the major themes for the book. It consists of three pieces. The 1988 Alaska speech, "Beyond Gorbachev: A New Russia," in which I first set forth the idea that Gorbachev's perestroika will inevitably lead to the emergence of a new post-Communist Russia, the Russia of Solzhenitsyn, may serve as a sort of preview for the book. The essay, "Solzhenitsyn's 1973 Blueprint For Reforms," recapitulates the main ideas of his *Letter to the Soviet Leaders*. Unacknowledged by Soviet leaders and ignored by Western policy-makers, the *Letter* is treated as the original blueprint for fundamental reforms, of which Gorbachev's perestroika is but a pale and distorted copy. The third piece is devoted to Solzhenitsyn's latest pamphlet, *How Can We Make Russia Livable?*, in which the exiled novelist has re-formulated the ideas of his previous *Letter* to suit the country's present circumstances. I treat the pamphlet primarily as an intellectual and cultural event which may well serve as a catalyst for a new alignment of political and social force that is necessary to bring about the birth of the new Russia.

Chapter 2, "Beyond Marxism-Leninism: Voices of Glasnost 1987-1988," is a survey of articles by more than a dozen Soviet authors. Directly or indirectly, they challenge Gorbachev's assertions that perestroika has been inspired by the ideas of Marxism-Leninism and that the country's problems can be solved on the basis of its present socialist system. Some of these authors express ideas that are considerably closer to those of Solzhenitsyn than either Lenin or Marx. Collectively, these "voices of glasnost" form, as it were, a polyphonic choir whose repertoire goes far beyond the restrictions of "socialist pluralism" that Gorbachev prescribed as mandatory. They represent a genuine non-Marxist new thinking, often of a distinctly Russian national orientation.

Chapter 3, "Beyond Communism: Voices of Glasnost 1989," is a continuation of the former. It offers an overview of the latest manifestations of Russian cultural rebirth. As in the previous chapter, the authors were deliberately chosen from different ideological camps. Their articles reflect a radicalization among Soviet intellectuals along the lines of what Solzhenitsyn has called Russian national and religious rebirth. They evince a growing realization that the Soviet Empire has been far more "evil" toward its own people than has been commonly suspected in the free world. They make clear that Soviet economic, inter-ethnic, and ecological problems cannot be solved without a thorough rejection of the entire Communist system. Compared to the authors in Chapter 2, the 1989 authors show a stronger tendency toward new thinking in terms of creating a Russian national alternative to the Communist regime.

Chapter 4, "Russia and Revolution," is a case study of the ideological schism that has polarized Soviet intellectuals in the wake of glasnost. It is devoted to a public debate between two prominent Soviet intellectuals, Vadim Kozhinov, reputed to be a Russian nationalist, and Benedikt Sarnov, reputed to be a liberal Westernist. Although they discuss such traditional Russian questions as "Whose fault?" and "What needs to be done?", the chief animus of the debate has to do with the respective roles of Jews and Russians in the Communist revolution. The two are sharply divided on the issue of "Russian anti-Semitism." The chapter consists of two parts. In the first part, the major arguments of this debate are reviewed. The second part consists of my own extensive commentary, based on a number of Western sources, unavailable to the two Soviet debaters.

Chapter 5, "Toward a New Russia: Building an Infrastructure," deals with the latest developments in the USSR in regard to the "Russian problem." Reflecting a change in the official attitude (evinced in concessions to the Russian Orthodox church and the Politburo decision to publish Russian non-Marxist philosophers, for example), these latest developments include a number of public initiatives aimed at building an infrastructure of a future Russian state. In retrospect it seems clear that both Boris El'tsin's election to the Russian presidency and the subsequent proclamation of Russia's sovereignty have been prepared and facilitated by these early initiatives.

As an author, I aim to give a hearing, before an American audience, to as many "voices" of Russian national thinking as possible. I endeavor to mediate, as it were, between three distinct political cultures: (1) the American on the one hand, (2) the declining Soviet and (3) the emerging Russian on the other. Besides the Introduction and Conclusion, my authorial "voice" will predominate only in Chapter 1. In the remainder of the book my role will be limited to that of an observer. While letting others speak up, I will limit myself to explaining some linguistic problems, such as the use of Aesopean language by Soviet authors, which inevitably arise in the conditions of a Marxist-Leninist monopoly. Although I have arranged, as it were, these voices to be heard across the Atlantic, I have done so only as an impresario or, perhaps, a conductor, rather than as a composer. I treat those voices as an integral part of a polyphonic choir. They may sing in different tones, but they have a number of tunes in common. I have not written those songs. But I have intoned a number of their leitmotifs. One of them will be recognized as a funeral dirge, for Communism. Another is a requiem for an old Russia that was slain. A third one heralds that the arrival of a new Russia is imminent.

In conclusion, I shall summarize the main achievement of the above "concert." Assessing the chances of transformation of the Soviet system into a new polity, I will offer a few suggestions for Gorbachev and U.S. foreign policy-makers as to how such a transformation can be achieved in the least painful way. Although the main focus of the book is on the Russian national alternative, I hope to pave the way for a wide-open discussion, both in the West and in the East, of whatever constructive alternatives to Communism may have a realistic chance to peacefully succeed it.

The book is supplied with three appendixes, containing published articles of mine. The paper, "Pamyat: A Force for Change?", which I presented at the AAASS conference in Honolulu, Hawaii, in November 1988, deals with the controversial group of Russian nationalist extremists. Treating Pamyat as a marginal phenomenon, I argue that the best antidote to Pamyat's judophobic rhetoric lies not in a blanket condemnation of Russian nationalism but in recognition of its legitimate aspirations as articulated by such people as Solzhenitsyn and Likhachev. The second appendix is a newspaper column, "Why Not Solzhenitsyn?," in which I argue, by analogy with Czecho-Slovakia, Poland and Hungary, that in Russia "no one is better qualified for the role of a national leader than the Nobel Prize winning novelist." The third appendix, the article "From Communism's Red Flag to Russia's Tricolor," is devoted to what I regard as the main political event of 1990, the election of Boris El'tsin to the Russian Federation presidency and the subsequent proclamation of the republic's sovereignty.

CONCEPTS AND TERMINOLOGY

A few words about the conceptual framework and key terminology used in this book. First of all, I regard the present polity of the USSR as fundamentally totalitarian. More precisely, it is Left Totalitarian. It is totalitarian in political structure (one-party system), in economy (state ownership of most means of production), in governmental structure (no division of powers), and in the unitary structure of the multi-national "Union" (the dominance of the Russian-speaking central authority). Until recently, it was totalitarian *de jure* because its constitution guaranteed the "leading role" for the Party.

To be sure, Gorbachev has demonstrated a considerable departure from totalitarian mentality by embarking on the path of reforms. One might say that he has thus initiated an authoritarian phase of Soviet history. By authoritarian methods he has managed to democratize the system more than any previous Soviet leader. But even though Gorbachev's reforms have undermined some of its pillars, the totalitarian structure of the Soviet Union remains basically intact. Moreover, Gorbachev's own attitude toward the totalitarian system remains ambiguous. Does he want to mend or to dismantle it? On the one hand, he said in his book that perestroika was intended only for restructuring, not dismantling, the existing system. On the other hand, he has lately been assuring his audience that his reforms are aimed at changing the Soviet system "radically and fundamentally." In my view, no reforms in the USSR can be radical or fundamental enough unless they are aimed at dismantling the entire totalitarian structure.

It is meaningless to analyze the current political situation in the USSR in terms of people being for or against perestroika. It makes more sense to analyze it in terms of support for different concepts of perestroika. As one Soviet author put it, there are at least two perestroikas going on at the same time. One is perestroika-coercion (*perestroika-prinuzhdenie*), the other, perestroika-liberation (*perestroika-osvobozhdenie*). The former, organized from above, is being pushed on the people. The latter is a spontaneous response by the people below. They are becoming more and more emboldened to assert their rights by taking advantage of the rulers' being divided, nervous, and confused. There can be no doubt that, while the goal of the "coercionists" is to repair the cracks in the totalitarian system, the goal of "liberationists" is to dismantle it.

Gorbachev appears to straddle the fence between the two camps. In his book, *Perestroika: New Thinking for Our Country and the World*, Gorbachev called the program of reforms he initiated a "revolution." Lest his readers might associate the word "revolution" with some frivolous ideas, Gorbachev explained that he was talking about a "revolution from above," that is, "profound and essentially revolutionary changes implemented on the initiative of the authorities themselves, but necessitated by objective changes in the situation and in social moods."[7]   Then, as if in an afterthought, he added that perestroika is at the same time a "revolution from below," which fact best guarantees "its success and irreversibility."   Gorbachev clearly wished to pay lip-service to Lenin, from whom he borrowed the two expressions.   Yet this was also an indirect acknowledgment of the impotence of perestroika-coercion, which could prolong the agony of the regime, but which cannot make the people work.

Now Gorbachev clearly has more on his hands than what he bargained for when he solicited the "revolution from below." As long as Gorbachev refuses to state unequivocally that he wants to dismantle, not repair, the totalitarian system, his "revolution from above" will be equated with perestroika-coercion. If so, it will be negated rather than helped by the "revolution from below." It is to the latter that this book is dedicated, even though I prefer to see it as a rapid evolutionary process rather than a revolution, much less a civil war.

Conditions of totalitarian society render largely inoperative the conventional terminology for describing a political situation or a spectrum of ideological views.   Such words as "right" and "left," "conservative" and "liberal" are of little help in the USSR today. Sometimes they are downright misleading.   Therefore, I find it more useful to describe a Soviet person's political views in terms of adherence to perestroika-coercion or perestroika-liberation.   In addition, I would use another criterion for defining one's views, namely: What does one see as the ultimate goal of perestroika, the good of the Communist Party or the good of the country?   This question is reducible to the choice of one's priorities: *Partia* or *Patria*?

The main ideological line dividing Soviet people today is that between the *partiots* and the *patriots*. The *partiots* are those who see the ultimate goal of reforms as strengthening the Communist system. The *partiots* may be ready for "radical" reforms, but only as long as the Marxist-Leninist one-party system remains intact. These *partiots* do not need to be Party members, even though the majority of them are. But aren't these *partiots* basically internationalists? Perhaps they are, but only in the perverted Marxist sense of being committed to international Communism. They have nothing to do with real internationalism as the term is commonly understood in the free world, that is, in the sense of commitment to international cooperation rather than to a political doctrine. Thus, there are many *partiots*, usually of Russian origin, in the non-formal group Interfront ("Internationalist Front"), which is opposed to the national liberation movements in the Baltic republics and which purports to defend the interests of the Russian-speaking minorities there. Soviet soldiers who fought in Afghanistan were always called "internationalists" in the official Soviet press because they allegedly performed their "internationalist duty" of helping to spread Communism.

The *patriots*, on the other hand, see the ultimate goal of reforms as the good of the country, regardless of whether the present system survives or not. Some of them might still believe in Communism and be Party members, but they would not hesitate to abandon both if they were to discover, as some have, that the Party, in its present totalitarian structure, is either unable or unwilling to subordinate itself to the interests of the country.[8] The question would naturally arise: What does Patria refer to? Armenia? Lithuania? Russia? It could be each of these, or any other place which a person regards as the land of his fathers. It could even refer to the Soviet Union as a whole, but not to its political or economic system. In my view, there are many Armenian, Lithuanian, and Russian *patriots*, and their number is rapidly growing; but there are fewer and fewer "Soviet *patriots*," as they are called in the Russian Sovietese language. However, since this book is devoted to Russian national problems, the term *patriots* refers primarily to the Russian *patriots* whom I will also call the *Russites*.[9]

They could also be called Russian nationalists. However, although I have occasionally used the term, I have done so only reluctantly. There are two reasons for this reluctance. The first has to do with current usage of the term "nationalist" in English. While the "nationalism" of smaller nations is usually tolerated, often excused, sometimes sympathized with, and occasionally admired, "Russian nationalism" usually evokes negative emotions. Some people equate it with "chauvinism" and worse. The second reason has to do with the Russian Sovietese language, in which all nationalisms within the USSR, including Russian nationalism, have been regarded as "bourgeois" and subversive. Until recently, the term was actually incriminating and could earn a jail sentence to anyone so labelled. Understandably, many Soviet citizens eschew being called nationalists, even though some of them feel they are. Under the circumstances, for me to call my Soviet authors "nationalists" would be tantamount to informing on them. For the above two reasons, I prefer to call them either Russites or *patriots*.

The reader should be aware, however, that when I occasionally call them nationalists, it is only because I regard nationalism as a major liberating force against the totalitarian Soviet system.[10] This applies equally to Armenians, Estonians, Jews, Russians, etc. Of course, there are bigots, extremists, and chauvinists among all nationalities, including the Russians. There are certainly some Russites who agree with the *partiots* on the need to preserve the Soviet Empire. However, the majority (and their number is growing) are more concerned with the survival of the Russian nation and its consolidation on a smaller territory. Such Russites should be able to find a common language with all other *patriots*, regardless of nationality, as to how the empire could be peacefully undone.

Notes

1. The persistence of this never substantiated assumption is largely due to the susceptibility of Western intellectuals to Marxist and other Left Totalitarian teachings. Julien Benda has called it "the treason of the intellectuals." Jean-Francois Revel has called it "the totalitarian temptation." Paul Hollander in his book, Political Pilgrims: Travels of Western Intellectuals to the Soviet Union, China, and Cuba 1928-1978 (New York: Oxford University Press, 1981), has shown how "the best and the brightest" of the West have succumbed to worshiping Communism. No amount of empirical evidence could disabuse them from praising Stalin and other Communist dictators. Faced with the tragic failure of Communism in one country after another, they have been merely changing the destination of pilgrimage from the USSR in the 1930s to Mao's China in 1960s, Cuba in the 1970s, Vietnam, Albania, Angola and Nicaragua in

the 1980s. Alas, most of these "pilgrims" never thought of themselves as Communists, nor were they known as such. Among them were many outstanding Western writers, artists, scholars, and even conservative politicians and clergymen. In fact, Hollander's "scroll of pilgrims" reads like a "Who's Who" of the Western cultural establishment. One major reason why the Communist Utopia has stayed in power for so long and with such a devastating effect on the East was precisely that so many leading Western intellectuals have lent their talents, names, and authority to sustaining it.

2. A notable exception is Donald Wilhelm's book, Creative Alternatives to Communism: Guidelines for Tomorrow's World (London: MacMillan, 1977). Professor Wilhelm correctly predicted that "We shall be saying farewell to conceptually-outmoded nineteenth-century Marxism, and we shall be welcoming a new philosophy geared to the twentieth and twenty-first centuries" (p. ix). Pointing out that "Western non-Marxist philosophy has lately been becalmed and stuck fast in a sargasso sea" (p. 50), Wilhelm predicted that it will be the Russians who will create a philosophical alternative to Marxism: "There is every reason to believe that their common sense, rooted in the soil and in their magnificent artistic heritage, will in the end prevail. Eventually they will supersede the alien Marxist import, and they will reshape and humanize the technological one" (pp. 152-153). Noting that in the West "little systematic and highly-motivated attention has been devoted to the matter [of creating such an alternative]" (p. 153), Wilhelm warned that "Communism will unfailingly tend to breed far-right reactions to itself--unless, that is to say, viable moderate alternatives are readily available" (p. 43). Alas, his call fell on deaf ears, and his book was largely ignored by the very people to whom it was addressed--Western liberals.

3. When Aleksandr Solzhenitsyn pointed out a number of such misconceptions in his article, "Misconceptions about Russia Are a Threat to America" (Foreign Affairs, Spring 1980), the majority of American sovietologists refused to take him seriously.

4. Alexander Shtromas and Morton A. Kaplan, eds., The Soviet Union and the Challenge of the Future, Vol.1 (New York: Paragon, 1988).

5. Idem. Vladislav Krasnov, "Images of the Soviet Future: The Emigre and Samizdat Debate," pp. 357-396.

6. The reader should be aware, however, that Soviet authors writing in government-controlled publications are often unaware of either their dissident predecessors (such as Solzhenitsyn) or even of each other. Moreover, they are often inhibited by fear of censorship which the policy of glasnost has not abolished. In this respect Solzhenitsyn and other authors in my 1985 selection have not only a head start in alternative thinking but also an advantage in freedom and clarity of expression.

7. Mikhail Gorbachev, Perestroika: New Thinking for Our Country and the World (Harper & Row, 1987), pp. 49-50.

8. For the purpose of this book, I shall use these two terms, _partiots_ and _patriots_ in italics in the text, to emphasize their political rather than moral denotation. The first neologism, _partiots_, is necessitated by the fact that it is not synonymous with Party membership. It is wrong to see the main conflict in the USSR today as that between the Communists and non-Communists. The Soviet regime was never a partocracy in the sense of a dictatorship of the Party. It was rather a dictatorship of Party elite. There are undoubtedly many Party members who want to see the totalitarian system dismantled. Moreover, the term _partiot_ cannot be replaced by the English "partisan" because a similar word in Russian, _partizan_, suggests a heroic guerrilla fighter rather than a defender of one's group's interests.

9. The word _Russites_ has been used in the past two decades in Soviet samizdat publications as synonymous with the neo-Slavophiles and Russophiles, both of which suggest that they are ideological descendants of the nineteenth-century Russian Slavophiles. Although I do not deny such a connection, I think the term Russites is a better choice because it is emotionally neutral and lacks the narcissistic quality of the -philes, a derogatory misnomer given by the Westernists to their intellectual opponents. Moreover, I use the word Russite in a sense that transcends Russian ethnicity (_russkii_) as it may also mean _rossiiskii_ patriotism, that is, the love of Russia as the common historical home of many ethnic groups.

10. One of the few American scholars who has studied Russian nationalism, John B. Dunlop, has come to a similar conclusion. See his The Faces of Russian Nationalism (Princeton University Press, 1983) and The New Russian Nationalism (Praeger, 1985).

1

Beyond Gorbachev

BEYOND GORBACHEV: A NEW RUSSIA[1]

Many of you saw Mikhail Gorbachev's interview with NBC's Tom Brokaw just before the summit (December, 1987) in Washington. One of the last questions was: "How do you want us Americans to remember you and the Gorbachev era, say, in ten years?" In his reply Gorbachev made it clear that ten years from now is not some distant future, but a "dynamic present." "Only then," said Gorbachev, "shall we witness the full development of what we have just. . . started to do. . . and the seeds we now plant will begin to sprout." The reply no doubt suggests Gorbachev's firm intention to stay in power for an unlimited tenure. Gorbachev evinces no humility about his, and perestroika's, political mortality.

What I want to do today is to sketch a possible future of the USSR that is far different from what Gorbachev wants us to imagine. My basic contention is that, even though perestroika is usually associated with Gorbachev, he does not own it. Gorbachev had little choice whether or not to start it when he took office in 1985. And now neither Gorbachev nor his opponents are free to stop it at will. The tide of change is sweeping the USSR; it obeys its own momentum, and it may well take us into a future beyond Gorbachev.

When in March 1985 the palsied old men of the Politburo elevated their youngest colleague to the position of General Secretary, it was an emergency measure. Two interrelated dangers frightened the gerontocrats. Internally, they saw a sagging economy; externally, they saw a weakening of Soviet power in the world. They set for Gorbachev a two-pronged task: to revitalize the Soviet economy and to reverse unfavorable trends in the global balance of power. To achieve that task, they gave him a rather broad mandate, but on one condition: the Party controls should not be weakened.

I shall not dwell too much on the external difficulties which made the old masters of the Kremlin hand power to a relatively untested "youngster." Suffice it to mention the Solidarity movement in Poland that threatened their dominion in Eastern Europe; the quagmire in Afghanistan and Cambodia; tensions with China; the rise of anti-Communist liberation movements in Ethiopia, Mozambique, Angola, and Nicaragua; the falling price of oil, a chief Soviet export; and such clumsy actions as the downing of the Korean airliner and the murder of Major Nicholson. All of the above pushed Soviet prestige in the world to an all-time low. To top it all, President Reagan not only made it more difficult for the "Evil Empire" to obtain credits and technology in the West, but restored the will of the West to defend itself, a will that was nearly paralyzed after Vietnam.

As to the domestic situation, Gorbachev quickly discovered that it was even worse than had been thought. As he acknowledges in his English-language book, *Perestroika*, he found the economy in a state of "stagnation" and "near crisis." The problems were not limited to the economy: widespread alcoholism, a weak work ethic, low living standards, inferior health care, low birth rate, high divorce rate, massive waste of natural resources, ruthless despoliation of the environment, and, of course, ubiquitous corruption.

Worst of all, these problems were not even supposed to exist under socialism. At a time when the information revolution was sweeping the world, the General Secretary didn't even have reliable figures for a proper assessment of what was wrong with the country. Why? Because the "propaganda of success--real or imagined--was gaining the upper hand"; "a credibility gap" had developed, and people "put in question. . . everything that was proclaimed from the rostrum and printed in newspapers and textbooks. . . . A decay in public morals began," says Gorbachev, and he concludes: "On the whole, society was becoming increasingly unmanageable."

Faced with such a situation, Gorbachev had little choice but to embark on perestroika, or restructuring, of the Soviet economy, moving in the direction of less centralization and planning, more initiative at the work place, and more respect for market forces. Just how far in this direction he intends to go, or will be allowed to go, nobody knows. But perestroika has already acquired a momentum of its own and cannot be easily stopped either by Gorbachev or by anybody else. This momentum applies particularly to such aspects of perestroika as glasnost [openness], *demokratizatsiia* [democratization], and "new thinking." Introducing the policy of glasnost, for instance, Gorbachev realized that, for the economy to succeed, the credibility gap between propaganda and reality had to be narrowed. And it is the policy of glasnost that may eventually lead the country into a future beyond Gorbachev's control.

To be sure, glasnost is not the same as freedom of the press. It abolishes neither censorship nor Party control. But under glasnost one can begin to describe reality as it is. One can even criticize that reality as long as the sacred cows of Socialism, Communism, Lenin, the October Revolution, and the Party remain untouched. However, the more one describes reality as it is, the more apparent it becomes that current problems are intimately linked with exactly those cows that give no milk, especially the Party. Here is a sample of revelations that now fill the pages of Soviet publications.

According to an article published last year, official Soviet statistics are utterly unreliable. For example, while official statistics say that the national income during the 1928-85 period grew by ninety times, the authors estimate the growth at only six to seven times. Notice the discrepancy: it is not ten or even a hundred percent, but about thirteen times!

Basing his calculations on data scattered in recent Soviet publications, my colleague at Hoover Institution, Mikhail Bernstam, estimates that "about 40 percent of the Soviet people live below the Soviet poverty line, which is itself about one-third lower than the U.S. poverty line."

Evgenii Chazov, Soviet Minister of Health, admitted recently that the USSR is behind Barbados, the United Arab Emirates and some fifty other nations in the rate of infant mortality. However, Chazov's figures do not include the premature and underweight babies who die within a week, and the addition of their numbers would probably increase Soviet infant mortality by 15 to 25 percent.

The most surprising thing about such admissions is not the Soviet failure. It is rather the fact that for years Soviet propaganda deceived not only the Soviet people and Western sovietologists, but also the Soviet leaders. As Soviet scholars point out, "For a planner, statistics are the same as a map for a navigator." Now Gorbachev faces a dilemma: let glasnost flourish--and it will tear apart the carefully crafted propaganda image of Communist success; stifle glasnost'--and find yourself in the turbulent sea of perestroika without a map.

In his book Gorbachev denies that his reforms have been necessitated by "disenchantment with socialism." But the more one listens to the voices of glasnost', the clearer it becomes that disenchantment with socialism as it has been practiced in the USSR for seventy years is widespread. For all practical purposes, Marxist-Leninist ideology is dead in the minds of the most farsighted intellectual advocates of perestroika. More than that, it is increasingly seen as the main obstacle to genuine new thinking.

One Soviet author, Larisa Popkova, in an article titled with the rhetorical question, "Where Are the Pies of Plenty?", gives an unequivocal answer: they are in the countries of free enterprise. According to her, socialism has failed not only in the USSR, but in all countries where socialists are in power. She ridicules the official efforts to base perestroika on the writings of Marx and Lenin, both of whom had little respect for market forces. One cannot be "half-pregnant" with free market ideas, says Popkova. She suggests that present Soviet problems stem not from deviating from Marx and Lenin but from following them too blindly.

Another Soviet author, Iurii Korkhov, in an article, "In the Cobweb of Coercion," condemns the entire Soviet educational system as a "system of emasculation of creativity." He distinguishes between two competing concepts of perestroika: the one which he calls "perestroika-coercion" and the other which he calls "perestroika-liberation." Suggesting that "perestroika-coercion" still has the upper hand, Korkhov warns that only "perestroika-liberation" can mobilize the creativity of the nation to solve its problems.

As the above sample shows, at times it is difficult to distinguish what is now written in the pages of the Soviet press from what we have heard for years from Soviet dissidents, defectors, and emigres. Long before Gorbachev, Solzhenitsyn demanded glasnost as the very minimum point from which to start. Now he is in Vermont and *persona non grata* in the USSR. Long before Gorbachev, my classmate and friend from Moscow University, Vladimir Osipov, practiced glasnost by publishing the samizdat magazine *Veche*, in which he denounced corruption and advocated an anti-alcoholism campaign. After serving fifteen years in the gulag, he is now free, but is not allowed to publish in the Soviet press. Long before Gorbachev, Soviet dissidents were called *inakomysliashchie* (heterodox) precisely because they engaged in new thinking. Now Gorbachev himself says things for which people used to be put in jail. We can hardly expect Gorbachev to give credit to his predecessors, but we should not for a minute forget that whatever "good" things we associate with Gorbachev are not just a result of his good will, but were bought for a high price by the courage, imagination, and suffering of the "heretics" who dared to describe Soviet reality as it is.

But if the Soviet "heretics" proved right in their diagnosis of present Soviet ills, then, perhaps, we should pay more attention to what they have proposed as a cure and a path to the future. One such "heretic" is Aleksandr Solzhenitsyn. Before being expelled from the USSR in 1973, Solzhenitsyn wrote his remarkable *Letter to the Soviet Leaders*. In that letter he proposed a path of reforms that would guarantee a peaceful, orderly and constructive escape from the dead end to which the Party was leading the country. Knowing the Soviet leaders' mindset, he did not ask them to relinquish their power and disband the Party. Nor did he ask them for free elections.

What Solzhenitsyn did ask was to put the good of the country above their narrow partisan interests. He suggested that the Party should share power with the local Soviets which gave the country its official name, the Soviet Union, but which had no power. He also proposed "free art and literature." Above all, urging free competition among all ideological currents, Solzhenitsyn asked Soviet leaders to renounce Marxism-Leninism, not as their personal creed, but as a state ideology which suppresses all new thinking and thus is the principal "roadblock on the path of our salvation."

We do not know whether Gorbachev has read Solzhenitsyn's *Letter*. But there is little doubt that he has heard of it. He may have even gotten its main message, namely, that unless the Party transcends its partisan interests in favor of the country's *national* interests, it will find itself presiding over a national catastrophe. Even though Gorbachev might never admit hearing Solzhenitsyn's voice, the country that he rules seems to be irrevocably moving toward Solzhenitsyn's path.

We can see this movement, first of all, in the policy of glasnost. Although it falls short of Solzhenitsyn's demand for "free art and literature," glasnost offers considerable leeway to express unorthodox ideas. We can see this movement in the publication of a number of Russian classics which for years were suppressed as "anti-Soviet." More and more Soviet authors are following Solzhenitsyn's famous farewell injunction, "don't live according to a lie." Under the restrictions imposed on glasnost, they cannot yet state the truth and openly declare that the king is naked, but they refuse to cover that nakedness with a shroud of lies. We can see the country moving toward Solzhenitsyn's path in a mushrooming of all sorts of "non-formal" groups and associations which emphasize Russian patriotism and national self-awareness, honor the pre-revolutionary cultural and religious heritage, work without pay on the restoration of historical monuments and churches, advocate preservation of nature, but--show no interest whatsoever in Marxism-Leninism.

This movement of Soviet society from ideological to spiritual, from "international" to national, from formal to non-formal, from rigid to spontaneous, from Marxism-Leninism to no "isms" at all, from partia to patria, from things Communist to things Russian--this movement is the most significant and, to my mind, the most hopeful development during the last three years. And it is this movement that Western sovietologists have largely failed to notice.

Of course, the Soviet Union is not just Russia, but a multi-national entity embracing more than a hundred ethnic groups. I am reminded that ethnic Russians are hardly fifty percent of the population and soon might become outnumbered by Soviet Muslims. How does this drift toward Russia square with the interests of national minorities? My answer is that Russian national revival is actually beneficial to the minorities' struggle for national self-expression. The more leeway ethnic Russians obtain from the government, the more reason national minorities have to ask for the same.

Some Western sovietologists and politicians see the main threat to freedom and world peace in the allegedly "Russian imperialism" of

Soviet leaders. I do not need to explain how erroneous and harmful such a misconception is for the West. Solzhenitsyn has done it more eloquently. But I would like to point out that among all national disturbances of the Gorbachev era--the bloody riots in Kazakhstan, the demonstration of the Crimean Tatars in the Red Square, and several demonstrations in the Baltic republics--none worried the Kremlin sponsors of "perestroika-coercion" as much as the demonstrations on the streets of Moscow of the "non-formal" association named Pamyat last May. Since then virtually every major Soviet newspaper has sounded an alarm about Pamyat and condemned at least some of its activities.

On the surface, the condemnation is focused on the alleged anti-Semitism of Pamyat. It is true that Pamyat's leaders made statements to the effect that the so called "Jewish-Masonic conspiracy" among Moscow architects was responsible for the destruction of Russian historical monuments. It is true that they blame the "Zionists" for many problems in the USSR and abroad. In my opinion, these Pamyat leaders are petty demagogues, deserving all the condemnation they received on that account. We should not forget, however, that anti-Semitism is not the main worry of the official press. Why indeed should the Soviet press worry about anti-Zionist statements when the Soviet government itself is officially committed to the policy of combatting Zionism and Israel? What worries Soviet authorities most is the freedom, spontaneity, and popularity of Pamyat, which pledges patriotism and loyalty to the country but defines these values in non-Marxist and non-Communist terms.

Pamyat has an unusually large following in Moscow and several other cities. Among its members there are many Christians, but it keeps its doors open to atheists and even to Communist Party members as long as they are concerned with the preservation and restoration of the *memory* (that's what Pamyat means in English) of Russia's pre-revolutionary heritage. It is widely believed that Pamyat has adherents even in the Party hierarchy. In spite of the vehement media campaign against Pamyat, authorities seem unable to forbid it altogether. Nor do they seem capable of putting Pamyat completely under Party control. But what they cannot control they try to manipulate. It is quite possible, therefore, that the KGB has infiltrated Pamyat's leadership and feeds it the anti-Semitic line in order to discredit Russian nationalism among Soviet intellectuals and the Western public.

Pamyat is not the only "non-formal" organization concerned with the preservation of Russian national roots. There are also "non-formal" groups and seminars that are primarily concerned with Russia's religious heritage, which has been under assault during the entire seventy-year rule of the atheistic government. Besides the "non-formal" groups, Russian national and religious themes are being increasingly reflected in Soviet art, cinema, and literature, especially in the writings of the so called "village school" of Russian prose. Lately Dmitrii Likhachev, a leading Soviet specialist on ancient Russian literature and member of the Academy, spoke out against the government's interference in religious affairs and suggested that Soviet morality and the work ethic cannot be improved without a return to the Ten Commandments.

In short, what we are witnessing in the USSR today is a sort of contest between the Communist Party and the "Russian Party." The Communist Party says that the primary experience of the Russian people is the seventy years of Soviet rule, and whatever went on before 1917 is either secondary or unimportant. The "Russian Party" says that the hundreds of years before Communism--and this year, 1988, Russia celebrates the millennium of its Christianity--are at least as important as the seventy years under Communism. That importance would no doubt grow even more as soon as the people were allowed to restore their links to the past that the Party has been trying so hard to destroy.

There is, of course, no Russian party as a political organization. But if one takes account of all recent manifestations of Russian nationalism, one realizes that such groups as Pamyat are but a tiny visible tip of a huge iceberg that for the first time in Soviet history seriously threatens the Communist Party's monopoly on power. We can call this iceberg Russian national and religious revival. But whatever we call it, we should not forget that its course is essentially divergent from the goals of the Party as we know it.

Like any other nationalism, Russian nationalism is susceptible to the temptations of demagoguery, chauvinism, and xenophobia. But in its essence it is a healthy, natural and beautiful phenomenon. In political terms, it is still a baby. Like any baby it needs to be washed. However, this baby is in constant danger of being thrown out with the dirty water of Soviet bigotry. The baby's ultimate fate will be decided by the dynamics of Soviet politics. But the West can assure its survival by an early recognition of its existence, lest the Communist Party's totalitarian wing try to get rid of the newborn on the sly. In due course, perhaps in ten years, the baby might grow up strong enough to lay claim to the Soviet future.

All Soviet leaders were adept at co-opting Russian patriotism, but their success was only partial. They were most successful in that they convinced first Hitler and then the West that the Communists and the Russians are just about the same. But if they failed to completely subjugate Russian nationalism after seventy years of trying, the chances are they never will. Gorbachev is aware that the main opposition to reforms comes not from the Russian nationalists but from the totalitarian Marxist-Leninist bureaucrats who enjoy the *status quo*. He might well decide to broaden the social base for his reforms by appealing to the national sentiments of Russians, who constitute the majority both in the party and among the workers.

He can do so first by renouncing the most aggressive "internationalist" aspects of Marxist-Leninist ideology, such as the theory of class struggle and world Communist revolution. In that case, the Marxist-Leninist tandem is likely to become more "Leninist" than "Marxist." As a sort of National-Bolshevik one-party system, this may satisfy some nationally-minded Russians but not for long. It would only postpone the second phase, the abolition of Marxism-Leninism as state ideology, which alone can guarantee a genuine ideological co-existence and detente at home and abroad. Eventually it would lead to the formation of opposition parties among which Russian nationalists will certainly play a major role.

Around what political program are Russian nationalists likely to rally? Basically, they want a new Russia. Domestically, they want freedom of religion first. They want a mixed economy, comprised of state, cooperative, and private enterprise. They want basic political freedoms, such as a free press and the right of free speech and assembly. In respect to the multinational structure of the country, the majority of Russian nationalists would favor national self-determination for minorities, including the right to secede from the Union. I think that an ultimate solution would be the replacement of the Soviet Union with some sort of Russian Commonwealth of Nations in which each member would choose its form of association.

In foreign affairs, the Russian nationalists want most of all to abandon the notion that their country should lead a Communist world revolution. In practical terms, they would stop sending arms to any violent revolutionary movement. They would withdraw Soviet troops from Afghanistan and Eastern Europe. They would seek friendship and cooperation with the West in establishing peace, justice, and stability in the world. They would still want their country to be great, but they would seek its greatness through internal development so that it could become an example to inspire others.

Some might say that the new Russia I've described is just a dream. Perhaps. But if I am dreaming, one must grant me this much: I am not dreaming in the empty Marxist-Leninist sky where I was raised. Now I am down to earth, and doubly so. I dream of a new Russia while my feet are firmly planted on former Russian soil, and I countenance a new Russia from what is now American soil--the beautiful Alaska. I don't remember the Russians ever giving a bad deal to the Americans before 1917.

What can we, as Americans, do in order to help the transformation of the Soviet Union into a new Russia? First, we should abandon the notion that Communism is a permanent and unchangeable system. Second, we should abandon the fear that a Russian national alternative is worse than the present regime, a fear which translates into our *de facto* support of the status quo in the USSR. After all, it is only prudent to let nature take its course. And if that course leads to a national Russia, so be it.

It sounds as if I am not asking for much. But I am asking for a lot more than what we have been doing so far. We spend millions of dollars every year on broadcasting to the Soviet Union. But our broadcasting is largely ineffective. It is ineffective because it is chiefly focused on the needs and interests of national and religious minorities, particularly those wishing to emigrate. We largely ignore the needs and interests of the Russian majority without which there can be no serious challenge to the present regime. It is about time we understand that "the mystic chords of memory stretch from every battlefield and patriot grave to every living heart and hearthstone" not only for Americans, but for every other nation, including the Russians.

LETTER TO THE SOVIET LEADERS: SOLZHENITSYN'S 1973 BLUEPRINT FOR REFORMS

> Silently spins the Earth in its orbit
> Because great events happen in silence
>
> -Nietzsche

In the gay din of glasnost and in the more somber bustle of perestroika, there is but one voice, one sound that rises high above everyone. It is the voice of Aleksandr Solzhenitsyn. It is the sound of silence in which the most renowned critic of the Soviet regime so enigmatically indulges himself. With ever-increasing intensity, this sound of silence emanates from his secluded residence in Vermont and then, as if transmitted by a satellite, hovers over the USSR, enveloping that huge country in an exhilarating presentiment of things to come. For some few, it is a presentiment of a threatening unknown. For many more, it is a presentiment of the long-overdue vindication of their hopes and beliefs. For all, it is the presentiment of the inevitable.

Solzhenitsyn's name has been popping up with growing frequency in the pages of Soviet publications ever since Sergei Zalygin, the editor of *Novyi mir*, announced in February 1987 his intention to publish Solzhenitsyn's work, only to retract his statement later. Since then there have been ups and downs in the unfolding struggle of Soviet readers for the complete and unconditional return of the world-renowned author to his motherland.

In April 1989 Zalygin announced, once again, that his magazine would start publishing a selection from *The Gulag Archipelago*.[2] The announcement was a surprise to many because on November 29, 1988, no less a figure than Vadim Medvedev, who was just appointed Party chief ideologist, declared that "to publish Solzhenitsyn's work is to undermine the foundations on which our present life rests." But those who have watched the scene more carefully are hardly surprised. They know that the events in the USSR no longer obey the dictates of its Communist leaders, least of all those charged with ideological watchdog duty. True enough, late in June 1989 the *Washington Post* reported Zalygin as confirming that *Novyi mir* would "without doubt" proceed with the publication this year.[3]

In a May 12, 1989 article entitled "The Hermit of Vermont," one Soviet journalist, A. Vasil'kov, wanted to know why the "hermit" so "enigmatically keeps silent" and utters not a word about the "events in our country which have captured the attention of the whole world?" Vasil'kov speculated that, after having "cursed" his country and pronounced Communism "unregenerate and incompatible with Russia," Solzhenitsyn needs the silence for "sobering up" and "re-evaluating his views."[4] A word of praise for perestroika, the journalist intimated, would help Solzhenitsyn's return. So why does the famous exile keep silent?

The plain answer is this: Solzhenitsyn has already said just about everything that needs to be said about glasnost, perestroika, or new thinking. In fact, he paved the way for many of the changes that are now occurring in the USSR under those names. In 1962 the publication of his novel, *One Day in the Life of Ivan Denisovich*, lifted the taboo from the theme of Stalinist labor camps that now has again become popular. In 1967 he fought the Brezhnevite "stagnation" (*zastoi*) by demanding the abolition of literary censorship and publication of the "anti-Soviet" and emigre authors (such as Nikolai Gumilev, Osip Mandel'shtam, Evgenii Zamiatin, Andrei Platonov, Boris Pasternak, and Vasilii Grossman) whose works are now being published. In 1969, in an open letter to Soviet writers, he defined glasnost as "the first requirement of a healthy society." "Those who deprive our fatherland of glasnost," he wrote, "do not wish to rid us of our social malady."[5]

In his polyphonic novels he has practiced ideological pluralism beyond the limits of the so-called "socialist pluralism" that Soviet authorities now allow.[6] In the novelistic cycle, *The Red Wheel*, on which he is still working, he has exposed the roots of the Communist revolution. His *The Gulag Archipelago* remains an unsurpassed expose of the entire penal system of the USSR, not just of its Stalinist phase. Last but not least, Solzhenitsyn's polemical articles, written prior to his expulsion, such as "Don't Live According to a Lie," *From Under the Rubble*,[7] and, most explicitly, *Letter to the Soviet Leaders*,[8] have anticipated, urged, and prepared the way for the spiritual and intellectual catharsis that has now gripped the country. Had Solzhenitsyn's works been made freely available to the Soviet public, Vasil'kov would have realized that Solzhenitsyn has said *more* about perestroika than some people in the Kremlin want the Soviet public to hear. It is this *more* that he has said that makes his silence pregnant with meaning.

What Did Solzhenitsyn Propose?

In retrospect, *Letter to the Soviet Leaders* is an astonishingly precocious plan for reforms similar to Gorbachev's perestroika.[9] Written on September 5, 1973, at the height of the Brezhnev "stagnation era," it uncannily anticipates, predicts, and urges many of the changes that have been occurring in the USSR since 1985. Receiving no reply from members of the Politburo, to whom the Letter was originally mailed in several copies, Solzhenitsyn made it public only after being thrown out of the country.

One of the Letter's most distinguishing features, when compared with dozens of other dissident visions of the Soviet future, was its pragmatism.[10] Realizing that dissidents had no levers of power to implement their noble visions, Solzhenitsyn proposed that Soviet Party leaders *themselves* undertake a *peaceful*, gradual, and orderly transformation of the totalitarian and expansionist Communist empire into a normal nation-state, in which national interests and domestic needs take precedence over everything else. But isn't this what Gorbachev has been trying to do? It would seem so. There are, however, some crucial features in Solzhenitsyn's master plan which are sorely missing in Gorbachev's perestroika. As I shall try to demonstrate below, they account for perestroika being presently stalled and out of breath.

Let us now take a fresh look at this well-conceived, ill-received and long-forgotten Letter. This must be done because in the West, too, the Letter has not elicited the response it deserves. Western critics particularly took Solzhenitsyn to task for advocating "authoritarian rule." They failed to notice, however, that in his language "authoritarian" implies considerable improvement over "totalitarian," a term he reserves only for Nazism, Fascism, and Communism. Moreover, he advocated "authoritarian rule" only as a transitory stage to assure a smooth descent from "the icy cliff of totalitarianism" to whichever form of government Soviet citizens would choose after they had access to information. He did not rule out democracy, but he suggested that the latter be based on Russia's indigenous traditions rather than merely copying the West.[11] This view is fully consistent with George Kennan's old advice not to judge the Russians according to "whether they answer to our concept of 'democratic.' Give them time; let them be Russians; let them work out their problems in their own manner."[12]

Let the Party Rule, But . . .

Unlike other dissidents, Solzhenitsyn realized that Soviet leaders would never relinquish their power without a struggle which might undermine civil order in the country. Therefore, declaring himself "an opponent of all revolutions and all armed convulsions," he opted for "a dialogue on the basis of realism." Conceding that "you will not tolerate *real* elections, at which people might not vote you in," Solzhenitsyn proposed that Soviet leaders retain political power.[13] But only on one condition: they must start dismantling the structure of the totalitarian state. As the first step, he proposed the abolition of the Party's ideological monopoly so that other ideologies, religions, and political and economic theories could grow and compete with one another in producing ideas for the betterment of life.

Calling for a series of political, economic, educational, and cultural reforms, he proposed an overall change in the government's priorities: switching the country's resources from an expansionist foreign policy to caring for urgent domestic needs. In order to transform the totalitarian state into a normal nation-state, Solzhenitsyn made a number of specific proposals. As part of domestic democratization, he proposed a gradual scaling down of the Party's total dictatorship to a sort of benevolent authoritarian rule. "Let it be an authoritarian order, but one founded not on an inexhaustible 'class hatred,'" wrote Solzhenitsyn in reference to one of the mandatory principles of Marxism-Leninism, "but [rather] on love of your fellow men." He called on Soviet rulers to show "magnanimity and mercy" by freeing political prisoners and "renouncing, once and for all, the psychiatric violence and secret trials, and the brutal, immoral camps where those who have erred and fallen by the wayside are still further maimed and destroyed."[14]

He made it clear, however, that Soviet leaders should regard their authoritarian mandate as a temporary arrangement, conditioned upon their undertaking further democratization. Thus, to prevent abuses of power, they should base the authoritarian order on the rule of law. The actual division of power into the legislative, executive, and judicial branches should be a starting point. Under his plan, the Party should also start sharing power with the local Soviets, which, though they gave the name to the country, have been rendered powerless by the concentration of all power in the Party apparatus in Moscow.[15]

"And from then onward let posts in the state service no longer depend on Party membership as they do now. In doing so you can clear your Party of the accusation that people join it only to further their careers," said Solzhenitsyn, emphasizing the need for a transition to a non-partisan, non-ideological approach to the affairs of state.[16] "Give some of your other hard-working fellow countrymen the chance to move up the rungs *without* having to have a Party card--you will get good workers, and only the disinterested [in personal privileges enjoyed by the *nomenklatura* class] will remain in the Party."[17]

Domestic Reforms

In the field of economics, the first step should be the speedy abolition of the involuntary collective farm system.   "With an impending world-wide shortage of grain," Solzhenitsyn argued, "there is only one way for us to fill the people's bellies: give up the forced collective farms and leave just the voluntary ones."[18] Invoking the name of the great Russian pre-revolutionary reformer, Petr Stolypin, he suggested that Soviet leaders can learn from his success in promoting more efficient, market-oriented, private farming.

Solzhenitsyn further called for the creation of a "stable economy," based not on ideologically-motivated goals of "catching up and overtaking" capitalist America, but on the material, biological, and spiritual needs of the people. Foremost is the need to restore (at least, to prevent from further deteriorating) the ecological balance in the USSR. "If we are to stop sweating over the short-term economic need of today and create a land of clean air and clean water for our children, we must renounce many forms of industrial production which result in toxic waste" and which are dictated by needless military competition with the West, said Solzhenitsyn.[19]   Countering the official propagandistic "projects of the century," aimed at showing the world that socialism can do anything capitalism can, he proposed "an economy of *non*gigantism with small-scale though highly developed technology,"[20] a proposal that seems to parallel that of E. E. Schumacher, the author of *Small Is Beautiful: Economics as if People Mattered.*[21]

Solzhenitsyn also suggested trimming down "our gargantuan civil service" and improving the work ethic at factories where "people don't put any effort at all into their official duties. . . but cheat (and sometimes steal) as much as they can" because they cannot "earn a living from wages alone." He called on the government to abandon its ambivalent attitude toward the spread of mass alcoholism, warning that "as long as vodka is an important item of state revenue nothing will change."[22]

Solzhenitsyn also proposed the abolition of compulsory military service, "which exists neither in China, nor in the United States." Saying that the government has created huge armed forces not for legitimate defense needs but "solely out of military and diplomatic vanity--for reasons of prestige, conceit [and] expansion abroad," he suggested that, at the very least, "the period of service could be greatly reduced and army 'education' humanized."[23] He also proposed ending military-motivated space programs, lessening the burden of overworked Soviet women, and raising salaries of underpaid school teachers.

Contingent upon the abolition of the Party's ideological monopoly, Solzhenitsyn strongly advocated a free market of ideas and genuine freedom of conscience. "Allow competition on an equal and honorable basis--not for power, but for truth--between all ideological and ethical currents, in particular between *all religions*," demanded Solzhenitsyn. As a first practical step, he suggested granting all denominations "the right to instruct and educate children, and the right to free parish activities." (In parentheses, he expressed his personal belief in Christianity "as the only living spiritual force capable of undertaking the spiritual healing of Russia." However, he asked for "no special privileges for it," only that it should not be suppressed.) "Allow us a free art and literature, the free publication of. . . philosophical, ethical, economic and social studies," wrote Solzhenitsyn pleading for ideological coexistence and pluralism, "and you will see what a rich harvest it brings and how it bears fruit--for the good of Russia."[24]

Foreign Relations

Solzhenitsyn called absurd the official propaganda about the threat to Soviet borders from the West. The only real threat he saw was coming from Communist China. Pointing out that one of the principal reasons for the Sino-Soviet conflict was ideological, namely, the competition of the two Communist giants for hegemony over world Communism, he proposed that Soviet leaders leave the Communist dogmas to the Chinese.

"Let the Chinese leaders glory in it for a while. And for that matter, let them shoulder the whole sackful of unfulfillable international obligations, let them grunt and heave and instruct humanity, and foot all the bills for their absurd economics (a million a day just to Cuba), and let them support terrorists and guerrillas in the Southern hemisphere too, if they like."[25]

At the same time, Solzhenitsyn expressed sympathy for the "ordinary Chinese." Not only "will our people soon be cured of this disease [the ideology of Communist world revolution]," Solzhenitsyn prophesied, but "the Chinese too. . . and it will not be too late, I hope, to save their country and protect humanity."[26]

As Solzhenitsyn summarized his plan for reforms:

> We must not be governed by considerations of political gigantism, nor concern ourselves with the fortunes of other hemispheres: this we must renounce forever, for that bubble is bound to burst. . . The considerations which guide our country must be these: to encourage the inner, the moral, the healthy development of the people; to liberate women from the forced labor of money-earning--especially from the crowbar and the shovel; to improve schooling and children's upbringing; to save the soil and waters and all of Russian nature; to re-establish healthy cities and to develop the Northeast. Let us hear no more about outer space and the cosmos,

no more 'historic victories of universal significance,' and no more of
dreaming up international missions. . .[27]

Seventeen Years Later

Rereading this Letter, one cannot help thinking how provident
and *prophetic* its author was then, seventeen years ago. Unfortunately,
Gorbachev's predecessors not only refused to take the path of reforms
that Solzhenitsyn proposed, but went on doing exactly the opposite.
Instead of focusing on domestic problems, they went on a spree of
those "historic victories of universal significance" (Vietnam, Laos,
Cambodia) which were already in their dream pipeline. Then they
dreamt up new "international missions" (Ethiopia, Angola,
Mozambique, Grenada, Nicaragua, El Salvador, and Afghanistan).

The Letter seems especially prophetic when compared with the
path the country has taken since 1985. In fact, the Letter anticipates
virtually all major initiatives undertaken under Gorbachev: the anti-
alcohol campaign, the release of prisoners of conscience, the
introduction of glasnost, the lessening of suppression of religion, the
tinkering with individual farming, enhancement of the role of the local
Soviets, as well as "de-ideologization" and "new political thinking" in
foreign policy. Furthermore, it anticipates the authoritarian ways
which Gorbachev has employed to promote democratization.

Perestroika's Unacknowledged Blueprint

Comparing the Letter with Gorbachev's own (or his
ghostwriters') book, *Perestroika: New Thinking for Our Country and the
World*,[28] it is hard to avoid the impression that the latter is but a
watered-down version of the former. So striking are the similarities
that one might even suspect plagiarism. One must certainly wonder: If
the Letter was not used as a blueprint for perestroika, wasn't it at least
one of its chief sources? Or is it just a case of "great minds running in
similar channels?" Regardless of how one explains the similarities, the
primacy of Solzhenitsyn's plan is beyond question and must be
acknowledged and recognized.[29]

It is not just a question of fairness to Solzhenitsyn. Rather, it is a question of fairness to all patriotic Soviet citizens who, like Solzhenitsyn, have been offering their ideas about finding an exit from the country's increasingly dangerous impasse. Nor is it just a question of historical accuracy. Rather, it is a question of the future of perestroika and the country. For it is enough to take a closer look at what has been happening lately in the USSR to conclude that, while Gorbachev's 1987 book has already become hopelessly out of date, Solzhenitsyn's 1973 Letter has largely retained its fundamental validity and acquired a new sense of urgency.

Multi-Ethnic Empire

Take, for instance, the nationalities issue. "Against the background of national strife, which has not spared even the world's most advanced countries," Gorbachev boasted in his book, "the USSR represents a truly unique example in the history of human civilization. . . in building a harmonious multi-ethnic state."[30] As a cure for the remaining few problems, such as "nationalist narrow-mindedness, chauvinism, Zionism, and anti-Semitism," he prescribed the usual panacea of Marxist-Leninist "internationalism" and "Soviet patriotism." In fact, Gorbachev completely misjudged the actual situation. A few months later he had to swallow his words about "a harmonious multi-ethnic state," admitting that the USSR has its share of nationalities problems, *like* any other state. Today it is obvious that it has more than its share, *unlike* many other states. Far from having been resolved on the basis of Marxism-Leninism, nationality problems have merely been covered up and allowed to fester. Gorbachev's book certainly provides no guidance to restructuring Soviet multi-national relations.

As for Solzhenitsyn, not only did he foresee the rise of nationalism in the USSR, but he welcomed it as a liberating force against the deadening grip of the Marxist-Leninist "internationalism" holding the Soviet empire together. He had especially high hopes for Russian nationalism as manifested in its liberal-democratic mainstream, the so called *vozrozhdentsy,* or Russian national-and-religious renaissance movement.[31] He envisioned that a Russian national revival would play a decisive role in dismantling the totalitarian regime. That's why, while writing his *Letter* as a calculated appeal to the Russianness of Soviet leaders, he made it just as clear that he did not regard the national aspirations of other peoples forcibly drawn into the Soviet empire as contrary to Russian national interests.

In fact, the key provision of his program was the conviction that Russia's future lies neither in an expansionist policy abroad, nor in domination over Central Europe (the Warsaw Pact members) and the Western and Southern borderlands of the Soviet Union itself, but "in putting her own house in order." It lies in consolidation and development of Russia's interior, particularly its Northeast (which he roughly defined as the European North and Siberia), a sparsely inhabited area, uncontested by any major nationality.

While acknowledging that small ethnic groups scattered across the vast territory of the Northeast have their legitimate claims that need to be addressed, he realized that "of all ethnic problems facing our country this is the least." As to larger nationalities, he fully recognized their right for self-determination by unequivocally stating that "no peripheral nation should be forcibly kept within the bounds of our country."[32]   In his other works, he condemned extreme manifestations of Russian nationalism both inside and outside the official Soviet establishment, suggesting that multi-ethnic conflicts can be best solved on the basis of mutual "repentance and self-restraint."[33]

Ecological Catastrophe

Another crucial difference between the two blueprints concerns the ecological issue. Whereas in his book Gorbachev hardly mentions it at all, in Solzhenitsyn's *Letter* the ecological issue occupies center stage. Gorbachev merely proposes to lower Soviet economic ambitions from surpassing the United States to achieving "world technological standards." Solzhenitsyn, on the other hand, was so concerned with the ecological malady of the country that he proposed getting out of the rat race of endless economic growth entirely. He insisted that economic perestroika must be subordinated to the need of restoring the country's ecological health.

Again Solzhenitsyn proved more prescient. As A. Koval'chuk, then chairman of the newly created State Committee for Preservation of Nature (*Goskompriroda*) of the Russian Federation, warned in April 1989, the ecological catastrophe (*katastrofa*) has already begun and might become irreversible.[34] And there are no reasons to believe that the situation is much better in other Soviet republics. The ecological issue has been adopted as one of the key issues by both Russian nationalists and Popular Fronts in Soviet republics. The Soviet "green" movement has already become a potent force which the government can ill afford to ignore. But it does. As Koval'chuk complained, the government refuses to provide his committee with either funds or authority to enable it to do something more than merely bemoan the damage already done.

A New Threat from Beijing

Likewise, Solzhenitsyn proved more far-sighted on the issue of Sino-Soviet relations. Whereas Gorbachev devoted just one short paragraph to them, for Solzhenitsyn it was one of the two foremost issues (the other was the ecological crisis) that prompted him to write the *Letter*. Of course, Solzhenitsyn could not foresee that the Chinese Communists would realize the fatal defects of socialist economy *before* their Soviet rivals, *themselves* taking "the revisionist road" which they so vehemently denounced in Khrushchev's case. Consequently, his concern with the danger of war with China may now seem exaggerated. However, as the bloody suppression of the Beijing Spring of 1989 has shown, that danger has far from disappeared. The handling of the students' pro-democracy demonstrations on Tiananmen Square by China's Communist rulers has raised once again the question implicit in Solzhenitsyn's *Letter*: Can Communist rulers who base their mandate to rule not on popular vote but on their ideology ("Power comes from the barrel of a gun," as Mao put it) be trusted with reforming a country out of its totalitarian coffin?

By writing his *Letter*, Solzhenitsyn seemed to give a cautious 'yes.' But he knew that the credit of trust could be extended to Communist reformers only on two conditions. First, they must *themselves* realize that the kind of socialism they created does not work. (Both Deng and Gorbachev have given ample evidence that they do realize that.) Second, they must assure people that their reform drive is irreversible. To do so, they must start dismantling the main pillars of totalitarianism, such as the Party's monopoly on ideology, news and information (glasnost in the USSR has largely undone that pillar, while in China it was one of the students' principal demands); on the economy (here China has gone much further); and on political power (the Soviets are just beginning to assert themselves vis-a-vis the Party apparatus). Solzhenitsyn did not ask Soviet leaders to renounce their Party convictions. He merely asked them not to impose theirs on all people. "I am certainly not proposing that you go to the opposite extreme and persecute or ban Marxism. . . *All you have to do* is to deprive Marxism of its powerful state support and let it exist of itself and stand on its own feet."[35]   In short, Marxist-Leninist ideology (and, by implication, atheism) must be separated from the affairs of state.

While China's Communist reformers have failed to assure the irreversibility of their reforms, in the USSR that second condition has been largely met through glasnost and political reform (allowing non-formal organizations, multi-candidate elections, etc.). As a result, Soviet publications are now filled with articles in which Marxism-Leninism is either subjected to full-fledged revisionism (often in an effort to save it) or more or less covertly attacked, ridiculed, or simply ignored.[36]   Contrary to Gorbachev's hopeful view, Marxist-Leninist "dialectics" no longer inspire Soviet intellectuals, even those within the Party ranks.

The Ball Is in the Kremlin's Court

Solzhenitsyn has certainly said a lot about perestroika--so much so that he appears to be its chief architect, whereas Gorbachev is but the on-site superintendent. But as long as the chief architect remains on the sidelines, the doubt will persist whether his blueprint is fully understood and properly executed. Solzhenitsyn's *Letter* certainly says much *more* about the direction perestroika must now take than the conservative wing of the Gorbachev leadership wants the Soviet public to hear. Therefore, the question, "Why does Solzhenitsyn keep silent?" should be addressed not to the writer, but to the Kremlin. After all, he did mail several copies there, and it is up to the Kremlin to decide whether and how to respond to this challenge. The speedy publication of *The Gulag Archipelago* is a step in the right direction. But giving full glasnost to perestroika's original blueprint seems even more urgent.

Solzhenitsyn's silence under the circumstances only validates the Russian proverb, "A word is silver, but silence is gold." It is the silence of the Kremlin about the unanswered *Letter* that is both unnatural and unwise. Solzhenitsyn hardly needs Gorbachev's help to write his novels. It is rather Gorbachev who needs Solzhenitsyn's, that is, if Gorbachev is serious about building a national consensus for solving the country's problems. Times have changed. It is no longer a question of "rehabilitating" Solzhenitsyn. It is rather a question of rehabilitating the Party-sponsored reforms. To do so, Gorbachev must publicly apologize, on behalf of the Politburo, for banning from the country its greatest writer and most faithful patriot. Only then will it be up to Solzhenitsyn to decide whether to return or not. Meanwhile, the ball remains in the Kremlin's court.

HOW CAN WE MAKE RUSSIA LIVABLE? SOLZHENITSYN'S HUMBLE REFLECTIONS ON HOW TO SAVE RUSSIA

> But the Miracle will not be bestowed upon those who do not strive toward it.
>
> -A. S. Solzhenitsyn

A portentous event took place in Moscow on September 18, 1990. The Communist Youth League's newspaper, *Komsomol'skaia pravda*, brought to its nearly 22 million readers the long-awaited "word" of Solzhenitsyn, his pamphlet, *How Can We Make Russia Livable* [Kak nam obustroit' Rossiiu]. The following day the weekly *Literaturnaia gazeta* offered the same to an additional 4.5 million readers.[37] The event was extraordinary by any standard. Only five years previously, these newspapers had berated the exiled author as "that vile scum of a traitor"; and as little as a few months earlier, Vadim Medvedev, then the Party's chief ideologist, denounced Solzhenitsyn for "undermining the foundations on which our present life rests." Did the Party change its mind about Solzhenitsyn? Or about "the foundations"? Or did it realize that there might be life after "our present life"? Whatever the reason, the double-barrelled publication of Solzhenitsyn's pamphlet may have mortally wounded Communist control over glasnost and over the hearts and minds of the Russian people.

What is the relationship between this 1990 brochure and the 1973 *Letter*? In what respects are they similar? In what do they differ? What does Solzhenitsyn propose now that he did not propose then?

Two Pieces of a Whole Cloth

Despite the seventeen years separating them, the two documents are pieces of the same cloth. Both are based on the same set of beliefs: that Communism is intellectually untenable and morally irredeemable; harmful to the interests of people of all nationalities, it is particularly destructive to the Russians; and that the best way to get rid of it is through the revival of the spiritual traditions of the Russian people, the foremost victim and the main carrier of the Soviet regime. Both documents exude an air of unabashed patriotism--the author's unswerving love of and faith in non-Communist Russia. Both aim at opening a way to a better future for the Russians and their neighbors. Both seek to assure that the descent from the "icy cliff of totalitarianism" be smooth and peaceful. In terms of this study, both documents aim at providing a peaceful means for dismantling totalitarianism and leading Russia away from and beyond Communism.

Whatever the differences are, they are due not so much to the evolution of the author's views as to the historical changes that have occurred in the past seventeen years. The most important of these changes is the fact that Communism has plummeted from the zenith of its global power during the seventies to its nadir at present. Solzhenitsyn compresses this change into three epigraphic lines. "The death knell of Communism has tolled," reads the first. "But its concrete structure has not yet collapsed," reads the second, alluding to the futility of Gorbachev's efforts to "restructure" Communism. "It could yet happen that instead of being liberated, we will all be crushed under its ruins," warns the third. To help avert such a tragedy is the main purpose of the pamphlet. Its first part, "The Nearest Term," focuses on the most urgent steps that are needed to rescue the country from the shadow of the collapsing structure. Its second part, "Farther Ahead," gives a deeper historical perspective to Solzhenitsyn's vision of Russia's future.

One important difference is that while in the *Letter* Solzhenitsyn put some trust in the ability of Soviet leaders to transcend their partisan interests and undertake reforms for the sake of the country they rule, in his "humble reflections," as the pamphlet is subtitled, he entertains no such hope. In fact, it is addressed not to Soviet leaders, but directly and primarily to their Russian subjects. Although Solzhenitsyn makes no references to his 1973 *Letter*, the pamphlet's ultimate effect largely depends on the fact that he did offer Soviet leaders a chance for "rehabilitating" themselves by reforming the country out of its totalitarian mold. Alas, as I have argued in the previous section, the Soviet leaders have largely forfeited that chance, allowing the country to slide to the brink of an abyss.

A Russian National Alternative to Perestroika

Those who hoped that Solzhenitsyn would jump up on the perestroika band-wagon will find no solace in his *Reflections*. Although he does not mention Gorbachev by name, Solzhenitsyn minces no words in repudiating the Party-sponsored reforms that Gorbachev has embodied. The "noisy 'perestroika'," says Solzhenitsyn, has amounted to little more than "re-shuffling posts within the Central Committee [of the Party]" and creating an "ugly, artificial electoral system," designed to keep the Party in power. Saying that nearly six years were wasted, he dismisses the laws passed under Gorbachev as "flawed, convoluted, and indecisive." It is not enough to abolish Article Six of the constitution proclaiming the Party's monopoly on power. The Party must be deprived *de facto* of all means of interfering in economic and administrative life. Unless this is done, "the people's path to solving the most urgent problems" will remain barred, says Solzhenitsyn.[38]

The pamphlet is an effort to outline "the people's path" out of the impasse to which the Party has led the country and from which Gorbachev's perestroika provides no exit. It lays out an intellectual and spiritual framework for the creation of a political alternative to Gorbachev's perestroika. This challenge is signalled in the brochure's title, *How Can We Make Russia Livable?* First, the focus is not on the "Union" of which Gorbachev is President, but on Russia proper. Second, although the title's verb, "obustroit'," has the same root as "perestroika," it suggests a task that is both less ambitious and more vital for the country than Gorbachev's "restructuring." Why should the Soviet system be "restructured" when it is obvious that it stands on a rotten foundation? The most one can do under the circumstances is take certain emergency measures ("obustroit'") in order to protect people's lives from the debris of the collapsing Soviet state. Since Solzhenitsyn's primary concern is with the peoples of Russia, not of the larger Soviet Union, "the people's path" means, for all practical purposes, a Russian path. Lastly, the pronoun "we" (*nam*) proclaims loud and clear that Solzhenitsyn and the viewpoint he represents can no longer be excluded from making decisions on the country's future.

The Soviet "Empire" or the Russian Union?

In addition to the removal of the Party from power, the other most radical proposal is to dissolve the "Empire" on the initiative of the Russians. Solzhenitsyn proposes an immediate "separation" of all "Union" republics, except Russia, Belorussia, the Ukraine, and parts of Kazakhstan where Russians form a huge majority. The remaining three East-Slavic nations would unite into a new political entity which he calls the Russian (*Rossiiskii*) Union. Radical as it sounds, the proposal should not surprise anyone familiar with Solzhenitsyn's previous work. More than once Solzhenitsyn had denounced the involuntary nature of the "Union." Consistent with that view, in his *Letter* he advised Soviet leaders that "no peripheral nation should be forcibly kept within the bounds of our country."

Now, that old advice has become a matter of practical necessity. Analyzing the current situation, Solzhenitsyn came to the conclusion that centrifugal tendencies are already so overwhelming that they "cannot be stopped without violence and bloodshed." Reproaching those Russian nationalists (among both the monarchist Russian emigres and Soviet "National-Bolsheviks") who take pride in the fact that the Soviet "Empire" has largely preserved the borders of the Empire of the Tsars, Solzhenitsyn says: "We should not be 'proud' of that, nor should we stretch our paws toward foreign lands. We must realize that our people are in the throes of a debilitating malaise--and we must pray for God to send us recovery and wisdom to follow it through." The choice the Russians are facing is thus "between the Empire, which, first of all, destroys us, on the one hand, and the spiritual and physical salvation of our people, on the other."[39]

Only when the separation is achieved, may the "cure" (*lechenie*) become effective, leading Russia to "recovery" (*vyzdorovlenie*) within its own territory. It will not be easy. "During the past three quarters of a century we have so impoverished ourselves, have become so depraved, exhausted and desperate, that many of us have lost all hope. So it now appears that only a Heavenly intercession can save us," says Solzhenitsyn. "But the Miracle will not be bestowed upon those who do not strive toward it,"[40] Solzhenitsyn admonishes his fellow countrymen. Convinced that the ultimate cause of all current Soviet problems is spiritual, namely, Russia's subversion by the atheistic, Communist, utopian idea, Solzhenitsyn warns that no cure from this mortal malady would be effective unless the Russians build their future on the rock of "our millennial [Christian] past."

Economic Cure

He then offers a number of proposals aimed at "curing" the ailing Russian economy (agriculture and industry), regional and central governance, church, family, and education. His economic proposals are clearly inspired by Petr Stolypin's agrarian reforms rather than by Lenin's New Economic Policy, which Gorbachev said he wanted to emulate. Gorbachev, like Lenin, wants to use a certain amount of privatization and free-marketization, chiefly in the form of trade concessions to westerners, in order to reanimate the moribund socialist economy. Solzhenitsyn, on the other hand, aims at creating an infrastructure of indigenous Russian private enterprise. This cannot be done without first getting rid of the Marxist-Leninist injunction against private property, a task which Gorbachev cannot carry out without ceasing to be a Communist. Not only is private ownership contrary to Communist ideology, but it creates a class of people who are economically independent of the omnipotent Communist state.

Solzhenitsyn bases his economic program on the firm belief that the extension of private ownership to as many people as possible will not only enhance economic activity, but will create an independent citizenry. That belief underlies Stolypin's reforms, which Lenin feared because he knew that the emergence of a large middle class of independent citizens would dash all hope for communist revolution. "There can be no rule of law until there is an independent citizen," Solzhenitsyn quotes Stolypin. "Therefore, the creation of a social order [based on the independence of private owners] should take precedence over all political programs."[41]

Solzhenitsyn's economic program is consistent with his fundamental view that private property, if equitably distributed, is not only a source of prosperity, but also a guarantee of civil liberty. In agriculture, he wants to complement personal land-leasing (which Gorbachev has allowed) with full private ownership, which he believes would encourage industriousness and "creative freedom" among the Russians. In industry, he argues for a speedy abandonment of "our centralized, idle, and ideologically-regulated economy which has impoverished the country." He proposes a three-tiered economy in which state, cooperative, and private enterprises compete with each other on equal footing. His vision is of "a healthy, honest, and intelligent private commerce which enlivens and unifies society."[42]

Leaving the details to be worked out by economic experts, he argues, however, against "thoughtless copying of an alien type of economy" from abroad without taking into account Russia's specificity. The result of such slavish copying, he cautions, might be domination from abroad. The price of our exit from Communism should not be the give-away of our land, forests, and natural resources to foreign capitalists, says Solzhenitsyn. He also emphasizes the urgency of protecting the Russian environment against despoliation in quest of foreign currency. Thus, in economics, as in the sphere of politics or culture, Solzhenitsyn insists that Russia should find its own way--the way that best suits its history, religion, geography and the character of its people.

He warns against the concentration of land and money in the hands of the few. If undertaken under the present corrupt administration, warns Solzhenitsyn, privatization may well end up with the "anonymous shadow-economy speculators" seizing control of economic life. These semi-criminal manipulators, he points out, are just about the only group which presently has enough money to purchase private property. (The other group, one might add, are corrupt officials who previously made their careers out of denouncing capitalism.) To counter the concentration of wealth in dishonest hands, Solzhenitsyn proposes that all citizens, including city dwellers, be entitled to a certain amount of land for free, paying only when the limit is exceeded.

Solzhenitsyn knows that transition to a market economy would inevitably entail severe hardships for millions of workers. Therefore, he proposes the creation of a social safety net to be financed by the savings accrued from a massive layoff of the "parasitic [management] apparatus." Furthermore, "the social evil of greed and egotism" should be restrained by anti-monopoly legislation, which would protect "healthy private enterprise" from domination by big money, foreign or domestic.

While defending all capitalist economies against the Soviet propaganda "caricature" of them, he finds particularly inspiring the example of Japan. The Japanese, according to Solzhenitsyn, "have risen from the fall [of World War II] not thanks to foreign investments, but by their superior work ethic." The main emphasis of his economic program is on fostering industriousness and entrepreneurial skills among the indigenous Russian population at the grass-roots level. Arguing for de-centralization, Solzhenitsyn urges a revival of some forty regional capitals, including those in Siberia, as centers of economic and cultural activity. "The path of our recovery is from the bottom up," he says. Believing that the native talents of Russian workers were wasted under Communism, he is confident that "as soon as the state oppression. . . is lifted and the pay [for workers] is fair, our workmanship will improve and our craftsmen will shine again."

Healing the Family

Among countless problems besetting the country, none is as urgent as the problem of raising a young generation. Alarmed by a falling birthrate, a growing infant mortality, unsanitary conditions of hospitals, and the abuse of women by men and the state, Solzhenitsyn is convinced that "unless *this* is straightened out today, it is pointless even to talk about our future." Saying that "the family is now the main link in the salvation of our future," he urges taking immediate steps to enable women "to return to the family to raise children." Without going into details, he says that men should be able to earn sufficient wages to relieve women from the double burden at workplace and at home. (He is aware, however, that many women must now work simply to make ends meet.)

Contrary to the common Western misperception of Soviet education as superior, Solzhenitsyn says that "our schools have long been teaching poorly and fostering badly." As a result, "our young generation has been drawn either toward criminality or toward a senseless and barbaric emulation of whatever seems alluringly foreign." Solzhenitsyn suggests a complete overhaul of the entire educational system. As a first step, he proposes an immediate de-ideologization of public education, a proposal that is consistent with the demand in his *Letter* that the Marxist-Leninist ideological monopoly be abolished. All school programs in humanities and social sciences, he says, should be "thrown out or completely rewritten" and "atheist indoctrination must cease immediately." This elimination of "ideological hogwash" should start at the colleges where school teachers are trained. Urging a greater attention to provinces rather than "the capital cities," Solzhenitsyn envisions that private schools, under the control of local districts, would play a major role in improving education for all Russians.

While aware that Marxist indoctrination has been counterproductive, Solzhenitsyn is more concerned that today's young Russians are too much attracted to the capitalist West. Unfortunately, they can consume only the cheapest and the least savory products of the West. "The historical Iron Curtain was effective in insulating our country from all that is good in the West: its civil liberty, respect for the individual, variety of personal pursuits, universal prosperity, and charitable movements. But the Curtain did not reach all the way down. And that's where the dung-wash of licentious and degrading 'pop-mass-culture' [...] has seeped through."[43] Scorning Soviet television for "subserviently broadcasting these filthy streams around the country," he mentions that in Israel, too, concerns have been raised about the threat that "American cultural imperialism" poses for Hebrew culture. It is his long-held conviction that not everything in the West is worth borrowing or emulating.

Political Overhaul or Spiritual Catharsis?

Solzhenitsyn's proposals about political reform contain a clear repudiation of the three principal forces presently contending for power: the so-called "conservatives" who attack Gorbachev from "the right"; the so-called "new democrats" who attack him from "the left"; and the Gorbachevite centrists who desperately cling to power by balancing between the two.

He dismisses the "conservatives" by denouncing the new Russian Communist Party formed under the leadership of Ivan K. Polozkov in the summer of 1990. Cognizant of the fact that some Russites have supported the idea of a separate Communist Party for the Russian Federation in the hope that it would advance the interests of ethnic Russians, Solzhenitsyn unequivocally condemns the RCP as the wrong way to advance the Russian cause. A "shameful extension" of the Communist Party of the Soviet Union, the RCP should not be allowed to "stain the name of Russia with all the blood and filth" associated with its progenitors.

Likewise, Solzhenitsyn wastes little time criticizing the mainstream CPSU and its General Secretary. Its removal from all levers of power is a precondition without which the country cannot be healed. In a chapter entitled "The Most Urgent Measures of the Russian Union," he proposes the confiscation of the "vast property" of the CPSU and recommends that Russia "stop feeding. . . the entire *nomenklatura* bureaucracy, the many million members of the parasitic administrative apparatus." The same goes for the KGB, which "has neither justification nor the right to exist." As in his *Letter*, Solzhenitsyn urges the cancellation of the development of offensive weapons, suspension of military-related space programs, and cessation of all support for Communist-led "tyrannical regimes." The money saved would be used to finance all other reforms.

As to the third political force, the so called "new democrats," Solzhenitsyn pays them considerably more attention than he does the other two. Apparently, he feels that, unlike the two Communist-led groups, the "new democrats" are on the rise, and that worries him. He is afraid that their schemes for reform, no matter how radical or well-intended, may do more harm than good. His brochure can be seen as a polemic with the "new democrats" on these two questions: What should a future, non-Communist Russia look like? What are the best ways to achieve it?

His fundamental disagreement with the "new democrats" is not as to whether a future Russia should be democratic or not. He emphasizes that the Russian Union will need democracy "very much."[44] But it is not enough to proclaim democracy. One must prepare the ground for democracy, find suitable seeds, choose a right time for planting them, and then carefully cultivate the strongest sprouts, protecting them from all natural and man-made adversities. Instead, the "new democrats" hope to advance democracy by cheap sloganeering, wishful thinking, demagoguery, and parroting the West. In so doing, Solzhenitsyn suggests, they are merely repeating the errors of the February Revolution, when their ideological predecessors succeeded in taking power from the tsar only to surrender it eight months later to the Bolsheviks.

Solzhenitsyn accuses the "new democrats" of wishing to destabilize "The System" to the point beyond which the country might well be plunged into chaos. A convinced evolutionist, he argues that "certain elements of our present state system have to be accepted, for the simple reason that they do exist." One such element is the institution of strong presidential power. Without mentioning Gorbachev by name, Solzhenitsyn seems to give him some credit for creating a stronger presidency, which "might be very useful for us for many years to come."

Although he may sound as radical as any of the "new democrats" in demanding a complete and immediate removal of the Party from power, Solzhenitsyn balances his radicalism by insisting, as he did in his *Letter*, that a transition to a new non-Communist Russian polity must be gradual, smooth, and non-violent. "If we do not crave another revolution," he says, the transition to a new polity must occur under conditions of "smooth continuity and stability." His entire program of political reform may be summed up in this sentence: "While retaining strong central authority [we must] patiently and persistently widen the rights of *local* life." [45]

The chief error of the "new democrats," Solzhenitsyn suggests, is rooted in their profound disregard for Russian history and blissful ignorance about the West. Failing to learn the lesson of 1917, they now push for a new "February Revolution" in the belief that it would lead straight to the establishment of a Western-style democracy in Russia. Denouncing their "self-delusion that there is no need to search for our indigenous way, that there is nothing to think about--just borrow as quickly as possible 'the way it is done in the West'," Solzhenitsyn challenges them with "We must search for *our own* way." Each Western country set up its democracy in its own way, determined by its history, but "Only we do not seem to need to look back and listen to what our [Russian] wise men had to say [on that score] before we were born," says Solzhenitsyn. While his pamphlet bears a strong personal imprint, it also offers a remarkable synopsis of pre-revolutionary and emigre Russian scholarship on the subject that for many decades was taboo in the USSR.

Solzhenitsyn's central idea is that the particular form of government and economy is secondary to a nation's spiritual foundations. "If the spiritual resources of a nation have dried up," he says, "then not even the best form of government, nor any sort of industrial development, can save it from death." One of the chief sources of the present malady is precisely the fact that the Communists reversed the order of priority by putting the "cart" of economic and political power before the "horse" of spirituality of human relations. As a result, not only the country's political institutions, economy, and ecology but also "the souls" of the people were destroyed in the name of the Marxist Utopia. "The destructions of our souls during the past three-quarters of a century--that's what is most terrible."

There could be no cure for Soviet economy or politics, Solzhenitsyn argues, unless it is preceded by a spiritual catharsis (*ochishchenie*). Unfortunately, the six "noisy" years of perestroika and glasnost saw little of this. But it might not be too late yet. While demanding the removal of the Party from power, Solzhenitsyn offers yet another olive-branch to Party leaders. "One wishes that this [the removal of the Party from power] would not happen by push and shove--but by the Party publicly [admitting and] repenting the fact that through a chain of crimes, cruelty, and absurdities it has led the country to the brink of an abyss, and that it does not know how to get out."

Such an act, says Solzhenitsyn, may greatly improve the "densely oppressive moral climate" suffocating the country.

Public repentance is expected not just from the Communist bureaucrats. Solzhenitsyn makes the same demand on "the glorious progressive forces of glasnost and perestroika," as he calls, tongue-in-cheek, pro- and anti-Gorbachev reformers. He particularly targets the new moguls of Soviet mass media and the new pundits of the Soviet educational establishment, "the smatterers," who by now have largely displaced the old-line apparatchiks.

> The word catharsis is not among their fashionable vocabulary. All the filthy mouths who for decades were subservient to totalitarianism have rushed into new glasnost. Three out of four troubadours of today's glasnost are former Brezhnevite sycophants. But which of them, even while cursing the impersonal 'stagnation,' has uttered a word of his own repentance? Those who for decades befouled students' minds from lecterns in the departments of humanities and social sciences, still continue to mouth their views with the same self-conceit. Tens of thousands of our intellectual smatterers have soiled themselves with hypocrisy and opportunism. Shouldn't we expect their repentance? Or shall we drag this pus with us into our future?[46]

These are harsh words. But they do not come from a fire-and-brimstone preacher. They come from a realist who knows that it is in the nature of a totalitarian regime to co-opt and corrupt all and everyone, with the exception of the few who dare to defy it openly. Solzhenitsyn is neither vindictive nor partisan in urging all his fellow citizens to repent. No layer of society is exempt from the need to repent. This includes the Orthodox church. "Alas, even today when all the country is on the move, the Orthodox hierarchy has hardly been touched by this revival of courage," observes Solzhenitsyn. "Only when the Church finds in itself the inner strength to free itself from the yoke of the state, will it be able to help us heal our society." He puts more hope, however, in "the revivalist movement from *below*, from the ordinary clergymen, the unified congregations and unselfish laymen."[47]

According to Solzhenitsyn, West Germany's economic "wonder" did not commence until after it had been showered by "the cloud of [universal] repentance" for the crimes committed by the Nazis. Why do our high-ranking "butchers and persecutors" continue to retain their posts or receive honorary pensions, he wonders. "In Germany, all such people, even the [Nazi] officials at lower ranks, were put on trial, but in our country, it is *they* who threaten to take us to court." Their public repentance is the least their victims can expect. Solzhenitsyn concludes that without such a catharsis "our development will be skewed," a conclusion that harks back to the motto familiar to all Americans, "The truth shall make us free."

Unrestrained Human Rights or Self-Restraint?

Solzhenitsyn also takes issue with human rights, "the most fashionable slogan of today." First of all, he points out that various groups define human rights differently, depending on their own group interests. Thus, while "our intelligentsia from the capital cities" demands freedom of speech or the right to emigrate, they deny to the provincial "plain folks" even the right to move into the capital cities. In short, every group wants to appropriate for itself as many "human rights" as possible at the expense of other groups. "No constitution, neither laws nor votes can in themselves create a balance in a society, because it is human nature to pursue one's own interests," says Solzhenitsyn. Therefore, a stable society can be built only on the basis of "conscious self-restraint when we realize that we must always yield to [the inner law of] ethical fairness." Russia will not be able to extricate itself from its present woes unless its people start abiding by the law of self-restraint. This task is even more formidable than the liberation from the Tartar yoke because "then the backbone of the [Russian] people was not crushed, nor was the Christian faith undermined among them."

Farther Ahead

In the second part of the essay, "Farther Ahead," Solzhenitsyn provides a historical perspective for a more remote vision of a future Russia. It is out of place to discuss it here in any sort of detail. Suffice it to say that he envisions a home-grown Russian democracy which he calls "democracy of the small localities."[48] He proposes that today's local Soviets (*sovety*) be replaced by self-governing bodies of the *zemstvo* type. The latter had flourished in the wake of Alexander II's reforms. After the October revolution, they were replaced by the Soviets, which "from the very beginning were subordinate to the Communist Party." Pointing out the *zemstvo*'s affinity with American townhall meetings and the self-governance of Swiss cantons, Solzhenitsyn urges a restoration and development of the *zemstvo* system, crowned by an indirectly elected All-Russian Assembly. He suggests that such "democracy of the small localities" be balanced by a strong central authority embodied in a president elected through direct universal vote.

Although political parties will exist, their role must be curtailed to prevent professional politicians from subverting democratic process through personal ambition and partisanship, argues Solzhenitsyn. According to him, the current Soviet electoral system gives unfair advantage to elitist candidates from "the capitals" who usually enjoy the support of the centralized mass media. Solzhenitsyn suggests a number of changes to assure a better representation for local interests so that "democracy of the small localities" would work from the bottom up.

Basing his vision on a broad spectrum of political philosophies, both Russian and foreign (Aristotle, Montesquieu, Alexis de Tocqueville, Oswald Spengler and Ronald Reagan are cited), Solzhenitsyn argues that democracy, like any other form of government, is bound to degenerate unless it is built on strong ethical foundations. Although "originally, the European democracy was filled with the spirit of Christian responsibility and self-discipline," says Solzhenitsyn, now it has largely lost that spirit. Pointing to the moral relativism of the Western "intellectual pseudo-elite," he cautions Russians against uncritically emulating it. Instead, he urges them to look at the West with "eyes that are wide-open, not bedazzled." Only then can the search for a better Russian future be fruitful.

Gorbachev Relegates Solzhenitsyn to the Past

Solzhenitsyn's "word" on Gorbachev's drive for reform had been eagerly awaited by various segments of Soviet society. Would

Solzhenitsyn throw his moral authority and world fame behind Gorbachev? Or would he side with Gorbachev's opponents? Which ones? Those who attack Gorbachev from "the conservative right"? Or Gorbachev's opponents from "the liberal left," the so-called "new democrats"? Early responses indicate that while Solzhenitsyn bitterly disappointed all three major political forces, he has encouraged non-partisan patriotic thinking among Russians of virtually all political persuasions and walks of life.

It was ironic that the first to respond to Solzhenitsyn's pamphlet was a successor to those who had snubbed his 1973 *Letter*. A few days after the pamphlet's publication, during a joint session of the USSR Supreme Soviet, a deputy from Kazakhstan asked Gorbachev what he thought about it. Gorbachev thus had a chance to make amends for his predecessors by striking a conciliatory note, without having to agree with everything in the pamphlet; but he did not do so. Although he did say that he respected Solzhenitsyn as a writer and "a great man," he still rashly dismissed him as a political anachronism.[49] "As a politician, I find Solzhenitsyn's political views alien to me, [because] he is entirely in the past, Russia's past, the tsarist monarchy," said Gorbachev, repeating a worn-out stereotype unsupported by the text of the pamphlet.

Gorbachev then portrayed Solzhenitsyn's proposals as "destructive," "out of the context of Soviet reality," anti-democratic, and ultimately irresponsible. The portrayal was self-serving because Gorbachev presented himself as "a democrat, inclined toward radical views" and yet endowed with a sense of historic responsibility. He even implied that because Solzhenitsyn proposed dissolving the "Union," he was less Russian than himself. (Since Gorbachev defined his "Russianness" and "democratism" in terms of adherence to Lenin, one American scholar aptly called him a National-Bolshevik.[50]) Even though Gorbachev said that he read the pamphlet twice, his comments show he was not an attentive reader. They also belie his reputation as a shrewd politician, for despite the support he received from two Ukrainian deputies, Boris Oleinik and Iurii Shcherbak, who accused Solzhenitsyn of Russian "great-power chauvinism," Gorbachev failed to set the tone for the country, especially among Russians.[51]

Moderate Russites Come to Solzhenitsyn's Defense

The primary reason for Gorbachev's failure was the support Solzhenitsyn received among those Russian nationalists whom I have called moderate Russites. It is hardly surprising that several of the authors who had been included in my selection (see Parts Two and Three) prior to the publication of Solzhenitsyn's pamphlet spoke up in his defense. I selected them precisely because an affinity of their ideas with those of Solzhenitsyn could be discerned.

Iurii Kariakin

One of the first to come to Solzhenitsyn's defense was Iurii Kariakin, a literary critic and people's deputy of the USSR. When interviewed on Central Soviet Television during the very same program "Vremia" in which Gorbachev's remarks had been broadcast the day before, Kariakin vigorously defended Solzhenitsyn. Without naming Gorbachev and the two other high-handed detractors, he advised them to read Solzhenitsyn more attentively lest they mistakenly ascribe to him monarchism, chauvinism, and other such "isms." Kariakin also sided with Solzhenitsyn by describing [the Gorbachevite conception of] perestroika as inadequate for the country's needs. What the country needs is "salvation, resurrection, and transfiguration," none of which is possible without a dialogue with such "great people" as [the late] Andrei Sakharov and Solzhenitsyn, said Kariakin in a double rebuke to Gorbachev, who had berated both.

He singled out for praise Solzhenitsyn's ideas on private property, a strong presidency, the need to do away with offensive weaponry, and the need for the Party to repent of its crimes and errors. Kariakin also endorsed Solzhenitsyn's proposal to dissolve the Soviet "Empire." He did it in full awareness that this proposal antagonized not only Gorbachev, but also many conservative "super-patriots" who, suffering from "imperial intoxication," have been urging Gorbachev to take stronger measures against separatists.[52]

Igor' Vinogradov

Igor' Vinogradov, another moderate Russite and a proponent of the "Russian Idea," came to Solzhenitsyn's defense in the liberal weekly *Moskovskie novosti*. Vinogradov virtually accused Gorbachev of "hastiness," if not deliberate slander, in respect to Solzhenitsyn. He challenged the President to find a single line in the pamphlet that would suggest a desire to return to the "tsarist monarchy." Vinogradov also defended Solzhenitsyn from unwarranted accusations of "great-power chauvinism." While expressing reservations in regard to some of Solzhenitsyn's proposals (indirect elections, e.g.), Vinogradov agreed with the main one, namely, that no exit from the current impasse is possible without the emergence of Russian national self-awareness, which alone is capable of producing "a truly national idea" to unify Russia and save it from impending catastrophe.[53]

Whereas Kariakin pointed out the disappontment that Solzhenitsyn's pamphlet has produced among the "super-patriots," Vinogradov took to task the other extreme, the "radical democrats." The latter failed to notice that Solzhenitsyn's national idea has a distinct "liberal-democratic orientation." Far from being hostile to the West, as his critics have asserted, Solzhenitsyn rejects only a thoughtless copying of Western experience.   Since Solzhenitsyn advocates a free market, private property, and political democracy, Vinogradov suggested, his national program is fully compatible with Western values. It would be foolish of the "radical democrats" to reject the "powerful moral support" which Solzhenitsyn gives to "our nascent *democracy*," argued Vinogradov. He was clearly inspired by the belief that Solzhenitsyn could help unify genuine Russian patriots and "radical democrats" into a single national-democratic opposition capable of producing a workable alternative to Communism.

Alla Latynina

A third author from my selection, a literary critic and a member of the editorial board of *Literaturnaia gazeta*, Alla Latynina, gave the most penetrating assessment of the impact of Solzhenitsyn's pamphlet on the debate about Russia's future.   In an article published by

Russkaia mysl',[54] a Russian emigre newspaper based in Paris, Latynina took to task not only Soviet detractors of Solzhenitsyn, but also "third-wave" emigres (mostly Jewish) and members of the Western left-liberal establishment. As an example of the latter she quoted *The New York Times* editorial comment which she heard on the Voice of America: "Intolerant of parliaments and elections, Solzhenitsyn calls for the creation of autocracy, founded on Orthodoxy and Russian nationalism." Saying that this statement consists of falsehoods and inaccuracies, Latynina suggested that *The Times* itself suffers from intolerance and bigotry. According to her, both Gorbachev's "cliches" and *The Times'* "hurried response" stem from the same source: "superficial [play at] democracy, the herd instinct, passion for platitudes, and a religious faith in progress, against which none dare to stand!"

As to the "third-wave" emigres, Latynina singled out for criticism Aleksandr Yanov, Maria Rozanova, Andrei Siniavskii, Vladimir Abovin-Yegides, and Vadim Belotserkovskii. Having participated in an "anti-Solzhenitsyn campaign in the West" as contributors to Radio Liberty's broadcasts, these emigres were abusing glasnost by manipulating the Soviet mass media. They were trying to persuade Soviet people, Latynina wrote, that "Solzhenitsyn is a staunch enemy of democracy" and that his "hopelessly retrograde views have horrified and repulsed the entire progressive West." She quoted Belotserkovskii's interview with a Moscow newspaper:

> For Solzhenitsyn, Communism is an absolute evil which Jews spread in the conditions of democracy. Consequently, these three things [Communism, Jews, and democracy??] must be annihilated. Therefore, Solzhenitsyn regards the democratic movement in the USSR as a great sin.

Everything is a lie in this passage, Latynina wrote, except that, unlike Belotserkovskii, Solzhenitsyn indeed sees Communism as the opposite of democracy.

Latynina had no compliments for the "liberal" Soviet press either. She accused the monthly magazine *Znamia* of trying to prejudice Soviet readers against Solzhenitsyn by publishing Andrei Sakharov's critique of Solzhenitsyn's 1973 *Letter* in full knowledge that neither the *Letter* nor Solzhenitsyn's response to Sakharov was available to Soviet readers.[55] She also criticized such darlings of the "liberal" Soviet intellectuals, as Roy Medvedev, Mikhail Shatrov, and Sergei Chuprinin for portraying Solzhenitsyn as "a reactionary," a "Russian Khomeini" and an antipode to Sakharov. Even such "democratic parliamentarians" as Galina Starovoitova, says Latynina, are "incapable of digesting the audacity of Solzhenitsyn's program."

According to Latynina, Solzhenitsyn's brochure produced the greatest disappointment in the ranks of the "bloc of patriotic forces," that is, those Russian nationalists who have failed to differentiate Russian national interests from those of the Soviet "Empire." "We Russians are a highly talented, heroic and courageous people, mighty in spirit," quotes Latynina from a manifesto of the "patriotic bloc."[56] Solzhenitsyn ridiculed these bombastic lines, says Latynina, when he enjoined the Russians not to "be puffed up with pride," but "to pray for God to send us recovery." Since these "Soviet patriots" had hoped that Solzhenitsyn would side with them, they were bitterly disappointed with his proposal to dissolve the "Union."[57]

Latynina argues that it was foolish to expect Solzhenitsyn to side with one or another faction of Soviet intellectuals. She questions whether politicized Soviet intellectuals are capable of understanding Solzhenitsyn's profoundly non-partisan program, which combines "political and spiritual radicalism" with absolute devotion to Russian traditions. While this unexpected combination of the "radical" and the "traditional" confuses Solzhenitsyn's critics, doesn't it promise "a series of bold reforms that would take us into a future across a bridge whose beach-head rests on our thousand-year history?" asks Latynina. Latynina's criticism of all major trends of Soviet politics may have accounted for the fact that her article was published only abroad.

Aleksandr Tsipko

Latynina's theme of whether politicized Soviet intellectuals are capable of understanding Solzhenitsyn was picked up by another author whose recent writings are reviewed in this book as an expression of the emerging Russian national thinking. He is Aleksandr Tsipko, a deputy director of the Institute of Economics of the World Socialist System, who quit the Party after the twenty-eighth congress in July

1990. In an interview carried by the "liberal" weekly *Ogonek* Tsipko criticized, first of all, the radical Soviet politicos for their partisanship.[58] They awaited Solzhenitsyn's "word" in the hope it would help *them*. But as soon as they discovered that the exile had a mind of his own, "It turned out that he was not needed here. They don't want to listen to him." Tsipko explains why. "If our politicos were not so deeply involved with their struggle for democracy," says Tsipko sarcastically, "they would be able to appreciate the writer's noble impulse, his pain and his wisdom."

Tsipko particularly reproached two of the most influential radical politicians--the mayor of Moscow, Gavriil Popov, and the mayor of Leningrad, Anatolii Sobchak--for their failure to support Solzhenitsyn. First of all, they should have admitted the correctness of his observation about "the radicals' unpreparedness for power." Referring to Sobchak's admission that many radical mandates were won thanks to "the tide of hatred" [of the voters against the regime], Tsipko questioned the opposition's ability to do "constructive work." Because Solzhenitsyn "clearly perceives the disease that plagues [our] society," argues Tsipko, he correctly warns against the "utopian illusions and radical deviltry" in the style of the February Revolution. The radicals' indulgence in sloganeering can only aggravate Russia's condition.

Tsipko particularly praised Solzhenitsyn for basing his "analysis of our situation on an authentic historical basis." Furthermore, he approved of Solzhenitsyn's appeal to give up the idea of imperial expansion, to concentrate on domestic affairs, and to "return to civilization." Tsipko also endorsed the idea that there could be no recovery unless the failure of the entire Communist experiment was recognized and a "return to our sources" initiated.

Like previous authors, Tsipko defended Solzhenitsyn against the attacks of the two Ukrainian writers and Gorbachev. Pointing out that Solzhenitsyn offered his "humble reflections" to spur a national dialogue for finding the means to avert an impending catastrophe, Tsipko condemned all three attacks as gratuitous. "I understand the complexity of Gorbachev's situation. Nonetheless I consider his comments a flop. It is time we stop pasting labels [on people], especially false ones," said Tsipko, alluding to the effort to dismiss

Solzhenitsyn as a man of the past. He went on to explain why Gorbachev's comments might have hurt his own political fortunes.

"Solzhenitsyn supports strong presidential power, and Gorbachev needs such authoritative support," argued Tsipko in reference to the one point of the pamphlet on which Gorbachev gave no comment. "I am struck by one fact. . . If Gorbachev had the courage and wisdom to phone Sakharov in Gorky to invite him to Moscow, what is to prevent him from placing a phone call to Vermont [where Solzhenitsyn resides]?" asked Tsipko. A mere invitation to return would not do, however. Gorbachev must *ask* Solzhenitsyn to return, and this he cannot do without first apologizing to the writer. "All of us are guilty before this man, and we still fail to offer him our apologies," said Tsipko.

Tsipko probably had in mind two main reasons for feeling "guilty." First, many of today's "troubadours of glasnost" either applauded Brezhnev's decision to exile Solzhenitsyn or lacked the courage to defend him as the first true champion of glasnost. Second, today's reformers have yet to acknowledge Solzhenitsyn's 1973 *Letter* as one of the first blueprints for genuine reform. Realizing that making apologies requires moral courage, Tsipko suggested that the potential benefits might outweigh the embarrassment. "The leadership of the country, no less than its intelligentsia, need to unite with the people. To achieve that unity, they must perform [moral] deeds which people could really appreciate," said Tsipko. To make sure Gorbachev got the message, Tsipko appealed to his own sense of reality. "Even if one thinks in terms of Bolshevism," said Tsipko, alluding to Gorbachev's admiration for the early Bolsheviks who are variously seen as pragmatic or Machiavellian, "it is, after all, to our own advantage [to have Solzhenitsyn's moral authority on our side]."

Tsipko's words should carry a special weight for Gorbachev. Tsipko is one of the few "troubadours of glasnost" who was not tainted by the sycophancy of the Brezhnev era. A moderate Russite, he seems to be on good terms with Westernizers and "democrats." Above all, he was one of the few influential reformist intellectuals who did not desert Gorbachev when El'tsin won the Russian presidency and began to assert himself at the expense of "central authority." It was Tsipko who refused to go along with the crowd, questioning whether El'tsin's drive for Russia's sovereignty was not caused by his personal rivalry with

Gorbachev rather than concern for Russia.[59] Arguing that it was "impossible to quit the USSR without completely destroying Russia," he warned that Russia's sovereignty may become an escape route for those who want to avoid responsibility for the fate of Russia's historical neighbors. At any rate, Gorbachev can ill afford to ignore Tsipko's advice in regard to Solzhenitsyn. For, waiting in the wings, is El'tsin himself.

Boris El'tsin

It is hardly surprising that El'tsin expressed a much more favorable view of Solzhenitsyn's pamphlet than Gorbachev.[60] He even took credit for making photostat copies of the pamphlet for the benefit of all RSFSR deputies, "so that they could read it very attentively." Saying that "there are a lot of interesting ideas there," El'tsin suggested that some of them--he did not specify which--might be included in his political agenda. Still, even though he later told the Russian parliament that he was "intrigued by the idea of a union of the three Slavic republics,"[61] he stopped short of unequivocally endorsing any of Solzhenitsyn's ideas. One has the impression that El'tsin's attitude toward Solzhenitsyn depends on political rather than moral considerations. Like Popov and Sobchak, El'tsin seems to ignore Solzhenitsyn's call for repenting one's own role in building the tottering structure of the Soviet state.

Toward a Demo-Patriotic Coalition

It is quite natural that virtually all moderate Russites welcomed Solzhenitsyn's pamphlet enthusiastically. It is hardly surprising that those professing "Soviet patriotism" were taken aback at his proposal to dissolve the "Empire." Nor was it unexpected that the "troubadours of glasnost," whether those in the Party or those who quit it, have generally ignored the pamphlet. What *is* surprising is the fact that in spite of being debunked or ignored by the Gorbachevite centrists and their opponents on the left and on the right, the pamphlet proved its power to appeal across ideological and political divisions (with the exception of die-hard Communists).

This is apparent from the comments of people not known to belong to any particular camp. Several such authors have suggested that Solzhenitsyn's brochure may help overcome ideological divisions among the Russians. Noting that "Solzhenitsyn belongs to no party," L. Surazhskii proclaimed him "the only prophet of our Fatherland," whose ideas, he added, are not incompatible with those of Andrei Sakharov.[62] Mikhail Sokolov of *Sobesednik* likewise thinks that Solzhenitsyn is an ally rather than an opponent of "Europhile Russia." By renouncing "imperial totalitarianism," says Sokolov, Solzhenitsyn made a significant step toward a "compromise between [today's] Westernizers and Slavophiles."[63] Sokolov suggested that now it is the Westernizers' turn to reciprocate by adopting some of Solzhenitsyn's ideas in the draft of the Russian constitution. Iurii Makartsev, the political observer of *Rabochaia tribuna*, also emphasized the pamphlet's relevance for today. In spite of being largely ignored and even "silenced"[64] by the Soviet mass media, says Makartsev, Solzhenitsyn's brochure has the potential to decisively influence the country's future development. Like Sokolov, Makartsev is convinced that the current debate on the future Russian constitution would be meaningless unless Solzhenitsyn's ideas are taken into account.

Finally, comparing the USSR to a sinking ship, Viacheslav Kondrat'ev recalled that Solzhenitsyn's *Letter to the Soviet Leaders* was an early warning for the ship of state to change its fatal course.[65] It was precisely because the warning was ignored that the ship is now in peril. A well-respected novelist himself, Kondrat'ev suggested that Solzhenitsyn's pamphlet offered a last chance for preventing the ship from sinking. Exasperated by the tendency of Soviet intellectuals to "split into [warring] groups," Kondrat'ev expressed the hope that the pamphlet may yet become a focal point for "the consolidation of all progressive forces." Unless such consolidation occurs, "nothing would come out of even the best thought-out plans for reforms, whether economic or political," concluded Kondrat'ev.

Western Reaction

Western reaction to Solzhenitsyn's pamphlet has ranged from stereotypes of the author as an incorrigible "autocrat" to admiration, not just for his vision of Russia's future, but also for his critique of the flaws in modern Western democracies. I have already discussed what Latynina thought about *The New York Times*'s editorial comment. As an expression of the left-liberal attitude, that comment was hardly surprising. Nor was it surprising that *The Times* echoed Gorbachev so closely (was it the other way around?). After all, the left-liberal establishment's support for Gorbachev's "reform Communism" has naturally evolved from its former dalliance with Gorbachev's totalitarian predecessors. More surprising is that the conservative *Washington Times*, which never agrees with *The New York Times* on anything, did agree on Solzhenitsyn's "anachronism." It advised the Russians not to take Solzhenitsyn for "a rational politician offering a correct plan for the future."[66]   *Time* magazine was more cautious. Conceding that the pamphlet "may liberate [Solzhenitsyn] from his reputation as an advocate of authoritarianism," *Time* no longer found Solzhenitsyn to be anti-democratic. But it skirted the question of his relevance for today.[67]

Then there is the opinion of Michael Scammell, perhaps the foremost Western scholarly authority on Solzhenitsyn. Comparing the recent pamphlet with the 1973 *Letter to the Soviet Leaders*, Scammell found that Solzhenitsyn's vision was "stuck in the nineteenth century" and "though changing in many details, has not varied as much as some had expected in response to the radical changes of the past five years." Calling him "a crusty conservative," "a patriarchic populist," "an incurable romantic," and "a Slavophile dreaming of a Russian golden age," Scammell accused Solzhenitsyn of "myopia" that "almost certainly will undermine his reputation." Due to "myopia," he now "has gone even further than he did in 1973 with a detailed political and economic program that is likely to be ignored, if not laughed out of court," Scammell predicted.[68]

In a more recent assessment of Solzhenitsyn's pamphlet, David Remnick, a veteran *New York Times* reporter, took a revisionist view that may help improve the exile's image in his adopted country. In a lengthy article published in *The New York Book Review* and datelined

Moscow, January 17, 1991, Remnick analyzed Solzhenitsyn's pamphlet and its impact on the USSR without the bias that distinguished his newspaper's editorial.[69] He even attacked Gorbachev for distorting Solzhenitsyn by "exploiting the recurrent stereotype of his views." (Or was it a sneak attack on his own newspaper, which did much to create and perpetuate the stereotype?) An essential part of that stereotype is the allegation of Solzhenitsyn's anti-Semitism. "But despite years of rumors and innuendoes from his critics, no one has yet made a cogent, sustained textual case that Solzhenitsyn is himself an anti-Semite," says Remnick. Even when Solzhenitsyn puts "[his] passions and his rhetoric in the service of Russian national renewal," he "shows no sign of fanaticism."

To be sure, Remnick finds some problems with Solzhenitsyn, "But I would argue--and reactions in Moscow bear me out--that Solzhenitsyn cannot be counted in any way with the hysterical nationalists who edit *Nash sovremennik* and *Literaturnaia Rossiia*, the black-shirted anti-Semites of Pamiat', and the pathetic monarchists who all so desperately wanted to claim him as their own." Once again hailing Solzhenitsyn as "an essential voice of resistance" against "the Lie" [of "reform Communism"], Remnick stopped short of predicting a political role for him. "While Solzhenitsyn may be a polemicist," says Remnick, "he is no politician."   Yet, referring to Solzhenitsyn's condemnation of "the much-celebrated perestroika," Remnick admitted that while "that judgment seemed almost incredibly harsh when it was published in September," now, merely four months later, "the brutal crackdown in Lithuania and Gorbachev's disdain for the democratically elected government there give it the painful ring of truth." More than anything else, this admission explains why a revision of Solzhenitsyn's "recurrent stereotype" in the West is in order. History has been teaching its lessons in accordance with Solzhenitsyn, not with the politicians in Moscow and their admirers in New York.

On the other side of the Atlantic, several observers emphasized the brochure's relevance not just for Eastern Europe, but also for the West. Writing in the conservative *Le Figaro*, Philippe Beneton, a French legal scholar, praised Solzhenitsyn for drawing attention to the "crisis of liberal democracy" in the West. "The worst thing we could do for our brethren in Eastern Europe is export to them our [moral] relativism," says Beneton.[70] Calling Solzhenitsyn a "prophet," Enzo

Bettiza, an Italian journalist, compared him with Vaclav Havel, a dissident-turned-president of Czecho-Slovakia, "except that he should be enlarged to the size of Russia." Bettiza predicted that eventually Gorbachev, the pagan "Emperor," would bow before Solzhenitsyn the Christian and proclaim, just as Julian the Apostate once did: "You've won, Galilean!"[71]

In an article that also appeared in Russian translation in *Literaturnaia gazeta*, Vittorio Strada, an Italian specialist on Russian literature, wrote that events in the USSR have borne out Solzhenitsyn's prophetic warning in *Letter to the Soviet Leaders*: "A time of peril will come, when [just as in World War II] you will again call upon this [Russian] people, not world Communism. And your fate--even *yours*--will be in *our* hands." In an appeal to the common sense of the West, Strada virtually equated Solzhenitsyn's pamphlet with the new political reality emerging in the East: "A new Russia, the Russia of Solzhenitsyn, is teaching us a lesson on how to fuse political realism with profound morality. [Even for its own sake] the West must enter into a dialogue, and free partnership, with this Russia--in order to acquire a new vitality."[72]

Conclusion

Although he had no illusions about the Brezhnevite leadership to whom his 1973 *Letter* was addressed, Solzhenitsyn may have hoped that the Kremlin's institutional memory would preserve and forward the *Letter* to reform-minded successors. This must be one of the reasons why he remained silent for so long. After Gorbachev came to power in March 1985, it appeared for a while that Gorbachev might be a leader capable of putting the country's national interests above those of his Party. After all, Gorbachev did give up on Communism's "world historic mission," shifting attention to domestic problems, exactly as Solzhenitsyn demanded in the *Letter*. Perhaps Solzhenitsyn wondered whether Gorbachev might not somehow realize that as long as reforms were handed down by the Party they would have no popular support, conversely, that only reforms leading away from and beyond Communism had a chance to succeed. Then Gorbachev would stand a chance of becoming a true reformer and national leader for whom *Patria* invariably stands above *Partia*.

Alas, this did not happen. Instead, as I have argued elsewhere in this book, Gorbachev's perestroika became but a parody of Solzhenitsyn's plan for reforms spelled out in his *Letter*. As a result, the country is now in worse shape than it was seventeen years ago. Many of its problems have become so acute that it is no longer a question of the "socialist" country reaching "world technological standards," as Gorbachev defined the goal of perestroika. Having wasted six more years, the Party has proved itself totally incapable of either reforming the country or reforming itself out of its totalitarian mold. The grace period, or the benefit of doubt, that Solzhenitsyn tacitly bestowed upon Gorbachev has now expired. It is now a question of averting the catastrophes of chaos, famine and civil war. Without the revival of Russia those catastrophes cannot be averted.

Notes

1. A speech delivered by the author at the Alaska World Affairs Council, Anchorage, February 12, 1988. Printed in Vital Speeches of the Day, LIV:13, April 15, 1988, pp. 393-396, used with permission.

2. See Solzhenitsyn's interview with David Remnick, Washington Post, April 21, 1989.

3. As reported by the Washington Post Service on June 25, 1989. That the pro-publication campaign is gaining momentum was further underscored by the announcement that in 1990 the publishing house "Soviet Russia" would publish a collection of Solzhenitsyn's prose. See Literaturnaia Rossiia, May 26, 1989.

4. A. Vasil'kov, "Vermontskii otshel'nik," Trud, May 12, 1989, p. 4.

5. A. Solzhenitsyn, "Otkrytoe pis'mo sekretariatu Soiuza Pisatelei RSFSR, November 12, 1969 (Sobranie sochinenii, vol. 6)

6. See Vladislav Krasnov, Solzhenitsyn and Dostoevsky: A Study in the Polyphonic Novel (University of Georgia Press, 1980).

7. Alexander Solzhenitsyn, ed., From Under the Rubble (Boston: Little, Brown, and Co., 1975).

8. Alexander I. Solzhenitsyn, Letter to the Soviet Leaders (Harper and Row, 1975).

9. One person to notice the similarity was Lev Losev, an emigre poet. However, even though he treats Solzhenitsyn with sympathy, Losev hardly makes the writer's ideas more palatable to the West by dubbing them "Slavophile" without explaining it. See his column, "Finally, the Slavophiles Triumph," The New York Times, March 31, 1989.

10. A number of other dissidents (Igor Ogurtsov, Andrei Sakharov, Sergei Soldatov, Roy Medvedev, Anatoly Fedoseev, Igor Glagolev, e.g.) have offered their plans for reforms, but none was as pragmatic as Solzhenitsyn's. See my chapter, "Images of the Soviet Future: The Emigre and Samizdat Debate," in The Soviet Union and Challenge of the Future, eds. Alexander Shtromas and Morton Kaplan (New York: Paragon, 1988).

11. For more on this see Solzhenitsyn's "Misconceptions About Russia Are a Threat to America," Foreign Affairs, April 1980, and Vladislav Krasnov, "The Social Vision of Aleksandr Solzhenitsyn," Modern Age, Vol. 28, Nos 2-3, Spring/Summer 1984.)
      A measure of Western lack of appreciation for the Letter may be seen in Michael Scammell's Solzhenitsyn: A Biography (New York, Norton, 1984). Failing to see Solzhenitsyn's pragmatism, Scammell reproached him for "[coming up] with a totally surprising suggestion--to bring back the soviets of the twenties (p.867)." One of the first political moves of Gorbachev was exactly trying to revive the soviets.

12. George Kennan, "America and the Russian Future," American Diplomacy, 1900-1950 (Univ. of Chicago Press, 1951), p. 136.

13. Letter, p. 67. Most of the quotations were checked against the Russian original, "Pis'mo vozhdiam Sovetskogo Soiuza," in Aleksandr Solzhenitsyn, Publitsistika (Paris: YMCA-Press, 1981). It is noteworthy that Solzhenitsyn does occasionally use the word perestroika for his program of reforms. For example, on p. 144 (see "Pis'mo,") he calls for a "renewal and restructuring (perestroika) both in the West and the East." In his introductory essay for From Under the Rubble he stresses the need for "restructuring moral outlook" (perestroika soznaniia) as a precondition for political reforms (p. 18). For the Russian original see Iz-pod glyb (Paris : YMCA Press, 1974), p. 21.

14. Letter, pp. 76 and 77.

15. Letter, p. 73.

16. Some American scholars agree with Solzhenitsyn that the Marxist-Leninist ideological monopoly is one of the pillars of totalitarianism. See, e.g., Carl A. Linden, The Soviet Party-State: The Politics of Ideocratic Despotism (New York: Praeger, 1983).

17. Letter, p. 74.

18. Letter, p. 43.

19. Letter, p. 45-46.

20. Letter, p. 49.

21. E.F. Schumacher, Small is Beautiful: Economics as if People Really Mattered (New York, 1973).

22. Letter, p. 44.

23. Letter, p. 47.

24. Letter, p. 77 and 78.

25. Letter, p. 19.

26. Letter, p. 20.

27. Letter, p. 75-76.

28. Mikhail Gorbachev, Perestroika: New Thinking for Our Country and the World (Harper & Row, 1987).

29. It is possible that when he assumed power in March 1985, Gorbachev had not read Solzhenitsyn's Letter, but he must have, at least, heard about it and known of its main thrust. Certainly, since 1985 he had had plenty of time to read the Letter. If he somehow failed to do so, it must be regarded as a dereliction of duty.

More surprising is the fact that while lavishing all praise on Gorbachev, the West failed to duly acknowledge the contribution of Soviet dissidents, including Solzhenitsyn, to the process of change.

30. Gorbachev, Perestroika, p. 119.

31. Dr. John B. Dunlop of the Hoover Institution discerns several "faces" of modern Russian nationalism, including its chauvinistic, anti-Semitic, and xenophobic sidestreams and undercurrents. However, he describes its mainstream, represented by Solzhenitsyn and other proponents of the "national-religious renaissance," as defensive, liberal-democratic, centrist, moderate, and generally wholesome. See his The Faces of Contemporary Russian Nationalism (Princeton Univ. Press, 1984) and "The Contemporary Russian Nationalist Spectrum" (Special edition of Radio Liberty Research Bulletin of december 19, 1988). Other scholars, such as George Gibian, Darrell Hammer, Donald Treadgold, and Adam Ulam, have also pointed out the liberating potential of Russian nationalism of the Solzhenitsyn stripe.

32. Letter, pp. 39 and 40 fn.

33. See Solzhenitsyn's essay, "Repentance and Self-Limitation in the Life of Nations," in From Under the Rubble, esp. pp. 119-120.

34. See V. Ivanitskii's report, "Na chasakh prirody," Sovetskaia Rossiia, April 28, 1989.

35. Letter, pp. 64-65.

36. See, for instance, Vasilii Selyunin, "Istoki," Novyi mir, No. 5, 1988; Aleksandr Tsipko, "Istoki Stalinizma," Nauka i zhizn', Nos. 11, 12 (1988),1, 2 (1989); Andrei Vasilevskii, "Stradanie pamiati," Oktiabr', No. 4, 1989; Igor' Zolotusskii, "Krushenie abstraktsii," Novyi mir, No. 1, 1989. These authors are discussed in parts Two and Three.

37. Aleksandr Solzhenitsyn, "Kak obustroit' Rossiiu: Posil'nye soobrazheniia," quoted below from an edition that appeared as a special supplement to Russkaia mysl' , a Russian emigre weekly, No. 3846, September 21, 1990. Translation to English is my own.

38. Ibid., p. 13.

39. Ibid., p. 6.

40. Ibid., p. 12.

41. Ibid., p. 15.

42. Ibid., pp. 16 and 17.

43. Ibid., p. 20.

44. Ibid., p. 35.

45. Ibid., p. 21.

46. Ibid., p. 23.

47. Ibid., pp. 23-24.

48. In addition to zemstvo, he sees the precedents of such democracy in the Russian village commune mir], in town assemblies [veche] that existed in a number of medieval Russian principalities, and in Cossack self-government. For more about Russia's democratic tradition, see Sergei Pushkarev, Self-Government and Freedom in Russia, Westview Press, 1988.

49. A transcript of Central Soviet TV, September 25, 1990.

50. John B. Dunlop, "Russian Reactions to Solzhenitsyn's Brochure," RL 504/90, December 10, 1990.

51. The non-Russian responses are outside of the scope of this study. Still, a brief summary may be useful. Early responses indicate a mixed reception for the idea of an immediate dissolution of the Union. While the Balts seemed to welcome it, there was a strong negative reaction among the Kazakhs who especially object to Solzhenitsyn's suggestion that part of Kazakhstan would stay with Russia. Several Ukrainian and Belorussian critics were incensed by the idea of a Russian tri-Slavic union. They largely ignored the fact that Solzhenitsyn insisted that that union must be strictly voluntary. Some of the non-Russian criticism seems valid and should be treated seriously. Its exclusion from this study implies no disrespect. For more, see "The Solzhenitsyn Debate," Radio Liberty's Report on the USSR, Vol. 2, No. 40, October 5, 1990.

52. Central TV, September 26, 1990.

53. Igor' Vinogradov, "Glazami ne vostorzhennymi, a iasno otkrytymi," Moskovskie novosti, No. 40, October 7, 1990.

54. Alla Latynina, "Kto uslyshit Solzhenitsyna?", Russkaia mysl', No. 3849, October 12, 1990.

55. About Znamia's (No. 2, 1990) publication of Sakharov's critique of Solzhenitsyn see R. Gal'tseva and I. Rodnianskaia, "Spor vopreki uchastnikam, Literaturnaia gazeta, No. 10, March 7, 1990.

56. "Pis'mo pisatelei, deiatelei kul'tury i nauki Rossii," Nash sovremennik, No. 4, April, 1990.

57. According to Latynina, Solzhenitsyn's pamphlet put the "patriotic forces" in disarray. Although she mentioned no names, she may have been referring to such well-known but less than moderate Russites as Valentin Rasputin, Stanislav Kuniaev, and Igor' Shafarevich, all three included in this book. Since Rasputin was the first to publicly suggest the idea of Russia's secession from the Union, his response to a similar idea of Solzhenitsyn's is somewhat surprising. In an interview with Iurii Makartsev (Rabochaia tribuna, November 28, 1990), Rasputin said that he, "of course, disagreed with the dissolution of the Union." But he admitted that the pamphlet contains an "enlightening meaning" (prosvetlennyi smysl). In another interview he said that he recognized Solzhenitsyn as a greater moral authority than the late Sakharov (Reported by Conor O'Clery, The New Republic, November 19, 1990). Kuniaev was reported as saying that Solzhenitsyn remains "a spokesman for the ethical views of Nash sovremennik," of which Kuniaev is the editor.

As to Shafarevich, he responded with a curious article, "Mozhno li eshche spasti Rossiiu?", that appeared in Komsomol'skaia pravda on October 18, 1990, a month after Solzhenitsyn's pamphlet was published there. While seemingly disagreeing with Solzhenitsyn (whose name he hardly mentioned at all), he actually endorsed all of his major proposals. Among other Russites, Vasili Belov, a people's deputy, defended Solzhenitsyn against Gorbachev. Viktor Afanas'ev, Vladimir Krupin, and Vladimir Bondarenko also spoke favorably of the pamphlet. Unlike "democrats," the nationalists tend to agree with Solzhenitsyn's ideas on indirect elections, the zemstvo, and "democracy from below."

58. Aleksandr Tsipko, "Ostorozhno: Bol'shevizm," an interview, Ogonek, No. 47, November 17-24, 1990.

59. Aleksandr Tsipko, "Russkie ukhodiat iz Rossii?", Izvestiia, May 26, 1990.

60. See El'tsin's interview in Komsomol'skoe znamia, September 30, 1990.

61. Dunlop, "Russian Reactions."

62. L. Surazhskii, "Litsom k otechestvu," Nedelia (the weekly supplement to Izvestiia), No. 40, 1990.

63. Mikhail Sokolov, "Parlamentskaia Rossiia i Aleksandr Solzhenitsyn," Sobesednik (the weekly supplement to Komsomol'skaia pravda), No. 39, 1990.

64. Iurii Makartsev, "Neudobnyi mudrets," Rabochaia tribuna, November 28, 1990. Makartsev probably has in mind not a deliberate "silencing" of Solzhenitsyn but rather the fact that leading Soviet politicians, such as Gavriil Popov, Anatolii Sobchak, Iurii Afanas'ev, and the majority of the "troubadours of glasnost," refrained from publicly discussing his substantive proposals. The same observation was made by Tsipko, Latynina, and Kondrat'ev. On the other hand, the pamphlet provoked quite a stir among ordinary readers. Both Literaturnaia gazeta and Komsomol'skaia pravda reported an "enormous" mail response, the latter receiving 1,070 letters within a month of the pamphlet's publication. Moreover, when Nedelia, a Sunday supplement to Izvestiia, asked six Soviet historians to comment on Solzhenitsyn's proposal to revive the zemstvo system, all six were virtually unanimous on the zemstvo system's superiority to the current Soviets and urged its revival, under whatever name, as a truly democratic institution. ("Chto moglo zemstvo," Nedelia, No. 48, 1990; the six scholars were Aleksandr Degtiarev, Kornelii Shatsillo, Vladimir Zots, Aleksandr Zamaleev, Valerii Kvartal'nov, and Grigorii Gerasimenko.)

65. Viacheslav Kondrat'ev, "Opiat' kak v 17-m?", Literaturnaia gazeta, No. 38, October 10, 1990.

66. Both editorials, The New York Times's and Washington Times's, appeared in Russian translation in the Soviet weekly Argumenty i fakty, No. 40, October 6-12, 1990. I am quoting in reverse translation into English.

67. For a review of Solzhenitsyn's brochure see Time, October 1, 1990.

68. Michael Scammell, "To the Finland Station? The Solzhenitsyn Factor in Russian Politics," The New Republic, November 19, 1990.

69. David Remnick, "Native Son," The New York Review of Books, No. 4, February 14, 1991.

70. Phillipe Beneton, "Solzhenitsyn stavit vse na svoi mesta," Russkaia mysl', December 28, 1990 (translation from Le Figaro of December 20, 1990).

71. Enzo Bettiza, "Otverzhennyi prorok," Russkaia mysl', October 19, 1990 (translation from a literary supplement to Stampa, September 26, 1990, Turin, Italy).

72. Vittorio Strada, "Pochemu Solzhenitsyn protiv 'imperskogo durmana'," Literaturnaia gazeta, November 7, 1990 (translated from the Italian newspaper Corriere della Sera, September 21, 1990).

2

Beyond Marxism-Leninism:
Voices of Glasnost 1987-1988

In the preface to his book, *Perestroika: New Thinking for Our Country and the World*, Gorbachev emphatically denied that perestroika "signifies disenchantment with socialism and a crisis for its ideals and ultimate goals."[1] He also implied that such a false interpretation of perestroika can come only from some inveterate anti-Communists in the West. In fact, as I will demonstrate in this chapter, there are some people in the USSR, even among Gorbachev's most ardent supporters, who are disenchanted with socialism, particularly with the only "true" kind practiced in the USSR. These people think of socialism more or less what Gorbachev ascribed to Western anti-Communists. Not only do they think so, but, thanks to glasnost, they articulate their ideas and sentiments with an increasing clarity and boldness in the pages of Soviet publications.

What follows is a brief survey of more than a dozen articles which, in my view, reflect genuine new thinking among Soviet intellectuals--a sort of "cultural revolution," except that, being neither sponsored by the Communist Party nor inspired by Marxism-Leninism, it may rather be seen as a "cultural counter-revolution." Although some of the authors in my selection openly defy the Party's authority on ideological matters, none challenges its political authority. On the contrary, all seem to be decidedly pro-perestroika and pro-Gorbachev. In this respect, their articles foreshadow that "revolution from below" which, Gorbachev has said, is necessary for his "revolution from above" to succeed, even though one may question whether it is what Gorbachev has bargained for.

The majority of articles were published in *Novyi mir*. This is not accidental. One of the best Soviet literary magazines, it has a long tradition of championing the liberalization and democratization of Soviet cultural and political life. It has been one of the principal conduits for glasnost and a barometer of change in the USSR since Khrushchev's "thaw."[2] Suffice it to say that it was *Novyi mir*, under the editorship of Aleksandr Tvardovskii, that published in 1962 Aleksandr Solzhenitsyn's novel *One Day in the Life of Ivan Denisovich* and thus at once lifted the then unknown author to world fame. After Tvardovskii's forced resignation in 1970, the magazine went through a period of relative decline, reflecting, as a barometer, the country's general stagnation of the Brezhnev era. However, after Sergei Zalygin became its new editor in September 1986, *Novyi mir* not only fully restored its former liberal reputation but assumed a new role as the principal forum for the moderate Russites. (For more on Zalygin, see Chapter 3.)

The policy of glasnost has created unusual opportunities for major periodicals to exert influence not only in forming independent public opinion but also in enlightening people in the ways of thinking beyond the limits of Marxism-Leninism. *Novyi mir* seized on that new opportunity with passion. "Our goal is to assist in the formation of a modern world view (*mirovozzrenie*) by means of enlightenment and glasnost. Our slogan is to publish what nobody publishes. . . . We need periodicals independent from the Party bureaucracy and state apparatus," said one of *Novyi mir*'s new editors, Anatolii Strelianyi.[3] Although Strelianyi did not stay in his job for very long, perhaps because his declaration of *Novyi mir*'s independence from Party bureaucracy was premature, there is little doubt that his formulation of the goal of the magazine has retained its validity even after his departure. Anyway, my sample would show that the magazine has made big strides in the "formation of a modern world view" to replace the antiquated Marxism-Leninism.

As to the direction of the search for a new world view, it has to do with the fact that Zalygin is not only one of the prominent "village prose writers" (*derevenshchiki*), but also a patron of this literary movement. His appointment reflects the increasing influence of the "villagers" not only as a literary school in opposition to Socialist Realism but also as a philosophical movement in opposition to

Marxism-Leninism. Although the "villagers" movement originated in the 1950s as a primarily literary school concerned with a truthful description of the fate of the Russian countryside under Communism, it has gradually evolved into a philosophy of life that is poles apart from Marxism-Leninism.[4]

It is out of place here to discuss this ruralist philosophy in any sort of detail. Suffice it to say that, whereas Marxism-Leninism is founded on the cornerstones of (1) class struggle, (2) violent revolution as the midwife of history, (3) the subjugation of nature to man, and (4) the primacy of economic "bases" over cultural and ethical "superstructure," the ruralists advocate social peace, promote national and international reconciliation, reject violence (advocating harmony between man and nature), and assert the primacy of ethical and religious values over the ever changing economic, social, and political conditions. Marx's indictment of "the idiocy of rural life" stands in sharp contrast to the ruralists' defense of the Russian village as the last bastion of traditional values against the onslaught of the Marxist utopians.

In short, the ruralist world view in general and their attitude toward the Russian peasantry in particular is much closer to that of Solzhenitsyn than to that of either Marx or Lenin. Considering the seminal influence that the early works of Solzhenitsyn, such as *One Day in the Life of Ivan Denisovich* and "Matriona's House," have exerted on a generation of Soviet readers, this is hardly accidental. Solzhenitsyn and the Soviet ruralists are particularly close to each other in the defense of the Russian peasantry as one of the last remaining repositories of Russian national culture and spirituality. The ruralist movement has gradually transcended its original orientation toward the peasantry as a social class to become part of a broader phenomenon, the revival of Russian nationalism. That revival manifests itself in a struggle for the emancipation of Russian national patriotism from co-optation by the so-called "Soviet patriotism."[5]

Within the broad ideological spectrum of contemporary Russian nationalism, both Zalygin and the academician Dmitrii Likhachev, who became a member of the magazine's editorial board in February 1987, have been identified with its moderate liberal-democratic mainstream. Solzhenitsyn is the best known spokesman abroad.[6] Like Solzhenitsyn, both Zalygin and Likhachev stress the need to develop Russian national self-awareness in order to assure the survival of Russia as a distinct cultural and political entity, regardless of the fate of the Communist system, which they regard as a time-bound episode in the incomparably longer course of Russian historical continuity.   I do not mean to suggest that their political views or ideological inclinations fully coincide with those of Solzhenitsyn.   On the other hand, it is hardly accidental that it is Zalygin who has championed publication of Solzhenitsyn's work in the USSR.

Although such village writers as Zalygin, Rasputin, Soloukhin and others included in the sample may not want to be called Russian nationalists or even Solzhenitsyn sympathizers, they agree with Solzhenitsyn on many other than purely literary matters. Their writings collectively represent the emergence of genuine new thinking among Soviet intellectuals. Contrary to Gorbachev's contention that the "new thinking" in the USSR is inspired by Marxist-Leninist dialectics and, particularly, by Lenin's "lofty thought," my sample shows that nothing could be further from the truth: the *Novyi mir* new thinking is clearly based on entirely different philosophical assumptions.

What were the criteria for selection? The first criterion was the originality and novelty of the authors' ideas measured against the ways of thinking in the USSR, that is, the official ideology of Marxism-Leninism.   At least some of the articles, such as those by Larisa Popkova, Nikolai Shmelev and Vasilii Seliunin, were so "new" and unprecedented that they became "news" even in Western media. The second criterion was that an article must be of general, rather than special interest, even though the cumulative purpose is to span a wide range of perestroika activities, such as the economy, education, the legal system, and statistics. Finally, I looked for polemical and even controversial articles. Consequently, the sample resembles a debate in which authors polemicize, either implicitly or explicitly, with each other, with Gorbachev and even with Western historians about Russian history, perestroika and the Soviet future.[7] This explains why, besides the *Novyi mir* authors, I have included Dmitrii Likhachev's interviews in *Literaturnaia gazeta*, Valentin Rasputin's interview in *Izvestiia*, and Vadim Kozhinov's article in *Nash sovremennik*.   But it must be emphasized that among all Soviet periodicals which champion perestroika, glasnost and new thinking, none is as close to the ideas and ideals of Aleksandr Solzhenitsyn as *Novyi mir*.

DMITRII LIKHACHEV ON MORALITY, RELIGION, AND RUSSIAN HERITAGE

We shall start with the only author in our group whose work under review does not appear in the pages of *Novyi mir* but who belongs to its editorial board. This is Dmitrii Likhachev, one of the foremost experts on ancient Russian literature and a member of the prestigious Academy of Sciences. Now an octogenarian, Likhachev suffered repression under Stalin, including a term at the dreaded Solovki labor camp. In spite of his advanced age, he is active in the defense of Russian nature and Russian culture against the onslaught of "modernization." The head of the Soviet Fund for Culture, he is universally respected both for his scholarship and his moral rectitude. Many consider him to be the spiritual and moral leader of perestroika.

Two articles of his appeared in *Literaturnaia gazeta* in 1987. Both are a sort of informal interview [*beseda*] that a reporter summarizes on behalf of the interviewee. The first such interview, "Pangs of Conscience" [*Trevogi sovesti*], appeared on the first day of 1987. It set the tone and introduced some of the major themes for much of the intellectual debate that goes on in the USSR today.[8] The title draws attention to a moral crisis in Soviet society, which Likhachev describes as the "dearth of public conscience" [*defitsit sovesti*]. This lack of conscience, or rather conscientiousness, among Soviet people is so pervasive that "we became used to a double life: we say one thing, but we do the other. We have unlearned how to tell the truth, the full truth," says Likhachev. Although Likhachev acknowledges that the advent of perestroika and glasnost has meant a turn for the better, he insists that much more needs to be done. He stresses the urgency of expanding the limits of glasnost if perestroika is to succeed. In a clear allusion to the current ideological restrictions, Likhachev says that "half-truth is the worst kind of lie because the lie is masked then as a truth."

Explaining the reasons for the "dearth of conscience," Likhachev says that many of his readers still fear punishment for telling the truth because, until recently, "the wrongs were done by people who occupied the key positions." But the main reason for the moral decay in Soviet society, Likhachev suggests, should be sought in the destruction of and disrespect for the pre-revolutionary Russian culture.

While noting some improvement in the government's attitude toward the preservation of the monuments of Russian history and culture, Likhachev doubts whether it is enough to make a difference. "It would seem that bitter experience has taught us a lesson to take better care of our culture of the past, and of our nature," says Likhachev in a linkage between cultural and natural ecologies typical for many Russian nationalists, "but did we learn it?" Likhachev credits emerging public opinion as the best guarantee of the preservation of Russia's culture. And he urges the public to do more. Citing Dostoevskii's heroes who passionately desired to visit Europe in order "to touch the stones" of its culture, Likhachev asks Russian readers: "Isn't it time for us to touch our own ancient stones, our own memory, and our own culture?"

This appeal may seem paradoxical to those foreigners who are used to regarding the Soviet regime as an expression of Russian national aspirations. But in fact Likhachev pinpoints one of the principal causes of the country's malaise: the Soviet state, in all its aspects--whether economic, political, social or cultural--has been built in violation, and at the expense of the Russian national tradition. If the Kremlin leadership is serious about creating a more humane society, Likhachev suggests that full recognition must be accorded to the remnants of Russian culture that have managed to survive to this day. He sends a clear message to Gorbachev when he warns that "without a change of climate in our culture, our economy will make no progress."

In the process of moral rebirth, says Likhachev, Russian literature must play a very special role. To him literature is "the conscience and soul" of society, and writing is not a profession, but a vocation to speak truthfully about life. Sadly, Russian literature, along with the rest of Russian culture, has also suffered enormously from a disruption of its ethical and aesthetic "ecology" through censorship of modern works and selective destruction of its heritage. Rejoicing at the fact that a number of Russian writers were rehabilitated and scheduled for publication in the USSR, Likhachev deplores the slowness of the process of returning the Russian literary heritage to Soviet readers. He particularly deplores the fact that even the works of such classics as Pushkin, Gogol', Lermontov, and Dostoevskii are not readily available to the public because the government fails to recognize the urgency of educating its citizenry on the moral precepts of Russia's national heritage. While focusing his ire against the higher-ups, Likhachev does not want to exempt anyone from the responsibility of telling the truth. "We should be afraid of but one thing--lying. Only then shall we assure a healthy atmosphere in our society." Saying that all Soviet people were guilty of accepting a lie as the truth, he enjoins his readers to admit their guilt and to choose "the path of repentance."

Likhachev's emphasis on the need for truthfulness no doubt echoes the same concerns expressed by Aleksandr Solzhenitsyn in his 1974 samizdat article, "Don't Live According to a Lie!" A measure of achievement in the process of spiritual emancipation may be seen in the fact that Solzhenitsyn's negative commandment has now been restated by Likhachev, in the positive, "Do tell the truth." Moreover, as I shall demonstrate later, the theme of repentance that has enjoyed considerable glasnost in the USSR since Abuladze's film, "Repentance," ultimately owes its origin to Solzhenitsyn's article, "Repentance and Self-Limitation in the Life of Nations," which was published only in the samizdat collection, *From Under the Rubble* on the eve of Solzhenitsyn's forced exile abroad.

If there were any doubts about the content which Likhachev imputes to the vital traditions of Russian culture, he dispelled them in his article, "From Repentance to Action" [*Ot pokaianiia - k deistviiu*], published in September 1987.[9] There he made it clear that he considers the Russian religious tradition an essential part of the Russian cultural heritage. Like the previous article, this one too is a sort of informal interview [*beseda*] recorded by a reporter. It is also a response to a number of letters received by the newspaper which published the first article.

Agreeing with one reader's suggestion that oppression of the church by the atheist state was one of the chief causes of the current "dearth of conscience" in Soviet society, Likhachev unequivocally stated that fundamental moral precepts are "stable and eternal." He thus directly challenged the Marxist-Leninist doctrine of the dependence of the "ethical superstructure" on the economic base of a given society, a doctrine that has been mandatory for Soviet citizens since the revolution. According to Likhachev, the Biblical commandments, such as "Do not kill," "Do not steal," and "Do not bear false witness," are as valid today as ever. Responding to his readers' complaints about the hostility of the official "atheist propaganda" against believers, Likhachev blamed the hostility on the absence in the

USSR of "the culture of democracy." He then elaborated on the positive role the Russian church has played throughout Russian history. Turning to the present day, Likhachev argued that the state's meddling in religious affairs precludes true separation of church and state in the USSR. A "complete and genuine separation of church and state" must be put on the agenda, said Likhachev. He demanded that the government stop preventing the church from publishing religious literature, including the Bible, to satisfy the needs of believers.

One reader reproached Likhachev for not speaking up for the truth earlier when it was more dangerous. Defending himself, Likhachev mentioned his punishment under Stalin in the labor camps, but he added that he did not become embittered by his personal fate. "We, all of us, are responsible for what has happened in the last few decades." Once again, reiterating the point of his first interview, he called on his readers not to accept a moral compromise, rather "to resist and to persist. To look for allies. To act, and to affirm one's life through action" and, if necessary, to accept "all discomfort, deprivations, and even disasters" for the sake of one's convictions, lest one slip back to "the state of serfdom" of the Stalin era.

LARISA POPKOVA ON SOCIALIST AND CAPITALIST PIES

One of the earliest challengers to Gorbachev's assertion that perestroika means "looking for the answers within socialism" was Larisa Popkova, an economist. In her article "Where Are the Pies of Plenty?" published in *Novyi mir* in May 1987, Ms. Popkova gave an unequivocal answer to the rhetorical title.[10] They are not in the socialist countries, but in the countries of free enterprise. According to her, socialism has failed not only in the USSR, but in all countries where socialists are in power. She disputed official efforts to base perestroika on the writings of Marx and Lenin. According to her, "neither Marx nor Lenin was mistaken" in his belief that "socialism is incompatible with market."

Quoting Likhachev's statement that "a half-truth is the worst kind of lie," Popkova accused Marxist-Leninist "fellow travelers" of perestroika of abusing the relative freedom of glasnost by telling "half-truths" rather than the full truth. She did not name anyone, but implied that such practice is standard. Those engaging in "half-truths," says Popkova, claim, for instance, that "in his juvenilia Marx indicated the possibility of an evolutionary, peaceful transformation of capitalism to communism." According to Popkova, the truth is that the quintessential Marx is not in the juvenilia or footnotes, but in "The Communist Manifesto," which unequivocally advocates a "revolutionary change in property relations that would destroy everything in the old, exploitative, and decaying society."

Likewise, she accused the "fellow travelers" of rereading Lenin for the purpose of finding quotations to support their version of "merchant socialism," while ignoring the fact that "we have built exactly the kind of socialism that Lenin bequeathed us." Popkova argued that the free enterprise system has proved to be more productive and more efficient and that "the Western world is still on the threshold" of an even greater development. While admitting that socialism offers greater job security, she is convinced that it is an inherently inefficient system. Arguing for an either/or proposition, she concludes, "one cannot be half-pregnant. Either plan or market, either command economy or competition."

Popkova's article provoked a strong rebuttal by a certain Otto Latsis, also an economist. The rebuttal appeared in the July issue of 1987.[11] Latsis took Popkova to task for not believing in perestroika because she implied that only free market capitalism could make the country's economy productive. "Since the reader knows that we don't want capitalism anyway," Latsis reasons, "that means that we have to give up on perestroika, and on the pies of plenty to boot." I do not know whether Popkova was given a chance to reply to Latsis, nor do I know how she would have defended herself. But the rebuttal indicates that there are definite limits to glasnost which Soviet intellectuals are still not allowed to transgress. It also shows that Marxist-Leninists stubbornly resist relinquishing their control over perestroika's direction.

Latsis obviously takes it for granted that perestroika excludes any possibility that the country eventually might take a non-socialist road. But what if all of the perestroika efforts along the socialist road lead nowhere and fail to turn the Soviet economy around? Will Marxist-Leninists then just wait for the country's collapse? Or will perhaps, the instinct for self-preservation make them try different options? Such questions do not occur to Latsis. He believes that the kind of socialism that has been built so far in the USSR "is not quite what Lenin bequeathed us." But he is just as sure that a better socialism, presumably of the true Leninist kind, will be built. And what are the reasons for his certainty? "I do not need to offer any arguments, except the fact that I think so," says Latsis.

This statement amounts to an admission that, at least for some Soviet scholars, socialism remains a secular faith. In their secular fanaticism they do not even notice that they violate the sensibilities, and, indeed, the conscience of their colleagues. They want to overrule the biblical commandments, and any other ethical norms, with their single commandment, "Do not dare to think, unless you think along socialist (actually, Leninist) lines." This explains one of the major reasons for the "dearth of conscience" in the USSR: the dominance of Marxist-Leninist dogmas over new thinking, over any thinking.

IURII KORKHOV ON THE TWO PERESTROIKAS

Another remarkable article, "In the Cobweb of Coercion," was published in the same May 1987 issue of *Novyi mir* as Popkova's article. It was written by Iurii Korkhov, an engineer, economist, and college professor from the provincial Ukrainian town of Rovno. Korkhov tells it all in the opening paragraph: "We are facing the difficult task of a slow, but steady destruction of the cobweb of coercion which has enveloped our life and to which people got so accustomed that they became lazy and lost all taste for and ability to take initiative or to be creative." The destruction of the cobweb is one of the most urgent tasks of perestroika.

Pointing out a difference in attitudes toward perestroika between the higher-ups and the grass-roots, Korkhov introduces a distinction that I find crucial for understanding the current situation in the USSR. According to him, there is not one perestroika going on, but two: the one which he calls "perestroika-coercion" [*perestroika-prinuzhdenie*] and the one which he calls "perestroika-liberation" [*perestroika-osvobozhdenie*]. Suggesting that these two perestroikas, or more precisely two concepts of perestroika, compete with each other, Korkhov leaves no doubt that perestroika-coercion is largely sponsored by the government (Isn't it Gorbachev's "revolution from above"?), while perestroika-liberation comes from the grass-roots and thus coincides with the "revolution from below." Putting all his faith in perestroika-liberation, Korkhov knows that "those who want no perestroika or else interpret it only as perestroika-coercion might take advantage of the habitual apathy of the people and start a counter-offensive against perestroika-liberation." However, only perestroika-liberation can mobilize the creativity of the nation to solve its problems, Korkhov warns the "coercionist reformers."[12]

Korkhov proposes to start the task of liberation by restructuring, first of all, the Soviet educational system. Why? Because "the greatest coercion occurs in our institutions of learning of all kinds and at all levels. Our educational system is, in essence, a school of emasculation of creativity. A person who has gone through it from the beginning to the end (from kindergarten to university) can function, as a rule, only as a performer." Referring to his experience as a college professor, Korkhov says that the government's decree about restructuring college education has had no practical effect because it was conceived and executed in a coercive manner. It was not based on the local initiative from colleges but was simply handed down as a directive from above.

Touching on other aspects of life inside the Communist "cobweb," Korkhov quotes from a novel by Valentin Rasputin, a "village prose" writer, to the effect that the only way a Soviet person can feel temporarily free from the cobweb of coercion is by getting drunk. He clearly blames the problem of alcoholism on the social system which suppresses all spontaneity. Korkhov argues for experimenting with greater variety in the forms of administration and management. To Korkhov, one of the best things that has happened during perestroika is the emergence of non-formal groups among young people. But he warns that official efforts to "ennoble them, and to direct them through the right channels" will ultimately kill them as a spontaneous expression of youthful creativity.

Although Korkhov mentions neither party controls nor Marxism-Leninism, his article challenges both. "We often talk about creativity of the masses," says Korkhov about one of the staple themes of Soviet propaganda. "But our talk is a bit hypocritical, because we want not creative self-expression, but correct, good, and error-free activity. And that is why we always want to organize it, to force it into the framework of a plan. But organizing initiative means a denial of it." Korkhov seems to challenge the basic Marxist-Leninist assumption that revolutionary violence and coercion are necessary for creating a better social system. "For the sake of this goal we are ready for everything. Hence our passion for violence and coercion." Korkhov makes it clear that this assumption was institutionalized in the form of Marxist-Leninist ideological monopoly, to which the Communist Party continues to cling even today.

ALEKSANDR IAKOVLEV ON THE LAW OF THE CONCRETE WALL

Korkhov's fear that perestroika-coercion might take the upper hand was echoed by Aleksandr M. Iakovlev, a distinguished doctor of jurisprudence and professor (not to be confused with former Politburo member, Aleksandr N. Iakovlev), whose article, "The Law of the Concrete Wall," appeared in *Novyi mir* in June 1987. Iakovlev focused his critique on the newly adopted Law on Individual Labor Activity and the Law on State Enterprise, the two chief measures of Gorbachev's economic reform. His basic contention is that the two laws are fundamentally flawed because they prescribe what people must do instead of allowing them to do whatever they want, except what is explicitly forbidden. "Coercion is effective, if it is used for restraint and destruction," says Iakovlev, "but it is powerless, if it is used to create."[13]

The Soviet system has no support from either grass-roots creativity from below or socialist legality from above, says Iakovlev. Instead, it is founded on the "law of the concrete wall." He explains it by the following parable. First, the authorities decide to build a park in the middle of town. Their intention might be good. But since they never correlate this intention with the interests of the local people, they build the park in the wrong place so that people constantly "trespass" on the park premises because it stands in the way to a bus stop or whatever. Then the authorities have no choice but to erect a concrete wall to protect the green lawns from traffic. No matter how many warnings or guards are posted around the wall, the people respond by making holes in it. The solution lies in allowing people to walk wherever they want, then paving the path they make with the "asphalt" of laws, says Iakovlev. He would let the grass of freedom grow everywhere else.

Pointing out that some of the new laws contradict the Constitution of the USSR or those of union republics, Iakovlev calls for an overhaul of the entire legal system on the firm foundation of the people's will and self-expression. "Democratization cannot move forward without democratization of the [Soviet] legal system." Even though Gorbachev himself was forced to admit the existence of a gap between Soviet propaganda and reality, Iakovlev makes it clear that this gap is nowhere greater than between the beautiful phraseology of Soviet laws and the rule of lawlessness in actual life. Iakovlev saw no change in this respect after two years of perestroika. "Divorced from life as it is, our legislature can perform a certain [useful] function," says Iakovlev sarcastically. "It can create the appearance of changes and substitute empty phraseology. . . for a fundamental and genuine perestroika."

Iakovlev suggests that the only solution for the country's economic problems is the "cardinal restructuring of the managerial mechanism" by tearing down the "concrete wall" erected by decrees from Moscow. "To what extent do the voices of teachers. . . decide the direction of school reform? To what extent do the voices of workers, foremen, and local factory managers decide the direction of economic reforms?", asks Iakovlev echoing Korkhov's disgust with the way perestroika has been carried out so far. He knows that those voices have no influence on decision-making. Repudiating the entire Soviet legal system, he affirms the basis of the Western "bourgeois" legality: "The most genuine and the most important rights are not those that are given, but those that cannot be taken away."

NIKOLAI SHMELEV ON "MARKET SOCIALISM"

Nikolai Shmelev, an economist, in his article "Advances and Debts," published in *Novyi mir* in June 1987,[14] argued that the existing Soviet economic system is fundamentally defective and that it can be straightened out only by a speedy return to the pragmatic approach of the NEP period. He challenged "the predominant belief in our country that the existing system of economic relations, including the property structure, is the very embodiment of Marxism-Leninism in practice and fully corresponds to the true nature of socialism as a social system." In an allusion to those dogmatic sponsors of perestroika who aim at a mere refurbishing of the existing system, Shmelev said that they are guided neither by facts nor by an honest desire for revolutionary change, but by nostalgia for the bygone era. To them he opposed the more heterodox scholars who now strive for "a true rebirth of our social thought and our national self-awareness."

According to Shmelev, NEP was not a temporary retreat from socialism, as Soviet propaganda asserted for decades, but a true "managerial socialism." Marx and Engels had no cogent theory of socialist economics, says Shmelev. What the two classics offered was just "guesswork." Lenin, too, was too much preoccupied with politics to give any systematic thought to the future economy. However, after the revolution, Lenin came up with the idea which Shmelev wholeheartedly endorses, namely, that "socialism is Soviet power plus the Prussian sense of orderliness on the railroads, plus American technology and corporate organization, plus the American system of public education." All one has to do in order to create an efficient and rational socialist economy, Shmelev suggests, is to fill the capitalist managerial forms with socialist content. The political contingency of "war communism" (1918-1921) forced Lenin to abandon his initial idea, says Shmelev. For a while, Lenin became convinced of the superiority of "administrative socialism" (totalitarian socialism, in my terminology). Only in 1921 did Lenin abandon "war communism" in favor of his initial view of socialist economy. He then introduced the New Economic Policy, which Shmelev calls a true "scientific approach" to the tasks of socialist economy.

In sum, Shmelev's article is an argument for the total overhaul of the current economic system along "the Leninist principles" of the NEP period. Shmelev's reverence for Lenin notwithstanding, his plan for economic restructuring remains too radical for the Soviet establishment because, among other things, Shmelev argues for the abandonment of political control over the economy and for direct participation of workers in its management. Soviet leaders, including Gorbachev, are clearly not ready yet to "return to Lenin's NEP" to the extent that Shmelev proposes. His article is a valiant but futile effort to bail out socialism from its present crisis by revising the official Marxism-Leninism to a pragmatic Leninism. It is also an expression of the "renaissance of our public thought and of our national self-awareness," which Shmelev says has begun in the wake of glasnost.

In his later article, "New Anxieties," published in the April 1988 issue of *Novyi mir*, Shmelev focuses attention on the public anxiety over the fate of perestroika.[15] The article was preceded by an editorial comment that among the many hundred letters received by the journal in response to Shmelev's first article, nine out of ten supported his stance. Summing up three full years of perestroika, Shmelev says that perestroika "awoke [the country's] creative forces and gave people hope for a realistic exit from the dead end we had reached during the years of stagnation." Nevertheless, public "anxiety over the future of the country and the future of the nation" is on the rise, says Shmelev. According to him, even on the eve of the Party Conference, "many among us still do not realize that there is no real alternative to perestroika, and that, as far as the economy is concerned, we are still at the edge of the abyss." Shmelev blames the Soviet press for propagandizing imaginary success and for creating the illusion that the situation is not so bad and that it will somehow get better by itself. He warns that unless both the government and the people realize the gravity of the situation, "we will land on the sidelines of history, and turn into an underdeveloped country."

Why has perestroika failed to fulfill its promises? Shmelev chiefly blames the failure on "a sort of silent conspiracy against perestroika" between local Party bureaucracies and a number of central governmental agencies. He quotes another Soviet journalist to the effect that this silent conspiracy has been poised for a counter-offensive. According to Shmelev, even if there was a certain increase in production during the last three years, that increase was due not to structural improvements but to the production of "unneeded products."

Shmelev especially scorns the lack of progress in agriculture where the system of collective and state farms resists any changes. "The crisis of our farming is payment for the more than fifty years of violence against common sense, against everything which makes people yearn for normal honest work," says Shmelev. His principal recommendation is a return to free market practices on the scale of NEP. Shmelev concludes his article by saying that "there has developed in the country a revolutionary situation" whereby "the higher-ups" can no longer rule as they used to, and the masses refuse to live as they used to. In an apparent allusion to Gorbachev's description of perestroika as both a revolution from above and a revolution from below, Shmelev says that neither of the two revolutions is easy to accomplish. He urges Gorbachev to proceed more decisively with his revolution and to "break the resistance of moribund social moods and structures."

OL'GA CHAIKOVSKAIA ON PUSHKIN

On the surface, Ol'ga Chaikovskaia's article, "Grinev,"[16] is a piece of literary criticism about the main hero of Aleksandr Pushkin's novel, *The Captain's Daughter*. Pushkin is revered in the USSR as the Russian Shakespeare, and his historical novel about the Pugachev peasant uprising in 1773-1775 is required reading in all Soviet schools. Chaikovskaia's article goes far beyond purely literary matter. Besides Pushkin's art, it tells as much about the Bolshevik revolution and perestroika. It is a passionate appeal to the nation to heal the festering wound that has been left unattended since the revolution and the fratricidal civil war. Chaikovskaia calls on the people to abandon the hatred that has been cultivated for decades under the banner of the Marxist-Leninist concept of class struggle and to unite in brotherly love in their search for the common good.

Chaikovskaia uses a 1984 academic edition of the novel as an example of the intellectual stagnation that has plagued the country since 1917 when the Marxist-Leninist ideological monopoly was imposed. Russian literature has suffered heavy losses from the excesses of the "sociological" approach (which subsumes the official theory of socialist realism), in which works of art were judged according to the social interests they might reflect. The influence of the "sociological" approach was so pervasive that "it is the real curse [of our society] that our creative imagination in general has become thoroughly sociologized," complains Chaikovskaia.

The editors of the 1984 edition portray Pushkin as a pro-revolutionary sympathizer. They claim that Pushkin was critical of his hero, Grinev, allegedly a naive representative of the "conservative gentry ideology." Chaikovskaia shows that in reality Grinev expresses Pushkin's own conservative philosophy when he says, "The best and the most durable changes are those that stem from an improvement of morals, without any sort of violent revolution."   According to Chaikovskaia, Pushkin says the same in his private letters.   She is convinced that when Pushkin wrote, "God save us from a Russian revolution that can be only senseless and merciless," he meant just that.

Chaikovskaia juxtaposes Pushkin's "classless" moral approach with the cult of class struggle that has been the main fare of Marxist-Leninist indoctrination of Soviet youth. She particularly denounces the glorification of the civil war (1918-21). To her, there is no greater horror than a civil war, in which "there is neither brother, nor son, nor friend; there are but two hostile camps." Meanwhile, "almost every day one sees on the screen how the Russians, as if in a trance, butcher each other. Almost every day our cinema and TV screens condition. . . our youth to get used to blood and murder," complains Chaikovskaia.

The propagandists of class struggle violence imagine that they teach the young to be courageous, but in fact they destroy and undermine "the idea of the country's unity [that] is as necessary as it is precious, and it is a crime to try to undermine it," says Chaikovskaia. Her words are an unmistakable challenge to Leninist doctrine, according to which Russian history has always flowed in two irreconcilable streams, the "progressive" and the reactionary. Denouncing the Marxist class struggle theory (from which Lenin's two-stream doctrine was derived), Chaikovskaia says, "a feeling of belonging to this unity must be present in the consciousness of every citizen of the country in all periods of its history, and especially at such crucial junctures as today."

Chaikovskaia counters the Marxist doctrine of class enmity with an ethical imperative: "To try to diminish the amount of evil in the world--this is the task for each of us, and, above all, for our statesmen and public figures. . . ."   According to her, this was the ethical imperative of classical Russian literature, as well as of such contemporary Soviet authors as Valentin Rasputin, Chinghiz Aitmatov, and Anatolii Pristavkin (especially his novel *Nochevala tuchka zolotaia*).

VALENTIN RASPUTIN ON ORDER IN A SOUL

Valentin Rasputin is one of the best and most widely read Soviet writers of the ruralist school. But in spite of his great popularity among Soviet readers, Rasputin was not exactly favored by the Soviet ideological establishment because the message of his early novels was at variance with Marxism-Leninism. It has been reported that in 1982 Rasputin was beaten up by a band of hoodlums, allegedly, at the urging of the KGB. However, Rasputin's fortune and his status in Soviet society dramatically improved with the advent of perestroika. Just as glasnost was beginning to gain momentum, he was awarded the title of hero of socialist labor in conjunction with his fiftieth birthday in March 1987. On that occasion *Izvestiia* published an interview with the writer which has established him as one of the foremost spiritual leaders of perestroika.

The moral thrust of the interview is reflected in its title, *Poriadok v dushe - poriadok v otechestve*.[17] Literally it means "an order in one's soul leads to an order in one's fatherland," but it could be best translated, "no country can exist without moral foundations." This may sound like a truism to those unfamiliar with Soviet political culture. But, in fact, Rasputin's emphasis on the need to restructure the soul of each Soviet citizen is as "anti-Soviet," or rather anti-Marxist, as the ideas of dissidents who used to be punished by jail terms, deportation, and exile abroad. More precisely, Rasputin's interview, like Likhachev's, echoes Solzhenitsyn's 1974 farewell to Soviet people, "Don't Live According to a Lie."

The writer points out, first of all, the change of the official attitude to the problems of Soviet society. Before perestroika we only pretended that everything was fine and invested in that pretense enormous monetary and intellectual resources, says Rasputin. Now we are finally admitting the truth of our situation to ourselves. "What we used to whisper about, today is being admitted loudly and openly." For the first time in many decades, says Rasputin, the views of the best of Soviet writers came too close to "the official viewpoint." Nevertheless, since "ethical and spiritual notions have been distorted and undermined," Rasputin doubts whether change in the official attitude will bring about a spiritual regeneration of the people any time soon. "We continue to talk a lot about morality, spirituality and patriotic moorings," says Rasputin, but "we do little to cultivate them" in actual life. And the major reason for this he sees in the domination of the "political idea" (of Marxism-Leninism) over genuine concern with these values.

Rasputin then picks up one of the most persistent themes of the ruralists, the theme of governmental endeavors to subordinate Russian nature to megalomaniacal dreams of socialist modernization. According to Rasputin, even "the flag of perestroika" has not prevented the government from making new disastrous mistakes because the government has not paid heed to "the long-term interests of man and his habitat." Rasputin says that bureaucrats lack that "protective feeling for the sacred heritage of our people" which alone can safeguard long-term interests.

When asked about his latest novel, *The Fire*, Rasputin left no doubt that the novel is not just about the destruction of the Siberian ecological balance but also about the dehumanization of Soviet people as a result of the megalomania of several generations of Soviet leaders, who ordered industrialization at any cost, wishing to subdue nature itself to their will. "Siberia is great, but the greedy hands of the ministries and other governmental agencies are long enough to reach to its most remote corners," complains Rasputin. Pointing out that so far there have been no changes in the official attitude, Rasputin accuses the government of treating Siberia as "not our own land, but as if it were a temporary holding or a concession."

While praising the policy of glasnost, Rasputin defines it more broadly than what was officially intended. Glasnost is not just objective information about the current state of affairs, but it is also "the necessity to tell the truth about the past, not to forget why and by whom the destructive and voluntarist decisions were made," says Rasputin, in a dual reference to the official decisions that have brought parts of his native Siberia, especially the Lake Baikal area, to the brink of ecological disaster, and to the forced collectivization of peasants. If, before collectivization, "a peasant knew how to follow the cycles [of nature] and tried to adapt to them, without squeezing his field of its last fertility," nowadays he has to "forcibly adapt the field to the figures and plans invented at a bureaucrat's desk." According to Rasputin, the endemic mismanagement amounts to plundering the Russian land and robbing future generations. "Without any moral restraint or compunction, without chewing or swallowing, today we are gobbling up something which does not belong to us. We behave as thieves in respect to the generations to come whom we doom to a life in desolation."

In his reply to a question about the role of literature in the process of perestroika, Rasputin admitted that there are some critics who warn against writers becoming too deeply involved in the politics of the day. Nevertheless, he justifies his own journalistic activities by saying that literature ought to provide a moral dimension to whatever problems concern society. In fact, Rasputin credits Russian literature with paving the way for perestroika. "For a long time, and especially in recent times, literature took upon itself the duty of [expressing] public opinion" says Rasputin, echoing Solzhenitsyn's dictum that Russian literature is the country's "second government." Rasputin makes it clear that the whole Soviet experiment amounts to a rape of Russia. It has created a "disorder" of the Russian soul. It has robbed the land of its ecological balance and the nation of its spiritual balance. Perestroika's economic, social, and political goals cannot be attained unless and until the spiritual order of things is restored. This must be done, first of all, by telling the truth about the history of Communist violence against Russian nature and the Russian nation.

VLADIMIR SOLOUKHIN: STANDING AGAINST ANTI-RUSSIAN POWER

Another outstanding Soviet writer, Vladimir Soloukhin, goes even further than Rasputin in denouncing the Communist system as both "anti-people" and "anti-Russian." Although he had been recognized as one of the finest ruralist writers even before perestroika, Soloukhin was frequently attacked by the Party's dogmatists for defending national Russian values. A Party member, he was reprimanded in the official journal *Kommunist* in 1982 for espousing religious views. Under glasnost Soloukhin's art has become even more "heretical." In September 1987 *Novyi mir* published his short story "The Burial of Stepanida Ivanovna."[18] Written in 1967, the story had to wait twenty years before the policy of glasnost gave it the green light.

The story is autobiographical and dedicated to the memory of his mother. It describes in graphic detail all the travail the author had to go through in order to fulfill his mother's last "earthly" wish: to be buried according to the rites of the Russian Orthodox Church, or, in her own words, "as behooves a human being." "In all times and among all nations the last wish of a dying person was respected, except when a country was seized by an occupying army, the barbarian invaders would terrorize and plunder it," writes Soloukhin. "Then, of course, one could hardly hope to have the last wish honored. But among all civilized nations the last wish of a dying person was regarded as sacred." The faithful son of Stepanida Ivanovna was ready to honor his mother's last wish. He flew from Moscow to Minsk, where his mother died. He then went through the travail of buying a generic unfinished coffin (there was no choice), finding someone who could line it with zinc, finding someone else to hermetically seal it, and then flying it from Minsk to Moscow whence it was taken by car to her native village, where she wished to be buried. In the process he had to contact a number of eminent writers, people's deputies, and even a government minister because funeral services are virtually non-existent in the USSR. He was lucky that virtually all the people he contacted were able to help him in one way or another.

But even when all the arrangements were made, and the coffin was finally delivered to his mother's native village, there was one more obstacle: there was neither a church nor a priest there. Undaunted, the author prevailed upon a priest from a neighboring village, but only after lying to him about having obtained permission to conduct the funeral service. It took another day to make sure that the priest would not be punished for breaking the law against "worshiping God under the open sky" (since there was no church in the village). The red tape that was necessary to fulfill his mother's wish to be buried "as behooves a human being" prompted the author to exclaim:

> If such a thing were to happen in a country at war, where the occupying forces so bridled and yoked the local population that they forbade them to bury their dead according to local rite, then it could possibly make some sense. But I do not know whether such occupying forces actually exist anywhere in the world and whether there is a nation willing to buckle under such a bridle.

Soloukhin thus equates the atheist system with a barbarian "occupying army," plundering Russia's Christian people. He suggests that a gulf separates the millions of Russians who continue to cling to their ancient traditions from the authorities who have always been hostile to any manifestation of Russian national or religious self-awareness. This story shows the falsity of the official portrayal of the Communist regime as "people's power." It also belies the widely held Western view that the Communist regime is an expression of the national aspirations of ethnic Russians.

If there was any doubt about Soloukhin's religious value system, it was dispelled in his new book of memoirs, *Smekh za levym plechom* [The Laughter from behind Your Left Shoulder], which, alas, did not fit within the confines of glasnost and was published abroad. "Neither professors who had taught me nor the writers whose books I managed to read bestowed on me such a clear and irresistible formula [of ethical conduct] as Stepanida Ivanovna did," said Soloukhin, thus acknowledging his indebtedness to the religious heritage passed on to him by his mother. "Wherever you go and whatever you do, remember that behind your right shoulder is an angel, and behind your left shoulder, Satan," his mother had advised him. "And whenever you do evil things, the angel behind your right shoulder will bitterly cry, but Satan behind your left shoulder will rejoice and laugh in his malice." As Soloukhin admits, though he tried to follow his mother's advice, he did not escape Soviet indoctrination. In his youth he fell for the cult of Lenin, and then "there was much sneering and laughing behind my left shoulder." Unlike many of his contemporaries, Soloukhin blames not only Stalin, but also Lenin for many of the horrible things that befell his country after 1917, particularly the destruction of the Russian peasantry in the wake of collectivization.

But what do Soloukhin's religious values have to do with perestroika? Well, as long as perestroika continues to be inspired by Lenin, there will be a lot of laughter behind its left shoulder. According to Soloukhin, under Lenin and Trotsky a plan was conceived "to turn free and enterprising Russian peasants into an impersonal army of landless, obedient and. . . virtually unpaid slaves." Under Stalin, "fifteen million peasants" were actually deported to the "desolate tundra to their suffering and death." There was a logic in that, says Soloukhin because, for the "anti-people and anti-Russian

[Soviet] power" to continue, it had to destroy "all the best people." "The task was to pump out of the Russian soil all its resources for the sake of the mythical world revolution, or just to stay in power with the help of the state apparatus and the military."[19]

Soloukhin's irreverent portrayal of Lenin was the chief reason why the book had to be, at first, published abroad.[20]

IURII KARIAKIN'S DEFENSE OF RUSSIAN LITERATURE

In form, Iurii Kariakin's article, "Why Step on the Rake?,"[21] is a defense of Boris Mozhaev's novel, *Muzhiki i baby* [Men and Women],[22] against a vicious attack by a "rather important person" who insinuated that the novel's author, an outstanding ruralist writer, was in league with "reactionary priests, Slavophiles, Hitler, and the White Finns." After the "important" reader demanded that his letter be published, the editors of the literary magazine *Znamia* asked Kariakin, a prominent literary critic, to respond to it, so that the attack on the novel would be balanced by an expert opinion. However, at the last moment the attacker asked to retract his letter. Nevertheless, Kariakin went ahead with his response to the "Incognito," who, in his opinion, personifies opposition to glasnost.

Using the Incognito's letter as a pretext, Kariakin writes a passionate defense not just of Mozhaev, but of all genuine Russian writers who have suffered from Soviet ideological watchdogs. That includes both "rehabilitated" authors, such as Boris Pasternak (author of *Doctor Zhivago*), Andrei Platonov (*Kotlovan*) and Anna Akhmatova (*Requiem*), as well as a number of contemporary Soviet authors whose works could not have been published before glasnost, such as Vladimir Dudintsev's *Belye odezhdy*, Daniil Granin's *Zubr*, Anatolii Rybakov's *Deti Arbata*. According to Kariakin,

> the past two or three years are unprecedented in the entire history of our literature. Never were so many works published during such a short period and at once, works which were produced in different eras, but which concern, essentially, the same thing. Never was there such a literary-social panorama created by the crossing of beams of light coming from different eras, by a polyphony of voices belonging

to both the living and the dead. A whole epoch of our recent history is depicted in these works.

What Kariakin is saying is that throughout a major period of Soviet history, "socialist realist" literature had more to do with propaganda than with art. It is only now that it has become possible to portray the Soviet past truthfully.

IGOR' KLIAMKIN: A NATIONAL-BOLSHEVIK?

Published in December 1987, Igor' Kliamkin's polemical essay, "Which Street Does Lead to a Cathedral?"[23] should rather have been titled "Which Street Does Lead to a Better Future for Russia?" In spite of Kliamkin's disclaimer that he does not "pretend to offer the answer," he makes it clear that there was no better street than the one paved by Lenin and built by Stalin. The chief thrust of his essay is to argue that there was no alternative either to Lenin's Bolshevik revolution or to Stalin's collectivization and industrialization.

According to Kliamkin, Stalin's slogan of "socialism in one country" was "the slogan of survival, self-preservation, and national defense. It was a slogan which allowed the idea of socialism to be combined with that of national independence, with the sense of national dignity deeply rooted in our people." Kliamkin admits that Stalin's methods in achieving this "unity" were "vulnerable not just from an ethical, but also from a criminal viewpoint." Nevertheless, Kliamkin justifies Stalin's rule by saying that "at that time victory was won by the strongest, and nobody but they could be the winners." He argues that no other project of "building the street" toward Communism was capable of competing with Stalin's collectivization. While defending Leninism unswervingly, Kliamkin wavers in his loyalty to Stalinism. "My soul is tormented by an unanswerable question: But couldn't everything have been otherwise, perhaps? My sober reason is implacable: No, it could not. But I wish my reason were in error."

It is hard to judge his sincerity. But there is little doubt that the duality of reason and moral sense Kliamkin exhibits is typical of many Soviet intellectuals today. It is no accident that, since Abuladze's film, "Repentance," the theme of repentance has become standard in much of Soviet journalism. Admitting that repentance is "not out of place" for him because of his former unquestioned belief in Stalin, Kliamkin asks:

> But before repenting, one wants to know why did we believe in it? What should we be repentant about? About the fact that we are we? After all, we were not born fifty years ago, and not even seventy. From what point should we start counting our sins? From Muscovite Russia? Or from the Russia of St. Petersburg? Or from the 1930s?

One question that Kliamkin fails to ask is this: "Why not start counting the sins from the Bolshevik revolution?" The absence of this question is conspicuous in view of the fact that a major part of his essay is devoted to a historical justification of the Bolshevik revolution. Perhaps the most remarkable thing about Kliamkin's essay is that he attempts to justify the Bolshevik revolution not from the official Marxist-Leninist viewpoint, but from that of the *Smenovekhovtsy*. The Smenovekhovtsy were a group of Russian emigres, some of them with strongly anti-Communist convictions, who nonetheless toward the end of the civil war accepted the Bolshevik revolution as Russia's "national" revolution. Not only did they recognize the legitimacy of the Communist government but they also expressed a willingness to cooperate with it. The group included such people as Iu. Kliuchnikov, N. Ustrialov, S. Luk'ianov and A. Bobrishchev-Pushkin. The group's name was derived from the collection of articles, *Smena vekh* (1921), the title of which meant to suggest a change [smena] of attitude as compared to the 1909 collection, *Vekhi*. Written by seven prominent authors, including such former Marxists as Petr Struve, Sergei Bulgakov, and Nikolai Berdiaev, *Vekhi* was the first attempt of Russian intellectuals to cope with their collective responsibility for the bloody upheavals that were to mark the twentieth century as a century of totalitarian horrors. In a mood of self-criticism and repentance, the authors of *Vekhi* condemned the Russian radical intelligentsia for its advocacy of revolutionary violence and its disregard for objective truth, religion, legality, and Russian national tradition. However, in the wake of the Bolsheviks' victory in the Civil War in 1921, the Smenovekhovtsy claimed that *Vekhi* was repudiated by history.

Kliamkin seems to endorse the Smenovekhovtsy historiography by assembling a six-page long collage (*montazh*) of quotations from their writings. Although he neither identifies the author of each quotation nor provides his own comment, Kliamkin skillfully builds the collage to a rhetorical crescendo:

> Russia can reach economic and general national health only through a mighty, intense, and willful power, only through it. Does it make any sense to try to destabilize this revolutionary power which has been created through much suffering without offering any other power and in a situation when the existing power makes heroic efforts to restore the household of the state?

Reading this passage, one realizes that Kliamkin's essay is more than an attempt to rehabilitate the Smenovekhovtsy, whom Soviet historians, until recently, tended to ridicule. Kliamkin clearly tries to resuscitate at least some of the Smenovekhovtsy ideas as a substitute for orthodox Marxism-Leninism, which no longer can hold the country together. Now, when the Communist regime finds itself in the most serious crisis since 1921, there is no alternative to the "mighty, intense, and willful power" of the Communist Party. Kliamkin suggests that, after all, this Party now, under Gorbachev, "is making heroic efforts to restore the household of the state." Kliamkin seems to believe that the Smenovekhovtsy ideology is better suited for rallying support for Gorbachev's "revolution from above" than the discredited orthodox Marxism-Leninism. Without polemicizing against the official Marxist-Leninist ideology, as if it were irrelevant to the problems of perestroika, Kliamkin clearly tries to reanimate it by infusing it with certain Smenovekhovtsy ideas to enable it to stand up against the challenge mounted by a growing number of the *Vekhi* proponents. According to Kliamkin--in spite of the fact that the *Vekhi* were never republished in the USSR--its ideas are extremely popular right now because they "correspond to certain moods" in the country. He particularly notes the popularity of the *Vekhi* thesis that "no genuine renewal of the world is possible unless preceded by a profound and exacting moral self-improvement." Kliamkin complains that "many have been attracted to the *Vekhi* due to this and other such ideas."[24]

Siding with the Smenovekhovtsy, Kliamkin roundly dismisses the *Vekhi* ideas on the curious ground that they were "doomed" by the Bolshevik revolution. But he has no faith in the future of Communism in Russia either, that is, unless it adapts itself to the needs of the

Russian state. Kliamkin's thrust is evident in the last paragraph of his collage:

> Do not think, that we have changed by recognizing your red banner [wrote Smenovekhovtsy to Communist leaders on the eve of NEP]. We have recognized it only because it will eventually bloom in [Russia's] national colors. Do not think that we came to believe in your ability to implant Communism in Russia and to force the Bolshevik revolution into a world revolution. No. But we could tangibly feel the armor with which the country covered itself through you.

Like the Smenovekhovtsy, Kliamkin seems to define the needs of the Russian state very narrowly. The overwhelming emphasis is not on the rights of its citizens, but on the might of "the armor with which the country covered itself." In spite of his disclaimer that he cannot "underwrite each word" of the Smenovekhovtsy, Kliamkin's selection of their quotations speaks for itself. What is remarkable about Kliamkin's apologia of the Smenovekhovtsy is the fact that if in 1921 former anti-Communists tried to justify Communism with narrowly defined nationalist slogans of military might, now, after sixty-seven years of trying to force Communism on Russia, Communists, like Kliamkin (he may not be formally a party member, but he certainly reasons like one) try to do the same.

Editors supplied Igor Kliamkin's polemic essay with a footnote saying that this is the first in a series of articles they plan to publish "in which problems of Soviet history will be discussed from different viewpoints." It is certainly the case with Kliamkin's essay, in which Soviet history is presented not from the official Marxist-Leninist viewpoint but from the National-Bolshevik viewpoint of the Smenovekhovtsy. Whatever Kliamkin's intentions were, his essay underscores the fact that the USSR today is facing not just an economic or social crisis, but, above all, a spiritual, moral, and intellectual crisis. A profound intellectual revolution, or, to use Nietzsche's phrase, a "re-evaluation of all values," is rapidly gaining momentum. It may well end up with a real *smena vekh*, that is, the replacement of the Communist "signposts" with something entirely new. However, contrary to Kliamkin, that "new" is more likely to be based not on the Smenovekhovtsy ideology, but on the ideas of the

Vekhi. Most certainly, that new has to be better grounded in the country's soil than the allegedly "Russian" and "internationalist," but in fact simply utopian and anti-national, ideas of Marxism-Leninism.

VASILII SELIUNIN ATTACKS LENIN

One of the most daring and persuasive critics of the half-hearted methods of perestroika is Vasilii Seliunin. He first attracted national attention by writing an article (co-authored with Grigorii Khanin) in which he showed that the official figures on the growth of national income in the USSR between 1928 and 1985 were exaggerated by a factor of thirteen.[25] Then in the May 1988 issue of *Novyi mir* he published another remarkable article, "Istoki" [The sources] which made headlines in the Western press.

Seliunin's article was unprecedented in that he accused Lenin of creating the system of economic inefficiency and political repression. But there was much more in the article than this sensational accusation. It was perhaps the most perceptive critique--in a low key, factual, and balanced way--of the basic assumptions of world socialism ever to appear in the Soviet press. It was also a paean to the superiority of free enterprise. Implicitly, the article contained a reply to Kliamkin's questions about "the sources" of what went wrong with the country and "What should we repent about?"

Seliunin traces the sources of Soviet economic woes to the failure of "the classics"--Marx, Engels, and Lenin--to understand the role of material incentives in raising labor productivity. Once the material incentives were abolished in the new Soviet state, the government had no choice but to resort to "non-economic means of coercion" (*vneekonomicheskoe prinuzhdenie*) in order to increase productivity. Coercion was especially relied upon during the years of "war communism" (1918-1921). Citing Lenin on the need to use concentration camps to coerce "class enemies" to work, Seliunin says that soon "the limits of repression expanded beyond all bounds: first, it was used to suppress opponents of the revolution, then it shifted to potential opponents, and finally it became a means of solving purely economic problems." Hence, the system of labor camps (and other means of compulsion to work) in the USSR.

When Lenin and other Bolshevik leaders decided that the revival of private property and free-market trade must be stamped out because it might lead the Soviet state back to capitalism, they doomed the country both to economic inefficiency and political repression, says Seliunin. He singles out Leon Trotskii as the evil genius who in 1920 proposed both forming "labor armies" and turning the country "into a giant concentration camp." Although Soviet historians say that the ninth Party Congress rejected Trotskii's proposal, writes Seliunin, in fact, the proposal found its way into the Soviet economy both during "war communism" and later.

While emphasizing Trotskii's influence as one of the "sources" of the current economic malaise, Seliunin is just as critical of Lenin's ideas and methods. He points out that Lenin was possessed by the idea of collectivization of farming as early as 1902. After the revolution, in 1918, when Lenin was a member of a commission on "socialization of land," he rejected outright the suggestion of the left Socialist-Revolutionary members of the commission that the promise to give the land confiscated from the gentry to landless peasants should be kept. Instead, Lenin pushed through his own plan of creating state farms on the confiscated land, and that plan was rubber-stamped without much discussion.

Lenin's agricultural policy was contrary to the interests of the peasantry. Seliunin shows the central role this antagonism played in the Civil War. While the majority of historians, both Soviet and foreign, reduce the civil war to the conflict between the whites and the reds, says Seliunin, "there existed a third force, against which the greatest blow [of the war] was inflicted--the peasant rebellion." According to Seliunin, neither the whites nor the reds cared much about the peasants. This amounts to saying that, contrary to official claims, the revolution was not in the interests of the overwhelming majority of the country's population. For a while, the peasants tried to fend for themselves by balancing between the reds and the whites. But when a peasant uprising against the reds broke out in the Tambov district, and the rebels created their own military force, Antonov's army, it had such broad popular support that Lenin regarded it as more dangerous for the new Communist regime "than all the white armies combined together," says Seliunin. Moscow had to send against Antonov's army its best troops under the command of Tukhachevskii, and the fighting that ensued was "no less intense than against [Admiral] Kolchak's [White] army."

However, since the majority of red soldiers were peasants themselves, the Communists were forced to rely on the use of the so-called "internationalists," a sort of foreign legion, consisting of pro-Communist sympathizers chosen from among prisoners of war captured by the Tsarist army as well as from national minorities who sided with the Bolsheviks. Numbering 300,000 (an unusually large figure for any civil war, says Seliunin), these "internationalists" proved to be the most effective tool of the Communists in fighting the "third force." Thus he indirectly buttresses the argument of those who emphasize the anti-Russian character of the Bolshevik revolution.

Lenin soon realized the folly of Trotskii's ideas and switched to the pragmatic approach of the NEP period. But this realization came only after the Antonov peasant uprising, the sailors' rebellion in Kronstadt, and the workers' strikes made the survival of the Communist dictatorship precarious, Seliunin points out. Even then Lenin originally conceived of NEP as a temporary measure. Only in May 1921 did a party conference define NEP as a genuine long-term policy. As a result, the "war communism" economic mechanism was dismantled and replaced with NEP, which "in its main features is similar to the new economic mechanism that is being created now," says Seliunin reinforcing his argument in support of a more radical version of perestroika.

Seliunin praises Nikolai Bukharin and Feliks Dzerzhinskii, the founder of the secret police, for objecting to Stalin's policy of abandoning NEP in favor of forced industrialization and collectivization. This policy was in essence a revival of "war communism," except that Stalin favored the creation of concentration camps over "Trotskii's plan of the militarization of labor," says Seliunin. Seliunin makes it clear that collectivization of farms was based on Lenin's policy of preventing the rise of capitalism, of which private farming was seen as a vital manifestation. Paraphrasing Stalin's famous remark about 1929 being the breaking point in building socialism, Seliunin says that in fact it was the year when "the backbone of the nation was broken."

Comparing such Communist victims of Stalin's intrigue as (Sergei Mironovich) Kirov and (Nikolai Ivanovich) Bukharin with the millions of non-Communist victims of peasant and worker background, Seliunin asks his readers not to forget "the suffering of Ivan Denisovich behind the tragedy of Sergei Mironovich and Nikolai Ivanovich." Seliunin's plea is counter to the tendency of many Soviet intellectuals to concentrate on the suffering of Stalin's Communist victims rather than on the suffering of the nation as a whole. Seliunin obviously admires Solzhenitsyn, who first called attention to the suffering of ordinary people under Stalin in the novel *One Day in the Life of Ivan Denisovich*.

In a lengthy excursus into Russia's pre-revolutionary history, Seliunin polemicizes against historians who suggest that Russia is doomed to political despotism and economic inefficiency. He particularly challenges the view of Richard Pipes, the author of *Russia Under the Old Regime*, that "since Kievan Rus' there has been no private property in our country," that Russia's economy was always dominated by state controls, and that, politically, the Russians "were [always] slaves to the state." "According to Pipes," says Seliunin, "the history of Russia was not a development. . . but a repetition and variation of the same hopeless cycle, as if it were happening in a sleepy oriental despotism." Not so, says Seliunin. Citing, for instance, the rapid development of Russia's economy in the wake of the reforms of Alexander II, Seliunin suggests that Soviet reformers can take a lesson of successful perestroika and democratization from pre-revolutionary Russia.

The real hero of Seliunin's article is Petr Stolypin, the Russian prime minister from 1906 to 1911, when he was assassinated by a terrorist. According to Seliunin, this "outstanding statesman" and "revolutionary reformer" did more than anybody else for the development of Russia's productive forces by freeing the peasants from the yoke of communal property and granting them private land ownership. Alas, the Bolshevik revolution canceled the achievements of Stolypin's reforms which, Seliunin suggests, could have been an ideal exit from Russia's economic lag behind the West. Although he does not challenge directly the political legitimacy of the Bolshevik revolution, he condemns the "command socialism economy" it created. On the other hand, he praises capitalism not only for its economic productivity and efficiency but also for its economic freedom, which, he believes, translates into a better guarantee of individual rights and political liberties.

To assure the success of perestroika, Seliunin urges the adoption of a three-tier economic structure: state-owned, cooperative and private enterprises. People should be allowed to choose where to work. Every person can earn his living as he wants, as long as he pays taxes. While assuming that the state-owned sector will predominate in the foreseeable future, Seliunin insists that all enterprises should be wholly self-accountable. The government then would have no need for the "total command planning" that it exercises today. It would merely steer the economy in the direction that is most beneficial for the country. "The American economy today is better regulated by the central government than ours is," says Seliunin.

Like Shmelev, Seliunin calls the present situation in the USSR "revolutionary." He defines it by paraphrasing Lenin that "working people do not want to live as they used to, and the administrative apparatus cannot rule as it used to." Like Shmelev, he urges Gorbachev to opt for a speedy, decisive, and fundamental version of perestroika. He believes that "without radical changes, by the mid-1990s our economy will collapse, with all the consequences that would follow in social, foreign relations, military and other fields." Saying that now there are still some realistic possibilities to solve the problems, Seliunin doubts whether the state "apparatus" would choose the best course. "Has this apparatus always reflected the interests of the country?", Seliunin asks. "If it has, today we would have no right to complain about the period of stagnation."

Seliunin urges Gorbachev to act decisively. First of all, Gorbachev must do away with the overgrown (seventeen million people, Seliunin estimates) bureaucracy, which should be "either smashed or abolished." Once the bureaucratic obstacle to perestroika is removed, measures similar to those under NEP can turn the country around both economically and politically. Some might find it hard to accept his "radical version" of perestroika, says Seliunin. Still, this is "the only realistic way to remedy the economy (and not just the economy)" of the country. Unless such a course is taken, the total structure of the Soviet state [derzhava] might collapse, warns Seliunin.

Seliunin intended his article to show not only the sources of the current Soviet economic woes but also the sources of alternative development. Seliunin clearly established the failure of the classics of Marxism-Leninism to understand the importance of private property and free enterprise for maintaining the productivity of a nation. He also demonstrated that the founding fathers of Marxism-Leninism shared this failure with other utopian socialists and egalitarian revolutionaries of the West. As to the chief sources of alternative development, Seliunin left no doubt that one does not have to go outside of Russia to find them. He used as examples the two Russian statesmen, Tsar Alexander II (1851-1881) and Prime Minister Petr Stolypin (1906-1911), both of whom were not hostile to the West and yet introduced reforms which encouraged the indigenous traditions of free enterprise and personal responsibility.

As to Kliamkin's question, "What should we repent of?", Seliunin answers it implicitly, but unequivocally. If Soviet intellectuals are to aspire to the role of intellectual leadership, they should, first of all, repent the sin of presumptuousness which they inherited from their socialist mentors. That sin made them abandon common sense, renounce the indigenous traditions of the Russian people, and put their faith in the utopian ideas of the West. That sin made them subservient to Soviet dictators who sacrificed millions of ordinary citizens who refused to accept the utopia. And that sin causes them now to justify Stalinism in terms of the Russian people's alleged love for their despots.

In another article, "The Revenge of Bureaucracy,"[27] Seliunin elaborates on his thesis that "either the reform will do away with the bureaucrats, or the bureaucrats will behead the reform." He pays particular attention to a comparison between the "total command planning" in the USSR and the mechanism of central regulation in such capitalist countries as Japan and the USA. He comes to the conclusion that, whereas "total command planning" is ineffective because it stays in the hands of the bureaucracy, the "central regulation" in capitalist countries is more effective because it relies on the regulatory forces of free price formation. Seliunin argues, for instance, that when Japan decided to combat environmental problems, the government established such high penalties for the offending industries that they found it more profitable not to violate environmental rules. Therefore, environmental problems are being solved more successfully in Japan than in the USSR, in spite of the enormous concentration of power in Moscow.

However, Seliunin disagrees with Popkova that central planning and the free market are incompatible, and that a country should choose either socialism or capitalism. Seliunin believes neither. He rather advocates combining the central regulatory powers of a government, be it communist or socialist, with the self-regulatory mechanism of the free market. He argues that the countries which were able to find a proper balance of the two regulatory forces have created better economies.

VADIM KOZHINOV, IGOR' SHAFAREVICH, AND ROY MEDVEDEV ON STALINISM

We shall now discuss an article which appeared in April 1988 not in *Novyi mir*, but in *Nash sovremennik*,[28] a literary magazine which is usually identified with the conservative, "National-Bolshevik" opposition to perestroika. The author of the article is Vadim Kozhinov, a literary critic, whom many regard as a spokesman for the "anti-Semitic" and "chauvinistic" strain of Russian nationalism. Formally, the article is a review of Anatolii Rybakov's novel, *Children of the Arbat*, the darling of the self-proclaimed liberal "superintendents of perestroika." But, in essence, it has to do with "Truth and a Search for Truth" (as it is titled) in respect to the fate of Russia under Communism.

Kozhinov finds Rybakov's novel not only artistically weak, but "superficial and untruthful" in its main subject, a characterization of the Stalin era. He dismisses as "childish" Rybakov's efforts to explain away the Stalinist phenomenon as an accidental aberration--due to Stalin's psychological idiosyncrasy or whatever--from the allegedly true Leninist path. Kozhinov contends that in Rybakov's novel there is neither truth, in the sense of a courageous statement of a historical fact (because no courage is needed to restate what has been known since Khrushchev's 1956 anti-Stalin speech), nor a search for truth, in the sense of trying to understand the historical "why" of Stalinism. As long as Rybakov continues to obscure Stalinism's intimate connection with Leninism and "the world revolutionary movement," the Stalinist phenomenon can be neither understood nor prevented from repeating itself, says Kozhinov.

He builds his argument chiefly around two quotations from Lenin. The one shows that Lenin had fully expected Russia to turn into a "mutilated, anguishing in pain, half-dead morsel of flesh" as a result of the revolutionary "act of birth" of a new system. The other reads: "A scientific concept of dictatorship means such power that is completely unrestricted, unlimited by any law or rules and is directly based on force." Kozhinov says that the two quotations were fully consistent with the doctrine of Marx and Engels. As such they had more bearing on the brutality of the Communist regime under Lenin and Stalin than all the "Asiatic" traditions of the despotic Russian tsars in which the Soviet "liberals" see the main cause of the "Stalinist excesses," Kozhinov suggests.

Kozhinov accuses Rybakov of an exclusive preoccupation with Stalin's purge of the old Leninist guard in 1937-1938, while paying only scant attention to the terror of 1929-33 against completely innocent people. The latter fell victim to the Stalinist terror machine, which was set up by the former, Kozhinov points out. Whether he read *The Gulag Archipelago* or not, in his understanding of the Stalin era, Kozhinov clearly follows in the footsteps of Solzhenitsyn. Like Seliunin, Kozhinov affirms that the backbone of the nation was broken, not in the 1937-1938 purges, but in 1929 with the advent of mass collectivization of farms.

Like Solzhenitsyn before him and Seliunin after, Kozhinov claims that "Stalin's crimes" were not only a consequence of the way the Soviet state was set up by Lenin, but were in fact preceded by mass terror during Lenin's tenure. Citing several Soviet statistical sources, Kozhinov contends that during 1918-1922 alone, human losses amounted to about thirteen million, out of which no more than two million belonged to the "exploitative" classes, while the rest were peasants, working people and other plain folks. Kozhinov makes clear that the main cost of the "act of birth" of the Soviet state was paid with the blood of ordinary Russian people, who were later sacrificed again to the Stalinist terror machine. Kozhinov's argument closely parallels Seliunin's contention that the heaviest losses during the civil war were sustained neither by the reds nor by the whites but by the "third force," the Russian peasantry who were caught between a rock and a hard place.   In essence, Kozhinov accuses Rybakov and his "liberal" admirers of a kind of "group think." They denounce the Stalinist terror only to the extent that it victimized Communists, and do not give a damn about its non-Communist victims, Kozhinov suggests.

As to Kozhinov's alleged anti-Semitism, I could not find any overt anti-Jewish or anti-Zionist statements in this article. But one can, perhaps, read that into it, if one can prove that when Kozhinov cites some Jewish-sounding names among the creators of the Red terror machine, he does so either incorrectly or with the malicious intent of impugning all Jews as accomplices of Stalin's crimes. But then he does not appear to spare such obviously Russian villains as Kirov, Bukharin, Rykov, and Tomskii. It is worth noting that similar accusations were made against Solzhenitsyn when it was discovered that many of the creators of the Gulag had Jewish-sounding names. Since I do not believe that Solzhenitsyn cooked them up out of malice toward the Jews as a nation or religion or for whatever reason, I have every reason to suspect that the charge of anti-Semitism against Kozhinov is just as dubious. In any case, his contention that Stalinism was not an expression of Stalin's "Georgianness" or "Russian Asiatism," but a phenomenon inherent in Marxist-Leninist ideas can hardly be classified as "anti-Semitic."

In spite of a number of unfair reviews it received in the Soviet press,[29] Kozhinov's article further expanded the limits of glasnost from the official "half-truths" toward the "full truth" that Likhachev advocated in his January 1, 1987 interview. This is especially noteworthy because the article was published in the "conservative" *Nash sovremennik*. Kozhinov's article figured prominently in the debate on the origin of Stalinism sponsored by *Moscow News*. The debate was initiated by the letter of Igor' Shafarevich, a prominent Soviet mathematician and a Christian, in which he defended Kozhinov's article against the negative review in *Moscow News*. *Moscow News* then invited Roy Medvedev, an early self-avowed Marxist-Leninist critic of Stalinism,[30] to comment on Shafarevich's letter. Both Shafarevich and Medvedev were, until then, regarded as "dissidents" and therefore shunned by the Soviet press. Roy Medvedev had been "rehabilitated" a few weeks prior to the debate, but for Shafarevich it was the first public exposure.

Before focusing on this debate, a few words are in order about the negative review of Kozhinov's article. It was written by Dmitrii Kazutin, a *Moscow News* political observer. First, Kazutin denigrated Kozhinov's article by comparing it with Nina Andreeva's notorious letter. Then he hammered at it for deviating from the current party line. According to Kazutin, Kozhinov contributes nothing to the search for truth because the truth has already been established [by the party?] that "contrary to our ideological adversaries, the cult of personality [of Stalin, or of Lenin?] was not inevitable, and it was alien to the nature of socialism."[31]

In his letter to *Moscow News* Shafarevich pointed out a discrepancy between the enormity of Stalin's crimes, which the Soviet press now openly admits, and the triviality of the explanations of the phenomenon itself. According to Shafarevich, these explanations are usually reduced to twaddle about the "perfidy and cruelty of a single person and a coincidence of unfortunate circumstances." What is worse, says Shafarevich, many newspapers, including *Moscow News*, indulge in the "elitist" view that the Soviet people themselves, with their "love of a firm hand," deserved no better. Shafarevich suggested that such "explanations" offered by the "liberal" Soviet Marxists are close, in fact, to Nina Andreeva's position, which they so vehemently denounced. Why? Because, like her, they are more concerned with the preservation of the image of Lenin's infallibility than with the search for historical truth. Shafarevich pointed out the paradox that the Marxists fail to follow Marx in that all great historical phenomena owe their origin not to accidents or personalities of leaders but to fundamental laws of history.

According to Shafarevich, better explanations of the nature of Stalinism are offered by such works of Soviet literature as the novels *Kanuny* (Vasilii Belov's novel-chronicle about the 1920s, the concluding part of which was published in 1987 by *Novyi mir*), *Muzhiki i baby* (by Boris Mozhaev), Tendriakov's short stories and Kozhinov's article. As soon as the latter was published by *Nash sovremennik*, says Shafarevich, a strange thing happened: "the very same periodicals which have done much for 'overcoming stereotypes,' 'removing white spots,' and 'eliminating forbidden topics,' attacked it from all sides." Shafarevich singled out Kazutin's misleading review of Kozhinov's article. According to Shafarevich, the great merit of Kozhinov's article consists in the following observation: "Stalinism has deep global roots, [and it is no accident that] Stalin was either praised, or, at least, protected from criticism by the majority of leading western liberals." Citing the pro-Stalinist sentiments of such leading western writers as Lion Feuchtwanger, Bernard Shaw, Albert Einstein, and Jean-Paul Sartre, Shafarevich called for the study of Stalinism in clear view of "[its] international aspect." He concluded his letter by saying that obfuscation of the true "roots of Stalinism" in the "liberal" Soviet press might have more serious consequences than any action of "Nina Andreeva's type" because it may "estrange from perestroika exactly those people who are capable of being its main force."

Although Shafarevich expressed some doubt whether *Moscow News* would print his letter, *Moscow News* was liberal enough to do just that. But it also invited Roy Medvedev to give a rebuttal to Shafarevich, which in itself is certainly a sound journalistic practice. Still, the newspaper's bias is apparent in the way it entitled the two contributions. While Shafarevich's letter is headed by the interrogative title "Logic of History?", Medvedev's rebuttal is titled in the declarative: "The Roots of the Phenomenon." In his rebuttal Medvedev employed the usual tactic of portraying Stalin as an aberration from socialism, Leninism, and Marxism. As to the "roots of the phenomenon," he reduces them to Stalin's "intrigues" and such things as a "gradual liquidation of all organs of party and state control" and the "abandonment of the Leninist principle of party unity." But Medvedev failed even to raise the question why those things occurred in the first place. Besides, one could argue that it was precisely the Leninist principle of party unity that was used most successfully by Stalin to crush his opponents.

Medvedev makes much of Shafarevich's defense of Kozhinov's view that Stalin's crimes were due not just to Stalin's "perfidy," but also, as Medvedev puts it, to a "conspiracy of Western intellectuals (mostly of French and Jewish origin)." He thus clearly insinuates anti-Semitism on the part of both Kozhinov and Shafarevich. Medvedev also tries to divert attention from the main point of his opponents, namely, that Stalinism is rooted in Leninism. He does it by character assassination of his opponents. According to Medvedev, one cannot take Kozhinov's argument seriously because he is a "fanatic of Russian feeling," who is sorry about the bitter fate of Nicholas II and old Russia. (He apparently thinks that such a feeling is outside the limits of glasnost.) As to Shafarevich, Medvedev simply dismisses him because he is not only a Christian but the author of a book in which socialism was denounced as an "absolute evil."

All in all, Kozhinov's article marked a new height in the process of spiritual emancipation of the Soviet intelligentsia from the yoke of Marxist-Leninist monologism. Besides pointing out a genetic link between Leninism and Stalinism (at home and abroad), Kozhinov brought attention to one of the most urgent questions of perestroika: Wasn't the socialism we built under Stalin of the kind that Lenin bequeathed us? If so, don't we need to start perestroika by replacing the Leninist (and Marxist) foundations of the Soviet state? Kozhinov suggests affirmative answers. His article, therefore, is a significant step forward in-the restructuring of the way Soviet people think, in that "cultural revolution from below," without which Gorbachev's "revolution from above" has no chance to succeed.

KSENIIA MIALO ON THE DESTRUCTION OF RUSSIAN PEASANT CULTURE

If Soloukhin likens the Communist domination of Christian Russia with the lawlessness of a barbarian "occupation army," Kseniia Mialo compares it with some specific episodes of Russian and world history. According to her, the destruction of the Russian peasant way of life through collectivization was a "cultural catastrophe" on a par with the Mongol yoke. In terms of world history, she likens it to the Spanish destruction of the Inca and Aztec civilizations, the annihilation of the Albigensians and the Huguenots in France, and the decimation of the Indians in North America. Just as H. M. Stanley, in his colonizing missionary zeal on behalf of Western civilization, was incapable of understanding that the Africans have their own living culture, says Mialo, so the Soviet "leftists" had no respect for the "primitive" culture of the Russian peasantry on whom they forced both collectivization and "cultural revolution," with disastrous results, not just for the peasants, but for the rest of the country.

Mialo provides the above world historical perspective on Communist rule in her article, "The Thread That Was Torn: Peasant

Culture and the Cultural Revolution," which appeared in *Novyi mir* in August 1988.[32]   The title speaks for itself: the "culture" the Communists have tried to foist upon Russia since 1917 broke with the Russian past.   Mialo speaks with the authority of a cultural anthropologist who has done extensive field work in search of the remnants of the destroyed culture.   Noting an increased interest in the country in the "Epoch of the Great Break" (as collectivization used to be glorified under Stalin), Mialo says that so far interest has been limited to the negative economic and demographic consequences of this tragic experiment.   Boris Mozhaev was just about the only novelist who has described the "savage orgy" with which the Soviet press greeted the burning of the traditional Russian village commune on the pyre of collectivization.

Mialo charges Soviet historians and sociologists with either ignoring the tragedy of the Russian peasantry or "creating a myth according to which the victim was [just about] the sole perpetrator of the crime."   In particular, she challenges Igor' Kliamkin and A. Butenko, who had blamed the backward "patriarchic" Russian peasantry for providing "a social-psychological foundation of Stalinism."   Much like Kozhinov and Seliunin, Mialo argues that some of Stalin's victims of 1937, such as Bukharin, Bubnov, and Rykov, had dug the graves for millions of Russian peasants during the 1920s. These "Leftists" and the "ideologists of nihilism" failed to apply "the Leninist principle of developing the best traditions" of Russian village life in order to make it an integral part of "socialist construction" in the country, says Mialo, in the customary lip service to Lenin.   However, she makes it clear that whatever good intention Lenin might have had, there were no spokesmen for his views among his successors, and thus the peasantry was doomed.

According to Mialo, there was no economic necessity for collectivization and the destruction of the "primitive" Russian peasantry.   Far from being "an obstacle to modernization and industrialization," the traditional Russian peasantry, especially the Old Believers, could have advanced Soviet agriculture thanks to their spirit of enterprise, thrift, and openness to innovations.   Their entire way of life was at one with a "cosmocentric" world view, according to which all technical innovations must be balanced within the universal order of things.   "Only in our era of disruption of ecological balance on a global scale. . . did we realize that the intuitive knowledge of our ancestors. . . was impeccable," says Mialo, echoing, perhaps inadvertently, the idea of a stable and ecologically sound economy that Solzhenitsyn had advanced in his *Letter*.

Mialo warns perestroika zealots against the fallacy of starting all over again. For the rebirth of the country, says Mialo, in a typically Russite argument, we need a new cultural idea according to which no construction will succeed unless it is based on the firm foundation of the country's history. She does not believe it possible to restore the destroyed peasant way of life. Nevertheless, she does not want to relegate it to the past "because one cannot go forward without having seen the light of the past, as every person does during a spiritual crisis." She reminds her readers that the very word perestroika was popular among the "leftist" masters of the country during the 1920s, when it was used to justify the imposition of utopian schemes. It is then that they dug the "pit" (*Kotlovan*, as in the title of A. Platonov's 1932 novel just published in *Novyi mir*) for the millions of Russian peasants.

ALLA LATYNINA ON THE CULTURE OF POLEMICS

Alla Latynina's article, "A Church Bell Is Not a Prayer," was published in *Novyi mir* in August 1988. A literary critic and a member of the editorial board of the "liberal" weekly, *Literaturnaia gazeta*, Latynina is well-versed in both literary and political matters, and her article may serve as a sort of summary to the debate of all the previous authors, some of whom are named in it.[33] The reader should not be misled by the article's subtitle, "About Literary Polemics." As Latynina makes clear in the opening paragraph, the "polemics" are concerned with much more than "literary" matters. What is being debated, says Latynina, is not just the novels of a Rybakov or a Pasternak, but "views on various methods of national development, on its ideational and cultural heritage, and its history. . . ." She likens literary criticism to "a firing range, at which ideas are being tested and the formation of trends of social thought takes place." She is convinced that the future of the country depends on the results that this debate might produce.

Latynina clearly positions herself within the moderate and genuinely liberal mainstream of Russian nationalism. "The movement of history has shown that the utopia of non-national existence is not about to come true," says Latynina, summing up the Soviet social experiment undertaken on the basis of Marxist-Leninist faith in non-national internationalism.   Not only "[is] national self-awareness in itself creative," but "its goal--the preservation and the development of the organic, national existence of a people"--has been in direct conflict with the "divisive goals" of the "non-national" experiment, which reached its apogee in mass murders during the 1930s under the pretext of fighting "enemies of the people." On the other hand, no nationalist goal can be creative unless there is plenty of room for national self-criticism. "Without national self-criticism, national self-awareness can degenerate into national self-complacency," says Latynina.   She deplores the fact that "a low type of national self-awareness" has presently asserted itself, most notably in certain pronouncements of Pamyat leaders and their sympathizers among contributors to such nationalist magazines as *Nash sovremennik* and *Moskva*. Rejecting the idea of the existence of a secret conspiracy against Russian culture, Latynina argues that the "enemy-of-a-nation" myth is just as pernicious as that of the "enemy-of-the-people."

Latynina does not even bother to argue with the "bureaucratic opposition to reforms." She dismisses it by quoting from St. John's Apocalypse that although "you have the name of being alive, you are dead." (St. John, 3:1) But while she generally disagrees with the ideas of such "national-radicals" (as she calls them) as Vadim Kozhinov, Valentin Rasputin, V. Bondarenko, and Tat'iana Glushkova, she defends their right to participate in the country-wide dialogue. In fact, the main targets of Latynina's article are not the "national-radicals" of such "conservative" magazines as *Nash sovremennik, Molodaia gvardiia*, and *Moskva*), but the "liberals" from the "progressive" and "pro-perestroika" magazines, *Ogonek* and *Iunost'*). She particularly deplores the tendency of such "liberal" critics as Benedikt Sarnov and Tat'iana Ivanova to label "an opponent of perestroika" anyone who is less than enthusiastic about either the literary or the philosophical merits of the works of a Rybakov or a Shatrov.

While disagreeing with Kozhinov on the historiography of Rybakov's novel, Latynina agrees with him that the novel is weak from a literary standpoint. Latynina shares Kozhinov's view that Stalin's cult is a phenomenon of the world revolutionary movement and that there is little that is specifically "Russian" about Stalinism. As to Rasputin, "his art has already suggested to us many profound answers" to the questions about the roots of the "genocide disguised as collectivization," says Latynina.   However, she rejects Rasputin's journalistic effort to explain the same phenomenon in terms of the "indifference and bureaucratic parasitism" of Soviet authorities. Regretting the fact that "we are too much accustomed to looking for the root of evil in people rather than ideas," Latynina offers the following explanation of Stalinism: "The destruction of the churches and monuments was a logical consequence of the faith in the world historical mission of the proletariat."

Latynina agrees with Rasputin that the "liberal" Soviet press failed to accord Pamyat the right to be heard. The treatment the Soviet press accorded Pamyat was not only in violation of the ABCs of democracy, but reminded one of the condemnation of Pasternak's novel, *Dr. Zhivago*, in 1958 by Soviet writers who prefaced their speeches by saying, "I have not read the novel, but. . . ." She also praises Stanislav Kuniaev, the *bete noire* of the "liberals," for arguing in his article, "Everything Has Started from Labeling," that many victims of Stalin in 1937 were themselves enthusiastic proponents of revolutionary terror. She agrees with Kuniaev's explanation of the tragedy of these people, many of whom were outstanding poets, in terms of the corrupting influence of the ideas of the Third International on which they were raised.

Latynina's main concern, however, is that Soviet intellectuals have not yet learned the "culture of polemics." After decades of officially imposed ideological conformism [*edinomyslie*], they are still unaccustomed to a plurality of views, still unable to listen to and understand an opponent's viewpoint.   Consequently, failing to discriminate between the fruitful and not-so-fruitful ideas of an opponent, they tend to lump them all together in order to put down the opponent for ulterior motives. Their favorite "method of debating" is pasting on an opponent the label of "an enemy of perestroika," "an antagonist of perestroika," or "anti-perestroishchik." This "method" is morally indistinguishable from the one used during the worst times of Soviet history, when the labeling of one's opponent "an enemy of the people" often led to his arrest, imprisonment and death, says Latynina.

Paradoxically, the worst offenders belong to the "liberal camp." Latynina shows that the tradition of pasting a label on one's opponent stems from the practice of "liberal terror" in nineteenth-century Russia. Taking advantage of their dominant position in Russian periodicals, the left-liberal critics subjected to "moral ostracism" anyone who was suspected of harboring "reactionary" ideas (e.g., such Russian writers as Dostoevskii, Leskov, and Pisemskii). The conservative authors, on the other hand, often responded by insinuating that their left-liberal critics were "politically unreliable," which amounted to "an appeal to a policeman." Presently, says Latynina, the "liberals" combine both functions. Not only do they subject their "conservative" opponents to "moral ostracism" as their predecessors used to, but, since they are part of the Soviet propaganda apparatus, they also denounce them to the authorities (for example, for the failure to follow Marxism-Leninism).

Latynina's article is a calm and cogent argument for the need to restore the original meaning of the word *liberalism*, which, since the nineteenth century, "has been undergoing linguistic corrosion just as the idea of liberalism itself has been compromised by both the left and the right." She affirms liberalism as an ideology that is most consistent with freedom of conscience, human rights, and trust in reforms. She clearly condemns Marxism-Leninism when she says that the "ideas of change through violence" have outlived themselves.

"Isn't it then about time to abandon our customary contempt for liberalism?", Latynina asks. Realizing that "liberalism cannot be introduced by force," she identifies its main opponents with three groups: (1) the "conservatives" [*okhraniteli*], who stand for "ideational purity" and personal privileges (a clear allusion to the coalition of the Marxist-Leninist dogmatists and party bureaucrats); (2) the "national-radicals," who do not trust sufficiently the values of liberty, even though Latynina credits them with the expansion of the limits of glasnost; and (3) those Soviet "perestroika liberals" who profess the ideas of liberalism but fail to respect its values. It is the last group that bothers Latynina the most because they fail to value freedom of thought. She accuses them of espousing a new illiberal theory according to which enemies of "the progressives" should be suppressed and forced to shut up in order to prevent the victory of either the bureaucratic opposition to perestroika or national radicalism.

Latynina endorses Strelianyi's position in regard to the official condemnation of Nina Andreeva's letter: "Most of all I am afraid that we will force the conservatives to shut up. . . . By stifling their voice, we risk becoming similar to them. What is more, imperceptibly we will become them." Ringing a church bell is not the same as saying a prayer, and a shout does not make a dialogue, says Latynina, paraphrasing a Russian proverb. "Will we ever learn how to pray?" she asks. A debate is not a means for asserting one's views by shouting down all opponents, but a spiritual activity involving a mutual search for truth, concludes Latynina.

Notes

1. Gorbachev, p. 10.

2. See Edith Rogovin Frankel, Novyi mir: A Case Study in the Politics of Literature, 1952-1958 (New York: Cambridge Univ. Press, 1981).

3. Anatolii Strelianyi, who served on the board from February through October 1987, made the statement during a discussion with Moscow University students on May 15, 1987. See Posev, 9/87, pp. 2-5.

4. About the ideological orientation of village writers see Edward J. Brown, Russian Literature Since the Revolution,revised and enlarged edition (Harvard University Press, 1982) and Geoffrey Hosking, Beyond Socialist Realism (New York: Holmes & Meier, 1980).

5. See John Dunlop, Faces of Contemporary Russian Nationalism (Princeton, N.J.: Princeton University Press, 1983).

6. See, for instance, a samizdat article, "Moskva, god 1986-i ot R.Kh., 69-i god sovetskoi vlasti," signed by the initials V.P. and datelined September-October 1986, Moscow. The author draws a distinction between the "National-Bolshevik" right-wing Russian nationalists, such as the leaders of Pamyat, the painter Il'ia Glazunov, and some of the "villagers" grouped around the magazine Nash sovremennik, on the one hand, and the moderates, on the other. The latter, he says, are variously called "the liberal wing of the Russian Party," the "moderate Russophiles," and "the party of national renaissance," but he prefers to call them "National-Liberals." The author includes among the moderates Dmitrii Likhachev, Sergei Zalygin, Boris Mozhaev, Sergei Averintsev, and, possibly, Olga Chaikovskaia, all of whom are represented in this book. The author points out their closeness to Solzhenitsyn's "defensive nationalism" in that they tend to favor the secession of Russia from the Union.

7. In this respect, my sample represents an extension of the debate about the Soviet future among the dissidents, defectors, and emigres which I have described for an international conference in Geneva in August 1985 in a paper, "Images of the Soviet Future: The Emigre and Samizdat Debate," published in The Soviet Union & the Challenge of the Future, Vol. 1, eds. Alexander Shtromas and Morton A. Kaplan (New York: Paragon, 1988), pp. 357-399.

8. D. S. Likhachev, "Trevogi sovesti," Literaturnaia gazeta, January 1, 1987.

9. D. S. Likhachev,"Ot pokaianiia - k deistviiu," Literaturnaia gazeta, September 9, 1987.

10. L. Popkova, "Gde pyshnee pirogi?", Novyi mir, 5/87, pp. 239-241.

11. O. Latsis, "Zachem zhe pod ruku tolkat'?", Novyi mir 7/87, 266-268.

12. Iurii Korkhov, "Pautina prinuzhdeniia," Novyi mir 5/87, pp. 241-245. esp. p. 243.

13. A. Iakovlev, "Zakon betonnoi steny," Novyi mir, No. 6, 1987, pp. 260-266, esp. 261.

14. Nikolai Shmelev, "Avansy i dolgi," Novyi mir, No. 6, 1987, pp. 142-158.

15. Nikolai Shmelev, "Novye trevogi," Novyi mir, No. 4, 1988, pp. 160 - 175.

16. Olga Chaikovskaia, "Grinev," Novyi mir, No. 8 (August), 1987, pp. 226-244.

17. Valentin Rasputin, "Poriadok v dushe - poriadok v otechestve, Izvestiia, March 15, 1987.

18. Vladimir Soloukhin, "Pokhorony Stepanidy Ivanovny," Novyi mir, No. 9 (September), 1987, pp. 130-140.

19. All quotations from Soloukhin's book are according to Mikhail Nazarov's review article in RM, July 1, 1988.

20. However, in January 1989 the nationalist magazine Moskva started its publication, and at least one laudatory review, by Ye. Osetrov, appeared in Literaturnaia gazeta, No. 24, June 14, 1989. For more see my next chapter.

21. Iurii Kariakin, "Stoit li nastupat' na grabli?," Znamia, No. 9, 1987, pp. 200-224.

22. Mozhaev's novel was published in the literary magazine Don, Nos. 1-3, 1987.

23. Igor Kliamkin, "Kakaia ulitsa vedet k khramu?", Novyi mir, No. 11 (November), 1987, pp. 150-188.

24. Announcing that Vekhi will soon be published in Moscow, Aleksandr Tsipko called it the most important single book for understanding the meaning of perestroika. Its publication, he said, would mean a "restoration of common sense" and a hope for Russia's rebirth. (See his article "Neobkhodimo potriasenie mysl'iu," Moskovskie novosti, No. 26, July 1, 1990.

25. Vasilii Seliunin and Grigorii Khanin, "Lukavaia tsifra," Novyi mir, No. 2, 1987, pp. 181-201.

26. Vasilii Seliunin, "Istoki," Novyi mir, No.5, 1988, pp. 162-189. It was translated into English and, under the title "Roots," published in Soviet Law and Government, Fall 1988.

27. Vasilii Seliunin, "Revansh biurokratii," Novoe Russkoe Slovo, June 10, 11, and 12, 1988. Reprinted from the magazine Strana i mir, No. 1, 1988. This article was circulated in samizdat and printed without Seliunin's permission.

28. Vadim Kozhinov, "Pravda i istina," Nash sovremennik, No. 4 (April), 1988, pp.160-175.

29. See, for instance, the articles by Ven'iamin Sarnov, Ogonek, No. 19, 1988; Nikolai Erofeev, Sovetskaia Rossiia, May 5, 1988; and Dmitrii Kazutin, Moscow News, No. 19, May 8, 1988. See also a negative aside about Kozhinov's article in Vera Tolz's analysis of Seliunin's article in Radio Liberty Research Bulletin 244, June 13, 1988.

30. I. R. Shafarevich, "Logika istorii," and Roy Medvedev, "Korni iavleniia," Moscow News, No. 24, June 12, 1988, pp. 12-13.

31. Kazutin, see note 27.

32. Kseniia Mialo, "Oborvannaia nit': Krest'ianskaia kul'tura i kul'turnaia revoliutsiia," Novyi mir, No. 8, 1988, pp. 245-257.

33. A. Latynina, "Kolokol'nyi zvon - ne molitva," Novyi mir No. 8 (August), 1988, pp. 232-244.

3

Beyond Communism:
Voices of Glasnost, 1989

SOVIET HOLOCAUST

As I pointed out in the Alaska speech on February 12, 1988, the most hopeful development since Gorbachev came to power in 1985 was the intellectual movement "from ideological to spiritual, from 'internationalist' to national. . . from Marxism-Leninism to no 'isms' at all, from *Partia* to *Patria*, from things Communist to things Russian." Since then that movement has resulted in a virtual breakdown of the Marxist-Leninist monopoly on intellectual life in the USSR.

In Chapter 1, I argued that the best alternative to the present regime lies in the legitimation of the moderate, liberal-democratic mainstream of the Russian national rebirth movement as represented by Solzhenitsyn. In Chapter 2, "Voices of Glasnost 1987-88," I tried to demonstrate that the "revolution from below," which Gorbachev has welcomed, has inevitably entailed intellectual ferment and a movement, not only away from and beyond Marxism-Leninism, but also toward a new *national* Russia. In this chapter I will give a hearing to outstanding voices of glasnost in 1989, with the emphasis on the movement toward a new post-Communist *national* Russia. I shall focus on issues of the past (Stalinism), the present (the Russian national problem and perestroika) and a future Russian polity.

On all these issues Russian nationalist authors, the *patriots*, differ markedly not only from the *partiots*, but also the so called "liberals," also known as the "superintendents of perestroika." The *patriots*, not just the Russite, but of other nationalities as well, think that perestroika should go as far as necessary to improve the situation in whatever part of the Soviet Union they consider their Patria, or fatherland, be it Russia, Armenia, or Estonia. Some of them might be Party members and regard themselves as genuine Communists. But they would not hesitate to quit the Party if they were convinced that the Party acts contrary to the interests of their *Patria*. (I'm sure they can find some Lenin quotations for that.) The *partiots*, on the other hand, although they may sincerely wish well to whatever nation they belong to--Armenia, Estonia, or Russia--cannot conceive of the future without making sure that the Communist Party, the *Partia*, remains in charge. Meanwhile, the "liberals," the so-called "new democrats," often straddle the fence between the *patriots* and the *partiots*.

Among the issues of the past which now divide Soviet intellectuals, the foremost is the issue of the Stalinist terror. The *patriots* tend to regard Stalinism as a logical consequence of Marxist-Leninist ideas. They view the Stalinist terror as the culmination of the revolutionary terror under Lenin and Trotskii. They may support the government-approved decision to create a memorial to Stalin's victims, but they think that the memorial should be expanded to include all victims of the Communist terror throughout Soviet history. The Russite *patriots* especially regard this terror as a national tragedy and a "genocide" of the Russians (as well as all other Soviet peoples) and blame it on the Communist regime itself.

The *partiots*, on the other hand, usually prefer to see the scale of Soviet terror limited to the Stalinist era. They are often joined, on that issue, by some "liberals." Both groups tend to attribute the brutality of the Stalinist era to either Stalin's aberrant personality or certain flaws in the Russian national character. The peasants, they allege, have either passively yielded to Stalin's despotism or even actively promoted it. Preoccupied chiefly with the Party purges of 1937-1938, in which many of the "old guard" Bolsheviks perished, the *partiots* (and some "liberals") view the whole phenomenon of Stalinist terror primarily as a Party tragedy. Ignoring the fact that there were thousands of innocent victims both before and after Stalin, they want the memorial to honor only the victims of the Stalinist regime. Claiming that Stalinism has nothing to do with either Leninism or Marxism, they set before themselves the impossible task of divorcing Stalin from the principles on which the Soviet state was founded.

As has been noted earlier, since the advent of glasnost, Soviet publications have been filled with reports about the terror under Stalin. To give an idea of the extent to which millions of Soviet citizens have just recently become aware of that terror, I shall briefly review a few recent revelations.   In June 1988 there appeared a report in a Belorussian newspaper about Kuropaty, a mass grave near Belorussia's capital, Minsk, where more than 100,000 corpses of Soviet citizens were found. It appeared that all of them were shot during the 1937-1941 period.[1] The authors of the report based their findings on numerous interviews with local residents and on the expertise of professional archaeologists. Rejecting the suspicion that the victims may have been killed by Nazis during the war, they pointed out that after the war Soviet soldiers were ordered to conceal the deeper layers of the mass grave. Even at the height of Khrushchev's anti-Stalinist campaign in 1957, no investigation was made when numerous skulls and bones were found during a road construction.   Noting that Kuropaty was just one of several such sites in Belorussia alone, the authors of the report concluded that secret mass executions were part of "the Stalinist system of genocide."

After the nineteenth Party Conference in June 1988 approved Gorbachev's proposal to erect a memorial to the "victims of Stalinism," there have been new discoveries.   In March 1989, a government commission concluded that people buried at a mass grave near the village of Bykovnia in the vicinity of Kiev, Ukraine, were victims of "the Stalinist terror," not of the Nazis as the government had previously alleged.[2] The chairman of the commission, Viktor Kulik, confirmed that the analysis of the exhumed corpses showed that they were the so called "enemies of the people," that is, persons who were accused during Stalin's rule, on trumped-up charges, of "counter-revolutionary activities, high treason, and nationalism," and then summarily executed. The site was first discovered in 1987.   However, at that time the authorities denied that Stalinism had anything to do with the massacre, and in May 1988 a monument to the "victims of the German Fascist invaders" was erected at the site.   Only when eyewitnesses protested the official falsification of history was the Kulik commission set up. According to unofficial estimates, the Bykovnia site contained 200,000 to 300,000 corpses.

Since then more reports appeared about other Kuropatys and Bykovnias scattered all across the country. New mass graves were discovered in the Levashovo wasteland near Leningrad;[3] in the suburbs of Kuibyshev (former Kainsk, meaning the city of Cain!); in the Barabinsk district of the Novosibirsk oblast' in Siberia;[4] on the Lysaia Gora (meaning Bald Hill, that is Golgotha!) near the city of Cheliabinsk in the South Urals;[5] in the village of Rutchenkovo, near Donetsk, Ukraine, where Soviet miners recently went on strike;[6] and in the town of Kolpashevo in the Tomsk oblast' in Western Siberia.[7] There were also some Soviet television programs about the Stalinist terror, including a confession of a former NKVD soldier who repented for taking part in executing people in Babii Iar before the war. (During the war Babii Iar became the site of mass executions of Soviet citizens, primarily Jews, by the Germans.)[8]   And there were at least two documentary films made about the Gulag camp at the site of the former Solovki monastery.[9]

Most of the new Soviet reports are confined, however, to the crimes of the Stalin era. To my knowledge, there were no reports of Soviet inquiries into the Red Terror during the Civil War, neither against the whites, nor against the greens, nor against the Socialist-Revolutionaries or other leftist and nationalist opponents of the reds. However, there were some reports of inquiries into Bolshevik persecution of Russian clergymen.[10]   Moreover, the annihilation of Tsar Nicholas II Romanov's family on July 17, 1918, has been receiving increased attention from the Soviet media, which is a response to popular demand to know more about this macabre episode that came to symbolize the end of the old world and the birth of the new one.[11] All in all, new Soviet reports, which often appeared in defiance of the official limits on glasnost, tend to confirm, expand, and complement the *worst* estimates of the brutality of the Soviet regime made by Western scholars.

The report about the Kolpashevo mass grave might illustrate the difficulties in overcoming official efforts to conceal the truth. It was contained in an article written by a local journalist, Vladimir Zapetskii, in October 1987. However, the article was not published until May 1989, and even then only in a small-circulation local journal. According to Zapetskii, a mass grave near Kolpashevo was discovered in April 1979 when the sandy bank, known locally as Kolpashevskii Iar, collapsed into the river Ob'. To the horror of the local population the landslide exposed the macabre sight of skulls and bones, as well as fully preserved corpses, falling into the river Ob'. In an effort to conceal the incident, the local authorities sent to the site two tugboats whose crews were ordered to simply wash off the exposed corpses and let them sink in the river. However, many of the corpses were so well preserved in the drier layers of sand (eyewitnesses thought that even the faces were recognizable) that they began floating in the river in view of the townspeople. The authorities responded then by sending cutters and oar boats with police crews on board, charged with the task of sinking the corpses with metal and rock sinkers or simply crushing them into pieces with the oars. Although they worked day and night until May 9, 1979, weeks later, corpses were seen floating hundreds of miles down the river.

There were no reports of the incident at the time. Kolpashevo residents testify that, in trying to explain away the desecration of the mass grave, local authorities spread the rumors that it was the grave of war-time Soviet army deserters who, presumably, did not deserve to be re-buried. However, rejecting the official version, Zapetskii speculates that this was one of the killing fields of the Kolpashevo NKVD prison which during the 1930s served as a way station for exiled kulaks and other "enemies of the people." It is impossible to establish whether Zapetskii's version is fully justified since he was not an eyewitness himself. However, his article inspires confidence since it was recommended for publication by three scholars from the University of Tomsk.[12] The author donated his honorarium to the Memorial Fund.

Besides reports containing new evidence of the Stalinist terror, a number of new statistical assessments have appeared of the damage it caused for the country in terms of both direct and indirect (demographic) loss of human lives. In September 1987 Yu. Poliakov, a leading Soviet demographer, estimated that during the civil war, 1918-1922, the country's population decreased by thirteen million.[13] In March 1989, Roy Medvedev, a former dissident who has been recently restored as a Party member, estimated the total number of Stalin's victims (from 1927 to 1953) at forty million.[14] V. Pereverzev, writing in the Russite magazine *Molodaia gvardiia*, put the losses for the 1918-1939 period at 20.1 million.[15]

In April 1989 Vladimir Shubkin, in an article published in *Novyi mir*, suggested that the figures of such Western specialists as Robert Conquest, Barbara Anderson, Brian Silver, and Steven Rosefielde are more correct than Medvedev's figures, which he found too low, even for the Stalinist period. Shubkin pointed out that Soviet losses during World War II (which Stalin had put at seven million people) were probably considerably higher than the commonly accepted figure of twenty million, which owes its origin to Khrushchev's speculations. He implied that the extraordinary losses during the war, which Medvedev did not include in his tally, were chiefly due to the disregard of other Soviet leaders for human life.[16] In June, in an article published in the mass-circulation *Komsomol'skaia pravda*, O. Marinicheva estimated the total losses due to the brutality of the Soviet regime since 1917 at ninety million people.[17]

I have cited the above range of figures because none of them can be verified and all are approximations at best. Regardless of which figure is closest to the truth, for the first time in Soviet history, millions of Soviet citizens have been informed of the great extent of the Communist government's crimes against humanity.[18] Even if one allows a large margin of error, the figures suggest that an unprecedented peace-time holocaust was perpetrated by the Soviet regime against its own people. The above revelations have just begun to penetrate the consciousness of the Soviet people, and the names of Kuropaty and Bykovnia will no doubt be in the same category of twentieth century horrors as those of Buchenwald and Auschwitz. It is necessary to review how Soviet authors are beginning to cope philosophically with this information confirming the worst estimates of mass terror during the Soviet regime.

ALEKSANDR TSIPKO, "SOURCES OF STALINISM"

One of the most significant intellectual events of the year was the publication of a series of articles, "Sources of Stalinism," by Aleksandr Tsipko, Doctor of Philosophy, Party member and deputy director of the Institute of Economics of the World Socialist System, in the magazine *Nauka i zhizn'*.[19] Tsipko contends that the chief responsibility for the tragedy of Stalinism lies with Lenin's "old guard"

Bolsheviks, most notably Trotskii and Preobrazhenskii. "It was the old guard who created that political mechanism, that tool of absolute power which Stalin later used for his egotistical goals. . . ." says Tsipko, defining Stalinism as a form of "Leftist extremism." As to the social group from which it issued, Tsipko identifies it neither with the working class nor with the Russian peasantry, but with "bourgeois intellectuals," particularly those claiming to possess "theoretical knowledge about the future."

While acknowledging that both Marx and Engels, as well as Lenin, belonged to that kind of intellectual milieu, Tsipko stopped short of condemning them personally. Nor did he condemn the Communist experiment as a whole. Apparently his membership in the Communist Party prevented him from doing that.[20] Tsipko drew a distinction between the "left dogmatists," on the one hand, and the "true Communists," on the other. "The left dogmatists, all those revolutionary radicals of all denominations and levels of intellectual sophistication, have never been guided by the desire to help people, to alleviate their hardships," says Tsipko. He suggests that all such "Lefties" have been driven by "various, mostly egotistical, motives." To them Tsipko opposes the Communists whom he portrays as "people who care about the common good." However, since he offers no proof of the Communists being morally superior to the leftists he condemns, the distinction remains paper-thin. At any rate, it was inapplicable throughout the major part of Soviet history since Tsipko himself recognized Stalinism as a form of "leftist extremism." One has to conclude that, at best, Tsipko's description of the Communists applies to their future, not the past.

Tsipko's assertion of intellectuals' guilt contradicts such observers as Richard Pipes, Alexander Yanov, and Igor' Kliamkin, who attribute the brutality of Stalinism either to the despotic traditions of pre-revolutionary Russian rulers or to certain flaws in the Russian national character, as embodied in the Russian peasantry, whence allegedly many of Stalin's henchmen originated. Conversely, Tsipko gives credence to those who, like Seliunin and Kozhinov, emphasize Western rather than Russian sources of Left totalitarianism. Remarkably, Tsipko's article was published at a time when Peter Collier and David Horowitz, the two former American leftists, published a book in which they denounced their former intellectual comrades, including the American Communists, for the same lack of concern for humanity.[21]

Tsipko's suggestion that the sources of Soviet totalitarianism should be sought in the West did not pass unnoticed in the Soviet press. In an interview with a Soviet journalist, Tsipko was confronted with the fact that the proposition he has attacked has many adherents not just among Soviet "superintendents of perestroika," but also in the West, where "many sociologists. . . are convinced that we have been building socialism not according to, but contrary to, Marx."[22] Tsipko did not budge. Referring to Igor' Kliamkin's article, "Why is it hard to tell the truth?",[23] Tsipko accused him and like-minded Western observers of concealing "the main truth. . . that the economic strategy of war Communism was formed, above all, under the influence of the ideas of *The Communist Manifesto.*" "In principle, we have no reason to reproach Leon Trotskii for. . . his attempts to militarize peasant labor. . . [because] in that case he, as a Communist, acted strictly in compliance with the instructions of *The Manifesto,*" explained Tsipko.

Like Popkova before him, Tsipko accused the so-called "eurocommunists" and their Soviet acolytes of distorting Marx when they argued that Marx was not an opponent of private property and the market economy but a lover of liberty, humaneness, and civil peace. Admitting that some of Marx's juvenilia could be interpreted in favor of his humaneness, Tsipko argued that the core of Marx's teaching, which appealed to the "old Bolshevik guard," was both violent and utopian. Aware of the lesson Marx drew from the Paris Commune of 1871, namely, that the insurgent communards were defeated because they were insufficiently ruthless against their opponents, these Bolsheviks were determined not to make the same "mistake." They were inspired by Marx's saying that "the revolutionary terror [was] the only means" if the bloody birth of a new society was to succeed.

As to Tsipko's own attitude toward the Marxist theory of revolutionary class struggle, it was perhaps best expressed in this passage from a book he managed to publish at the height of the stagnation era:

> As experience has shown, prolonged civil wars are the greatest danger for a society as a social organism. Not only do these wars undermine the biological and economic roots of a society, but the

violence and cruelty [that accompany them] even in the name of humane ideals always carry within them something that destroys the spiritual foundations of humanity. . . There is nothing more terrible than the habit, the inertia, of violence. At first we kill our real enemies, then the imagined ones, and then our closest friends most devoted to the cause of the revolution. Therefore one should regard any fratricidal civil war as a historical tragedy, and violence, even in the name of progress, as a short-term contingency. A class struggle approach may help to understand the historical and social sources of this tragedy, but it cannot transform the cruelty and violence into something that is ethically good.

Although the book came out in 1980,[24] this passage prevented Tsipko from receiving his doctoral degree for six years. Up to the present day, Tsipko continues to be one of the most intelligent, daring and steadfast critics of both Gorbachev and his "liberal" opponents.[25]

IGOR' ZOLOTUSSKII, "THE BANKRUPTCY OF ABSTRACTIONS"

Another milestone on the road of emancipation of Soviet intellectuals from the yoke of Marxism-Leninism was Igor' Zolotusskii's article, "The Bankruptcy of Abstractions," published in the January 1989 issue of *Novyi mir*.[26] Being a literary critic, he wrote his article in the form of a review of some of the works of fiction which have appeared since the advent of glasnost, both by living Soviet authors and those posthumously rehabilitated. But in essence, it was an assault on the political controls of Russian literature. Referring to a high school textbook on Soviet Russian literature published in 1987, Zolotusskii accused its authors of trying to teach the young generation an "abstract love of the Party" and of propagating the tenets of socialist realism that have shackled Soviet literature for decades. He challenged the concept of "Leninist" perestroika, saying that its adepts (whom we have called the *partiots*), merely want to replace "the cult" of Stalin with that of the Party and Lenin. "There is no cult of Stalin nowadays," wrote Zolotusskii, "but there is the cult of the Party. The Party itself, as well as the idea it embodies, is always correct. Some Party activists make mistakes, but the Party--never. . . . But isn't this a new idolatry, except that now it is not personified, but collectivized?", asked Zolotusskii with bitter sarcasm.

The cult of the Party is linked with that of Lenin. "Everything Lenin wrote they turn into a 'teaching,' a commandment, or an instruction to be carried out. Once Lenin wrote that each culture consists of two cultures, the progressive and non-progressive, and Russian culture was divided and split in two," wrote Zolotusskii in reference to the one issue that is very central for all *patriots* and particularly for the Russites. The latter have always objected to official efforts to stamp out all vestiges of Russian culture that did not conform with the so-called "progressive" (that is, pro-revolutionary and pro-socialist) thought as "reactionary," "retrograde," "mystical" and otherwise suspect.

In evaluating recent Soviet literature, Zolotusskii gave, on the whole, higher marks to the works of the ruralists, several of whom he praised for their search for "spiritual answers to social questions" and for their staying close to the interests of the people. As to such "liberal" authors as Mikhail Shatrov, Anatolii Rybakov, and Daniil Granin, in Zolotusskii's opinion, they follow too closely the ever-changing Party line. "Instead of Stalin [they offer] Lenin (or Kirov), instead of full collectivization--NEP," wrote Zolotusskii about these modern fellow-travelers. According to him, by politicizing their work, they fall short of the higher, spiritual calling of art. "But the solution is not in replacement of one leader with another or even of one form of government with another. This is not enough for literature. Its ideal cannot be political. It should aim beyond the rule of one tsar or another, and even farther than a whole historical epoch," wrote Zolotusskii, denouncing the tendency of time-serving even if it be in the name of a "progressive cause."

"Where is the traditional Russian hero--an idealist hero? Where is the search for the meaning of life? Where is death and immortality? God or Devil?" asks Zolotusskii. Certainly not in the works of "the [current] state-sponsored literature (and Rybakov's *Children of the Arbat* represents this state literature, even though in a progressive sense) [which] offers no spiritual answers [because] its arsenal was borrowed from the sphere of politics, not from the spiritual realm," he answers.

Pointing out the increasing independence of new Russian literature from Party controls, Zolotusskii called on it to focus attention on "the critique of the idea of violence as a means of progress." This focus was characteristic not only of classical Russian literature, but also of the best of the Soviet writers who remained independent of party controls during the 1920s and early 1930s, such as Mikhail Bulgakov and Andrei Platonov. The latter showed, says Zolotusskii, that "the idea of violence warps the very nature of man, allowing a person to stretch on a drum the skin of his own father, so that the beat of the revolution could be sustained." Welcoming a tendency to return to the "old values and the old symbolism," Zolotusskii especially praised the evangelical symbolism in Chinghiz Aitmatov's novel *Plakha* [Executioner's Block] and Iurii Dombrovskii's novel *Fakul'tet nenuzhnykh nauk* [Department of Unnecessary Sciences]. He concluded with a call "to restore life to life, to return light to a soul, human warmth to an ideal--that's what our literature should aspire to today...."

VLADIMIR SHUBKIN, "A DIFFICULT FAREWELL"

Vladimir Shubkin is a survivor. Born in 1923, he belongs to the generation of those high school students who graduated in 1941 only to step into the deadly trenches of the war. However, having survived the violence of external war, Shubkin devotes his article to the even more harrowing violence of revolution and civil war, on which, according to him, the entire power structure of the USSR is founded. Taking as an epigraph Marx's famous affirmation of violence as the "midwife of history," Shubkin analyzes how that idea was embodied in the Soviet power structure.

The specificity of the Soviet power structure should not be confused with "either Western or Russian forms," he says. It consists of an extraordinary reliance on violence and coercion. Violence was the chief tool not just in the revolutionary seizure of power and the destruction of the "old world," but also in the construction of the new one. As Shubkin puts it, "Violence became the main instrument in the hands of the builders of the new world." Why so? Because from the very beginning, Lenin and his associates regarded the revolution in

Russia as a staging area for a world revolution. "The primary task then was to retain and to enlarge power, not to share it with anybody. It was necessary [for the Bolsheviks] to create an army for self-defense and for assistance to revolutionary movements in Europe and Asia."

But how could they make people work for such grandiose projects? The answer again was found in Marx, who suggested the need for non-economic coercion under Communism. Since the Bolsheviks at once abolished private property, as Marx advised, they had no choice but to resort to the coercive option, says Shubkin. Acknowledging that Seliunin had already shown the role of coercion in the post-revolutionary period (see Chapter 2), Shubkin concluded that, contrary to the beliefs of some dogmatic perestroika enthusiasts, the current "bureaucratic structure" had originated neither during Brezhnev's "stagnation era," nor under Stalin, but from the very first days of Bolshevik power. According to Shubkin, there were no serious disagreements among the leading Bolsheviks when they chose coercion as one of the cornerstones of the Soviet power pyramid.

Having traced current Soviet problems to Marx's theory of violence, Shubkin makes no apologies for Lenin either. In fact, he suggests that as the founder of the Bolshevik Party, Lenin was chiefly responsible for institutionalizing the Party's elitist "political mechanism" as a model for all Soviet governance structures. With its military chain of command from the top down, this model was ideally suited for concentration of power, at first among a very small group of professional conspirators and then in the hands of a single dictator.

The chief thrust of Shubkin's article is against the Leninist concept of the Party. This becomes obvious when the author approvingly quotes Plekhanov, the father of Russian Marxism, who split with Lenin precisely over the issue of Lenin's turning the Russian Social-Democrat Party into an elitist party of professional Bolshevik conspirators. Once the Bolshevik Party took power, its anti-democratic political mechanism was copied in all other Soviet governing bodies, from trade unions and the Young Communist League to local Soviets and the state apparatus. "The result was a unified center of all these hierarchic structures, the *nomenklatura*, which. . . has suppressed all forms of spontaneity, self-organization and initiative, and thus made coercion the fundamental principle of governance," says Shubkin.

Besides his analysis of the coercive nature of the Soviet power structure, Shubkin offered one of the first detailed accounts of the total human cost of the "war that the [Soviet] state has conducted against its own people."[27] Quoting from demographic research, Shubkin says that during World War I the country's population continued to grow in spite of the fact that about two million people were killed or died from wounds and disease. However, during the civil war, 1917-1922, the country's total population decreased by thirteen million, of whom about two million emigrated and the rest fell in battle or as victims of mass executions, pogroms, epidemics, and famine. (These figures are particularly instructive in view of the fact that the majority of those who supported the Bolsheviks did so for their promise to end the "exhaustive" war.)

Even more staggering are the figures that Shubkin cites for the victims of the peace-time violence--of the Gulags, purges, collectivization, and man-made famine. Thus, for the period from 1926 through 1939 these losses were between sixteen and twenty-six million, and in 1940-1950, at least ten million more perished in the Gulags alone. Shubkin attributes all these losses to the fundamentally coercive nature of the Soviet regime, calling some of the Party-sponsored measures deliberate genocide. Even the preliminary estimates make it abundantly clear, says Shubkin, that "the ordeals which [Soviet] people experienced since the October coup amount not only to a demographic, but also a genetic catastrophe, the consequences of which we and our descendants will continue to suffer for several decades and, perhaps, hundreds of years."

Shubkin shows that the cost of this Soviet Holocaust (he calls it *katastrofa*) is unprecedented, not just quantitatively, but also in terms of the damage it inflicted on the genetic pool [*genofond*] of the nation. As Shubkin points out, during the civil war the country lost its best intellectual minds (especially through emigration); during collectivization it lost its most diligent and enterprising farmers; and during the purges--the most active part of the new Soviet intelligentsia and working class. Moreover, those who managed to survive could not help having their minds warped under the "monstrous press" of official lies, hypocrisy, and intimidation.

But why did the Russian people tolerate such a regime? Didn't the Russians get the government they deserve? No, says Shubkin, it has nothing to do with the "servile patience of the Russian people," as some Western observers have suggested. "Dozens of other nations have tried the same Stalinist model both inside the USSR and abroad, [and] the result was the same," argues Shubkin as a typical Russian *patriot*. Explaining the triumph of Stalinism in terms of a universal decline of the human species, the *homo sapiens*, he even doubts whether the species deserves the adjective *sapiens*.

In order to explain what has happened in the USSR, he proposes to define the human species through a "triad" of its actual hypostases: the biological, social, and spiritual. Whereas in its biological hypostasis a human being is primarily concerned with individual physical survival, the social human being realizes the advantage of surviving as part of a group. Nonetheless, the social human being remains essentially a social animal as he lacks ethical standards that transcend his narrow and purely utilitarian group interests. Thinking himself to be a product of his environment, he is sure that he has an alibi for any crime. He is a hedonistic consumer devoid of conscience, religion and patriotism. Only in its third, spiritual (or religious) hypostasis does the human species possess a conscience, religion, and the ability to distinguish between good and evil on a global scale. According to Shubkin, the demographic and genetic catastrophe in the USSR has meant the elimination of both the spiritual and social "legs" of the triad and the reduction of the human species to its lowest manifestation, the biological man. "The majority of [Soviet] people were doomed to purely biological existence. Incredible hardships and deprivations. . . crowded from their minds all thought about rights and human dignity. The biological man has become the main hero of this time."

This was to be expected, Shubkin suggests, because Lenin's "simplified" approach to morality has become the unwritten law of the land. "We say," Shubkin quotes from Lenin, "that our morality is fully subordinated to the interests of the proletarian class struggle." As a result of the Party following this Lenin line, "for decades not a word was uttered about universal morality and values," says Shubkin in a clear challenge to Gorbachev's effort to portray "universal values" as rooted in Marxism-Leninism. Shubkin leaves no doubt that it was exactly Lenin's "simplified" approach to morality that was chiefly responsible for both the unprecedented suppression of all religious and idealist philosophical thinking and also the destruction of the Russian peasant culture.

Taking issue with Kliamkin, who had suggested that the peasants were the main protagonists of Stalinism, Shubkin rather sees them as the primary victims of the regime. Shubkin supports Mialo's typically Russite argument (Chapter 2) that the destruction of Russian peasant culture has had a most damaging effect on both the economic and spiritual "ecological balance" of the country. The destruction of the peasantry and religion, says Shubkin, amounted to the defeat of people's culture and morality. It facilitated the triumph of the arbitrariness, violence, and cruelty, without which Stalin would not have been able to run his machinery of repression.

Shubkin disagrees with those who suggest that a "spiritual revolution" is either less important or easier to accomplish than political democratization and economic restructuring. A real rebirth of public morals has not yet started, says Shubkin, and a spiritual revolution is even further away. The latter "is more difficult than seizing power, and occurs much less frequently than a political revolution." As a first step toward such a revolution, Shubkin suggests taking a better look at the "millennial experience of Christianity." According to Shubkin, Christianity has been able to play "its role of spiritual shepherd by affirming moral standards founded not on the transitory authority of one leader over another, but on something that was eternal and absolute." He suggests that no spiritual rebirth in the country will be possible unless we bid "farewell" (hence the title of his article) to Lenin's approach to morality and adopt instead that of Dostoevskii, namely, the primacy of the ethical ideal over the social one. He quotes Dostoevskii's famous utterance to the effect that each nation has to be founded on the basis of an ethical ideal, not just on the basis of a social contract.

While emphasizing the need for a spiritual renaissance, Shubkin is not oblivious to the need for fundamental political and economic reforms. But he warns that, if such reforms are conceived as a return to the "Leninist principles," they will inevitably result in a consolidation of the "totalitarian system." (Shubkin reproaches Gavriil Popov, now the mayor of Moscow, for euphemistically calling it the "administrative command system.") Neither the "merchants" (pro-capitalists) nor the "cavaliers" (pro-socialists) among Soviet reformers can solve the economic problem unless Soviet people elevate themselves to the status of "spiritual being," says Shubkin. Nevertheless, he sees the key to the success of both economic and political reforms in the reintroduction of private property, first of all in the form of farmers' land ownership. Only when people begin to feel that they are true masters over their production will they increase productivity and become active participants in the democratic political process.

Shubkin concluded his article by saying that the main threat to Soviet society today comes not from the political naivete of non-formal groups, but from the residual acceptance of violence as a means of solving problems. He called for bidding farewell not only to the class struggle morality but also to that violent Marxist "midwife of history" which promised a short-cut to progress but instead has become "a permanent fellow traveler in our life."

ANDREI VASILEVSKII REVIEWS GULAG MEMOIRS

As part of the revolution from below, Soviet citizens have been relentlessly expanding the limits of glasnost by daring to write on issues and topics that have been taboo for decades--and by offering ideas, opinions, and interpretations that are far removed from official ideology. One such taboo until recently was on the topic of Soviet forced-labor camps, better known under the name coined by Solzhenitsyn, the Gulag. To be sure, the publication of Solzhenitsyn's first novel, *One Day in the Life of Ivan Denisovich*, in 1962 at first signaled the readiness of Soviet authorities to lift the taboo, but this proved not actually to be the case. Although Solzhenitsyn's novel paved the way for the publication of a number of other works about the camps, censors were ever watchful that authors limit themselves to criticizing "the cult of Stalin" and nothing else.

They certainly could not stand anything like Solzhenitsyn's *The Gulag Archipelago*, all the more that it was not a work of fiction, but a documentary account, based on the testimony of hundreds of witnesses. It was a clear and incontrovertible indictment of the entire Soviet penal system from its founding by Lenin in 1918. Solzhenitsyn portrayed the Gulag as a Soviet version of holocaust. He showed it to be a logical consequence of Communist Party policies and of the

Marxist-Leninist ideology that underlay them. That is why Solzhenitsyn was expelled from the country in 1974 even though *The Gulag* had been published only abroad, and he had made no effort to circulate it as clandestine samizdat. Now, when Solzhenitsyn's *Gulag* is finally being published, does this augur that glasnost is about to turn into freedom of the press?

Perhaps, but even if not, it would certainly augur a qualitatively new intellectual and spiritual climate in the country. More particularly, it would raise the level of the Soviet people's understanding not just of the Gulag but of the entire Communist experiment. Just as during the 1960s, Solzhenitsyn's *Ivan Denisovich* raised the standards of Russian prose, so the publication of *The Gulag* today is bound both to enlarge the scope of "investigative reporting" on the malaise of the Soviet system and to raise the level of understanding of its root causes. This becomes apparent when one compares it with a relatively small but steadily growing stream of Soviet memoirs of the Gulag, a stream fed by the refreshing rain of glasnost. Andrei Vasilevskii's article, "Suffering the Memory," published in 1989 in the "liberal" magazine *Oktiabr'*, offers a helpful assessment of these recent Soviet memoirs.[28]

Vasilevskii's main concern is not with the veracity of documentary evidence presented by each author about everyday existence in the camps. He believes all of them and has no intention of siding with one or another as to the truthfulness of their respective accounts. What interests him most is how each author understands the historical significance of what he describes. And that understanding varies considerably because it depends not so much on the events but on the personality of the author who describes them.

Among the some twenty authors of memoirs under review are Evgeniia Ginzburg, Nadezhda Mandel'shtam, Galina Serebriakova, and Varlam Shalamov (to name a few whose works were originally published in the West).[29] In addition, Vasilevskii reviews the works of a number of new Soviet authors, such as Alla Andreeva, Evgenii Gnedin, Sofia Kelina, Galina Koldomasova, A. Larina (Bukharin's widow), Boris Mazurin, Z. Maslenikova, Nikolai Murzin, Lev Razgon, Trude Richter (a German Communist), Vitalii Semin, Sof'ia Shved, Iakov Shestopal, Il'ia Taratin, Iulian Tarnovskii, and Anatolii Zhigulin.[30]

One theme is common for many of them, says Vasilevskii. That common theme is alluded to in the article's title, "Suffering the Memory," that is, suffering not only from having to relive the horrors one describes, but also from realizing one's inability to come to terms with those horrors which defy all efforts to fit them into any sort of rational explanation. To clarify that common theme, Vasilevskii refers to the memoirs of Vitalii Semin, the only author who described the experience of being an *Ost-Arbeiter*, that is, a forced-laborer under the Nazis. "To that which has not been explained, our memory constantly returns," says Semin, from whom Vasilevskii borrowed the title. At least, says Vasilevskii, Semin could blame his misfortune on the "Fascists." But what about those who were subjected "not to foreign organized violence, but to our own?" asks Vasilevskii.

That is the question--and the common theme--that unites all the authors. None of them, Vasilevskii says, has given a satisfactory answer. All seem to suffer their memory in incredulity and disbelief that such unthinkable things could have happened. But at least, says Vasilevskii, today Soviet people are beginning to ask the right questions in trying to comprehend what has befallen their country in this twentieth century. "Atonement for the attempt to carry out a 'proletarian' revolution in a peasant country? The crushing failure of the effort to build a society with predetermined characteristics? A result of leftist adventurism? 'The Devils' (an allusion to Dostoevskii's prophetic novel about what would happen if Russian revolutionaries took power)? Power of the 'New Class' (an allusion to Milovan Djilas's book about the new Communist bureaucracy)? God's wrath?" It is this kind of questions that ought to be asked if we are ever to find a more or less satisfactory answer, says Vasilevskii.

But even though all the authors have suffered through their memory, they offer very different interpretations of what has happened. For one thing, they tend to identify their arrest with the beginning of the country's tragedy. Since the majority of the memoirists were arrested after 1936, they tend to ignore or minimize the scope of the Stalinist terror that occurred prior to that date. Hence the theme, "the 29th contra 37th." Hence the difference in the understanding of Stalinism. While the majority of the memoirists tend to identify it with the 1937-38 purges of the party ranks, the minority date its fearsome progress from 1929, when collectivization produced the first rich crop of peasants in the Gulag. But why is it a minority? Were there fewer peasants than intellectuals in the camps? No. But there are fewer memoirs about the peasant tragedy because the victims' cultural level, even illiteracy, precluded them from producing works of psychological depth and intellectual sophistication comparable to those of their intellectual brethren. Moreover, when one intellectual died in the Gulag, his memory continued to live in the minds and writings of his colleagues and relatives, "but millions of peasants and workers have vanished into the memory hole without a trace," says Vasilevskii.

Nonetheless, Vasilevskii singles out the memoirs of Nikolai Murzin. Among other things, Murzin described the cannibalism among the exiled peasants in 1934, when they were treated worse than cattle "whom one had to feed." Murzin offers sufficient evidence for Vasilevskii to conclude that the beginning of the phenomenon of Stalinism should be dated 1929 rather than 1937. In fact, he accuses the 37thers of a "narrow partisan interpretation of the people's tragedy." That interpretation may have been suitable for the level of historical understanding under Khrushchev but is definitely outdated now, Vasilevskii suggests. Not known to belong to the Russite camp, Vasilevskii nevertheless finds more understanding of the spiritual significance of Stalinism in Stanislav Kuniaev's poem, "All has started from Nikolai's children," than in any of the memoirs he has reviewed. He endorses the idea that Stalin's terror against old guard Leninists was indeed historical retribution for their espousal of the class struggle morality, of which the last Tsar's children ("Nikolai's children") were the first publicly known victims. (For more on this topic, see the Kozhinov-Sarnov debate in Chapter 4.)

Of course, not all intellectual memoirists are 37thers. Some have empathized with the people's tragedy. Nadezhda Mandel'shtam, for instance, has understood the system as the absolute evil. Because of that, Vasilevskii speculates, her memoirs have not yet been published in full. The late Varlam Shalamov was another example. At the other pole, however, are such intellectuals as Galina Koldomasova and Trude Richter. The former put all the blame on Stalin's personality, while completely exonerating the system. The latter, a German Communist, even took pride in having contributed, through her work in the Gulag, to the "construction of socialism." According to

Vasilevskii, memoirists of this kind "have learned nothing" from their bitter experience. The rest of the memoirists are positioned between these two poles.

Vasilevskii mentions a number of other themes. One is the theme of popular resistance to the regime. The poet Zhigulin, for instance, in his autobiographical novel, *Black Rocks*, has described an underground youth group in the city of Voronezh in the 1960s. Members of this group risked their lives to oppose the regime, even though they did so from what they believed were Marxist-Leninist positions. Vasilevskii praises Zhigulin for the dual courage of having been a member of that group and of preserving the memory of its activities. Yet he reproaches Zhigulin for giving the impression that resistance was limited to unorthodox intellectual Marxist-Leninists. Not so, says Vasilevskii, arguing that resistance existed at the grassroots. According to Vasilevskii, Alla Andreeva showed in her memoirs that there were actually uprisings of the Gulag slave-laborers in Norilsk, Vorkuta, and Karaganda, the last-named one suppressed with tanks. (This theme is most prominent in the last volume of Solzhenitsyn's *Gulag*, of which Vasilevskii seems to be only vaguely aware.) Vasilevskii points out that Lev Tolstoi's followers, whose travail in the Gulag was described by Boris Mazurin, offered a greater inner resistance to their masters than did the imprisoned Communists. At any rate, Vasilevskii is convinced that the full story of what he calls "anti-totalitarian resistance in our country, both before and after Stalin," has not yet been told.

Vasilevskii also notes the theme of American politicians aiding and abetting the Stalin regime. He cites Il'ia Taratin's memoirs about a visit of an American delegation to a Kolyma camp. Although the camp authorities displayed for the occasion the proverbial "Potemkin village," Vasilevskii doubts that the Americans were actually fooled (Taratin offers no opinion on the matter). Vasilevskii believes, rather, that the Americans were more cynical than naive. "Like our side," he says, they were "interested in the concealment of the truth," as long as they were assured that the gold that the prisoners dug continued to be delivered as payment for the lend-lease assistance.

Another theme that Vasilevskii finds remarkable is the theme of affinity between the Stalinist totalitarianism and the Hitlerite one. That theme is prominent in the memoirs of Evgenii Gnedin, a former

Soviet diplomat, and Evgeniia Ginzburg. Citing a couple of recent Soviet articles on the subject, Vasilevskii finds at least one plus for Hitler compared with Stalin. Hitler was more candid in his brutality because, unlike Stalin, he never swore that he loved the Jews and the Slavs, nor did he expect praise from those whom he was about to kill.

Compared with the scope of the Soviet Holocaust, the number of publications about it, although growing, remains "blasphemously small," in Vasilevskii's words. And although the memoirists have not yet approached the level of Solzhenitsyn or Lev Tolstoi, he says, at least they make readers ask the right questions about the paramount event of the century.

SERGEI ZALYGIN, "ON THE QUESTION OF IMMORTALITY"

Sergei Zalygin's article, "On the Question of Immortality," is interesting both in itself and as an indication of the complicated relationship between moderate Russites, for whom Zalygin's *Novyi mir* serves as the principal forum, and perestroika-from-above.[31] Excessively long and convoluted, the article is not easy to read or to review. It is full of lofty sentiments, sober insights, and vivid reminiscences from the author's long and vibrant life. But it is also full of spontaneous digressions and other extraneous matter. Above all, it is full of glaring contradictions.

These contradictions reflect a great deal of confusion, not just in Zalygin's mind, but in the minds of Soviet intellectuals and in society itself. This confusion is not necessarily a bad thing. Nor is it boring. It can hardly be blamed on those confused. Rather, it is an unavoidable result of glasnost, which, falling like long overdue rain on a parched land, has been dumping on Soviet citizens a torrent of information and ideas without granting them a moment of respite to absorb them. No wonder that many seeds thought to be dead sprouted, including those of weeds. Perestroika is, above all, the discovery of what a fertile but long-neglected and abused land can produce. As Zalygin puts it, perestroika is self-discovery.

The mood of the article is decidedly apocalyptic. The possibility of the end of the world seems to Zalygin very real. But what world? On a cerebral level, Zalygin seems to be worried about the fate of the whole world, the planet Earth, facing the dual threat of a nuclear war or ecological catastrophe. (Common to many Russites, this concern with the survival of the planet was strongly expressed in Solzhenitsyn's *Letter*.) But viscerally, he seems to be more perplexed by the end of the world the birth of which he witnessed in his adolescence, the Communist world. Actually, he hardly uses the word "communist" at all. Like the majority of reformers, Zalygin speaks instead about socialism, and even then in such broad terms that one can hardly recognize it as a specific historical formation.

That is where his contradictions start. On the one hand, he clearly chooses socialism over capitalism because, he says, only the former can guarantee the survival of mankind. (As it turns out, his article is not about personal immortality, but about the "immortality"-- which he equates with "survival"--of mankind, presumably a civilized one.) On the other hand, he admits that so far socialism has been a complete failure not just in the USSR but everywhere on the globe. In the USSR it failed not only economically, but also politically, spiritually and culturally.

Moreover, it failed in the one area which has been especially dear to Zalygin, both professionally and personally: the ecology.[32] In fact, he accuses the authorities, even today, of "concealing from our population the scale of the approaching catastrophe, not allowing people to use Geiger counters (nor producing them), not permitting them to publish data about the effect of herbicides, nor about the degree of atmospheric and water pollution." (This statement alone would suffice to set one in an apocalyptic mood.) Yet, despite such life-threatening failures of socialism, Zalygin continues to believe in it, not in its practical achievements, but rather as an idea opening "new possibilities" and a "form in search of a content." He even takes pride in the fact that while Americans know how to work, do business and be pragmatic, Russians are masters at pursuing utopias.

Although he is the only editor of a major Soviet periodical who is not a Party member, at times Zalygin sounds like one, and a very orthodox one to boot. He seems to believe that the "capitalist world" is driven by the profit motive to war and exploitation of other countries. He even suggests that the arms race between the USA and the USSR is mostly due to greed for profit on the part of American arms manufacturers. (As a member of Gorbachev's entourage, Zalygin met

Reagan, who, he says, failed to answer his question on this issue.) Like Gorbachev, he praises Lenin for his theory of imperialism, as well as for introducing NEP. He even credits the October Revolution with raising an obstacle to the "apocalypse" (he does not explain how), while admitting that it failed as a world revolution and in just about all other respects.

On the other hand, Zalygin has no illusions that the revolution has been subverted and, since Stalin, has "degenerated" into a "Bonapartism" which has lasted through both the Khrushchev and the Brezhnev eras. Like Seliunin, Kozhinov and Shubkin, he believes that the backbone of the nation was broken in 1929. And yet he claims that at the very top of the Party "hierarchic ladder" there are some people who have retained "genuine socialist ideals" which can be saved only through "democracy" and "people's power." Unless democracy is implemented now, "the catastrophe is unavoidable, all of us will perish, and together with us will perish socialist ideas, this time forever," says Zalygin.

He is aware of the scope of the Communist Holocaust. He knows that it was portrayed by such Russian writers as Bulgakov and Platonov, in strongly apocalyptic terms. In his article one looks in vain for a single good thing that the revolution has brought to the Russian people. The only good thing Zalygin says about the revolution is that it forced Western capitalists to raise living standards for *their* workers. He even attributes the survival of the Social-Democratic parties in the West to the protective influence of the USSR. At the same time, however, he believes that the most fortunate countries are those where "capitalist" and "socialist" economic approaches are mixed. He even suggests that some steps in that direction had been made in Russia *before* the revolution.

Similar contradictions abound when Zalygin speaks of ideology and culture, religion and science, revolution and counter-revolution. On the one hand, he rejects outright all "invented ideologies," that is, those which are not derived from practice, as "the greatest sin and vice of mankind." That Marxism-Leninism is a prime example is understood because, in the same breath, Zalygin says: "We have nothing to eat, but we have plenty of ideology!" Ridiculing those who have advocated socialism as a panacea for all ills, Zalygin counsels getting rid of "all that is invented in our ideology." On the other hand, he praises all revolutions as a vehicle of social progress. Surprisingly, Zalygin calls them a "European invention" and a product of "Christian conscience." Revolutions are inspired by faith, not science, he says, admitting that, like any religion, a revolution can lead to fanaticism.

But the greatest praise Zalygin reserves neither for socialism nor for science, but for literature, which alone can understand and explain human nature, he says. And in Russia this means literature in the tradition of Tolstoi and Dostoevskii.

> That society which has retained the spiritual potential [of that tradition]. . . has the best prospects for the future. . . We have greatly undermined our foundations. . . But we have deeply realized our loss, and that means not everything is lost. Russia, the country of Tolstoi and Dostoevskii, went through a terrible history of suffering in the twentieth century. But the suffering not only kills and tortures--it also elevates. . .

He realizes, however, that the Russians of today are far from being spiritually elevated. Why? Because "we ourselves have let our national heritage be diluted and compromised, more so than any other republic," says Zalygin, echoing a theme that is common for Russites of all persuasions, from Pamyat and Kozhinov to Likhachev and Solzhenitsyn. While Americans have wisely benefited from their national heritage of the last two hundred years, says Zalygin, "we have been using our millennial heritage only for footnotes and denunciations." He especially deplores the lack of direction in contemporary Russian culture. "We have a culture, but there are no [real] directions in it, there are only squabbles about who gets the largest print runs," says Zalygin in an allusion to the squabbles between Soviet periodicals and authors who tend to measure their popularity by the size of their print runs, even though that size often depends on the allotment of paper by the government.

It is disconcerting that, while praising the unnamed (but obvious) "revolutionaries from above" who "have been pushing us toward democracy," Zalygin shows little appreciation for the dissidents, who, he says, "played no role in the change of our course [toward perestroika]." And yet Zalygin is the man who has done the most to return to the country the greatest dissident of all--Solzhenitsyn. This probably has to do with the fact that Solzhenitsyn's dissidence has always been of a different kind, a kind that is most in line with that spiritual tradition of Russian literature for which Zalygin has the highest hope. It is to Zalygin's great credit that he is able to appreciate the art of a man whose views on such controversial topics as revolution, religion, and socialism he hardly shares. By returning Solzhenitsyn to his countrymen, Zalygin will have helped to provide at least one firm direction to Russian culture.

It was because of his commitment to the spiritual tradition of Russian literature that Zalygin was able to make *Novyi mir* a forum for a genuine Russian national debate. Ironically, after praising Russian "utopianism" in the article, he ended by enjoining his readers to, first of all, do the "[practical] job of helping, supporting, and participating [in the affairs of the country]." He may have occasionally gone too far in his lip service to the "revolutionaries from above" and underestimated the spiritual force of the "revolution from below," but he is definitely not a *partiot*.

SERGEI AVERINTSEV ON VLADIMIR SOLOV'EV

Besides Dmitrii Likhachev (see Chapter 2), Sergei Averintsev is one of the most respected scholars among all Soviet authors associated with the Russite movement. A prominent specialist on the history of Byzantine, the country from which Russia adopted Christianity, he is also a leading "culturologist," that is, a student of cultural development and the relationships between the cultures of various nations. Like Likhachev, Averintsev is one of very few Soviet scholars who have made it to the very top of the Soviet cultural establishment (he is a corresponding member of the Academy of Sciences) in spite of being a Christian. While professionally interested in the past, as a citizen he is deeply involved with the politics of today and with Russia's future. He certainly does not isolate himself in an ivory tower. He is a member of the Congress of People's Deputies, an honor he shares with Likhachev, Zalygin and Rasputin. We shall return to his activities as a deputy later, after reviewing a sample of his recent writing.

Averintsev's attitude towards the problems of perestroika is perhaps best expressed in this passage from his 1988 brochure published as part of the *Ogonek* Library series:

> We live at a time of great hope and even greater anxiety. While one
> cannot deny that the circumstances of our life are changing for the
> better, people, alas, are changing for the worse. And the latter
> change outpaces the former. We must either stop the momentum of
> [this moral] disintegration with concerted moral efforts or face a
> threat never seen before.[33]

Reading this assessment of the current situation in the USSR, a secular
Western reader might want to yawn, as he probably did when he read
Likhachev and Rasputin--or when he heard Solzhenitsyn speak in the
West. Isn't this yet another fire-and-brimstone preacher of whom we
have had enough and whom we would rather see removed from our
TV screens and confined to Sunday school preaching?

A first-rate scholar, Averintsev can indeed sound like a latter-
day moralist. But he is also one of the most widely-read advocates of
cultural perestroika. He is a moralist precisely because one of the
reasons for the need of cultural perestroika now is the fact that the
Bolsheviks got rid of all the traditional moralists, wherever they were
found: in places of worship, Sunday schools, Russian literature and
philosophy. Thousands of them were executed, driven to the Gulag or
abroad, their books burned, their names vilified. And then the
Bolsheviks seized the monopoly on preaching the class struggle
"morality," a monopoly they are still trying to retain.

However, with the current unraveling of Marxist-Leninist
ideology, there has emerged a dangerous vacuum not just in the
ideological but also in the ethical education of the Soviet people.
Reacting against stagnation-era "morality" based on the principles of
class struggle, proletarian internationalism, and "Soviet patriotism" (all
defined by the state, of course), Soviet youths often reject the need for
any morality. That rejection makes them the most volatile and
potentially dangerous group in the country. "There are already walking
among us young people. . . who don't even want to stretch their hand
toward the heritage of [our] culture," sadly observes Averintsev. He
points out that this lack of interest is not due to their laziness, but
rather is a sign of an active rejection of culture in favor of anti-cultural
surrogates. As a scholar, Averintsev sees his duty as reminding the
young generation that before both the Marxist-Leninist and Western
consumerist surrogates of culture, there was a genuine culture in

Russia of which all Russians can be rightfully proud. The Russian cultural tradition was fundamentally Christian, and as such it was both nationally distinct and universal by being part of the Judeo-Christian cultural circle.

Speaking of the distinctiveness of Russian culture as compared to that of Western Europe, Averintsev says that one may regret that we had neither minnesingers nor troubadours. But if we had had them, we might have never produced either Andrei Rublev or Tolstoi or Dostoevskii, because "each culture has its own laws, and an elementary historicism requires that we respect their provenance." Averintsev rejects the notion that the culture of intellectuals is inherently superior to that of either workers or peasants. However, he thinks that at present there is a greater urgency for the creation of a culture for the people of non-intellectual professions because the majority of them have no roots in either urban or rural culture (See Mialo's article about the destruction of the Russian peasant culture in Chapter 2).

In spite of Averintsev's reverence for the *old* Russian culture, he is a new moralist. As Iurii Kublanovskii, a Russian emigre critic, pointed out, Averintsev's moralism is informed not only by scholarship but also by the twentieth-century horrors brought about by the rejection of the Russian cultural tradition. Averintsev is different from both the Russian pre-revolutionary intelligentsia and today's Western intellectuals in that he rejects their positivism and moral relativism. It is hard to disagree with Kublanovskii's assessment of Averintsev's world view as a synthesis of the Russian cultural *pochvennik* movement (of "people of soil," the nativists), in which many Russites find an inspiration, and European humanism. Averintsev seems to be equally close to both. And he is equally alien to both the "progressivist naivete" of Western secularists and their Soviet followers and the "Slavophile utopianism" to which some of the Russites seem to be susceptible.

One of the most attractive personal traits of Averintsev is his aversion to partisanship. "I think that one of the most urgent duties of an intellectual is to stand against the evil of group-think which threatens to denigrate cultural activity to the level of rooting for our team," says Averintsev in an apparent allusion to the partisan squabbles among Soviet "liberals" and "conservatives," neo-Slavophiles and neo-Westernists. (As one may recall, Zalygin has also complained about such squabbles because they tend to be not about truth or ideas but about winning government favors.)

Averintsev's scholarship stands him in particularly good stead in the publication of the works of Russian "idealist" philosophers which were banned until the advent of glasnost. In his introduction to a collection of articles and letters by Vladimir Solov'ev (1853-1900), published in January 1989 in Zalygin's *Novyi mir*,[34] Averintsev carefully steers a middle course between the extreme views of some of the Russites and the equally extreme views of their Westernist "liberal" opponents. He defines the "Russian philosophy" as everything that has been created in the Russian language in the context of Russian life. Such a definition obviously includes pre-revolutionary Slavophile philosophers, whose works until recently were proscribed by the government as "reactionary" and "mystical."

On the other hand, Averintsev rejects the tendency of some of the Russites to ignore Russian philosophers of "Westernist" persuasion on the grounds that they are not "genuine" Russians. An excessively zealous national feeling, says Averintsev, is a mirror image of the "national nihilism" [of Marxist-Leninists] in that both regard foreign sources and influences as incriminating or suspect. Solov'ev's work is a case in point precisely because he was close to both the Slavophiles and the Westernists. While he shared with the Slavophiles an appreciation of the distinctiveness of Russian culture and the Orthodox Christianity that inspired it, he was never oblivious of the fact that Russia and the West have a common Christian heritage. Moreover, being both "philo-Catholic and philo-Semitic," Solov'ev consciously strove for a reunification of Christianity, says Averintsev.

Solov'ev was one of the first Russian thinkers to fully realize the importance of solving the nationalities problem of the Russian Empire. He thought he had found a solution to it. The current exacerbation of the nationalities problems in the USSR was no doubt a contributing reason for *Novyi mir* to start republication of Solov'ev's articles on the nationalities issue. It is out of place here to discuss in detail Solov'ev's approach. Suffice it to say that he believed that a solution could be found in Christianity itself if it were properly understood. According to him, although Christianity does away with nationalism, it saves each nation as a distinct community. Christianity is supranational, but it is not nationless. "A nation which wishes to save its soul within a cloistered and exclusive nationalism will lose it," warns Solov'ev. "But a nation which dedicates itself to the *supranational* and universal work of Christ, will also save its [national] soul." As utopian as he might sound, Solov'ev suggested one very practical precondition for such a solution: implementation of full freedom of religion.

The *Novyi mir* collection includes Solov'ev's 1895 letter to Tsar Nicholas II, in which he tried, as a loyal subject and a fellow Christian, to persuade the Emperor to grant full religious freedom to all his subjects, including Russian Christian sectarians, Catholics, Lutherans, Jews, Buddhists, and Muslims. When Christ said "I am the door," argued Solov'ev, He meant neither keeping people inside nor turning them away. Orthodoxy is the purest form of Christianity, and Russia's essence is in its Orthodoxy. Therefore, argued Solov'ev, if there is for Russia a Christian mission to fulfill, it must be the mission of uniting the world not by arms, but by spirit and truth. Russia cannot even begin to carry out this mission as long as the Orthodox Church enjoys privileged status and governmental support, while freedom of conscience is denied to the non-Orthodox citizens of the Empire.

Solov'ev died in 1900, and only the 1905 revolution persuaded the Tsar to grant freedom of religion to all citizens of the Empire. Unfortunately, by that time, the virus of atheist fanaticism had taken hold of the most "progressive" among the Russian intelligentsia, and twelve years later the whole country succumbed to an orgy of religious persecution unprecedented in its scope and viciousness. This time freedom of conscience was denied to *all* people who failed to conform to the new atheist "religion" of Marxism-Leninism. It is in the vestiges of this new religious unfreedom that Averintsev now sees as the main obstacle to perestroika.

In his "undelivered" speech[35] at the Congress of People's Deputies, Averintsev demanded a revision of the article of the Soviet Constitution which, though superficially proclaiming freedom of conscience, in fact condemns believers of all religions and denominations--Christians, Muslims, Jews and Buddhists--to the status of second class citizens. The discriminatory practice of the atheist state against all believers is based on the provision of the article which allows unrestricted "atheist propaganda," while "freedom of conscience" for believers is limited to worship alone, and even then only on the premises of churches registered by the government. If we are ever to implement civil equality between atheists and believers in the eyes of our secular state, argues Averintsev, we cannot tolerate the fact that unrestricted propaganda of atheism is being carried out at the expense of all taxpayers, including believers. Mandatory instruction in atheism in all Soviet schools also violates the principle of the civil equality of all citizens. In a secular state, one should not be forced to listen to either atheist or religious propaganda, says Averintsev.

Averintsev was not the first to suggest that perestroika cannot succeed until freedom of conscience is constitutionally guaranteed and fully implemented. Solzhenitsyn drew attention to this problem when he suggested in his 1973 *Letter* the urgency of abolishing the Marxist-Leninist ideological monopoly, which in itself violates the freedom of conscience of all those who do not believe in Marxism. Separation of the Soviet state not only from the church but also from atheism was high on the list of demands of various dissident groups of Russian Orthodox Christians.

Unfortunately, by focusing almost exclusively on the undeniable manifestations of both popular and state-sponsored judophobia in the USSR, Western scholars have failed to pay enough attention to the fact that the Soviet state has been denying the most fundamental human and civil rights not only to the Jews, but to millions of Muslims, Catholics, Lutherans, Buddhists, Russian Christian sectarians, and--no less viciously--to the largest group of all, Russian Orthodox Christians, whose number is estimated at some fifty million. As Averintsev points out, the massive denial of fundamental human rights to the Orthodox Christians continues even now. Even while the millennium of Russian Christianity was celebrated in Moscow with Gorbachev's approval, provincial authorities refused to return to the believers their churches, some of which had been desecrated and turned into public toilets. Moreover, all believers, including Orthodox Christians, continue to the present day to be discriminated against in the Soviet army, where they are usually confined to construction battalions. The immensity of the abuse of human rights in the USSR, in addition to that connected with judophobia, becomes apparent when the situation of the allegedly "dominant Russians" is taken into account.

Contrary to the common belief in the West that the Soviet army is the stronghold of "Russian" chauvinism and an instrument of the "Russification" of non-Russian minorities, the army continues to be as anti-Russian as it is anti-Georgian or anti-Estonian. The Soviet Army is certainly "de-Russified" in the sense that no Russian, no matter how patriotic or professional, can ever become an officer if he professes the Orthodox Christian faith under the banners of which the Russians had defended their country from the invasions of the Mongols, Teutonic knights, Swedes, Poles, French and Germans, all of whom at one time or another threatened Russia's survival as a distinct national entity.

Averintsev's humanity and true Russian patriotism were manifested when he praised Andrei Sakharov's speech at the Spring 1989 session of the Congress as a heroic civic act. "He did what we have failed to do; he took the floor without waiting for permission. He, and people like him, had paid dearly for the right to speak--for themselves and for all of us." Referring to Aleksandr Solzhenitsyn, Averintsev reproached the Congress for its failure to instruct the Supreme Court of the USSR to reverse its decisions, according to which the most courageous people were deprived of their homeland. In a July 16, 1989 interview for a Latvian Popular Front bulletin,[36] Averintsev took pride in the fact that at the Congress he voted for all proposals that were defeated. He said that he would rather belong to the defeated minority than to the majority which tried to "overwhelm" everyone by the "march-like" manner of applauding the speeches that were more befitting to the era of stagnation than to that of perestroika.

GALINA LITVINOVA ON THE PLIGHT OF THE RUSSIANS

Galina Litvinova's article on the plight of the Russians, which appeared in May 1989 in the Russite magazine *Nash sovremennik* was an important step in public recognition of the Russian problem as one of the most serious problems facing the Gorbachev regime. The article was polemically entitled, "*Starshii ili ravnyi*" [Elder or Equal].[37] The title suggests that, far from playing the role of "big brother" in the Union, the Russians have fallen behind their "smaller" national-minority brothers and now crave nothing but equal treatment. Dr. Litvinova, a leading scholar at the Institute of Government and Jurisprudence at the Academy of Sciences of the USSR, devotes her article to the striking proposition that the ethnic Russians, who are usually regarded in the West as the masters of the Soviet Union, are, in fact, one of its most disenfranchised ethnic groups. On Lenin's instructions, the Soviet government has, since 1917, put a heavier burden on Russians so that the minorities could sooner achieve actual (that is, not just before the law, but also in economic, political, and cultural spheres) equality with the Russians, says Litvinova. As a result, the pace of development of the Russians was deliberately slowed down in comparison with that of the non-Russian peoples.

While justifying it by the needs of "a united international socialist state" for the earlier period, Litvinova argues that this policy should be abandoned because it has outlived its original purpose. After Lenin's death, Soviet leaders failed to heed his warning against basing their policy "on abstract and formal principles instead of a concrete economic situation," says Litvinova. At any rate, even though actual equality of minorities with the Russians was largely achieved "in the early 1940s," the policy of favoritism toward minorities continues to the present day, says Litvinova. As examples of favoritism toward border-area republics, she cites subsidies from the all-Union budget, lower taxes, higher pay for their collective farmers and higher state-set prices for their agricultural products in comparison with those in the Russian Federation. As a result, the Russians (as well as the two other Slavic nations, the Belorussians and Ukrainians)[38] are not only rapidly sliding to the status of backward nations, but are on the brink of demographic catastrophe.

Litvinova illustrates her thesis with statistics derived from the 1979 population census. According to her, the Russians have one of the lowest living standards of all the union republics. Their birth rate is also one of the lowest and falling still further. While the Russians have one of the highest percentages of industrial workers among them, their percentage of engineers, technicians, researchers, and creative intelligentsia is one of the lowest in the Union. Even the high percentage of Russians in the Party and state administrative apparatus is misleading. While these bureaucrats use the Russian language, their objectives are far removed from the interests of the Russian population, says Litvinova.

The policy of favoritism toward national minorities has influenced a dramatic change in the ethnic composition of the country. In 1913 the Slavs formed 82.9 percent of its population while the share of Central Asians was 8.1 percent. By contrast, in 1986 the respective figures were 61.5 and 29.2 percent. Calling this trend alarming,

Litvinova criticizes the government for their failure to stop it. Although the depopulation of the Russian countryside was first noticed in 1959, Soviet leaders have done nothing to stop it. For the past few years about three thousand Russian villages per year have disappeared from the region where the government plans to produce about 90 percent of the country's food, complains Litvinova.

Not only is the demographic situation bad and getting worse, but the Russians have no means to fully assess and to publicize its true scope. While each of the Central Asian republics has its own Academy of Sciences with a department of demography in each, the Russians have none. Worst of all is the fact that when the Russians try to express their concerns, they are automatically accused of "great-power chauvinism" and even "anti-Semitism," says Litvinova echoing a common complaint of the Russites.

As a remedy for the actual inequality of the Russians, Litvinova proposed raising the status of the Russsian Federation to that of the fourteen minority republics. This could be done, she suggested, by creating the Central Committee of the Communist Party of the RSFSR, as well as similar bodies in the *Komsomol* (Young Communist League), and trade unions. As was mentioned before, Litvinova also urged the creation of an Academy of Sciences and a mass media network for the Russian Federation, as distinct from those for the USSR. Further, she proposed a number of budgetary measures, such as putting minority republics on self-accounting and introducing legislation that would economically stimulate two-to-three children families, a measure that would equalize the rate of population growth for all republics. Above all, Litvinova insisted on *de jure* and *de facto* implementation of "the principle of proportionate national representation" in all political and social structures of the country.

Saying that no particular nation, "neither the Uzbeks nor the Belorussians nor the Russians," could be blamed for the alarming situation of ethnic Russians, Litvinova blamed it on the "bureaucratic administrative apparatus that does not want to implement the principle of social justice." Thus, although she fell short of faulting the Soviet system as such, she admitted, in fact, that the Russians, who have been commonly regarded in the West as the privileged "big brother" of the Soviet Empire, have actually regressed as a nation under Communist rule.

Therefore, Litvinova's pledge of allegiance to the "socialist system" and the "principle of proletarian internationalism" at the end of the article sounds especially hollow. On the other hand, her article anticipates the subsequent recognition of "the Russian problem" by Soviet politicians. The creation of a separate Communist Party of the Russian Federation, El'tsin's election to the presidency of the RSFSR and the proclamation of Russia's sovereignty - all these events taking place within a year - show just how popular the initial concerns of Litvinova and the Russites in general have become.

DMITRII BALASHOV APPLIES LEV GUMILEV'S THEORY

I turn now to an article by Dmitrii Balashov, "The Formation of the Russian Nation and Contemporary Problems of Our National Life,"[39] published in *Literaturnaia Rossiia* on February 13, 1989. Although the topic of the article is unusually broad, the author, a historian and novelist, offers a rather concise and cogent survey of the development of "Muscovite" Russia as an ethnic group distinct from its European neighbors. "Is Russia one of the European countries that must develop according to a Western model? Is its 'backwardness' a result of its failure to conform to the Western model? Or does Russia have its own messianic task within this choir of nations?", asks Balashov, reviving the old Westernist-Slavophile dispute.

"We are neither better nor worse. We are different," Balashov replies, acknowledging that he borrowed the words from Lev Gumilev. Gumilev is the son of the poet Nikolai Gumilev, executed by the Bolsheviks in 1921, and of Anna Akhmatova, one of the foremost "dissident" poets (she died in 1966). A former prisoner of the Gulag, Gumilev is a leading Soviet anthropologist with a strong interest in Asia. He is the author of the controversial "passionary" theory of ethnogenesis, which, until glasnost, was tolerated but hardly accepted by the academic establishment. Now, thanks to glasnost, Gumilev's major works are being published,[40] and his "passionary" theory has been increasingly gaining ground at the expense of Marxist-Leninist assumptions about the transience of nations, assumptions which Balashov casually dismisses as "vulgar sociologism."

According to Gumilev's theory, a nation (actually Gumilev uses the word *ethnos*) is not just a product of social history, as Marxism claims, but part of an ecological system. Each ethnos goes through about a fifteen-hundred-year cycle of birth (through a burst of energy, or "passionary" impulse), maturation, blooming, a longer period of maturity with its ups and downs, a sort of mid-life crisis (*nadlom*), decline, and death (usually through an absorption into another more energetic, "passionary" nation). The destiny of each nation is then determined not just by such factors of social history as the Marxian "class struggle" or technological inventions, but also by biological, geographical, psychological and even cosmic factors. If this is so, Gumilev seems to be saying, then it is wiser to accept ethnic differences as the indispensable means of adaptation of each nation to its environment than to fight them as obstacles to international progress. His theory challenges the entire Soviet policy on the nationalities as being based on wrong assumptions. Instead of trying to submerge ethnic differences in a single Soviet nation, as the Soviet government had attempted to do, it should strive to achieve their peaceful symbiosis, Gumilev suggests.

Balashov's article is an attempt to apply Gumilev's theory to the Muscovite Russian "ethnos," as distinguished from both European nations and the Russians of Kievan Rus'. According to Balashov, the character of the Russian "ethnos" (of which ethnic Russians are the modern descendants) was chiefly determined by the adaptation to the conditions of life in the forests and swamps of Northern Europe, including a short agricultural cycle and the need to interact with their neighbors from whom they were not separated by natural barriers. Faced with these challenges, the Russians created a unique civilization and national statehood, says Balashov.

According to him, having originated around the fourteenth century, the Russian state attained maturity before the time of Peter the Great. The first signs of decline appeared when Tsar Peter made the fateful mistake of westernizing the Russian nobility and thereby isolating it from the culture of the Russian people. As a result, for all its "brilliance," the Russian aristocratic culture of the nineteenth century brought little benefit to the Russian people. Failing to learn the art of economic husbandry in harmony with Russian nature, the westernized Russian gentry remained "ecologically illiterate." Their efforts to organize the Russian economy according to French, British, and Dutch patterns were bound to end in a fiasco, because they never took into account either the ecological peculiarities of Russian nature or the historical traditions of the Russian people.

If the above interpretation of Russian history sounds familiar, it is because it is close to that of the nineteenth century Slavophiles, to whom Balashov acknowledges his debt. What is new is his attempt to reinforce the old Slavophile argument with the help of Gumilev's theory. It is out of place here to dwell on the details of Balashov's reading of the Russian past. However, his view of the 1861 abolition of serfdom is noteworthy. Although he praises the general thrust of this reform, he sees its chief flaw in the twin failure to introduce an "ecological literacy" and to bridge the cultural gap between the educated classes and the Russian people. It was this twin failure that ultimately led to the revolution, says Balashov.

Stolypin's 1907 agrarian reform offered a last chance to "restore health" to Russian agriculture and thereby avert the revolution. However, this was not to be. By cancelling Stolypin's reforms, the revolution produced a sort of prolonged crisis, or *nadlom*, from which the country is presently trying to "climb out," says Balashov, explaining the historical roots of perestroika. Should the Russians be able to do so, they might well be on the threshold of a "Golden Autumn" period of gradual, dignified, and satisfying decline, says Balashov. But he knows that it will not be easy to overcome the *nadlom*. Why? Because collectivization was an unmitigated disaster, the effects of which weigh heavily upon Russians to the present day. According to Balashov, collectivization amounted to a "second serfdom" and a "counter-revolution" which destroyed not only the traditional Russian art of agriculture but the land itself. Balashov is especially worried by the destruction of the land, a process which, he says, continues unabated because the "bureaucracy" (most notably, the Ministry of Water Resources and Amelioration charged with the construction of hydroelectric power stations) continues to ignore ecological needs. As a result, instead of successfully "climbing out" of its nadlom, the Russians might soon find themselves on the brink of irreversible biological degeneration.

While the fate of the Russians is the focus of Balashov's attention, he is also concerned with the fate of small national minorities scattered across Siberia, the Far East and Kamchatka. According to Balashov, by trying to impose on these peoples "our cultural standards," we have destroyed their way of life, just as we destroyed ours in a futile effort to imitate the West. "The very notion that there are underdeveloped and developed countries is false," says Balashov, condemning "the cosmopolitan idea that all nations need a single way of life copied from a Western European model."

It is hardly surprising that Balashov's program of overcoming the nadlom is predicated on healing Russia's national roots. His program has three main objectives: (1) restoration of the ecological balance; (2) restoration of national agricultural traditions; and (3) restoration of Russian national culture. To fulfill the first objective, he proposes such measures as closing all nuclear power stations and "the majority" of chemical plants, reduction of heavy-industrial production (class A) to a bare minimum, re-forestation of all de-forested areas and release of water from all dammed reservoirs.

The second objective, Balashov says, cannot be attained until the kolkhoz and sovkhoz system is abandoned and the land is returned to those who till it, that is, to individual peasants. However, he does not expect this to be done overnight. Nor does he recommend unlimited private land ownership, but only "hereditary land-holding" (nasledstvennoe zemlepol'zovanie) which, he says, is more in tune with Russian traditions. He also proposes a country-wide cadastre of all land, both rural and urban, to determine its value for the purpose of differentiated taxation. Only when industrial enterprises and governmental agencies start paying taxes on the land on which they sit will they learn how to manage it wisely, and only then will self-accounting become meaningful. In agriculture, huge tractors which damage the texture of soil should be replaced by small ones used by individual farmers. Farmers of each region would know best how to follow in the footsteps of their ancestors, who managed to maintain the ecological balance for centuries.

As to the third objective, "the restoration of national culture and national ethical norms," it cannot be attained without the help of the church. To secure such help, says Balashov, the church should be freed from the "Egyptian persecution, both economical and political," from which until recently it greatly suffered. In addition, "our schools must be different, and our textbooks should change too," says Balashov, advocating in fact domestic de-ideologization, that is, freeing the entire Soviet educational system from the Marxist-Leninist monopoly.

Only by attaining these three objectives will the Russians be able to "climb out" of that nadlom which now threatens their national existence. Only then will they get out of harm's way and enter the "Golden Autumn" period of a "quiet, prosperous, and cultured" life. But these objectives cannot be attained without a concerted national effort on the part of all layers of society. Nor can they be attained without love, a "love of one's own people, land, truth, and justice." Nor can they be attained without "respect of other peoples of our multi-national Fatherland and of their traditional way of life," Balashov concludes.

WHO ARE THE RUSSITES?

We have considered so far eight Soviet authors--Tsipko, Zolotusskii, Zalygin, Shubkin, Vasilevskii, Litvinova, Averintsev and Balashov--whose 1989 articles bear witness to a restructuring of the very thought patterns of Soviet intellectuals. There is no doubt that the main line of the restructuring is not only moving away from Marxism-Leninism but heading toward Russian national thinking. The "national" here should be understood in two senses. In a broader sense it has the same meaning that is implied, for instance, in the expression "U.S. national security" or "French national interests," that is, "security" or "interests" defined not in partisan--Republican or Democrat, capitalist or socialist--terms, but in terms of country-wide consensus. (The emergence of such national thinking in the USSR was facilitated by Gorbachev's own slogan of de-ideologization, which he may have wanted to restrict to foreign affairs but was clearly unable to do.)

In a narrower sense, Russian national thinking means thinking along the lines of Russian non-Marxist and pre-Communist ideas which have managed, often in a mangled, unattractive, and "Sovietized" form, to survive Marxist-Leninist domination. Such *national* thinking naturally focuses on the interests of ethnic Russians (about 50 percent of the Soviet population), but it also includes the interests of the peoples, mostly within the Russian Federation, who have either been assimilated (many Tatars, Mordvinians, Jews, Germans, etc.) or might be willing to continue their centuries-long symbiosis with the Russians. (Balashov, as Solzhenitsyn before him, was particularly emphatic in admitting "our guilt" toward many such peoples in Siberia and the Far East.)

It is primarily in this narrower sense that I have called this group of authors Russites. However, by calling them so I do not wish to suggest that there are no substantial differences between them. Tsipko and Litvinova, for instance, are Party members,[41] and Zalygin at times sounds like one (although he is not). Averintsev, Shubkin, and Balashov, on the other hand, clearly are inspired by Christian ideas. But for all of them the interests of historical Russia (both as an ethnic and a supra-ethnic entity) take precedence over those of the Communist Party. In this sense, all of them are Russites, and all are *patriots*, not *partiots*.

Although I am convinced that this group is fairly representative of Russian national thinking, there are, no doubt, some other important authors whose contribution might be no less significant. As in my selection for 1987-1988 (see Chapter 2), my main criterion for selection was whether an article or author was able to add to the larger picture of Soviet intellectual debate on a wide range of topics (religion, philosophy, literature, politics, economy, intra-ethnic relations, etc.). I also looked for authors who would appeal to Soviet readers across ideological lines. For that reason, four out of eight authors in my selection were chosen from the centrist-liberal *Novyi mir*, two (Litvinova and Balashov) from the "conservative" *Nash sovremennik* and *Literaturnaia Rossiia*, and two (Tsipko and Vasilevskii) from the "liberal," "internationalist," and "leftist" journals *Nauka i zhizn'* and *Oktiabr'*.

The selection would counter, I hope, two fallacies that hamper Western efforts to understand the process of change in the USSR. One fallacy consists of either ignoring Russian nationalism altogether or focusing on its least fortunate manifestations, such as Pamyat (see Appendix 1). The other fallacy consists in the failure to establish an adequate taxonomy on the emerging spectrum of political opinion in the USSR. Since I have already discussed the first fallacy elsewhere, I shall now say a few words about the second.

That the problem of taxonomy exists is evident, for instance, in the debate of Alla Latynina with her non-Russite challenger Sergei

Chuprinin in the pages of *Literaturnaia gazeta*.[42] Latynina suggests that it is wrong to approach the Soviet political spectrum with the customary pair of opposites, such as "conservative" versus "liberal," "right" versus "left," "reactionaries" versus "progressives." To illustrate her point she told the following story. Once, in an interview with *Moscow News*, she suggested that the "repressions" of the 1930s were a direct consequence of the terror of civil war and that, therefore, a memorial should be erected to all victims of fratricide so that the very idea of violence would be condemned. Having read this interview, one of her acquaintances among the literati praised her for the courage of expressing such a "humane idea" whose time, he said, has come. However, a month later, he reversed his opinion, warning her against linking the violence of Stalinism with that of the civil war "because that's what the rightists do."

That argument created a dilemma for Latynina. On the one hand, believing that the "leftward movement" is a movement toward liberty, she has always regarded herself a leftist. On the other hand, in the context of the Soviet political debate of today, the sign "Left" usually marks efforts to justify terror, the sign "Right"--its condemnation. Likewise, the Leftists continue to praise the works of Soviet literature of the 1920s in which the ideas of violence, hatred, class struggle, and world revolution were cultivated. The Rightists denounce them. The Leftists support the establishment views on Stalinism, but the Rightists call for a deeper examination of Stalinism's ideational sources. So says Latynina, suggesting that the true proponents of the most radical and fundamental perestroika are to be found more often among the Rightists than among the Leftists.

In the past the above terms had a definite meaning. "Today they mean nothing. We [Soviet intellectuals] can no longer be divided in two halves, the Left and the Right, the westernizers and the Slavophiles," says Latynina. She refused to condemn a number of authors whom Chuprinin criticized for the mere fact that they had submitted their articles to "conservative" magazines. Although she disliked some of their ideas, says Latynina, she reserved for herself the right to grant them the benefit of the doubt in respect to other ideas. Rejecting Chuprinin's suggestion that her standing "above the struggle" amounts to a morally questionable neutrality, Latynina defended her centrist position as "a position of culture" that is both more "profound" and pragmatic.[43] According to her, it was precisely because *Novyi mir* assumed a similar centrist position that it was able to contribute most to widening the "boundaries of freedom."

Latynina argued that the national revival among the Russians has nothing to do with the spirit of divisiveness, as it is fully consistent with political centrism. She particularly rejected Chuprinin's suggestion that Solzhenitsyn's brand of Russian nationalism could be likened to fomenting revolution in the manner of an Iranian "ayatollah." Citing a book about Solzhenitsyn by Dora Shturman,[44] a Soviet emigre now living in Israel, Latynina said that, far from being a "reactionary and chauvinist," as some "unconscientious" authors have suggested, Solzhenitsyn represents a major moderating force in the current political polarization of Soviet society. Not only is he a "religious moralist," but he is also "a liberal in the classical sense of the word and a convinced centrist in politics."

There are "dark forces" in every nationalism, says Latynina. But these forces cannot be stopped by (official) exhortations of "internationalism."   Such exhortations have become indelibly associated in the minds of Soviet people with Soviet propaganda appeals to class struggle and hatred. Therefore, the country needs "other enlightening ideas" and "an authoritative voice" to articulate them. She left no doubt that Solzhenitsyn is such a voice.

Latynina's argument suggests that the customary western taxonomy of the Soviet political spectrum needs major revision. For instance, what does the adjective *conservative* mean when applied to *Nash sovremennik*, *Molodaia gvardiia*, *Moskva* and other Russite publications? In what sense are they conservative? Are they "conservative" in the sense of being *contra* perestroika and *pro* the status quo, as the predominantly "liberal" Soviet (and Western!) media allege? Or are they "conservative" in a Western sense, that is, when we speak, for instance, of Thatcher's Conservative party and of the Reaganites as conservative Republicans?

In light of Latynina's argument, the first proposition is simply false. The readership of these magazines may include people sympathetic to the views of a Nina Andreeva or a Ligachev, both of whom could be called "conservative" only in the sense that they want to "conserve" the current Leftist-inspired one-party system. But their predominant readership and their main thrust is not against

Gorbachev's perestroika *per se*, but against conducting it on the terms of the *partiots* rather than those of the *patriots*. Such Russite authors as Soloukhin, Kozhinov, Shafarevich, and Shubkin, who have been identified with these "conservative" magazines, are in fact considerably more radical in their criticism of the Soviet system (Communism) in general and Stalinism in particular than the more "liberal" authors, such as Sarnov and Kliamkin. Nor are these magazines interested in merely maintaining the status quo, even though they are definitely more wary (than *Ogonek*, e.g.) of the danger of de-stabilizing the situation to the point of the total breakdown of civil order.

But are they conservative in the Western sense? Yes, fundamentally they are. Like Western conservatives they emphasize the importance of cultivating national traditions in respect to religion, economies, ecology, politics, literature, and art. However, unlike their Western colleagues, who are used to having considerable clout in society at large (excepting, perhaps, in the media) and therefore tend to be both self-confident and complacent, the Soviet conservatives, especially the Russites, are the true "have-nots" of the Communist world. Not only are they the underdogs in the Soviet political establishment, but they find little sympathy and understanding from the West, even from their ideological kin. It is no wonder some Russites tend to take needlessly anti-Western and radical positions. A revised Western taxonomy of the Soviet political spectrum could help to cool down hotheads on both the Right and the Left. It might also help the realignment of Soviet political forces in accordance with the principle of political balance between the Left and the Right, the conservative and the liberal, that is fundamental to an open society.

Notes

1. Zenon Pozdniak and Evgenii Shmygalev, "Kuropaty - doroga smerti" [Kuropaty - the road of death], Literatura i mastatstva, Minsk, June 3, 1988. Reprinted in Novoe Russkoe Slovo, June 24, 1988.

2. See the AP report of March 24, 1989, based on the data provided by TASS. Also Novoe Russkoe Slovo, March 25-26, 1989.

3. See M. Belousov's report from Leningrad in Trud, June 5, 1989.

4. G.T. Khomich, "Sibirskie Kuropaty?" Sel'skaia zhizn', July 4, 1989.

5. See A. Terekhin's report from Cheliabinsk entitled "Ural'skie Kuropaty?" Sotsialisticheskaia industriia, July 9, 1989.

6. See B. Glotov's report from Donetsk in Pravda, July 4, 1989.

7. Vladimir Zapetskii, "Kolpashevskii iar," special issue No. 5, 1989 of Molodost' Sibiri.

8. See Radio Liberty Soviet Media Digest for a transcript of a Soviet Central TV program, "Vzgliad," including a letter from Vladimir Tsvetov. The commentator said that newspapers in Kiev refused to publish Tsvetov's confession.

9. See Radio Liberty Soviet Media Digest about the film, "Gde vykhod iz labirinta?", shown on Soviet TV on June 12, 1989; see also interview with Marina Goldovskaia, director of the film, "Vlast' solovetskaia," in Russkaia mysl', May 19, 1989.

10. During a meeting on December 27-28, 1988, the Holy Synod of the Russian Orthodox Church formed a commission to investigate the persecution of clergy and laymen since 1917. However, when the chancellor of the Moscow patriarchate was asked during a March 1989 interview if he could add anything to the figure that from 1918 to 1938, about 250 bishops of the Russian Church were "repressed" and only four (three metropolitans and one archbishop) stayed out of prison, he replied "not yet." See Argumenty i fakty, No. 10, 1989.

11. For more on the Romanovs' massacre, see, for instance, Gelii Riabov's "Prinuzhdeny Vas rasstreliat'," and Genrikh Ioffe's "Dom osobogo naznacheniia," Rodina No. 5, 1989. Riabov, who claims to know where the remains of the last Tsar are, refuses to reveal the site until there is permission to give them a Christian burial. He condemns the Bolsheviks for "spilling innocent blood." Ioffe, a historian, likewise concludes that the Romanovs were not treated in accordance with the "principles of humanity" by either the Provisional government or the Bolsheviks. He accuses the latter of putting their "class interests above ethical considerations."

Vladlen Sirotkin, in his article in Nedelia, No. 25, 1989, points out that on July 16-17, 1918, in Ekaterinburg there were executed, besides the tsar, his wife, five children, and four of their loyal servants. Moreover, there were other executions of Romanovs: on July 13 the tsar's brother Mikhail was shot in Perm'; on July 18 in Alpaevsk there were executed eighteen other members of the Romanov family, and on July 22 in Tashkent uncle Nikolai Konstantinovich was shot. Sirotkin blames the massacre on the Bolshevik central authority. It was not only immoral but also counterproductive, because it set the "third force," the Russian peasants, against the Bolshevik regime, says Sirotkin. Finally, there were reports that the first public memorial service for the Romanovs was held at Donskoi Monastery in Moscow on July 17, 1989, in which at least 300 people took part.

12. There are reports that Egor K. Ligachev, a former Politburo member and rival to Gorbachev, was sued in a Russian court for his alleged role in the Kolpashevo affair during his tenure as first Party secretary of the Tomsk oblast'. See the article "O budushchei knige" in Knizhnoe obozrenie, No. 48, November 30, 1990.

13. See Iu. Poliakov's article in Literaturnaia gazeta, September 30, 1987.

14. See a compilation of Medvedev's data in "Tragicheskaia statistika," Sobytiia i vremia, No. 6, March 1989.

15. V. Pereverzev, "Dvadtsat' millionov: Zametki o demograficheskom razvitii v SSSR v 1918-1939 godakh," Molodaia gvardiia, No. 7, 1989. The total losses for the period include the 10.7 million lost in the civil war (of which 5.9 million died of starvation) and 9.4 million who lost their lives "in the process of de-kulakization and forced collectivization." Pereverzev says that the figure could have been higher, were it not for the "unselfish" help from the West, especially from the American Relief Agency, a fact which, Pereverzev points out, has not yet been duly acknowledged by Soviet historians.

16. Vladimir Shubkin, "Trudnoe proshchanie," Novyi mir, No. 4, April 1989, pp. 165-184.

17. O. Marinicheva, Komsomol'skaia pravda, June 22, 1989.

18. Robert Conquest, the author of The Great Terror, said in an interview with Moscow news (No. 13, March 26, 1989) that new Soviet data suggest that his estimate of human losses was too low. This is noteworthy because many Western scholars, suspecting an "anti-Communist bias," found Conquest's figures too high.

19. Aleksandr Tsipko, "Istoki stalinizma," Nauka i zhizn', Nos 11 and 12, 1988, and 1 and 2, 1989. Tsipko quit the Party after its twenty-eighth Congress in July 1990.

20. See previous note.

21. Peter Collier and David Horowitz, Destructive Generation: Second Thoughts about the '60s (New York: Summit Books, 1989). For more on this book see Chapter 4.

22. Aleksandr Tsipko, "Uberech' dostoinstvo" (interview with Vladislav Starchevskii), Nedelia, No. 11, 1989.

23. Igor' Kliamkin, "Pochemu trudno govorit' pravdu," Novyi mir, No. 2, 1989. See also my discussion of Kliamkin's previous article in Chapter Two.

24. Aleksandr Tsipko, Sotsializm: zhizn' obshchestva i cheloveka, Moscow, 1980.

25. Tsipko's thesis was rebuked by A. K. Masiagin, a Central Committee ideologist, in his article, "Kredit doveriia," Pravda, February 13, 1989. Masiagin admitted that the Party shares responsibility for Stalinism, but he disagreed with Tsipko's contention that Stalin followed Lenin's line. Masiagin's attack did nothing to dissuade Tsipko from his convictions. His latest article, "Khoroshi li nashi printsipy?" [Are Our Principles Sound?] is a bold challenge to the very fundamentals of the Soviet state. Tsipko places responsibility for Stalinism and the current impasse of Soviet society not only on Lenin, but also on Marx and Marxism. He urges Soviet reformers to abandon their Marxist delusions and follow the example of their colleagues in Central Europe in "de-ideologization" of their country (Novyi mir, No. 4, 1990, pp. 173-204).

26. Igor' Zolotusskii, "Krushenie abstraktsii," Novyi mir, No. 1, 1989.

27. Vladimir Shubkin, "Trudnoe proshchanie," Novyi mir, No. 4, April 1989.

28. Andrei Vasilevskii, "Stradanie pamiati," Oktiabr', No. 4, '1989.

29. Evgenia Ginzburg, "Krutoi marshrut," Iunost' No. 9, 1988; Nadezhda Mandel'shtam, "Memoirs" in Iunost', No. 8, 1988 (in English, Hope Against Hope); Galina Serebriakova, "Smerch'", Pod'em, No. 7, 1988; Varlam Shalamov, Novyi mir, No. 6, 1988.

30. Alla Andreeva (widow of poet Daniil Andreev), "Memoirs" in Moskovskii komsomolets, November 30, 1988; Evgenii Gnedin, "Sebia ne poteriat'," Novyi mir, No. 7, 1988; Sofia Kelina, her memoirs in Moskovskii komsomolets September 25, 1988; Galina Koldomasova, "V te dalekie gody," Nauka i zhizn', No. 3, 1988; A. Larina, "Nezabyvaemoe," Znamia, Nos. 10-12; Z. Maslenikova, "Memoirs" in Neva, Nos. 9-10, 1988; Boris Mazurin, "Rasskaz i razdum'ia ob istorii odnoi tolstovskoi kommuny," Novyi mir, No. 9, 1988; Nikolai Murzin, his memoirs in Ural, Nos. 9-11, 1988; Lev Razgon, "Zhena prezidenta," Ogonek, No. 13, 1988; Trude Rikhter, "Dolgaia noch' kolymskikh lagerei," Za rubezhom, No. 35, 1988; Vitalii Semin, Nagrudnyi znak OST; Iakov Shestopal, "ChP v lagere," Nedelia, No. 25, 1988; Sofia Shved, "Vospominaniia," Ural, No. 2, 1988; Il'ia Taratin, "Poteriannye gody zhizni," Volga, No. 5, 1988; Iulian Tarnovskii (former KGB agent), "Memoirs" in Daugava, No. 9, 1988; Anatolii Zhigulin, "Chernye kamni," Znamia, Nos. 7-8, 1988.

31. Sergei Zalygin, "K voprosu o bessmertii," Novyi mir, No. 1, 1989, pp. 3-50.

32. A former professional hydrologist, Zalygin was instrumental, together with a number of other Russites, in the defeat of the governmental project to reverse major Russian rivers to irrigate dry lands of the South. For more, see Nicolai N. Petro, "The Project of the Century: A Case Study of Russian National Dissent," Studies in Comparative Communism 20:3/4, Autumn/Winter, 1987, pp. 235-252.

33. Sergei Averintsev, "Popytki ob'iasnit'sia," Ogonek Library Series, No. 13, Moscow, 1988. Quoted from Iurii Kublanovskii, "Kul'turologiia Averintseva," Russkaia mysl', September 23, 1988.

34. Vladimir Solov'ev, "Stat'i i pis'ma," Novyi mir, No. 1, 1989, pp. 194-234.

35. Sergei Averintsev, "K sovesti," Sovetskaia kul'tura, June 15, 1989.

36. See Averintsev's interview with Atmoda's Aleksandr Kazakov, July 16, 1989.

37. Galina Litvinova, "Starshii ili ravnyi," Nash sovremennik, No. 5, 1989.

38. Although Litvinova's article is focused on ethnic Russians, she makes it clear that many of her arguments are applicable to the Belorussians and Ukrainians, as well as the Baltic peoples.

39. Dmitrii Balashov, "I nuzhna liubov': formirovanie russkoi natsii i sovremennye problemy nashego natsional'nogo bytiia," Literaturnaia Rossiia, No. 8, February 24, 1989; reprinted in Veche (Novgorod), May 1989.

40. According to Gumilev's interview (Izvestiia, June 23, 1989), his book, Etnogenez i biosfera Zemli has been published. In 1990 it came out in English, Ethnogenesis and the Biosphere (Moscow: Progress Publishers). Gumilev acknowledges his indebtedness to the Slavophiles and the "Eurasians," a school of Russian emigre historians who stressed Russia's Asian heritage and whose work was suppressed in the USSR. In his article, "Biografiia nauchnoi teorii, ili avtonekrolog" [A history of scientific theory, or a self-obituary] (Znamia, No. 4, 1988), Gumilev accuses the academician Iurii Bromley, who has dominated Soviet anthropology for years, of suppressing, distorting and plagiarizing his "passionary" theory. See also Gumilev's letter to the editor, Voprosy filosofii, No. 5, 1989; and his article, "Korni nashego rodstva," Sputnik, No. 5, 1989. Gumilev emphasizes that the Soviet nationalities' problems cannot be solved without further democratization.

41. Tsipko quit the Party after its twenty-eighth Congress in the Summer of 1990.

42. Alla Latynina versus Sergei Chuprinin, "Dialogue of the Week," see the four installments in Literaturnaia gazeta, Nos. 14-17, April 5, 12, 19 and 26, 1989.

43. Latynina's own "political centrism" has attracted the attention of at least one American scholar, John B. Dunlop. See his article, "Alla Latynina: A Self-Proclaimed Centrist Calls for Political Realignment," Radio Liberty Report on the USSR, 275/89, June 8, 1989.

44. Dora Shturman, Gorodu i miru (Tretia Volna Publishing House, 1988).

4

Revolution and Russia

A very important public debate took place in March 1989 in the pages of the "liberal" weekly, *Literaturnaia gazeta*, whose readership exceeds six million. It was the debate between two well-known literary critics: Vadim Kozhinov, reputed to be a Russian nationalist (see Chapter 2), and Benedikt Sarnov, who belongs to the "liberal" camp. The debate ran for four consecutive weekly installments.

The four installments' titles are suggestive of the main interrelated themes of the debate. (1) "Who Is to Be Blamed?", that is, who is responsible for the tragedy of mass terror, the scope of which far exceeds the Nazi Holocaust? (2) "Russia and the Revolution," that is, was the Communist Revolution carried out for the sake of Russia, or was Russia sacrificed for that revolution's universal purpose? (3) "Crime and Punishment," which echoes one of Dostoevskii's novels and suggests that no crimes, including those of the Communist revolution, will go unpunished. (4) "What Needs To Be Done?" that is, how to get the country out of its current crisis. The above four themes clearly exceed the bounds of what is usually expected in a debate between literary critics. In fact, these four themes have become four crucial political, philosophical, and moral issues which currently sharply divide Soviet intellectuals. This chapter is therefore entirely devoted to them. After reviewing the debate in the first part, I shall attempt to put it in a larger historical perspective in the second.

171

DEBATE

Who Is to Be Blamed: The Jews or the Russians?

The debate was started by a discussion of Rubashov, the main protagonist of Arthur Koestler's novel, *Darkness at Noon*, which had just been published in the USSR for the first time. A Communist who dedicated his life to the cause of world revolution, Rubashov was involved in dangerous terrorist activities in several European countries. In a twist of irony, he is finally arrested, for no apparent reason, in the country where his cause has seemingly triumphed. Tortured by his Communist interrogators, the brave Communist admits to various counter-revolutionary crimes he never committed. His interrogators want him to sacrifice his life "for the Party." Only in the face of execution do the scales fall from his eyes. Rubashov finally realizes that, just as he used to sacrifice people "for the Party," now it is his turn to be sacrificed.

Agreeing with a recent Soviet review of the novel, Sarnov praised Koestler for showing that Rubashov, Koestler's autobiographical character, suffered from the "syndrome" of loyalty to the cause which forced many Communists to abandon all logic and slander themselves during the Stalinist "show trials." The same "syndrome" afflicted not only Russian revolutionaries, Sarnov agreed with the reviewer (M. Zlobina), but also the best and the brightest of the West, such as Bernard Shaw, Romain Rolland, Lion Feuchtwanger, Theodore Dreiser, and Louis Aragon. The difference was, however, that whereas Bukharin and Rykov admitted to uncommited crimes under torture, their Western counterparts faced no tortures. Sarnov credited the reviewer with the insightful observation that many Western Communists chose to remain apologists for Stalin "out of loyalty to the cause" even though they knew better and faced no danger if they chose to speak the truth.

At this point Kozhinov reminded Sarnov that many of Stalin's Communist victims had either been executioners themselves or, at least, had helped create the system of lawlessness and terror. The phenomenon of Stalinism itself cannot be fully understood unless it is treated as part of Western intellectual history, argued Kozhinov. Disagreeing with him, Sarnov accused Kozhinov of juggling facts to serve his "scheme" and questioned Kozhinov's dedication to the search of truth. Kozhinov parried by saying that such a "presumption of guilt" was not conducive to a dialogue. Without questioning his opponent's commitment to truth, Kozhinov suggested that perhaps they have been searching for the truth in different spheres. Whereas Sarnov wants to find it in the tragedy of the Rubashovs and Bukharins, intellectuals obsessed with the "romantic" idea of world revolution, he, Kozhinov, is more concerned with the tragedy of the people who were made to suffer the consequences of that obsession.

Kozhinov then explained how the late literary scholar Mikhail Bakhtin (1895-1975) helped him gain deeper insights into the history of the revolution. A specialist on Dostoevskii, Bakhtin was arrested in 1928 "by the Rubashovs" who, says Kozhinov, were trying to cut off Soviet intellectuals from the tradition of Russian spirituality, embodied in such religious philosophers as Sergei Bulgakov and Nikolai Berdiaev. After a term of exile, Bakhtin was allowed to teach at Saransk University in Mordovia where Kozhinov befriended him in the 1950s. According to Kozhinov, Bakhtin was never formally rehabilitated, nor did he ask for rehabilitation. As the executor of Bakhtin's will, says Kozhinov, he is "not about to ask for the rehabilitation [of Bakhtin] either." Only after learning Bakhtin's "lessons" did Kozhinov begin to see the meaning of the revolution in a different light.

To show how the intellectual Rubashovs have invited a disaster not only on themselves but also on millions of innocent people, Kozhinov gave Sarnov a number of examples. In 1920 Bukharin justified the red terror as "a method of creating Communist mankind from the material of the capitalist epoch." In 1930 Bukharin proposed to talk to the kulaks (well-to-do peasants) "with the language of lead [bullets]." According to Kozhinov, even Stalin refrained from publicly threatening people with bullets. Quoting from Eevgenii Losev's recent article,[1] Kozhinov argued that Iakov Sverdlov (1885-1919), one of the Soviet revolutionary heroes, was chiefly responsible for *raskazachivanie* ("de-Cossackization"), that is, the mass annihilation of the Russian Cossacks. Iona Iakir (1896-1932), a Stalin victim, himself advocated the decimation of a certain percentage of the population, across the board and regardless of whether they were "rich" or otherwise "guilty," simply for the sake of intimidation of the rest. "It is a duty of every

Communist to inform [on each other]," Kozhinov quoted another influential Communist leader of the 1920s, S. Gusev (Drabkin). It was exactly the Communist ethical nihilism of the 1920s that opened the bloodgates of the terror of the 1930s, argued Kozhinov. Objecting to his being labelled a "Stalinist" by the "liberals," Kozhinov said that his approach to the phenomenon of Stalinism was "much more 'radical' than that of my accusers, who refuse to see [in Stalinism] anything more than the tragedy of the Rubashovs."

At this point Sarnov, who is Jewish, launched a fierce *ad hominem* attack on his opponent. Accusing Kozhinov of hypocrisy, Sarnov alleged that by differentiating between the tragedy of the Rubashovs and the tragedy of the people, Kozhinov was, in effect, blaming the Jews for everything tragic or evil that the revolution has entailed. "People who are more delicate blame the Freemasons, those still more delicate blame de-nationalized elements. But those who are candid enough, bluntly accuse the Zionists, a world Jewish conspiracy, etc.," said Sarnov, in an effort to link Kozhinov with Pamyat's anti-Jewish propaganda. He alleged that, while Kozhinov secretly shared the Pamyat leaders' views, he chose to express himself more "delicately" by *selectively* focusing only on the misdeeds of revolutionaries of Jewish extraction. (Although neither debater identified the origin of the revolutionaries they discussed, both seemed to assume that the majority of Soviet readers know that Trotskii, Kamenev, Zinov'iev, Sverdlov, Iakir and Gusev, as well as Rubashov and Koestler, were Jewish.)

Sarnov suggested that Kozhinov's differentiation between 'they' who made the revolution and 'people' who suffered its consequences stems from "Solzhenitsyn's idea. . . that pre-revolutionary Russia was a prosperous, flourishing country, engaged in a victorious war, etc." In Sarnov's view, "the problem of the revolution and the problem of the people are one and the same." "You say 'world revolution,' but I would rather call it 'Russian revolution,'" said Sarnov. "I am convinced that the Russian revolution is the most legitimate offspring of Russian history. There was a profound, long-neglected crisis, which was unsolvable because of the chronic inability of the Russian governments to solve such problems." It was this "chronic inability to reform" that led to the revolutionary explosion, concluded Sarnov.

"Revolution for Russia or Russia for Revolution"?

The second round of the debate began with Kozhinov's observation that Sarnov had started the first with the statement, "We have frequently been engaged in a shoot-out between us." Kozhinov denied that he ever "shot" at Sarnov. He wrote about Sarnov only twice: once praising him as a promising literary critic, and then defending another author from Sarnov's "utterly aggressive attacks." Asking Sarnov to refrain from personal attacks, Kozhinov called for the abandonment of the "presumption of guilt" on the part of one's debating opponent, a "sinister practice dominant in the 1920s and 1930s." "I admit I 'shot' at you much more frequently than you at me," Sarnov replied. "But what we are engaged in is not a duel, but, as we say nowadays, a civil war. And you can hardly deny that in this 'war' you and I are on the opposite sides of a front line." Replied Kozhinov: "Let us engage not in a 'war,' but a peaceful dialogue. To do so, we should not invent disagreements."

I quoted the above exchange in full to illustrate the respective positions of the two camps, the so-called "liberal pro-Western" and the "conservative Russian nationalist," in the unfolding national debate on the historical roots of the country's current crisis. While the "liberals," like Sarnov, often see perestroika as a return to the "romantic" era of the revolution and civil war, the "conservatives," like Kozhinov, see it as an opportunity to assert such "bourgeois" values as civil peace and the need for a dialogue on the basis of mutual respect and ideological pluralism.

When Kozhinov asked Sarnov not to "invent disagreements," it was a request not to hit below the belt. For even though glasnost has dramatically expanded the area of the permissible, it has not guaranteed full freedom of expression. In 1989 there were still a number of "sacred cows" that remained untouchable, certainly in the pages of a national newspaper like *Literaturnaia gazeta*. In this instance Kozhinov meant that Sarnov "invented" a disagreement about the character of the October Revolution. "I have no doubt that the revolution was both Russian and the people's," said Kozhinov. (He may be sincere in believing this, but Sarnov left him with little choice.) "It was an expression of the striving of various layers of society. . . toward the ideals of justice and brotherhood." (This is too general a statement, one which is more applicable to the February revolution, but Kozhinov apparently dares not kick the "sacred cow" of the revolution.)

"What you refuse to see," Kozhinov charged, "is the fact that the revolution was torn between two completely different, even opposite, paths: the *Revolution for Russia or Russia for the Revolution.*" Explained Kozhinov: "The first path of the revolution meant the release of the talents of the people from their political and economic shackles. The second path, on the other hand, meant rejection of the time-honored popular heritage and use of the people as a bundle of kindling to be thrown onto the pyre of [world] revolution." According to Kozhinov, Lenin favored the first path, but "the majority of the most influential" Bolsheviks managed to pull the revolution to the second path. (Again, Lenin as a "sacred cow" remains untouched.)

Kozhinov then quoted from the letter to Lenin written by Mironov, one of the Red Army generals: "I cannot agree with the 'destroy-everything-to-create-anew' tendency. . . .   The life of the Russian people should be built in accordance with its historical, cultural and religious views, and let time take care of the rest."[2] According to Kozhinov, in 1921 Mironov was secretly murdered on Trotskii's order. "Mironov's fate, as that of millions of other people, was a result of the triumph of the second path," concluded Kozhinov. Sarnov replied by quoting the Russian religious philosopher Georgii Fedotov (1886-1951) that "a great revolution is characterized by the depth and power of the cataclysm it produces." It was the Russian people themselves who wanted to destroy their heritage, and the "aliens" such as Trotskii, Sverdlov, and Iakir had nothing to do with the wantonness of that destruction, Sarnov insisted.

Sensing that Sarnov was again reading "anti-Semitism" into his position, Kozhinov replied that when he emphasizes the "alienness" of many revolutionaries, he has in mind not their ethnic origin, but rather an "emigre problem." Citing such revolutionary leaders as Bukharin (a Russian), Trotskii, Kamenev, Zinov'ev, and Sokol'nikov, Kozhinov said that they spent too much time in emigration and therefore did not know Russia well. (However, Kozhinov failed to include Lenin in that "emigre" category, and Sarnov missed a chance to score.) The others, like Radek and Rakovskii, were international revolutionaries who immigrated to Russia in order to start world revolution and therefore could not care less for the country's heritage. As a result, said Kozhinov, "a revolution against the capitalists and nobles [as it was allegedly conceived by Lenin] was turned into the greatest violence against people."

Sarnov retorted that Lenin, too, regarded Russia as a base for Communist world revolution. Even while introducing NEP, Lenin still believed that in "ten to twenty years [our] victory on a global scale will be assured," argued Sarnov. Although he failed to cite Kozhinov's own article, in which Kozhinov himself argued that Lenin was fully prepared to sacrifice millions of Russians for the sake of world revolution (see Chapter 2), Sarnov scored a major debating point by showing that even the "pragmatic" Lenin of the NEP period continued to regard Bolshevik Russia as a beachhead for world revolution.

Kozhinov tried to recover lost ground by saying that Lenin was opposed both to Trotskii's 1919 plan to send the Red Army to India and to Bukharin's 1922 slogan of "Red intervention." However, the current fifty-five-volume *Complete Works* of Lenin undoubtedly gives more support to Sarnov's position that Lenin remained a believer in world revolution to his death. At the same time, even though Sarnov managed to outscore Kozhinov in enlisting Lenin's authority on his side, he was unable to negate the acuity of Kozhinov's distinction between the Revolution for Russia and Russia for the Revolution.[3]

"Crime and Punishment"

The focus of the third round again shifted to the question of responsibility for the unexpected consequences of the revolution, such as the Stalinist purges, in which a far larger number of Communists were killed by other Communists than by their anti-Communist adversaries. Why such a cruel irony? To address this question, Sarnov called Kozhinov's attention to two poems. The first, by Soviet poet Stanislav Kuniaev, who is reputed to be an extreme Russian nationalist, was recently published in *Nash sovremennik*. The second poem, written by Naum Korzhavin, a Soviet Jew who later emigrated to the U.S.A., was published in 1963.

Kuniaev's poem is devoted to the execution of the last Tsar of Russia, Nikolai II, and his entire family, including wife, children, and family doctor. The execution was carried out in Ekaterinburg (now Sverdlovsk) in June 1918 by a revolutionary squad headed by Iurovskii, a Jewish Bolshevik. That execution, Kuniaev suggests, unleashed the bacchanalia of terror which, during the 1930s, did not spare even children of the leading Communists. Their fate is described in such Soviet novels as Vladimir Rybakov's *Children of the Arbat* and Iurii Trifonov's *The House on the Embankment*. "If one happened to slip in a pool of blood [during the 1930s] and then came to one's senses somewhere at a tree felling site [in the Gulag], one should thank one's father for that," reads Kuniaev's poem. Kuniaev suggests that the Stalinist purges that swallowed the lives of thousands of Communists (including many Jews) was a historical, even cosmic, vengeance for the crimes of their fathers as symbolized in the execution of the Tsar's innocent children.

This theme of historical retribution is intoned in the line, "All has started from Nikolai's children." Kuniaev chooses to focus on the children because, whatever crimes could have conceivably been imputed to the Tsar, his children were certainly innocent. This theme has special appeal to the Russians for two reasons. First, it reinforces the theme of repentance which had been first articulated by Solzhenitsyn and then made popular through Abuladze's film, "Repentance." Second, it harks back to Dostoevskii's well-known saying that he would not want to live in a paradise built on the tears of innocent children. Soviet readers are bound to ask themselves: Would one want to live in a Communist paradise (even if perestroika succeeded in erecting one), in the foundation of which there are the seas of tears and mountains of bones of the innocent?

Saying that he had no wish "to exonerate the guilty ones," Sarnov did not challenge the poem's main theme. But he objected to Kuniaev's polemical thrust suggested in the poem's title, "Reflections in the Old Arbat." Kuniaev's distinction between the suffering of the Rubashovs and their children, on the one hand, and the suffering of the much more numerous kulaks, on the other, was unfounded and immoral, Sarnov argued. Referring to Kozhinov's own critique of Trifonov's novel, Sarnov accused him of making the same distinction as Kuniaev. Why does he empathize with the children of the kulaks, while feeling only malevolence toward *The Children of the Arbat* and *The House on the Embankment*?, asked Sarnov.

Kozhinov replied by citing the fate of Bukharin. Saying that Sarnov himself once called Bukharin a "criminal," Kozhinov wondered why Sarnov tries to "whitewash" him now by equating his suffering with that of the innocent kulaks. "Bukharin, who in 1930 demanded to speak with the kulaks in the language of lead (bullets), had himself fully and directly prepared the [historical] vengeance that struck him later," said Kozhinov.

Sarnov countered by juxtaposing Kuniaev's poem with Korzhavin's "Naivete," devoted to the fate of peasant victims of the "cruel experiment" [of collectivization and deportation to the Gulag]. While both poets are at one in their condemnation of the "experiment," Korzhavin's stance is morally superior, said Sarnov. Whereas Kuniaev curses Communist "experimenters" as "aliens," Korzhavin curses them as his own people and acknowledges his personal responsibility for this "main blood" of the Stalinist terror. "As long as I keep silent, that blood remains on my conscience," Sarnov quoted from Korzhavin's poem.

Kozhinov replied that he liked Korzhavin's poem too. But he liked better Kuniaev's condemnantion of those who regarded Russia only as "material" for their revolutionary "experiment." Kozhinov then quoted Lenin's allegedly last words, in which Lenin not only recognized the Bolshevik failure to win the Russian people but also warned against imposing the new system on Russia lest the use of force would turn the country into an "all-Russian meat-grinder."[4] According to Kozhinov, Kuniaev's poem is more consistent with this Leninist line, because it condemns only those who did indeed turn the Revolution into a "meat-grinder."

Sarnov responded with a series of quotations which, one has to agree, confirm Lenin's own complicity in turning the country into a "meat-grinder." He accused Kozhinov of indulging in the old "scheme" according to which "a tiny group of 'devils' (with non-Russian names, unlike in Dostoevskii's novel, *The Possessed*) rapes the gigantic country and millions of its people." Calling attention to Vasilii Grossman's 1960 novel, *Life and Fate*, which had recently been published in the USSR,[5] Sarnov quoted the inner monologue of the Communist Shtrum, the novel's Jewish protagonist, who finally realized that it is just as wrong to persecute people for their ethnic origin (as the Nazis did), as for their social origin (as the Communists did).

> Hitler says that nothing counts, except whether one is a Jew or not. This goes against the grain of my convictions, and I protest. But don't we apply a similar principle [in the USSR]--when we judge people according to whether they belong to the gentry, kulaks, or merchants? What is worse, in our [Soviet] personnel forms they ask those questions of children and grandchildren. Is then being a noble, a merchant, or a clergyman in one's blood, like being a Jew? This is absurd. . . .

Grossman's ability to see injustice regardless of whether it is inflicted on one's own people or on "aliens" distinguishes him from Kuniaev, contended Sarnov. Kozhinov replied by saying that "there are lots of people [in the USSR] who continue to regard those [Communist criminals] as their own." He then challenged Sarnov to disassociate himself from "these criminals." Taking up on Grossman's analogy between the Nazis and the Communists, Kozhinov asked: "You aren't going to defend those of Hitler's henchmen whom he later executed, for whatever reason. . . ." Then why cover up for Bukharin who used to boast that "we have carried out a mass annihilation of defenseless people, with their wives and children. . . ."?

Sarnov failed to respond to this challenge. He did not dissociate himself from either those responsible for the "main blood" of Stalinism or those who continue to cover up for them. Kozhinov certainly won this round of the debate by showing that his search of the roots of Stalinism is more consistent with the demand of open inquiry than Sarnov's. In fact, Kozhinov's attitude on this issue is similar to that of Solzhenitsyn who has always maintained that, unlike in West Germany, there are still "lots of people" in the Soviet government and party apparatus who have no interest in identifying either the historical roots or the actual perpetrators of the Soviet Holocaust that swallowed at least fifty million lives, according to Soviet sources.[6]

"What Needs to Be Done?"

In the first round of the debate Kozhinov did not respond to the charge of anti-Semitism that Sarnov fired at him. In the next two rounds Sarnov renewed the charge. He accused Kozhinov of following

Solzhenitsyn in regarding Tsarist Russia as a prosperous country in which nobody but Jews wanted a revolution (as Sarnov reads Solzhenitsyn). He then insinuated that Kozhinov's views (and, presumably, Solzhenitsyn's) were not very different from those of Pamyat. Although Kozhinov again ignored Sarnov's challenge, a mutual "judophobe-russophobe" animus was clearly present during the first three rounds of the debate.

In the fourth and final round Kozhinov decided that he had enough. "I have re-read all previous rounds of our debate and, as it turned out, in each of them you tried to put the nationality issue to the fore, accusing me, for starters, of 'displaying' a number of names," Kozhinov said. "In fact, the name I 'displayed' most prominently was Bukharin, who was Russian." As to others, said Kozhinov, he could not discuss the October Revolution and the Civil War without naming the top seven Bolshevik leaders, four of whom were Jewish (Trotskii, Kamenev, Zinov'iev, and Sverdlov), one Georgian (Stalin), and two Russians (Lenin[7] and Bukharin).

Kozhinov not only denied having anything to do with "anti-Semitism, that is, a negative attitude toward Jews as Jews," but in turn accused Sarnov of indiscriminately pasting the label of "anti-Semite" on anyone who dared utter critical remarks about Jews, even when no malice was intended. As an example, Kozhinov cited Sarnov's recent article, in which he accused Anton Chekhov, the classic of Russian literature, of anti-Semitism, because he once complained that "Jews who knew nothing about the grass-roots of Russian life and who were alien to it" were nonetheless dominant among the literary critics of St. Petersburg. Pointing out that throughout his literary career Chekhov portrayed Jews with great sympathy, Kozhinov concluded that, if one applies Sarnov's criteria, then "all great [Russian] writers, from Pushkin and Belinskii to Blok and Sholokhov," have to be declared "anti-Semitic."

Should one, for instance, regard the foremost "proletarian writer" Maxim Gor'kii (Aleksei Peshkov, 1868-1936) as an "anti-Semite" because in 1924 he called Trotskii "the most alien (*chuzhoi*) person to the Russian people and Russian history?," Kozhinov asked. One of the staunchest radical defenders of Jewish equality in Russia, Gor'kii nonetheless condemned Trotskii's sinister role in the Revolution. (Kozhinov conveniently "forgot" to mention that Gor'kii condemned Lenin as well, for using people for the revolution as a "chemist uses matter for a laboratory experiment.") "Those who have read my books and articles know that I value highly--at times, exceptionally highly--many contributors to Russian culture. . . 'of Jewish origin' because I consider that 'origin' absolutely unessential," said Kozhinov, adding that he did not mind being in the company of Pushkin, Chekhov, Gor'kii and other Russian classics unfairly accused of anti-Semitism.

Acknowledging the existence of the Russo-Jewish problem, Kozhinov volunteered his opinion as to "what needs to be done" to solve it. There are two solutions, said Kozhinov. The first is a complete assimilation of the Jews into Russian culture. According to Kozhinov, Boris Pasternak advocated this first solution as "the most beneficial for the Jews." The second solution was proposed by I. Gurland, an "outstanding journalist and a close associate of Stolypin," who advocated a sort of cultural autonomy for the Jews within Russia's borders. "And I am convinced," said Kozhinov, "that there must be complete freedom of choice between the two solutions."

Saying that neither choice is easy and may involve a "drama," Kozhinov professed his readiness to live with whatever choice the Jews make. (Surprisingly, he did not mention the third solution, advocated by the Zionists, that is, emigration from the USSR to Israel, a solution for which many Jews have already opted.) The only Jews with whom he has a problem, Kozhinov said, "are those who, without experiencing any sort of drama, stay in the mainstream of culture and politics of another people while remaining alien (*chuzhdy*) to its interests and to its very essence." Can one be legitimately called an "anti-Semite" for criticizing such "alien" people? No, said Kozhinov, and he explained why.

For one thing, "as a rule, these people are alien [not only to the host nation] but also to Jewry as such, for they either don't know [Jewish] culture, language, etc. or don't like it." Strictly speaking, these people can hardly be regarded as Jews, Kozhinov went on, and therefore charging one with "anti-Semitism" for criticizing them is absurd. Secondly, when he uses the word "alien," he does not restrict it to people of Jewish origin. There were and are many Russians who are either alien to Russia or even hate it. Again he cited the "russophobe" Bukharin whom he had repeatedly criticized throughout the debate.

Why is it acceptable to criticize the Russian "aliens," but as soon as one turns to "aliens" of Jewish extraction, one is immediately accused of "anti-Semitism, chauvinism, and even fascism," wondered Kozhinov. What is needed is not "charges" and "shouts" but a "calm, sober, and objective discussion of the problem," Kozhinov concluded.

Ironically now Sarnov ignored Kozhinov's challenge to debate the "Jewish question." Nor did he have any comment on the "aliens" within the revolutionary movement. He brushed aside all of Kozhinov's arguments by bluntly stating, "I don't like anti-Semites." Lest Kozhinov didn't get the message, he said that he particularly disliked "intellectual anti-Semites" who indulge in "misquoting." To Kozhinov's point that there were only two Russians among the top seven revolutionary leaders, Sarnov replied that it is meaningless to analyze their ethnic background. What is important is the fact that a "considerable part of the [Russian] people" did follow them and their ideas. Why? Sarnov quoted the following lines of the Russian religious philosopher Nikolai Berdiaev.

> The very internationalism of the Russian Communist Revolution is purely Russian and truly national. I am even inclined to think that the active participation of the Jews in Russian Communism is very typical of Russia and of Russian people. [For,] Russian messianism is akin to Jewish messianism. . . . The Russian people failed to fulfill their messianic idea of Moscow as the Third Rome. . . instead, they succeeded in establishing the Third International. . . . The Third International is not an International at all, but a Russian national idea.

Kozhinov admitted that Berdiaev's view of the revolution was worthy of debate. But he decined to do so, because it was "too complex" to be dealt with adequately in the format of their debate. Rejecting Sarnov's charges of "misquoting," Kozhinov, in turn, reproached Sarnov for refusing to seriously discuss the "nationality issue" which "you've imposed on me" only to display "[your] emotions." Replying that he was more interested in the question, "what needs to be done?" than "who is to be blamed?", Sarnov made an attempt to project Bukharin as a model for perestroika. According to Sarnov, the answer to the question, "what needs to be done?" lies in the return to Bukharin's 1925 slogan for the peasants, "get rich," which, Sarnov suggested, meant the cessation of government control over agriculture. Quoting a passage from Petr Stolypin's letter to Lev Tolstoi, in which Stolypin extolled the virtues of private land ownership, Sarnov concluded that Bukharin's 1925 approach to the peasantry was similar to Stolypin's. "And you are trying to declare this man [Bukharin] a proponent, together with Stalin, of a military-feudal exploitation of the peasantry!", Sarnov charged.

Kozhinov deflected the charge by saying that in 1925 Stalin himself defended Bukharin from the then politically dangerous comparison with the "reactionary" Stolypin. "To confuse Bukharin with Stolypin, as does Zinov'ev, means distorting Bukharin," Kozhinov quoted Stalin as saying. According to Kozhinov, in 1930 Bukharin repaid this debt of gratitude to Stalin by demanding to speak with the "enriched" peasants in the language of bullets. For the "aliens," like Stalin and Bukharin, "the peasantry, and Russia in general, were but 'material' [for the Communist experiment]," Kozhinov concluded. (He failed to point out that Sarnov contradicted himself by first declaring that the Tsarist governments were incapable of reforms and then portraying Stolypin as a model for Bukharin and, presumably, for perestroika.) Sarnov refused, however, to discuss the substance of the Kozhinov argument, and the rest of the debate was spent in squabbling about the accuracy of quotations.[8]

COMMENTARY

The very fact that such a debate, on issues which until recently were taboo in the USSR, took place at all is an important achievement in Soviet intellectual history. It signifies yet another breakthrough for glasnost, another victory in the struggle for emancipation from the yoke of Marxist-Leninist ideological monopoly. It has raised the level of Soviet intellectual debate to a new height, no matter how low it might appear by Western standards.[9] Besides the question of the respective role of Jews and Russians in the revolution and post-revolutionary terror on which the debate was primarily focused, it raised a number of larger, historiosophic issues succinctly suggested in the titles of each segment of the debate.

Poisonous Ideas

The first one, "Who Is to Be Blamed?", only superficially concerns Stalin's purges in the 1930s and the role of Jews and Russians in them. On a deeper level, it concerns the tragedy of the Revolution itself, as well as the present impasse of Soviet society. For every reader raised in the USSR, the segment title echoes that of the classical Russian novel, *Who Is to Be Blamed?*, by Aleksandr Herzen (1812-1870), a pre-Bolshevik revolutionary of socialist orientation. The second segment, "The Revolution for Russia or Russia for the Revolution?", challenges the fundamental Soviet assumption that the good of the Revolution was automatically the good of Russia. The third segment, "Crime and Punishment," echoes the Dostoevskian theme of the intimate connection between ends and means. It raises these questions: Didn't the use of evil means, whether under Lenin or Stalin, defeat the noble ends of the revolution? Isn't the Soviet Union still being punished now for the crime of the Revolution? Finally, the fourth segment, "What Needs to Be Done?", echoes the title of the well-known Russian novel by Nikolai Chernyshevskii (1828-1889), another pre-Bolshevik radical, who saw the answer in socialism. It suggests that the faith in revolution and socialism as a means of progress and modernization came to naught as progress proved elusive and the country now finds itself back at square one.

The debate shows that the Soviet people have become increasingly aware that the particular problem of perestroika--"What needs to be done to get out of the present impasse?"--cannot be solved without learning how the country got into that mess in the first place. Now they begin to understand that they got there not only through Brezhnev's "stagnation," but also through the tragedy of the Communist Holocaust which took millions of   lives. Just when President Reagan stopped calling the USSR "an evil empire," Soviet publications began to be inundated with revelations of the brutality of the system which precisely fit the description. The Soviet public now seems to realize that, unless recognized and healed, the trauma of the Communist Holocaust (also known as the Gulag and *katastrofa*) will prevent national reconciliation, thereby paralyzing perestroika and leaving the country in the deadly impasse.

Both debaters showed considerable resourcefulness in using the leeway of expression that glasnost has offered. Nonetheless, both were severely hampered by the limitations implicit in the policy of glasnost. They were also hampered by their overexposure to Marxist-Leninist schooling.[10] Both knew well that glasnost requires staying within the bounds of "socialist pluralism." Both knew that there was no better way to demonstrate their respect for these boundaries than by enlisting Lenin's authority on their side. Both knew that the historical legitimacy (or popularity) of the Bolshevik revolution cannot be questioned. Both knew how to stay away from challenging the Marxist-Leninist ideas underlying all politics of the Soviet regime. Hence, the onus of the question, "Who Is To Be Blamed?", turned on the ethnic origins of the Bolshevik leaders, not on their political convictions.

As a result, both debaters beat around the bush, neither one hitting the real target. While Sarnov was trying to prove that Lenin's position on such issues as world revolution or uprooting Russian traditions was identical with that of other top Bolsheviks, Kozhinov spared no effort to portray Lenin as virtually the only genuinely "Russian" revolutionary who opposed the pernicious influence of the "alien" Bolshevik leaders (four Jews, one Georgian, and one Russian-- Bukharin), who thought nothing of sacrificing Russia on the altar of world revolution. Kozhinov wanted to place Lenin in opposition not only to Stalin, but also to Stalin's would-be victims: Bukharin, Trotskii, Kamenev and Zinov'iev. Sarnov, on the other hand, capitalizing on the victims' current good-guy status, wanted to ally them with Lenin against Stalin.[11]

Neither admitted that all the above leaders were drinking from the same bottle of poisonous wine, whose "spirits" are equally alien to both the Jews and the Russians. Even if the "new" Lenin had indeed "sobered up" the morning after (the revolution) and realized the need to steer the revolution onto its "Russian" path, as Kozhinov likes to portray him, he still has the lion's share of responsibility for, first, serving that bottle of heady revolutionary wine to his "alien" comrades and then failing to prevail when they refused to sober up. Intoxicated with that "alien" substance, Stalin's would-be victims were no doubt happy to participate in the butchery of Russia until they found themselves on the butcher's block in the late 1930s.

The answer to the question, "Who is to be blamed?", should be obvious: all the Bolshevik leaders, with Lenin at the helm. All of them share personal responsibility for what has happened to the country after the revolution. As important as it might be from a historical viewpoint, however, the question of personal responsibility is hardly practical. It certainly should not be asked out of vindictiveness, especially since most of the culprits are dead, and some may have died as enlightened and as repentant as Rubashov. The practical question is not "Who" but "What is to be blamed?" In other words, what was it that made these undoubtedly intelligent people behave in such an inhumane, brutal, foolish, and ultimately self-destructive way? What kind of ideas determined their political behavior? The answer should be sought, first and foremost, in the ideas of Marxism-Leninism of which they regarded themselves the chief spokesmen. It is these ideas that have determined not just the events in Russia, but the entire totalitarian thrust of the twentieth century.

There is no need to go through the entire set. Suffice it to mention the ideas which have led to the most tragic consequences and which, alas, still retain virility to the present day. The Marxist idea of violence as the midwife of history is one of them. Incorporated into the theory of class struggle as a motive force of history, it gave a "scientific" justification, and even sanction, to any form and scale of violence as long as it could be argued that it served the cause of world revolution. It also gave free license and a perfect alibi for any criminal or psychopath clever enough to disguise his crimes under the banner of revolution. And it did not matter whether one was of Russian, Jewish, or Georgian origin.

Regardless of whether Stalin was a true Marxist-Leninist or a bona fide criminal (or both), it was the Marxist sanction of violence that not only opened the bloodgates for his reign of terror, but also assured the applause or consenting silence of the only influential group whose protest could have staved it off or minimized it--the Western intellectuals. Alas, the latter were more interested in the "progressive" march of history than in the fate of their Russian counterparts, much less in the fate of Russia's "ignorant and reactionary" masses. (Kozhinov was right that Western intellectuals shared responsibility for Stalin's crimes, but he did not explain why.)

Concomitant with the theory of class struggle was the idea of the historical transience of nations. Marx believed that the "working class has no country," that national differences are trivial, certainly not as important as social class differences and, at any rate, are bound to disappear in a classless socialist society. That seemingly innocuous idea proved to be completely false even during Marx's lifetime. Yet, when, contrary to all empirical evidence, the Bolsheviks tried to force it upon reality, it proved lethal for the Russians, the Jews, and the others.[12]   Having evolved into the Leninist policy of merging nationalities into one single "Soviet nation," this idea of Marx has been largely responsible for the decades of neglect and quackery in treating inter-ethnic conflicts. Only now, after some of these conflicts have already erupted into violence, has the government begun to realize that neither Marx nor Lenin offered any solution to nationality problems. Nowadays, Soviet publications customarily, albeit obliquely, refer to their ideas as "national nihilism." The Marxist slogan of internationalism has been so compromised that its use has become counterproductive in combatting nationalism because it only inflames the passions of those who remember that under this slogan many nationalities were either "Russified" or otherwise brought to the brink of extinction.

Then there was the Leninist idea that the "age of imperialism" made it unnecessary for Russia to wait until it was "mature" enough for the Marxist proletarian revolution. The Bolsheviks therefore went ahead with the "proletarian" revolution in an overwhelmingly peasant country (more than 80 percent of the population). As a result, the October Revolution did not have even the slightest chance of ever becoming "Russian" and "popular." Lenin was forced to give promises which went against the grain of his Marxist convictions: promises of land to peasants, self-determination to national minorities, and the promise to end the war. If the October Revolution was popular at all, it was so only as long as these promises were kept, which was not for long. The peasants soon realized that the land the Bolsheviks got for them (from the nobility) was theirs only as long as they gave all results of their labor to the government. The minorities soon learned that their self-determination was to be only under the Red banner. And everyone soon learned that the end of war with the Germans, in which the country lost about two million lives, meant the beginning of civil war, in which losses were many times higher.

Keenly aware that theirs was not the kind of revolution that Marx prescribed, the Bolsheviks went overboard in trying to "re-legitimize" it in the eyes of their Western comrades. They followed *The Communist Manifesto* to the letter, overcompensating, as it were, for the "heresy" of starting a "Western" revolution in the East. "The theory of the Communists may be summed up in the single phrase, abolition of private property," say Marx and Engels in *The Communist Manifesto*. Guided by this proposition, the Bolsheviks went on a spree of expropriation of private property that left the country's economy in a shambles. At first, the wave of expropriation hit the urban people. The Jews were its primary victims because of a high percentage of urban proprietors (shopkeepers, craftsmen) among them.[13] It was only when the confiscation expanded to rural population, especially through the infamous *prodrazverstka ,* that the Russians were hit more than the Jews. The fear that private ownership would inevitably lead to the restoration of capitalism became the cornerstone of Soviet economic policy for the years to come. Even now, while Soviet authors frequently describe Marxism as "economic nihilism," the fear of deviating from *The Manifesto* blocks Soviet economic reform both in industry and in agriculture.

The Bolsheviks also tried to follow *The Manifesto*'s demand for the "establishment of industrial armies, especially in agriculture," an idea which gave birth to both the command economy and the labor camps. (And if Trotskii was most active in the promotion of both, it was due less to his being anti-Russian, as Kozhinov suggests, than to his following Marx too closely.) Even the Bolsheviks' attitude toward the peasant majority was characterized by Marxist overkill. While on the level of economic relations, it was governed by Marx's injunction against private property, on the level of culture it closely reflected Marx's anti-religious views and his contempt for the "idiocy of rural life."

In their adoption of the one-party system the Bolsheviks also found considerable support in *The Manifesto*, which proclaimed that, even though "the Communists everywhere support every revolutionary movement," they and only they have "the advantage of clearly understanding the line of march, the conditions, and the ultimate general results of the proletarian movement." Even though they seized power with the help of other leftist parties, the Bolsheviks felt neither a theoretical nor a moral obligation to share it with those who were said to be incapable of seeing "the line of march."

Bolshevik intolerance not just to political opposition, but to any heterodox views, was largely founded on Marx's claim that his political and economic theory was the only "scientific" one. The Bolsheviks certainly took notice of how, in *The Manifesto*, Marx and Engels dismissed their potential opponents: "The charges against communism made from a religious, a philosophical, and, generally, from an ideological standpoint, are not deserving of serious examination." From this there was but a short step to silencing all authors of "undeserving" ideas and establishing an ideological monopoly which crowns the structure of the totalitarian state.

Bolshevik foreign policy, too, was largely determined by Marxist ideas, or rather by the impossibility of enacting them in Russia. Acutely aware of the fact that their "proletarian" revolution could never become "popular" in Russia, the Bolsheviks were constantly tempted to view it as a spark for world revolution. They felt a particular compulsion to expand it to the West. They knew from *The Manifesto* that "united action of the leading civilized countries (that is, England, Germany, France, and the United States) at least, was one of the first conditions for the emancipation of the proletariat." After all, in spite of their professed internationalism, they believed in Marx's arrogantly ethnocentric idea that there was but one "highway" of human progress--that of the West.

All these Marxist-Leninist ideas are inherently anti-national, anti-religious, anti-traditional, and--utopian. As such, they were and are equally "alien" to both the Jews and the Russians. They are "alien" to mankind at large. Not only are they conducive to violence, but they also are ideocidal, that is, lethal to all other ideas. Yet they appealed and continue to appeal, in a most obsessive way, to people of all nationalities. It was this obsession, particularly when these ideas were combined into a so-called Marxist-Leninist "science," that was chiefly responsible for the tragedy of the Communist Holocaust, under both Lenin and Stalin. It was the intoxication with these ideas that alienated the Bolshevik leaders from reality and made them abandon all logic, common sense and common standards of morality and decency. Their macabre fate during the 1930s is proof of the proposition that ideas have consequences, and that bad ideas produce bad consequences. The efforts to impose them on humanity are bound to end in disaster, including for the bearers of those ideas.

Without taking into account the influence of these ideas on the Bolshevik leadership, one cannot even begin to understand the tragedy of the twentieth century. Guided by these "alien" ideas, a Marxist revolution, which could have conceivably been "democratic" in a developed Western country where the majority of the population were industrial workers, was bound to be anti-democratic in Russia, an essentially peasant country. It was a revolution carried out by an elitist intellectual minority who knew that their power came through the barrel of a gun, not the power of the popular vote. (Neither debater mentioned that in the election of the Constituent Assembly the Bolsheviks received less than 25 percent of the vote.) They knew that they could stay in power only through force and deception. That is why they had to resort to divide-and-conquer tactics, of which setting Russians against Russians, Jews against Jews, Jews against Russians and vice versa, was and is an integral part.

The failure of both Sarnov and Kozhinov to draw attention to the Bolsheviks' political ideas shows that these tactics continue to entrap Soviet intellectuals. Thus, by affirming the allegedly "popular" and "Russian" character of the revolution (as the limitations of glasnost have required), Kozhinov and Sarnov derailed their debate to the secondary issue of whether the Jews or the Russians were most instrumental in making a "good" revolution go wrong. Meanwhile, the fundamentally anti-Russian and anti-Jewish character of the ideas that inspired the revolution remained untouched. In the final account, both debaters unwittingly burdened both the Jews and the Russians with more blame than either deserved.

Sarnov was particularly inept in defending the Jews against the charge that the Bolshevik revolution was "Jewish." On the one hand, he failed to acknowledge that a disproportionately high number of people of Jewish origin participated in the Bolshevik revolution, and an even larger number joined the Communist cause thereafter. This is a fact which has been acknowledged and openly debated by Western scholars, including Jewish ones, for several decades. On the other hand, he failed to point out two paramount considerations. First, that the Jews joined the Bolsheviks only to the extent to which they had lost or denied their Jewishness. Second, that the high percentage of Jews among the Bolsheviks did not mean that the *majority* of the Russian Jews supported the Bolshevik revolution. In fact, while the politically active Jews overwhelmingly supported the February revolution, not a single Jewish party, neither the socialist Bund, nor "United," nor Poale Zion, nor the Zionists came out in favor of the Bolshevik regime. Actually, the proportion of Jews in major all-Russian radical parties, such as the Mensheviks and Socialist-Revolutionaries, was, certainly before October 1917, considerably higher than among the Bolsheviks.[14]

Sarnov also failed to counter Kozhinov's charge that Jews had led the "anti-Russian" campaign of the 1920s by pointing out that during the same period the so-called Jewish Section of the Party (*Evsektsiia*), staffed by the Jewish Bolsheviks, conducted violently anti-Zionist and anti-Jewish policy. Finally, Sarnov failed to point out that there were some Jews who actively opposed the Bolshevik regime. For instance, Moisei Uritskii, the Jewish boss of the Cheka in Petrograd, whom Kozhinov accused of anti-Russian bias, was assassinated by Leonid Kenegisser, also a Jew. Another example may be seen in the abortive attempt on Lenin's life by Dora Kaplan, a Jewish member of the Socialist Revolutionary (SR) party.

Although Sarnov may have known some of these facts, he apparently chose not to rock the boat of glasnost. Ironically, he fell overboard himself when he suggested, by quoting Berdiaev, that the Third International was the fulfillment of the Russian "messianic" dream and that that dream was akin to Jewish messianism. What he conveniently "forgot" to mention was that Berdiaev, whose works until recently were proscribed in the USSR, made it just as clear that Bolshevik "messianism" was as much a travesty of Russian messianism (which is an arguable notion in itself) as Marx's "proletarian messianism" was a travesty of the Jewish messianism. Kozhinov, for his part, missed a chance to set the record straight. As a result, the reader was left with the impression that both the Jews and the Russians bear greater *national* responsibility for Communism than what actually was the case.

The fault rests only partly with the two debaters. Its major share rests with the very ideas that they did not dare to attack.

Congealed into the Marxist-Leninist monopoly, these ideas continue to distort, poison and mislead Soviet intellectual debate. Though severely undermined, this monopoly continues to block Soviet scholars' access to information. Since its inception the Soviet regime has destroyed, distorted, and concealed the true record of popular opposition to Communism, both among Russians and non-Russians. This is especially so in regard to the Jewish opposition, for the obvious reason that the regime has always counted on the support of pro-Communist Jews abroad. Even now the access of Soviet citizens to sources which might reveal a more accurate picture of what then happened remains restricted. To clarify the main issues of the debate I shall briefly review a number of such sources.

The Bickerman Collection

It is unlikely, for instance, that either Sarnov or Kozhinov had a chance to read the collection of articles, *Rossiia i evrei* [Russia and the Jews], published by a group of conservative Russian Jews in Berlin in 1923 (henceforth referred to as the Bickerman Collection).[15] Rejecting the myth of the "Jewish" character of the Bolshevik revolution, its authors argued that the Bolshevik regime was "the *greatest* evil. . . for both the Jews and all other nationalities of Russia." For the Jews, the balance sheet of the revolution included the loss of "countless lives and all our property" and the suppression of the most cultured and dignified Jews, who were doomed to a silent death in "sadness, poverty, and helplessness." "Our sacred relics are desecrated, our [secular] culture is uprooted and trampled down as well; just as the Russians, hundreds of thousands of Russian Jews are scattered" in this "second diaspora,"[16] they lamented.

First of all, pointing out the "excessively zealous" (*nepomerno r'ianoe*) participation of the Jewish Bolsheviks in the "destruction and suppression of Russia," the authors of the Bickerman collection not only recognized it as a fact (which can be disputed but not ignored), but recognized it as "a sin, which carries its vengeance in itself." However, unlike both Sarnov and Kozhinov, they just as clearly recognized the ambivalence of the Jewish role in the revolution. "For what misfortune could be greater for our people than the misfortune of seeing our sons go astray and yet be accused [that this misfortune is] a manifestation of our power, of our Jewish dominance," complained the authors about the common identification of Jewish Bolsheviks with the Jews as a people. Justifiably or not, "[among Soviet people of all classes] Soviet power is being equated with Jewish power, and the hatred toward the Bolsheviks translates into a hatred toward the Jews," observed the authors, suggesting that the misdeeds of the Jewish Bolsheviks, a tiny minority among the Russian Jews, became the greatest source of judophobia in the post-revolutionary period.[17]

In an appeal to "the Jews of all countries," they argued, "It is time for a Jew to stop fearing whether he is sinning against the revolution. There is a more urgent task at hand: not to sin against the ultimate, fundamental values of man and mankind, not to sin against one's fatherland and against one's own people." The authors made it clear that in respect to the Communist regime their interests coincide with those of the Russians: "For Russia and against her destroyers! For the Jewish people and against those who defile its name!"[18]

The collection consists of six articles by six conservative Russian Jews in emigration. Since the book has not been translated into English, a brief review of all six articles might be in order here. It will clarify certain points of the current Russo-Jewish controversy in which both Sarnov and Kozhinov found themselves so hopelessly mired.

In his lead article, "Russia and Russian Jewry," I. M. Bickerman set the overarching theme of the collection: the need to expiate the "excessively zealous" role of Jews in the Bolshevik regime. Jews have suffered from the revolution as much as Russians, says Bickerman. But their "main sin" is the refusal to admit their co-responsibility for the atrocities committed by Lenin, Trotskii and others. Yet the best way to disprove the charge of anti-Semites that the Jews destroyed Russia, says Bickerman, is to tell "the truth about Russia's catastrophe," including the Jewish contribution to it.

The truth is that "Russia was killed by the February revolution," of which the October coup was a logical consequence.[19] This would not have happened without the connivance of "very respectable and very influential groups [such as the overwhelmingly Russian Kadet party] which did everything to make the advent of [the Bolshevik] Satan possible and even inevitable."[20] By blaming the October coup on the Jews rather than on the Kadets, the Russian right-wingers merely divert attention from the real killers of Russia to "a flock of crows scavenging on its corpse."

"Neither caused by us nor carried out by us, the revolution is nonetheless being perceived by Jews as a great good for all, and especially for us."[21] Such a misperception of the revolution on the part of a majority of Jews is a serious mistake. Bickerman explains it by Jewish susceptibility to Marxism, a "subversive ideology" of "false-prophets teaching. . . that the proletariat has no fatherland, that it could lose only its chains and win the whole world." Hence Jewish indulgence in "verbal maximalism, and spiritual minimalism."[22] Hence Jews succumbing to the "worship of the Idol of Revolution."

Like the Samson of old, the Russian Jew fell for the charms of the Delilah of the revolution, says Bickerman. Betrayed by her, he was captured, blinded, and enslaved by his enemies. Alas, shorn of the "hair" of Jewish religious tradition, the Samson of today chooses to wallow in slavery and blindness, "relishing equality [with other slaves] under the rubble of the house he did not ruin."[23] Among the enemies of the new Samson, the worst are "the masters from *Evsektsiia*," says Bickerman, in reference to the special Party department whose Jewish bosses zealously persecuted religious Jews during the 1920s.

Contrary to the common notion that the revolution saved Jews from the pogroms, Bickerman argues the opposite: that the pogroms in 1917-1920 took incomparably more Jewish lives than those of the entire pre-revolutionary period. Contrary to Soviet propaganda, the majority of the post-revolutionary pogroms were perpetrated not by the White Army, says Bickerman, but by various leftist regimes that rose after the breakdown of civil order in February 1917: the Petliura regime of the Ukrainian separatists, whom Jews originally supported; the army of the Ukrainian anarchist Makhno; such leftist warlords as Grigor'ev, Zelenyi, and Angel;[24] and the Red Army itself. Bickerman especially notes the pogroms by the Red Army in Glukhov and Novgorod Severskii in the winter of 1918. The first wave of pogroms started right after the February revolution, says Bickerman. "Swallowing many Jewish lives," the pogroms in Tarnopol and Kalushche occurred because the Provisional Government was unable to assert its authority.[25] Reproaching all radical Jews for contributing to the breakdown of civil order in February 1917, Bickerman quotes from the Bible: "Those who sow the wind, shall reap the whirlwind."

As to the pogroms by the White Army, Bickerman says that they should be seen in the context of the Army's "fantastically heroic struggle against a huge, monstrously insolent and vicious enemy, as David against Goliath,"[26] to save the country from "Cain's crime." Never sanctioned by the army's command, these pogroms were spontaneous retaliations against the crimes of Jewish Bolsheviks, says Bickerman. A Jew held Red regiments together by taking "thousands of Russian people, old men and women, as hostages to force Russian officers. . . to serve their worst enemies." Another Jew ordered the execution of the whole Romanov family without a trial, says Bickerman, citing eyewitness accounts of how at railway stations Jewish Bolsheviks were sorting out Russian officers for summary execution. Why do we call these atrocities a "revolution," but the officers' response to it a "pogrom"? Why such an honor to Marx and his followers?, wonders Bickerman. "It was the curse of the time that anyone could give vent to his hatred, declaring a social class or ethnic group 'harmful' and then exterminating it ruthlessly,"[27] concluded Bickerman, long before Vasilii Grossman made a similar conclusion on the origin of the Soviet regime.

In the final account Bickerman blames both the Russian and Jewish intellectual leaders for failing to take advantage of the opportunities for reform that were opening up, certainly after 1907, when not only "the Russian people were becoming more prosperous [and] Russian culture was developing wide and deep," but "Russian Jewry was growing in importance and power."[28] "Despite the Pale of Settlement and educational quotas, despite [the pogroms in] Kishinev and Belostok, I was and felt myself a free man. . . who could prosper materially and grow spiritually and who could fight," writes Bickerman. "It would have taken five to fifteen years," he speculates, "before Jews would have attained full equality before the law, and we could have waited, because waiting meant to live, to work, and to fight."[29] By contrast, even though many individual Jews have prospered under the Bolshevik regime, theirs is the happiness of a slave, whereas Russian Jewry as a whole is dying out. However, "fate has not yet uttered its last word about Russia. . . . Russia will live, and her rebirth must become our national task, the task of all Jewish people and, first of all, of Russian Jewry."[30]

For this to happen, Jews must free themselves from the "superstition of revolutionary phraseology," a task in which they have fallen behind Russians.[31]   Saying that the weight of world Jewry "currently helps [Russia's] oppressors," Bickerman argues for shifting it in favor of Russia's rebirth.[32]   Unless that happens, world Jewry will remain open to anti-Semitic charges that it has conspired against Russia, warns Bickerman.   In fact, not only are these charges totally unfounded, he adds, but their anti-Semitic authors give too much credit to the wisdom of modern Jewish leaders.

> They portray us as the master race, a nation which seeks world domination and which has already half-succeeded in that. In fact, our prodigal thoughts only flutter over the surface of the world. We are not masters even over ourselves. And if we now are dangerous to anyone at all, this is only because we go with the flow of the [revolutionary] current which undermines the very foundation of European civilization already shaken by the tremors of the last few years."[33]

says Bickerman, alluding to World War I and subsequent Communist revolutions in Hungary, Germany, and Russia, each of which, one might add, having solved nothing, set the stage for the tragedy of World War II, the Nazi Holocaust, and the expansion of Communism over one-third of mankind.

Another contributor to the collection, G. A. Landau, devoted his article to the spread of revolutionary ideas among the Jews since the French revolution.   Referring to the "irrefutable facts of participation of the Jews in destructive processes in Europe,"[34] he explains them as a consequence of many Jews becoming infected with socialist ideas.   As a result, in the Jewish community there was gradually established "a hegemony of socialism. . . with its denial of civil society and modern state, and its condescension to bourgeois culture and the heritage of centuries." The spread of socialism was facilitated by the fact that many Jews had already rejected their own religious heritage in the "process of Europeanization" in the nineteenth century. Ironically, socialism was even less suitable for Jews than for Russians. "Can one imagine anything more absurd than the sermon of socialism among people whose majority consisted of petty bourgeois, craftsmen, merchants, intellectuals and middlemen?" asks Landau.[35]

When the Bolshevik revolution occurred, this absurdity turned into a nightmare, because the abolition of private property at once wiped out all sources of livelihood for the Jewish masses. While the majority of the Russians remained on land (the peasants) or at factories (workers), a typical Jew "was deprived of his income, his profession was abolished, and he had [no choice] but to go [begging] to the Soviet authorities" for his very survival. Since the revolution "overturned the entire societal pyramid, giving social power to have-nots, moral authority to human refuse, and cultural provenance to ignoramuses," argues Landau, "it was inevitable that it would drag to the surface the same elements from Jewry, thus giving a green light to impudence, expediency, and all sorts of opportunism. . . ." Moreover, since the Jews had the highest rate of literacy, they were preferred as new servants of the Soviet state. As a result, under the banner of socialist revolution there were marching not only Jewish idealists, but also all sort of "hooligans and scoundrels."

> What especially struck us, and what we expected the least among the Jews, was the cruelty, sadism, and violence, which seemed to be alien to a people far removed from a physical and military life; those who yesterday could not handle a rifle today turned up among cut-throat executioners,[36]

says Landau in his indictment of Jewish Bolsheviks. Even though "the Jewish community took an active part in the process of destruction [of the old regime], this destruction fell upon Jewry with especially devastating force."[37] Since "the destruction of Jewry was part of Russia's destruction, therefore the two [should seek] a common path to reconstruction,"[38] concluded Landau.

I. O. Levin's article was devoted to the reasons behind Jewish participation in the revolution. Admitting that discrimination against the Jews in Tsarist Russia was one of the major reasons for Jewish support for the Bolsheviks, Levin suggests that the other major reason was the "cultural disintegration" and "soillessness" of Jews, who found themselves "suspended in the air between old Jewish culture, from which they departed, and the Christian-European culture. . . which they didn't join." He condemns not only the Jewish Bolsheviks, but also those Jews who played a bloody role in the revolutions in Hungary and Bavaria where, Levin argues, there was virtually no discrimination against the Jews. Levin suggested that neither the Jews nor the Russians could be "healed" from Bolshevism unless a "revival of ethical-religious principles of national life takes place."[39]

D. O. Linskii, who fought against the Bolsheviks in the ranks of the White (Denikin's) Army, devoted his article to the "national self-awareness" of Russian Jews. Not denying that anti-Semitism was rife among White army rank-and-file, Linskii resolutely rejects the charge that the army's commanders either ordered or encouraged pogroms. He explains the spread of anti-Semitism among the Whites not only by the atrocities committed by Jewish Bolsheviks but also by the "unforgivable exaltation" with which many non-Bolshevik Jews accepted the revolution.[40] As a contributing factor he mentions the Bolshevik ploy according to which the Jews who opposed them were routinely accused of "bourgeois activities," while the more serious charge of "counter-revolution" was reserved for the Russians.[41] Whenever the White Army recaptured a town from the Reds, Linskii recalls, the local Jews welcomed it just as happily as the Russians. Linskii's conclusion is unequivocal: the White Army fought for freedom and human rights for all, including the Jews.

V. S. Mandel's article is devoted to "conservative and destructive elements" within Jewry. He argues that, although Jews have the reputation of being a nation of trouble-makers and rabble-rousers, their religion and customs are fundamentally conservative and anti-revolutionary. Dismissing the "Protocols of the Elders of Zion" as an "awkward and malicious forgery," he points out that Jews themselves contributed to the common perception of them as a revolutionary people. He cites, for example, the book, *Die Jude als Rasse und Kulture*, whose Jewish author, Fritz Kahn, boasted about "the legions of Jewish revolutionaries" who fought in the revolutions in Russia, Hungary, and Bavaria under the banner of Ferdinand Lassalle, "the leader" of modern Jewish "messianism."[42] When Amfiteatrov, a Russian judophile, praised Jews for their revolutionary and socialist "mission" in the world, Mandel' points out, Jews failed to repudiate him.

Even though Marx rejected Judaism in favor of German "ethical nihilism," says Mandel', his Jewish followers were instrumental in the "transplantation of this foreign fruit onto Russian soil."[43] Pointing out that radical Jews were active participants in every revolutionary movement in Europe since 1848, Mandel' opposes them to conservative Jews. The revolutionary Jewish "legions" do not represent the majority of the Jewish people, who remain deeply conservative and law-abiding people. One such Jew was the British prime minister Benjamin Disraeli (1804-1881). In spite of his conversion to Christianity, says Mandel', Disraeli retained a deep love of the Jewish tradition. Mandel' endorses Disraeli's observation on the destructive role of Jewish radicals in Europe: "God's people work together with the atheists, and those most capable of acquisition ally themselves with the communists."[44]

The concluding essay of the collection, "What Are We Striving For?", was written by D. S. Pasmanik. Jews should, first of all, recognize their co-responsibility for the crimes of the Jewish Bolsheviks, argued Pasmanik. Saying that "Jewish dominance" over Bolshevik Russia was not a mere invention of anti-Semites, Pasmanik recalled how Jewish members of Soviet diplomatic missions used to boast by telling such anecdotes as "Tea is Vysotskii's, sugar Brodskii's, and Russia is Trotskii's."[45] Calling for rejection of the "mindless and impractical" notion, popular among Jews abroad, that "Bolshevism is better than restoration," Pasmanik predicted the eventual downfall of Bolshevism and warned the Jews not to set themselves against the inevitable. The more actively Jews participate in the struggle against Bolshevism, the less will be the likelihood of Jewish pogroms. Citing Marx's anti-Semitism, Pasmanik argued that "the spiritual victory of the Bolsheviks over Judaism is more dangerous than all the pogroms." Therefore, it is the moral duty of the Jews to fight against Bolshevism, "a profoundly anti-cultural and reactionary phenomenon, disrupting the natural evolution of mankind and of Russia in particular," concluded Pasmanik.[46]

Although each author dealt with a different aspect of the relationship between Jews and Russia, a number of salient themes pervade the whole collection. They can be summarized as follows: (1) the Bolshevik regime is both anti-Jewish and anti-Russian; (2) it particularly threatens the survival of the Jews as a distinct people with a deep religious tradition; (3) Jews were both the victims of the Soviet regime and among its worst servants, and their role in the "class struggle" genocide of the Russian population should be admitted and expiated; (4) even though many Jews prospered under the Soviet regime, they did so at the cost of persecution of the Jewish majority; (5) the price tag of this "progress" must include the thousands of Jewish lives lost in the post-revolutionary pogroms which were mainly due to the breakdown of civil order in February 1917, to which Jews contributed; (6) the downfall of the Bolshevik regime is inevitable; (7) both the ethical principles and self-interest of the Jews dictate that they unite with the Russians to hasten this downfall; (8) to do so, Jews must stop worshipping the "Idol of Revolution," renounce the false prophets (Marx, Lassalle, Trotskii, etc.) and return to the tradition of Moses; (9) by acknowledging and expiating whatever revolutionary "sins" their "prodigal sons" have committed in Russia, Jews will assure their own survival as the people of the Bible and strengthen the Judeo-Christian foundations of European civilization; (10) if Jews as a people can be held accountable for the tragedy of the revolution, it is only because of their failure to rein in their own deracinated, violent minority, a failure that can be imputed equally to the Russians.

As we have seen, the Jewish contemporaries of the 1917-1922 events understood the role of Jews in the Communist revolution more deeply than either Kozhinov or Sarnov. They understood that from its very beginning the revolution was profoundly alien to both Jews and Russians. They knew that the revolution was destructive to both the Jews and the Russians. They did not regard it as an expression of the national aspirations of the Russian people. Nor did they regard it as Jewish or Zionist. They saw it, rather, as the logical outcome of a progressive "infection" of both Jewish and Russian intelligentsia with the debilitating virus of Communist ideas, a virus which eventually broke down the resistance of the body politic of many a nation to the assault of their deracinated "prodigal sons." Unlike Sarnov, they were not reluctant to acknowledge the "excessive zeal" of Jewish Bolsheviks in the atrocities of the regime. They knew that, far from representing the Jewish messianic tradition, Jewish Bolsheviks only profaned it.

Alexis Babine's Diary

Besides the Bickerman Collection, Kozhinov and Sarnov could have greatly benefitted from another important eyewitness account, that of Alexis Babine (1866-1930). A Russian intellectual, Babine had spent nearly twenty years in the United States where he graduated from Cornell University before returning to Russia in 1910. Babine witnessed the events of 1917-1922 in the provincial Volga city of Saratov where he was an English instructor at the university. An admirer of American democracy, Babine managed to return to the United States in 1922 with the help of the American Relief Administration (ARA), which was then fighting a famine in that region. He brought along a diary which he had wisely kept in English. Afraid of possible repercussions for his relatives in Russia, Babine refrained from publishing it before he died in 1930.

Published in the United States in 1988,[47] Babine's diary corroborates the view of the revolution, and of the role of Jews in it, expressed in the Bickerman Collection. His observations complement the Collection from the perspective of a Russian intellectual. Babine was neither a revolutionary nor a counter-revolutionary. His primary concern was with the breakdown of civil order, which he saw, much as did the authors of the Bickerman Collection, as issuing directly from the February revolution. According to one of his diary entries, "to the masses the overthrow of the monarchy seemed like the subversion of a time-honored and tried regime by a class of selfish and unscrupulous individuals."

On October 27, two days after the Bolsheviks took power in Petrograd, an appeal was published in the local newspaper to resist the Bolshevik takeover of Saratov. However, "owing to the unpopularity of Kerensky and his rule and to the physical and moral flabbiness of our Christian citizens, only 150 persons. . . answered the call to defend the city."[48] The following day the Bolsheviks took over. Immediately, "there [was] widespread dissatisfaction with the suppression of free speech. There [was] every reason to believe that people would prefer even monarchy to the present state of anarchy and wanton oppression just to get rid of Kerensky, Lenin, Bronstein [Trotsky], Rosenfeld [Kamenev] & Co.,"[49] writes Babine. The soldiers of the Saratov garrison apparently played a decisive role in the Bolshevik takeover in the city. These soldiers joined the Reds because they viewed them as less pro-Jewish than the Kerenskii government. Babine reports rumors about a Jewish pogrom. When the mobs began their "lynch law" rule in the streets, people did not expect any protection from these Red soldiers, but only from the Cossacks surrounding Saratov. On

November 12 all hope vanished. "Hoodwinked by the Bolsheviks," the Cossacks refused to enter the city and moved away. Since then Babine witnessed uninterrupted Bolshevik rule.

Just a week later, on November 18, "the air and the local Soviet's newspapers [were] full of soldiers' threats of a St. Barthlomew's Night for the bourgeoisie, the well-to-do, the liberals in general, and the non-Bolshevik socialists in particular." When "a dense crowd of citizens gathered. . . and discussed the Bolshevik oppression, abuse of power, and the general betrayal of the people's interest," a detail of Red soldiers "ordered it to disperse." Babine notes that the Red soldiers' ranks were soon swelled by common criminals released from Saratov's jails.

Babine's diary corroborates the contention of the Bickerman Collection that the Russian intelligentsia, among whom there were many Jews, was completely unprepared for the revolution it precipitated. While there were numerous demonstrations, strikes, and open insurrection against the Bolsheviks by church people, workers, porters, students, waiters, shopkeepers, and the general populace, the most Babine's university colleagues did in the way of protest was to interrupt classes for one day. This prompted Babine to comment: "The Russian tendency to protest against oppression and all sorts of barbarity by refusing to do any work, is, to me, as touching as the Russian incapacity to do anything to eliminate injustice."[50] While the railroad workers refused to work on Christian holidays, says Babine, "at the university the lectures are to take place as usual: the learned teachers have not the stamina of the common folk."[51] When a student was shot dead during a demonstration under the slogan "Down with the Bolsheviks," Babine commented: "The three hundred thousand inhabitants of Saratov are at the mercy of three or four thousand armed ruffians. Our so-called intelligentsia are flabby. Their brains and their will power are as flabby as their muscle."[52]

Disgusted with his colleagues' "advocacy of all sorts of 'rights' and with their practical inability to defend these rights," Babine wonders: "Can this be accounted for by the presence among [us] of so many members of a nation which through centuries of persecution has stood away from all physical struggle against oppression, which has always purchased for money what pittance of an existence it could get, or hired others, or inspired them, to stand the brunt of armed conflict?"

He was clearly alluding to his Jewish colleagues. However, lest one jump to conclusions, his next question was: "Or is it the purely Slavic amorality, immorality, and the physical and moral decrepitude of the polished and so-called educated and intellectual classes?"[53] He did not give an answer to either question. But the fact that he asked them suggests that his line of thought was close to that of the authors of the Bickerman Collection. Like them, Babine regarded the intellectuals as the chief protagonists of a gradual breakdown of civil order which resulted in a revolution they could not control.

By no means an anti-Semite,[54] Babine nevertheless noted the prominent role Jews played in the revolution. Much like the authors of the Bickerman collection, he shows that role to be much more ambiguous than what one could glean from the Kozhinov-Sarnov debate. On the one hand, Babine shows an early Jewish opposition to the new regime. On January 9, 1918, at a public protest meeting against random killings, "an excited young Jew expressed his belief that the Bolsheviks would shoot us and do with us anything they pleased as long as we did not repel them in kind." At another several persons, "mostly Jews and other aliens," spoke against the Bolshevik decree abolishing the right of property in real estate. When Mr. Maizul, a Jew, whom Babine calls "my friend," proposed to ignore all the decrees of "this band of highwaymen," Babine was delighted to note that "his resolution carried." On March 31, 1918, Babine notes that "Lieber, a Bund orator, spoke last week at the railway station on the tyrannical Bolshevik rule before an audience of some eight thousand railroad employees." When two Russian Bolshevik leaders tried to interrupt him, the crowd supported Lieber. Babine's sympathy is unmistakable. The same is true in respect to a certain Rabinovich, a printing press owner, who shot dead Press Commissar Alekseev, who tried to confiscate the Jew's property.[55]

On the other hand, Babine describes with disgust a certain Mr. Brovarskii, "a neighbor of ours, a baptized Jew," reputed to be a former member of the *Okhrana* [Tsarist secret police]. Having now become "a pronounced Bolshevik," Brovarskii speaks disparagingly about the bad temper and manners of Dr. Brod, who was murdered, allegedly for refusing to treat poor patients.[56] Noting that the leading troika of the local Cheka, M. Vengerov, Ivan Genkin, and M. Deutsch, were all Jews,[57] Babine describes how the latter shot a prisoner on the university premises after the suppression of the Menshevik and Socialist Revolutionary uprising in Saratov on May 16, 1918. He is indignant that "an order has been received from Bronstein [Trotsky] to show no mercy whatever."[58]

Refraining from personal comments, Babine reproduces what the common people had to say about the Jews. In the beginning the soldiers were more opposed to Kerenskii (whom they believed was a Jew) than to the Bolsheviks. On the day of the Bolshevik takeover, "it [was] rumored that the pro-Bolshevik soldiers [were] planning a Jewish pogrom."[59] A year later, Babine overheard one of the Red soldiers. After seeing one Jewish-looking Bolshevik official, the soldier said: "These Jews like money first-rate, and get all the best-paid positions."[60] At another point an unnamed Red Army instructor was overheard as saying that his soldiers complained of "waging war against our own people... Soldiers are not in love with Trotsky... peasants hate him."[61] On December 28, 1918, Babine wrote:

> In the line for bread this morning, between six and seven o'clock, the common men and women bitterly complained of the waste of time in all sorts of 'lines,' severely criticized the economic policy of the Bolsheviks, and pointed to the disappearance of meat from Soviet stores. 'Only the Jews have all the meat they want,' was the general refrain. A young worker said: 'We have twelve or fifteen of them in our office. When we began to blame them for the present state of affairs, they said, 'Remember the 1905-1906 [pogroms]. You dipped your fingers in our blood then. Now we are washing our hands in yours.' The worker was from the Soviet Supply Department. A woman seconded him. She had heard a Jew boast, 'We have put you into a bag; soon we will tie the bag.'[62]

Although Babine made no comments on the above, his diary shows that he understood well the difficulties the Jews were facing under the new regime. Contradicting Sarnov's assumption of "substantial" popular support for the Bolshevik revolution, Babine gives no indication of such support, from either the Jews or the Russians. To the extent that these two peoples remained true to their respective traditions, they were not actively involved on the side of the Bolsheviks. Babine's diary is filled with the reports of anti-Bolshevik sentiments among the overwhelming majority of the people in Saratov and the Russian villages he visited.

The people favored neither the Reds nor the Whites, but the Greens, a largely peasant army which tried to position itself between the two. On July 3-4, 1919, the Greens came close to capturing Saratov:

> The leading Bolsheviks are said to be leaving Saratov. The Jews are moving to villages near the city. . . . The working classes of Saratov are said to be in favor of surrendering the city without resistance, while the ardent Communists insist on defending it to the last. The Greens are beginning to attack, and to destroy, representatives of Bolshevik authority in villages within ten miles of Saratov, and even closer. Even the local Bolshevik paper frankly acknowledges the Green danger.[63]

The Bolsheviks eventually prevailed, but only after the suppression of pro-Green city residents with the help of a Latvian regiment. Still, even two years later, in July 1921, "rumors of a peasant insurrection all over Russia [were] a common topic of conversation. A Tambov rebel leader, Antonov, has become a sort of anti-Bolshevik hero."[64] Largely unknown in the USSR,[65] the story of the Green movement did not even enter the Kozhinov-Sarnov debate. Both debaters merely paid lip service to the myth of the popularity of the Bolshevik revolution.

But wasn't it popular at least among the oppressed national minorities? Besides telling of the Latvians suppressing the citizens of Saratov, the diary contains numerous other reports of Hungarians, Slovaks, Chinese, Volga Germans and other "aliens" fighting for the Bolsheviks. However, while reporting those instances, Babine never makes any generalizations. Apparently he understood that, like Jews, these other "aliens" were used by the Bolsheviks against the Russians, the majority of whom were unwilling to support them. This was part of the Bolshevik strategy of setting up one nationality against another, a strategy which produced the illusion of an "international revolution." Babine may complain occasionally that "the Jewish and German clique of the faculty. . . beat the native element."[66] But at the same time he writes with compassion about the fate of both Jews and Germans under Communism. "The city is beset by beggars--German colonists who have fled from their settlements after the bloody suppression of their unsuccessful insurrection against the Soviets,"[67] he noted on May 27, 1921.

The closest Babine came to a generalization about the Jews is at the end of the diary. On November 16, 1922, onboard an America-bound ship, noticing that it was "full of Jews," he made the following observation: "Many of them are fleeing from Russia, where life at present is impossible and where pogroms are expected against all the Jews for the sins of a few criminal anarchists who are Jews only in name, but who bring a curse on the entire Jewish race." Written from the perspective of a Russian intellectual who was well-disposed toward both Jews and American democracy, this conclusion is remarkable. It coincides exactly with that of his Jewish contemporaries, the authors of the Bickerman Collection. Like them, Babine was shocked at his first encounter with those Jews in the West who had been among the most fervent apologists of the Soviet regime. During a stopover in London, Babine ran into "a small crowd on a street corner around an orator. A youthful Jew was preaching Moscow Sovietism to a circle of English workers who apparently were already well informed about the Soviets and pressed the lout with questions that made him very uncomfortable." This was perhaps Babine's strongest outburst of anger in his entire diary. "Among other things, the Communist quoted Trotsky's maxim about dealing with the bourgeoisie: 'It is easier to shoot them than to argue with them,'"[68] notes Babine, as if to remind the West about the essence of the new regime.

Rabbi Chaim Bermant on Radical Jews

This latter episode brings us back to the "Rubashov syndrome" as an international phenomenon, from which the Sarnov-Kozhinov debate had started. "Strange as it might sound today, after the October Revolution, a pro-Soviet illusion started to spread among Jewish intellectuals, students, professionals, and especially among journalists and labor leaders," observed one Jewish author in a 1968 Russian emigre collection about Russian Jewry.[69] Made about the United States during the 1920s-30s, this observation has much validity for later periods and for other countries.

But didn't the situation change after the Moscow show trials, after the Nazi-Soviet pact, after the Nazi Holocaust and the emergence of Israel? No. Certainly not as much as would seem warranted by the bitter record of Jews under Communism. In the post-World War II period, pro-Soviet Jewish Communists and radicals, even though they were a minority within the Jewish community, continued to play a key role in the expansion of Soviet Communism throughout the world. As recent research indicates, Jewish Communists were very active in establishing Stalinist rule in Central Europe, most notably in Hungary and Poland.[70] Meanwhile, their counterparts and sympathizers in the West did their best to render the policy of containment largely ineffective.

But didn't the situation change after the world learned of Stalin's crimes from Khrushchev himself? Didn't Jews finally understand that in Soviet Communism they nurtured their own nemesis, implacably hostile to the state of Israel, to Judaism as a religion, and to Jews as part of the civilized world? Some did. But many did not. Even when they stopped praising Soviet-model Communism, they continued to espouse radical leftist causes which undermined the strength of the West in its stand against Soviet expansion. Moreover, when the New Left was born in the United States during the Vietnam war, it attracted a great number of Jewish radicals of affluent background. (See the last section of this chapter.) Again, even though they were a tiny minority within the anti-war movement, they were able to subvert the pacifist aspirations of the well-meaning majority of campus demonstrators into a violent anti-American revolutionary movement.

Why indeed have so many Western intellectuals, among whom Jews no doubt play a leading role, been attracted to Communism, to revolution, and to all sorts of leftist causes? Why have they been so susceptible to what Jean-Francois Revel has aptly called the "totalitarian temptation"? As far as the Jews are concerned, the best, albeit by no means exhaustive, answer was provided by Chaim Bermant, a British rabbi. In his book, *The Jews*, he devotes to the subject a whole chapter, "Eternal Radicals." Far from disputing the fact of extraordinary Jewish radicalism, Bermant regards it as a more or less permanent trait of Jews as a group. However, like the authors of the Bickerman Collection, he points to a paradox in the Jewish attraction to radicalism: "No people is so averse to change yet none in recent times has dissipated more of its energy on revolution."[71]

When a Tsarist minister told Theodor Herzl, one of the founders of Zionism, that, although Jews formed less than 5 percent of Russia's population, they accounted for more than 50 percent of its revolutionaries, Herzl was not surprised, notes Bermant. In a country where Jews were both poor and oppressed, Herzl was sure the reason was anti-Semitism. For Bermant such an explanation is only partly valid. As he points out, "most of the leading revolutionaries who convulsed Europe in the final decades of the last century and the first decades of this one, came from prosperous Jewish families."[72] Moreover, citing the examples of the New Left in America and the May 1968 upheaval in France, Bermant points out that Jews were just as prominent in revolutionary movements in the countries where the "existing order favors Jews."[73] In addition to anti-Semitism, he reasons, there must be some other reasons for Jewish radicalism. Karl Kautsky explained it in terms of a revolt against the "reactionary" character of Judaism. Isaac Deutscher suggested that the congenital position of Jews as outsiders predisposed them to revolution since "they were born and brought up on the borderline of various epochs." Werner Sombart pointed to Jewish rootlessness and a tendency to think in abstractions. The guilt feeling on the part of prosperous Jews for their "untroubled existence within the continuing order" might be yet another reason for Jewish radicalism, says Bermant, citing the example of Karl Marx.

All the above reasons are rooted in the uniqueness of Jewish historical experience and have nothing to do with anti-Semitism. Most of them were noted by the authors of the Bickerman Collection. What is new, however, is the way Bermant explains the Jews' attraction to Marx. He quotes the following passages from Marx's article "On the Jewish Question": "What is the secular cult of the Jew? *Haggling*. What is this secular god? *Money*! Well, then! Emancipation from *haggling* and *money*, from practical, real Judaism would be the self-emancipation of our time." Marx was convinced that this "Jewish" attitude to money dominates the Western world, says Bermant. "With the Jew and without him, *money* has become a world-power, and the practical spirit of the Jew has become the practical spirit of the Christian peoples. The Jews have emancipated themselves to the extent that the Christians have become Jews," Bermant quotes Marx.

An aversion to money, he says, was no doubt a factor in the spread of Marxism among young Jewish idealists, such as Rosa

Luxemburg or Chaim Zhitlowskii, a Russian *narodnik* who was repelled by the exploitation of the Russian peasantry by Jewish "capitalists." But there was more in Marx's attack on the Jews that appealed especially to secular Jews. There was his fundamental aversion to Judaism and intolerance toward religion in general. Noting that Marx "had an imperfect grasp of Jewish history," Bermant suggests that "the venom" with which Marx approached Judaism had something to do with the way he felt about his Jewishness: "a personal stigma" to be erased at all cost.[74]

Ironically, Marx failed even in that. As Bermant suggests, while the content of Marx's thought was clearly an affront to Judaism, the latter insinuated itself into its very structure. In fact, Marxism became a sort of secular *Shulchan Aruch*, the code of Jewish law which prescribes exactly what a believer must do. Marx's system, says Bermant, "laid down iron laws, operating irrespective of human will and human effort. . . . It suggested an inevitability to the course of human history; it promised certainties. . . . It cleared the mind for action." In short, "It was a *Shulchan Aruch*, and no one embraced it more enthusiastically than young Jews who had discarded the *Shulchan Aruch* of their fathers." In any case, when the chaos of World War I erupted in revolutions, "Jews were everywhere at the helm: Trotsky, Sverdlov, Kamenev, and Zinoviev in Russia, Bela Kun in Hungary, Kurt Eisner in Bavaria, and. . . Rosa Luxemburg in Berlin."[75]

Bermant may have overestimated the importance of the structural affinity of Marx's thought with the Jewish code of daily conduct as a source of Marxism's popularity among secular Jews. Yet, his explanation is significant in that it corroborates Berdiaev's suggestion that just as the Communist International was a travesty of "Russian messianism," so Marx's theory was a travesty of Jewish messianism. It had a special appeal to those secular Jews ("de-Judaized Jews," as Bermant calls them) who, like Marx, hated their Jewishness and wanted to dissolve it in a vision of a nationless world. As to the Jewish attraction to radicalism in general, Bermant speculates that "perhaps there is something in the Jewish character, or at least in the character of many Jews, which disposes them to upheaval for its own sake: perhaps they have lived so long amidst chaos that they find something unsettling in stability."[76]

John Cuddihy on the Jewish Ordeal of Civility

The importance, indeed the centrality, of the "Jewish question" for Marx and Marxism is examined in John Murray Cuddihy's book, *The Ordeal of Civility: Freud, Marx, Levy-Strauss, and the Jewish Struggle with Modernity.*[77] Contrary to the common view of Jews as a Western or at least Westernized people, a view which both Sarnov and Kozhinov seem to share, Cuddihy treats them chiefly as a case of "delayed modernization." In fact, the process of Jewish emancipation (modernization, assimilation, and Westernization) did not begin en masse until the nineteenth century, nearly a hundred years after Russia started a similar process under Peter the Great. Cuddihy shows that that process, involving a conflict between the medieval Judaism-centered culture of the ghettos and *stetlach* of Central and Eastern Europe, on the one hand, and the secular culture of the West, on the other, was neither easy nor complete.

"Unable to turn back, unable to completely acculturate, caught between 'his own' whom he had left behind and the Gentile 'host culture' where he felt ill at ease and alienated, intellectual Jews and Jewish intellectuals experienced cultural shame and awkwardness, guilt and the 'guilt of shame.'"[78] Cuddihy suggests that Marx's socialist ideology, although "universalist in its rhetoric and appeal," was fundamentally an attempt to solve the Jewish question, "which, for German Jewry generally, has always turned on the matter of the public misbehavior of the Jews of Eastern Europe (the proverbial 'Ostjuden')."[79] The latter include, of course, Russian Jews.

Although Cuddihy may have exaggerated the importance of etiquette in "the Jewish struggle with modernity," his study, like that of Bermant, helps to explain why Marxism exerted a strong appeal especially for Russian Jews. It may also explain why it exerted (certainly before 1917) a considerable appeal to the Russians. As Cuddihy admits, his study is "judocentric" only in methodology because what he says about the Jews might well apply to other cases of "delayed modernization," and Russia's was one of them. In a chapter comparing Jews and Irish (he is Irish-American) as "latecomers to modernity," Cuddihy quotes historian R. R. Palmer. Whereas the French Revolution "grew directly out of earlier French history," and the French were neither troubled "by any feeling of backwardness" nor strained "to keep up in a march of progress," says Palmer, the revolutions in Russia and China were "precipitated by contacts with an outside or foreign civilization, and by the stresses, maladjustments, feelings of backwardness and other ambivalences ensuing thereupon."[80]

In my opinion, this distinction is certainly valid for Russia. Although originally a European nation, the Russians had been isolated from European progress since the Mongol conquest in the thirteenth century. Even after freeing themselves from the Mongol yoke in the fifteenth century, they were unable to rejoin Europe because access to it was blocked by hostile powers. Only after Peter the Great forced his way into Europe were the Russians able to partake of European progress. But then their westernized elite, the noblemen, discovered that they were not quite as European as they thought they were. Nor were they accepted as such. They came to feel acutely the stigma of a "barbarian" and "Asiatic" people, possessed of a "strange" antiquated religion. They were ashamed of their lack of civility, and even more so of the "backwardness" of the Russian people: the peasants, craftsmen, and clergymen whom westernization had barely touched.

In their struggle with modernity, the Russian westernized elite, like the Jews, went through an ordeal of civility. They too felt shame and the guilt of shame for themselves and their countrymen. They were caught in a dilemma. On the one hand, they wished they could force westernization on the Russian masses as Tsar Peter forced it on them. On the other hand, they knew that such reforms might lead to the loss of their privileged status. In fact, the cost of their westernization was chiefly borne by those who were not westernized. Thus, a schism developed between the progressive, secular, westernized, and parasitic Russian elite, and the "barbaric," "Asiatic," religious and hard-working Russian people. The educated Russian elite was becoming increasingly alienated from the Russian people.

The savagery of the French revolution, especially its anti-religious drive and Jacobin terror, was the first reminder that the veneer of European civilization was rather thin. The second shock came with Napoleon. After the defeat of Napoleon, in which the "backward" Russian peasant-soldiers played a major role, some Russian noblemen concluded that not all European ideas were worthy of emulation. Some were as much a threat to Russia as to Europe. They concluded that the best way to protect Russia was by cultivating its own indigenous traditions, including Orthodox Christianity. These men came to be known as the Slavophiles.

The other Russian noblemen did not feel that Napoleon invalidated the essentially "progressive" character of the French Revolution. They came to be called the Westernizers. United in their rejection of Russian tradition, the Westernizers were, however, divided as to which way of modernizing Russia was better, the way of violent revolution and socialism or the way of peaceful evolution through reforms. The first were the radical Westernizers. The latter were the liberal Westernizers. Although the liberals prevailed for a while when Alexander II's reforms were enacted, the radical Westernizers among the Russian intelligentsia (which by then had succeeded the nobility as the country's intellectual elite) felt that the way of reform was too slow and ineffective. They were convinced that modernization could be achieved only by the revolution of Russian people (*narod*) against the oppressive Tsarist regime. After these *narodniki* failed to sell the idea of revolution to the peasants, their alienation from the Russian people became apparent. Some of them changed to the tactics of individual terror "on behalf of the people." Others, encouraged by the growth of Russian capitalism in the wake of Alexander II's reforms, found solace in Marxism.

Marxism was especially appealing to the radical Russian Westernizers because it seemed to integrate the "best" of Europe: the profundity of German philosophy; the practical experience of the British labor movement; and the tactics of French revolutions (from 1789 through the Paris Commune in 1871), which seemed to "improve" by becoming more radical, more socialist, and more violent. Above all, Marxism wrapped it all in a fool-proof package of "science." Young Russian Jews, for whom westernization often meant emancipation from the "shackles" of Judaism and assimilation with the "progressive" Russian culture, were among the early Marxist followers. Since they were often perceived by the Russians as more European than they actually were,[81] these Jews, in spite of being novices to modernity themselves, became the chief conduit of Marxism for the less urbane Russians. As a result, the blind were leading the blind.

After the assassination of Alexander II in 1881, the idea of violent change, whether through individual terror or a Marxist revolution, was widely accepted by the Russian intelligentsia. The bloody revolution of 1905-1906 followed. Although Prime Minister Petr Stolypin, after heading off the revolutionary terrorism, managed for a while to steer Russia back to the path of reforms, he got little support from either the bureaucratic conservatives or from the liberals in the Duma. After his assassination in 1911, by a Jew, the reforms were stalled and, contrary to his advice, the government allowed Russia to be drawn into World War One. The strain of war ultimately led to the February revolution, which paved the way for the Marxist experiment.

Marxism gave its followers that "feeling of the supremacy of the general over the particular experience, of law over fact, of theory over personal experience." This, Trotskii admitted, was the decisive factor in his becoming a Marxist. That feeling evinced, in fact, Trotskii's and other deracinated Russian Jews' alienation from reality, including the reality of their Jewishness. Trotskii's Russian comrades fully shared that feeling, except in their case it was alienation from the Russian people. It was the combination of the youthful arrogance of these two alienated groups that determined the direction which the Russian revolution took in October 1917. Both the Russian and Jewish Bolsheviks were alienated from the reality of Russia's history, but not because they had lived abroad for too long, as Kozhinov suggested. Rather, their ideology itself was a flight from the reality of historical experience. They became "aliens" in Russia by virtue of emigrating into the land of Marxist-Leninist utopia.

As latecomers to modernity, both the Russians and the Russian Jews were beset with all sorts of problems. One was the problem of identity. The Russians passionately desired to be Europeans. Yet they were seldom perceived as such by the bona fide Europeans. For assimilation-bound Jews wanted to be like Russians, albeit not like the actual Russians around them, but rather like the ideal "Europeanized" Russians of the future. Ashamed of their "barbaric" traditions, of their "odd" religion, of their illiterate people, of their despotic rulers, the intellectual Russians adored European rationality so much that they refused to admit that the "rational" premises of the French revolutionaries did not prevent them from the most bizarre irrational behavior.

To expand on Cuddihy's ideas, the psychological problems of the Russian Jews were further compounded by a number of complexes. Like the Russians, they suffered a complex of inferiority toward

Europe, that is, the Romano-Germanic Europe of France, Germany, England and North America. They were especially ashamed of their ancient and "reactionary" religion, just as the Russians were ashamed of theirs. They were also ashamed of their "barbaric" host country, Russia. They even felt an inferiority complex toward West European Jewry, especially the German Jews, who seemed superior in that they had succeeded best in both emancipation and assimilation. Marx, as a German Jew, must have seemed to them like a new Messiah who offered the final solution to the Jewish problem by formulating a fool-proof law of world revolution, the secular *Shulchan Aruch*, after which the whole globe would turn into a promised land.

What neither the Russians nor the Russian Jews realized was that, far from being scientific, Marx's theory was a sublimation of his desire to erase the stigma of his Jewishness by "emigrating" from the reality of facts to the utopia of fantasy. Marx needed the revolution as a steamboat for his own "emigration." They needed Marx as an opiate. Like Marx, they chose "law" over fact and a universalist theory over both personal and national experience. They particularly ignored the fact that, far from becoming a highway of universal progress, a Marxist proletarian revolution failed to materialize where and when it should have. As is often the case with people afflicted with an inferiority complex, they were soon stricken with an equally devastating superiority complex. If at first they merely wanted to catch up with the West by latching onto the bandwagon of an all-European Marxist revolution, now they wanted to become more European than the Europeans and more Marxist than Marx. Hence their opting for the Bolshevik coup d'etat in violation of Marx's law. Hence the tragedy of the Soviet Holocaust, which was as inevitable as the offering of a sacrifice to the demanding idol of revolution once its worship was established as a state religion. Hence the need for perestroika, that is, restructuring what had been built on the shifting sands of utopian theory. So much for modernization.

As to the goal of westernization, "they are like a crow that succeeded in leaving its flock, but failed to join the flock of peacocks." This Russian proverb aptly describes the USSR today. It equally applies to both the Jews and the Russians who wanted to become Europeans but only managed to lose their national identity. And so does the Russian fairy tale about a fisherman who, always fishing for a gold fish, got none. According to another Russian saying, the slower one moves, the farther one reaches. The revolution seemed like a shortcut but turned out to be a historical detour. The English proverb, "haste makes waste," warned of the same. Alexander Pope said that "fools rush in where angels fear to tread." Based on different national experiences, these sayings speak common sense. But it was common sense that Communists consistently ignored. They also ignored the New Testament parable of the Gadarene swine that Dostoevskii took trouble to elaborate upon in his novel *The Possessed.* Nor did they deign to look into the Talmud. Had they done so, they would have found what Rabbi Bermant has found for them: *Tofasto merubo lo tofasto.* He who seeks too much finds nothing.

What needs to be done? Both the Russians and the Jews have to realize, first of all, that "any theory is dead, and only the tree of life is green forever" (Goethe). A nation is not a thing that can be turned up and down and around at will. It is more like a tree. One can influence its development by pruning its dead branches and trimming its excessive foliage, but one cannot make it grow by cutting its roots. Like a tree, each nation needs to be cultivated. With unwavering love and steady care, each nation will in due course bloom and bring forth its fruit. But the roots of its national traditions should never be disturbed. Both the Jews and the Russians should not regard their ancient traditions as a stigma. Rather, they should regard them as an inheritance which may contain assets as well as liabilities.

I am not suggesting that Soviet Jews and Russians should abandon their quest for modernization or westernization and instead return to their respective Jewish or Christian orthodoxies. But they must stop being self-hating Jews and self-hating Russians. Only when they stop hating themselves can they begin to truly love other nationalities and mankind. They must stop regarding religion as an obstacle to modernization. On the contrary, they should consider how religion could best be adapted to modernization, providing it with a spiritual "ecological" balance.

Peter Collier and David Horowitz:
The Destructive Generation

Even while Sarnov and Kozhinov debated each other in the USSR, a book was published in America which has clearly demonstrated that the Communist experiment in Russia cannot be understood without taking into account that many influential Americans have been heavily engaged in what one of them called a "romance" with Communism.[82]   This is a 1989 book, *Destructive Generation: Second Thoughts About the Sixties*, written by two former leaders of the New Left, Peter Collier and David Horowitz.[83] The two authors, who during the Vietnam war era were editors of *Ramparts* magazine, the leading voice of the New Left, tell about their disillusionment with the revolutionary Marxist ideas which used to guide their lives.[84]   Three prominent themes are interwoven in the book.   One is the theme of totalitarian mentality of even the most intellectual, predominantly Jewish, leaders of the New Left.   Another is the theme of their kinship with Stalinism.   The third is the theme of the New Left's continuing influence, often disguised, on the American intellectual establishment.

Collier and Horowitz describe in detail the activities of Weatherman, a terrorist organization which was eventually taken over by hard-core Communists.   They tell about the intellectual pundits of the New Left who were, in their opinion, either Stalinists or apologists of Left Totalitarianism.   Belying the "pacifist" image of the American anti-war movement, they now admit that they were interested not in peace in Vietnam, but in the defeat of America.   According to Collier and Horowitz, their former comrades have deliberately obfuscated the record of atrocities committed in the name of Marxism.   As a result, "one of the large ironies of modern history" remains unrecognized: "Even though Marxist socialism is a doctrine that has exploited, impoverished and murdered more people than any other creed in our time, the Communist (and neo-Communist) Left remains part of respectable society in a way. . . that the heirs of Nazism never could be."[85]   Collier and Horowitz are certainly in a position to know what neither Sarnov nor Kozhinov (nor any other Soviet citizen) can even imagine: the extent to which the "respectable societies" of the West have been aiding and abetting the perpetrators of Communist atrocities.

They make no bones about the fact that the leaders of the radical Left were predominantly of Jewish origin. Such Weatherman leaders as Bernardine Dohrn, Mark Rudd, John Jacobs and Eleanor Stein were all Jewish. So was their ideological mentor Annie Stein (Eleanor's mother), "an unreconstructed Stalinist." Also Jewish were such other prominent New Leftists as Jerry Rubin, Abbie Hoffman (the late author of *Revolution for the Hell of It*), Saul Landau and Cora Weiss. Noam Chomsky, "the intellectual godfather of the post-Vietnam Left," is also Jewish. And so were the numerous lawyers, from Fay Stender (to whom they devote a whole chapter) to William Kunstler, who were defending, and covering up for, various terrorist acts committed by the Black Panthers and Weatherman.

What is important, however, is not the Jewishness of the New Left per se, but the fact that it was usually only nominal. They were usually deracinated Jews alienated from both Judaism and Jewish traditions. Occasionally, like Marx, they were self-hating and Jew-baiting Jews. Also like Marx, they belonged to the upper middle class. As such they were neither oppressed nor discriminated against. Like Marx, they joined the revolutionary cause precisely because they wanted to emigrate from their Jewishness to the land of utopia. The oddity of a Jewish revolutionary in a country where the established order actually "favors Jews," as Rabbi Bermant put it, is extensively dealt with in the autobiographical chapter of the book, written by David Horowitz, himself a Jew. Horowitz gives a frank account of his Jewish Communist family background:

> For nearly fifty years our parents' little colony of 'progressives' had lived in the same ten-block neighborhood of Sunnyside in Queens [New York city]. And for fifty years their political faith had set them apart from everyone else. They inhabited Sunnyside like a race of aliens--in the community but never of it--in cultural and psychological exile. They lived in a state of permanent hostility not only to the Sunnyside community but to every other community that touched them, including America itself.[86]

REVOLUTION AND RUSSIA   219

What Horowitz describes is, of course, the same phenomenon of purposeful alienation from reality which we have previously observed in regard to the Russian Jews.

But why did American Jews choose to live in their self-imposed ghetto? Because "the only community to which they belonged was one that existed in their minds: the international community of the progressive Idea." As to the actual meaning of their "progressivism," Horowitz explains: "All the activities of the Sunnyside progressives--the political meetings they attended five and six nights a week, the organizations they formed, the causes they promoted--were solely to serve their revolutionary Idea." But what was wrong with advocating a revolution for a better future for the whole mankind? "My father lived the sinister irony that lies at the heart of our common [Communist] heritage: The very humanity that is the alleged object of its 'compassion' is a humanity it holds in contempt." Their contempt was directed, first of all, at the religious Jews, "whose community center [my father] would never be part of and whose synagogue he would never enter." "To my father, the traditions his fellow Jews still cherished as the ark of their survival were but a final episode in the woeful history of human bondage, age-old chains of ignorance and oppression from which they would soon be set free."[87]

Horowitz describes his father as typical of a whole generation of American Communists who, after Khrushchev's anti-Stalin speech, may have left the Party and yet remained Stalinists at heart, not because they were evil or malicious people, but because their relation to the "progressive Idea" was pathologically obsessive. "Our parents," writes Horowitz in a letter to his former friend who denounced him for abandoning the cause, "were idolators in the church of a mass murderer named Stalin. They were not moralists but Marxist-Leninists. For them, the revolution *was* morality (and beauty and truth as well). For them, compassion outside the Revolution was mere *bourgeois* sentimentality." It was exactly the same idolatry of revolution to which the authors of the Bickerman Collection found secular Jews so susceptible. And it was this idolatry of revolution, this obsession with the "progressive Idea," which was chiefly responsible for the mind-boggling enormity of the Soviet Holocaust of which Jews were both victims and perpetrators.

Horowitz shows that it was from fathers like his that the New Left ideologically descended. Although it flaunted its rejection of Stalin and Soviet-model socialism, the New Left remained fundamentally totalitarian. "What motivates the Left is the totalitarian Idea: the Idea that is more important than reality itself... *Everything human is alien. . . .* This is the consciousness that makes mass murderers of well-intentioned humanists and earnest progressives,"[88] says Horowitz of the kind of mentality of which he himself used to be a prisoner. Remarkably, he describes it in much the same terms as Kozhinov did when he denounced the "aliens" and "emigres" among the Bolsheviks, one of whom, Trotskii, actually admitted his preference for "law over fact, of theory over personal experience." However, like myself, Horowitz stresses the alien and alienating character of the idea itself, regardless of what shape it assumes: Marxist, Leninist, Trotskyite, "Russian," or "Jewish."

Defining the essence of the "progressive Idea" as purely totalitarian, Horowitz suggests that there is something perverse and even satanic in the way its adherents embrace it.

> Totalitarianism is the possession of reality by a political Idea--the Idea of the socialist kingdom of heaven on earth, the redemption of humanity by political force. To radical believers, this Idea is so beautiful it is like God Himself. It provides the meaning of a radical life. It is the solution that makes everything possible; it is the end that justifies every regrettable means. Belief in the kingdom of socialist heaven is the faith that transforms vice into virtue, lies into truth, evil into good. For the revolutionary religion, the Way, the Truth, and the Life of Salvation lie not with God above but with men below-- ruthless, brutal, venal men--on whom the faith confers the power of gods.[89]

Isn't this what Berdiaev meant when he talked about the Communist travesty of "Russian messianism"? Or what Fritz Kahn has praised as the modern manifestation of "Jewish messianism"? Or what Bermant described as a secular *Shulchan Aruch*?

As to the cost of the "progressive Idea," "since 1917, perhaps one hundred million people had been killed by socialist revolutionaries in power; the socialisms they created had all resulted in new forms of despotism and social oppression, and an imperialism even more ruthless than those of the past." Nonetheless, admits Horowitz, "the weight of this evidence had failed to convince us. We were able to hold on to our faith by rejecting this experience as a valid test."[90]   In Vietnam alone "more people had been killed in the first two years of the Communist peace than in the thirteen years of America's war,"[91] says Horowitz. The New Left thus cannot escape its share of responsibility for the Communist genocide in the wake of the American defeat in Vietnam.

Horowitz makes it clear that there is no reason for the West to feel smug about the fact that Communism has spared it, spreading instead to the allegedly "backward," "barbaric," and "used-to-despotism" countries, like Russia and China. He seems to challenge the school of thought according to which Stalin was as "natural" for Russia as Ivan the Terrible.

> The Red Terror is the terror that 'idealist Communists' (like our parents) and 'anti-Stalinist' Leftists (like ourselves) have helped to spread around the world. You and I and our parents were totalitarians in democratic America. The democratic fact of America prevented us from committing the atrocities willed by our faith. Impotence was our only innocence. In struggles all over the world, we pledged our faith and gave our support to the perpetrators of the totalitarian deed.[92]

Horowitz does not limit his critique to the New Left past. According to him, the American liberal establishment has allowed itself to be so thoroughly infiltrated by New Left ideas that it too bears responsibility for the spread of Left Totalitarianism in the world. After a brief period of dormancy, argues Horowitz, the New Left has now reappeared in a new guise. If during the Sixties it flaunted its extremism and indulged in liberal-bashing, in the Eighties it has switched to the tactic of "popular front" moderation. This tactic allows it to infiltrate "the Democratic Party, churches, universities, and various liberal institutions."[93] In accordance with this tactic, Horowitz's former comrades deny that Gorbachev's reforms were necessitated by the need to move toward "the more humane standard and more productive institutions of the capitalist West." Instead, they portray these reforms "as indication that anti-Communism is mere ideological prejudice and western defense concerns were military paranoia."[94]

In the concluding chapter of their book, Collier and Horowitz recount a 1987 meeting of former leftists who, like themselves, turned to "second thoughts." The "rediscovery of patriotism was perhaps the most common ground of all [the participants]."[95] Recalling how they "had abused America" and its armed forces, the Second Thoughters admitted that the New Left had inflicted "tremendous damage (much of it still unrepaired) to America's values and institutions." A one-time radical student at Yale admitted that "it was a growing sense of his identity as a Jew" that helped him realize that his radical activities not only undermined America but jeopardized the very survival of Israel, which "might well have been defeated during the Yom Kippur War if not for the backing of U. S. arms."[96] He probably would have agreed with Rabbi Bermant's earlier assessment of Jewish leftists when he compared them to "Bourbons, who have forgotten nothing and learned nothing, and who, by struggling for the unattainable, threaten all that has been attained."[97]

This point underscores the irony of the fact that so many leftist leaders were of Jewish extraction. This irony did not escape the authors. Pointing out that it is the leftists who like to portray the lobbying activities of American Zionists on behalf of Israel as a fifth column, Collier and Horowitz argued that "The [real] fifth column that threatens this country. . . is not Jews who support America's Israeli ally but a Left that works on behalf of America's totalitarian enemies and whose influence grows unimpeded." Explain the authors:

> Unlike American Zionists, the openness of whose support of Israel allows others to judge their motives, American leftists are steeped in a tradition of conspiracy and deceit whose instruments are secretive 'vanguards' and 'popular fronts,' through which basic commitments are regularly concealed, and important agendas are always covert at the same time that charges of 'red-baiting' and 'McCarthyism' are being invoked to shield the underlying allegiances from the scrutiny they deserve.[98]

This observation takes us back to the Kozhinov-Sarnov debate. It is clear that this debate did not encompass the larger question of "who is responsible" for the spread of totalitarianism in the world. It is also clear that not only is the totalitarian idea itself of Western origin, but the Western intellectuals have been as susceptible to its virus as the intellectuals of any developing country. If the latter have fallen victim to this disease more freqently and with more devastating results than their Western colleagues, this was not due to their "backwardness." Having borrowed from Marx the idea that religion was the chief obstacle for modernization, they not only alienated themselves from their national grass-roots but "emancipated" themselves from all ethical constraints in imposing the "progressive [Western] Idea" on their nations.

Without taking into account this larger ambience, Kozhinov's and Sarnov's search for truth can hardly proceed. Both appear to be deadlocked in the unenviable position of having to blame a *world* problem chiefly on the two nationalities they identify with, the Russians and the (Russian) Jews. They can blame it on the Russian "judophobes" and Jewish "russophobes," Russian Tsars and the "Zionist-Masonic conspiracy," even on Russian and Jewish messianisms. But they cannot, dare not, challenge the "progressive Idea" itself. To be sure, the Russians and Russian Jews, have played a key role in the initial spread of Left Totalitarianism throughout the world. They are responsible for failing to rein in their violent fringe, the Russian and Jewish Bolsheviks, before disaster struck.

But then, where is the nation which has prevented leftist totalitarians from doing their destructive job at home and abroad? As Collier and Horowitz have shown, it is certainly not the United States. And where is the internationale of good people, about which the old Jew Gedali was dreaming? Had not Isaak Babel, the author of the story about Gedali, dismissed the old man as "antiquated," he may not have become a victim of the Soviet Holocaust. There are of course plenty of good people in the United States and elsewhere. But, as Edmund Burke has written, "The only thing necessary for the triumph of evil is for good men to do nothing."

Notes

1. Evgenii Losev, <u>Moskva</u>, No. 2, 1989.

2. Mironov's letter was published in <u>Don</u>, No. 12, 1988.

3. The final verdict has to be withheld until a new seventy-volume edition of Lenin's work is published to replace the currently available fifty-five-volume Complete Works,

even though the editors warn that it might be not quite "complete" either. See interview with Giorgii L. Smirnov, head of the Institute of Marxism-Leninism, Nashe nasledie, No. 5, 1988.

4. The authenticity of that utterance was later disputed on the ground that it was recorded by Bazhanov, a former Lenin secretary and defector who had heard it from other secretaries. See an article by Vladlen Loginov, Moscow News, No. 14, 1989.

5. Vasilii Grossman, Life and Fate (Regnery Gateway, 1988).

6. According to Roy Medvedev, there were forty million victims of Stalinism. Other Soviet sources indicate that at least ten million people perished before Stalin took power. See Chapter 3 on the Soviet Holocaust.

7. Actually, Lenin's Russianness is doubtful, because, besides Russians, he had Germans, Kalmyks, Swedes and Jews among his ancestors. See Adam Ulam, The Bolsheviks and Uno Willers, Lenin i Stockholm.

8. Both debaters relied heavily on quotations. I am not in the position to judge their authenticity, but it appears that both debaters were guilty of "misquoting." Thus, Kozhinov quoted Gusev (Iakov Davidovich Drabkin, a Jew) as saying that "it is a duty of every Communist to inform [on one another]," without saying that Gusev was approvingly paraphrasing Lenin. Sarnov, on the other hand, while indicating Lenin as a source for Gusev, concealed the fact that, to Lenin's "every good Communist must be a good Chekist," Gusev added the specific duty of informing. Kozhinov makes Sverdlov and Trotskii personally responsible for the policy of de-Cossackization and the murder of Mironov, while Sarnov argues that both decisions were made by collective bodies. N. A. Vasetskii, a Soviet historian, portrays Trotskii as the evil genius behind both decisions (Komsomol'skaia pravda, May 19, 1989). In my assessment of the two debaters I relied on the consistency, cogency, and tenor of their arguments rather than on the accuracy of their facts.

9. It was certainly a step forward compared with the bitter exchange of personal letters between two prominent Soviet intellectuals, the late Nathan Eidel'man and the village writer Viktor Astaf'ev, published in the emigre magazine Strana i mir, No. 12, 1986.

10. I do not know for sure, but both sound like Party members.

11. On the whole, Sarnov appears to be more in the right in regard to Lenin, certainly the way he was portrayed in Soviet propaganda throughout the major part of Soviet history. On the other hand, as the announcement of the publication of a new and considerably larger edition of Lenin's Complete Works suggests, there must have been some writings and utterings he made which his successors did not want to include in the currently available Complete (?!) Works which might lend greater support to Kozhinov's view. See note 3.

12. Only after millions of Soviet lives were lost at the start of the war with Hitler did the Stalin government realize that, contrary to Marx, the German "proletarians" were not about to be united with the Russians and that the Russians themselves fight better when they fight for their fatherland than for any "international" creed. Other millions were lost in consequence of the pre-war purge, in which more Soviet generals were killed than during the entire war with Hitler.

13. According to the 1897 census, out of the total of 5.185 million Jews of the Russian Empire, 31 percent were in trade and commerce, while about another third were artisans and craftsmen. (Quoted from Lionel Kochan, ed., The Jews in Soviet Russia Since 1917, Oxford University Press, 1978, p. 21). According to Sbornik materialov ob ekonomicheskom polozhenii evreiskogo naseleniia v Rossii, vol. 1, St. Petersburg, 1904, p. 201 (quoted in the same work), fewer than 3 percent of the total Jewish population were hired workmen. Among the Russians, the overwhelming majority of whom were peasants, the share of people in trade and commerce was less than 1.5 percent at the time of the census, and the situation did not change drastically on the eve of the Bolshevik Revolution.

14. See, for example, S. Ettinger, "The Jews in Russia at the Outbreak of the Revolution," in the collection The Jews in Soviet Russia since 1917, ed. Lionel Kochan (London: Oxford University Press, 1978). Ettinger says, for instance, that all Jewish radicals "constituted only a minority of the total Jewish public," among whom the Zionists enjoyed much greater support. "The Communist revolution put an end to the social, cultural, and national hopes of the Russian Jews," concludes Ettinger (p. 28). Zvi Gitelman, in A Century of Ambivalence: The Jews of Russia and the Soviet Union, 1881 to the Present (New York: Schocken, 1988) writes that before the October revolution the Bolsheviks attracted far fewer Jews than either the Mensheviks or the socialist Bund. But even the latter's 34,000 members were outnumbered by the 300,000 Zionists (pp. 90-91, 94).

15. I. M. Bickerman, G. A. Landau, I. O. Levin, D. O. Linskii, V. S. Mandel', D. S. Pasmanik, Rossiia i evrei, First Edition, a reprint (YMCA Press, Paris, 1978).

16. Bickerman, et al., p. 5.

17. Ibid., p. 6.

18. Ibid., p. 8.

19. Ibid., p. 21.

20. Ibid., p. 15.

21. Ibid., pp. 26-27.

22. Ibid., p. 32.

23. Ibid., pp. 31-32.

24. Ibid., p. 70.

25. Ibid., p. 61. Western scholarship tends to gloss over the issue of post-revolutionary pogroms. Encyclopaedia Britannica's entry, for instance, does not mention them at all, thus re-inforcing the tendency to associate them exclusively with Tsarist Russia. Moreover, research on post-revolutionary pogroms tended to focus on those by the White Army and the Ukrainian separatists. Virtually no inquiries were made into pogroms under the Provisional Government and those perpetrated by the Reds and their leftist allies thereafter. For titles, see note 14.

26. Bickerman et al., p. 53.

27. Ibid., p. 59.

28. Ibid., p. 85.

29. Ibid., p. 33.

30. Ibid., p. 93

31. Ibid., p. 83.

32. Ibid., p. 55.

33. Ibid., p. 56.

34. Ibid., p. 101.

35. Ibid., p. 107.

36. Ibid., p. 117.

37. Ibid., p. 116.

38. Ibid., p. 119.

39. Ibid., p. 138.

40. Ibid., p. 145.

41. Ibid., p. 146.

42. Ibid., p. 173.

43. Ibid., p. 199.

44. Ibid., p. 193.

45. Ibid., p. 209. Gitelman quotes a similar "anecdote" in Yiddish, according to which the initials of the first Soviet government, the VTsIK, were spelled out as meaning "vu tsen idn komandeven" (where ten Jews give the orders). See note 14, Century, p.96.

46. Ibid., p. 226.

47. Donald J. Raleigh, ed., A Russian Civil War Diary: Alexis Babine in Saratov, 1917-1922 (Durham and London: Duke University Press, 1988).

48. Ibid., p. 23.

49. Ibid., p. 28. In quotes the original spelling is retained.

50. Ibid., p. 31.

51. Ibid., p. 112.

52. Ibid., p. 47.

53. Ibid., p. 63.

54. It is very unfortunate indeed that the editor, Professor Raleigh, has prefaced the diary by stating that "Babine was anti-Semitic"(xvi). This is contradicted by the diary itself. For example, Babine describes with sympathy and even affection "my Jewish friend," Mr. Maizul, a shopkeeper, and his sister-in-law, "a sweet, modest girl of sixteen or seventeen." When Maizul risked selling him some extra food in defiance of Soviet authorities, Babine was moved to comment: "Had I met Mr. Maizul on my way home, I am sure I would have hugged him"(p. 126). Tracking down the Maizuls' story to their emigration to Poland in November 1921, Babine notes with compassion that their valuables were "confiscated at the border." Babine describes warmly the local Jewish "bourgeois" Imenitov and Mittelman, with whom he used to play cards. He pities the latter for being shot at and "compelled to pay an 'indemnity' of five thousand roubles to our conquerors"(78). He writes approvingly of Mr. Levikov, "a youngish Hebrew" watchmaker, who was wounded while emptying his Browning at the robbers. There is no evidence in the diary that Babine condemns Jews as a group. The unsubstantiated charge of anti-Semitism is therefore injurious to the honor of a man who, the editor would agree, rendered great service to humanity by recording the suffering of all peoples of Russia, including especially Jews, at considerable risk to his liberty and life.

55. Ibid., pp. 72-73.

56. Ibid., p.38.

57. Ibid., p. 79.

58. Ibid., p. 83.

59. Ibid., p. 23.

60. Ibid., p. 125-126.

61. Ibid., p. 134.

62. Ibid., p. 128.

63. Ibid., p. 148.

64. Ibid., p. 184.

65. See Oliver Radkey, The Unknown Civil War in South Russia: A Study of the Green Movement in the Tambov Region, 1920-21 (Stanford, 1976).

66. Raleigh, ed., p. 179.

67. Ibid., p. 183.

68. Ibid., p. 226.

69. See Il'ia Trotskii's article in Kniga o russkom evreistve (1917-1967) [Book about Russian Jewry], Ya. G. Frumkin et al., Eds. (New York, 1968), p. 400.

70. See, e. g., Istvan Deak exchange with Geza Jeszenszky and Maria Kovacs in The New York Review of Books, November 24, 1988. Deak maintains that "the great majority of the top Stalinist leadership were Jews: the Politburo members, the police generals, the cultural dictators, a group numbering a few hundred altogether." "The Jewishness of this small group still immensely complicates Gentile-Jewish relations in Hungary," says Deak, while admitting that "the majority of Jews had nothing to do with Stalinists, and many were victims." About Poland, see Julia Brun-Zejmis, "Polish Communists Speak," Slavic Review, Vol. 47, No. 2, Summer 1988, pp. 307-313. In this review article of a book of interviews with the former leaders of Communist Poland, many of whom were Jewish (Jakub Berman, Roman Werfel, Edward Ochab, e.g.), Brun-Zejmis raises the question of "the overwhelming Jewish presence" in the Polish Communist party.

71. Chaim Bermant, The Jews (New York: Times Books, 1977), p. 160.

72. Ibid., p. 160.

73. The prominence of Jewish radicals has attracted the attention of a number of scholars. See, for example, Robert Wistrich, Revolutionary Jews from Marx to Trotsky (London: George Harrap, 1976); Arthur Liebman, Jews and the Left (New

York: John Wiley and Sons, 1979); Stanley Rothman and S. Robert Lichter, <u>Roots of Radicalism: Jews, Christians, and the New Left</u> (New York: Oxford University Press, 1982).

74. Marx's attitude toward Christianity, his adopted religion, was just as shallow and hostile. He certainly failed to see the importance of religion as a factor of economic development. Max Weber, in his <u>The Protestant Ethic and the Spirit of Capitalism</u> (New York: Scribner's, 1958), makes a good case for the importance of the study of religion for economists.

75. Bermant, p. 162.

76. <u>Ibid.</u>, p. 178.

77. John Murray Cuddihy, <u>The Ordeal of Civility: Freud, Marx, Levy-Strauss, and the Jewish Struggle with Modernity</u> (New York: Basic Books, 1974).

78. <u>Ibid.</u>, p. 4.

79. <u>Ibid.</u>, p. 5.

80. <u>Ibid.</u>, p. 168.

81. For Russians, Jewish names of German derivation sound like the epitome of Westernism. Moreover, the Russians were impressed that Jews had the experience of living in virtually all European countries. This created a deceptive aura of cosmopolitanism about them in the eyes of the much less peripatetic Russians.

82. The phrase is taken from the title of Vivian Gornick's book, <u>The Romance of American Communism</u> (Basic Books, 1977). The author, a Communist sympathizer, tried to rehabilitate American Communists by arguing that "they were like everybody else, only more so (p. 21)."

83. Peter Collier and David Horowitz, <u>Destructive Generation: Second Thoughts About the '60s</u> (New York: Summit Books, 1989).

84. Their early precursor was Phillip Abbot Luce. In his book, <u>The New Left Today: America's Trojan Horse</u> (Washington, D.C.: Capital Press, 1972), Luce disputed "the purported newness of the New Left" and described his former comrades as totalitarians guilty of "all the evils usually associated with the Old Left, i.e. the Communist Party and/or the Trotskyites (p. xi)."

85. Collier and Horowitz, p. 226.

86. <u>Ibid.</u>, p. 283.

87. <u>Ibid.</u>, p. 284.

88. Ibid., p. 288.

89. Ibid., p. 287.

90. Ibid., p. 299.

91. Ibid., p. 148.

92. Ibid., p. 289.

93. Ibid., p. 218. Horowitz's observation on the spread of Marxist ideas in the academic establishment seems to be borne out by other observers. Even when in 1985 Gorbachev was beginning to look for a way out of the Communist impasse, Theodore Draper noticed a revival of Communist thought in America, so that the study of history of American communism "has become a minor academic industry." A long-time student of Communism himself, Draper wrote in 1985 a series of articles in which he reviewed some of the questionable products of these "new historians." (See "American Communism Revisited," "The Popular Front Revisited," "Revisiting American Communism: An Exchange," The New York Review of Books, May 9, May 30, and August 13, 1985.) While he confined his observations only to the study of American Communism, he noted that "Self-styled Marxist academics are now active in virtually every discipline, especially in the social sciences." Estimating their membership at 12,000, "the largest and most important cohort of left-wing scholars in American history," Draper attributed it to an influx of former New Left agitators into the haven of tenured positions at universities. (In his estimate he relied on Ellen Schrecker's article in Humanities in Society, Spring/Summer 1983, p. 136.) Whereas the New Left of the 1960s was contemptuous of the Communist Party, Draper observed, in the 1980s "these post-New Leftists have turned back to the Communist past in their search for new faith and visions."

"The growing number of Marxists" in the West was noted by another observer, Andrzej Walicki, himself a refugee from Poland. In 1985 he wondered "whether the wide-spread phenomenon of so-called Western Marxism (as opposed to both classical and Soviet Marxism) can be sufficiently explained by the intrinsic appeal of its lofty ideas and universalist aspiration" or simply due to the refusal of Western intellectuals to recognize the totalitarian structure of Marx's thought. ("Low Marx," The New York Review of Books, April 25, 1985.) Finally, Horowitz's thesis that the '60s generation has carried its destructive work into the present is borne out by two books published in 1990, Roger Kimball's Tenured Radicals: How Politics Has Corrupted Our Higher Education and Charles J. Sykes' The Hollow Men. Kimball complains, for instance, that "Instead of attempting to destroy our educational institutions physically, [the now tenured flower children of the '60s] are subverting them from within."

94. Collier and Horowitz, p. 248.

95. Ibid., p. 325.

96. Ibid., p. 326.

97. Bermant, p. 177.

98. Collier and Horowitz, p. 144.

5

Toward a New Russia:

Building an Infrastructure

THE REHABILITATION OF THE RUSSIAN IDEA

One of the most important events of 1988 (but hardly noticed in the West) was the May 12 decision of the Politburo to authorize the publication of works of pre-revolutionary and emigre Russian philosophers. That decision meant the extension of glasnost to the one area from which Marxism-Leninism can be most safely challenged. In fact, that decision amounted to a concession to Solzhenitsyn's 1973 demand to abolish the Marxist-Leninist ideological monopoly. We have already seen how *Novyi mir* took advantage of this decision by publishing Solov'ev's works on the nationalities' problems. A number of other non- and anti-Marxist Russian philosophers have now been made available to Soviet readers for the first time since the Revolution.

Among them none is perhaps more relevant for the intellectual debate of today than Nikolai Berdiaev (1873-1948). A former Marxist, Berdiaev was one of the authors of the 1909 *Vekhi* collection in which the anti-religious, anti-national, and pro-violent proclivities of the Russian intelligentsia were resolutely condemned.[1] In a way, like Collier and Horowitz's book, it was a collection of "second thoughts" about the 1905 revolution on the part of those who were either Marxists or sympathized with revolutionary violence. It was also a warning that, unless the Russian intelligentsia would stop instigating a revolution and become instead a force for reason and moderation, a worse fate may yet befall Russia and themselves.

Alas, this warning remained unheeded by Russia's "progressive" public-opinion makers of the time because of their strong pro-revolutionary bias. They met *Vekhi* with hostility, ridicule, and catcalls of "betraying the ideals of progress." Russia's slide toward violence and chaos continued. Within eight years, that revolution against which the *Vekhi* authors warned took place in Russia, and the present stage of world history was set. But even though the *Vekhi* authors were unable to prevent the tragedy, their work was proof that Russia was capable of producing an intellectual "antibiotic" against the virus of totalitarianism. Another hopeful sign may be seen in the collection, *Iz glubiny* (1918), in which several of the *Vekhi* authors, including Berdiaev, participated.[2] They were the first to assess the tragedy of the Bolshevik revolution and to foretell its dire consequences for the rest of mankind.

In his contribution to the collection, the essay "Spirits of the Russian Revolution," Berdiaev wrote that the Bolshevik revolution was the result of a "spiritual degeneration" of the Russian intelligentsia and, particularly, of its failure to learn the bitter lessons of the 1905 revolution. He darkly prophesied that "the [real] healing" might not occur until after "a horrible crisis when the entire body of the Russian people will be near death." Predicting that "the anti-Christian spirit of the revolution will give birth to the kingdom of darkness," Berdiaev nonetheless retained his hope that eventually "Russia's Christian spirit might reveal its strength." In 1922, Berdiaev was expelled from Lenin's Russia along with a group of eminent scholars and other intellectual leaders whose work was found to be incompatible with Communism. Never again did he set foot on the soil of his motherland, which indeed turned into the kingdom of darkness. Meanwhile Berdiaev became one of the founders of Christian personalist existentialism and the best-known Russian philosopher in the West.[3]

Unfortunately, some of Berdiaev's notions, expounded at the later stages of his career, gave rise to considerable confusion in the minds of those eager to blame Communism on Russia. Thus, due to the efforts of Alexander Yanov, a Soviet emigre, Berdiaev's catch phrase, the "Russian idea," has lately been given a bad name in the West. In his 1987 book, translated into English as *The Russian Challenge and the Year 2000*, Yanov depicted the Russian idea as the rallying cry of an imagined New Right coalition between neo-Stalinists and Russian nationalists--from Solzhenitsyn and Ogurtsov to the "Russian fascists"--all of whom he indiscriminately lumped together. According to Yanov, this Russian New Right is "a far greater threat" to the West than totalitarian Communism. By misidentifying the Russian idea with this mythical New Right, Yanov hoped to convince the West of the correctness of his own *idee fixe*: the need to prevent "Solzhenitsyn and his followers" from seizing power in the Kremlin and "ruining Gorbachev's reforms."[4]

Yanov's travesty of the Russian idea did not pass unnoticed in the USSR. In an article introducing Berdiaev to the "benighted" Soviet public, Renata Gal'tseva, an editor of a Soviet philosophical encyclopedia, takes issue with Yanov's and other such distortions.[5] Gal'tseva admits that Berdiaev indeed advanced the theory that "The Third International is not an International at all, but a Russian national idea" as he spoke of "proletarian messianism" falling victim to a "messianism of the Russian people." But she also makes it clear that neither these nor any other ideas of Berdiaev have ever been incorporated into official Soviet ideology. In fact, throughout the major part of Soviet history Berdiaev's work was banned in the USSR. Moreover, as profound a thinker as he was, says Gal'tseva, Berdiaev was at times ambiguous and contradictory, confused and confusing to others.

Although in the works of some Slavophiles who influenced Berdiaev, the Russian idea took on a certain messianic quality, and Russia was indeed envisioned as a champion of unified Christianity, the thrust of such "messianism" was diametrically opposed to everything Communism stands for, Gal'tseva points out. Therefore Berdiaev's equation of the Third International with the Russian national idea had more to do with his wishful thinking than with reality, Gal'tseva suggests, saying that Berdiaev's logic occasionally yielded to the "arbitrariness of his heart."

According to Gal'tseva, Berdiaev's tendency to identify the "messianic" aspects of Communism with the Russian idea has contributed to a common misinterpretation of Soviet Communism as a product of Russian national character and Russian cultural tradition. Calling it completely unfounded, Gal'tseva deplores the fact that this "baneful delusion of the twentieth century" has become "extremely popular" among Soviet emigres and even made some inroads into

Western sovietology. Worst of all, presently it is being vigorously propagated by the "speaking majority" of Radio Liberty beaming its programs back to the USSR.

Gal'tseva argues that the primary beneficiaries of this misinterpretation are Western "left-leaning ideologists" who quote Berdiaev out of context in order to exonerate Marx from any responsibility for Soviet totalitarianism. While alleging that true Marxism was "russified" and "orientalized," they use Berdiaev as a life-saver for Marx and themselves. To allege that the Communist revolution meant not destruction of Russia's traditional national life, but its renewal, is to flout all empirical evidence for the sake of a utopian theory, says Gal'tseva.

While deploring the fact that some of Berdiaev's ambiguous notions have contributed to Western confusion about the nature of the Bolshevik revolution, Gal'tseva concludes that, taken as a whole, his personalist "philosophy of freedom" far outweighs his ambiguities as it helps to "arm [us] with the knowledge of the true sources of twentieth-century totalitarianism." Gal'tseva particularly praises Berdiaev for defining totalitarianism as an expression of "misdirected religious needs." She suggests that Berdiaev's fundamentally Christian philosophy may serve as an antidote to the spread of totalitarianism in the world.

Gal'tseva was not alone in her defense of the Russian idea from its distortion into a bogeyman of the Russian nationalist threat to the West. In his June 11, 1989 article in the *Moscow News*, Igor' Vinogradov extolled the Russian idea as an antithesis not to the West, but to the "revolutionary theory" in which "moral norms are not absolute" but depend on the vicissitudes of class struggle. Attributing the formulation of this antithesis chiefly to Vladimir Solov'ev, Vinogradov defined the Russian idea as a fundamentally Christian approach to solving social problems, not by revolutionary violence but by a gradual and strictly voluntary application of Christ's teaching to social, national, and international issues.

According to Vinogradov, Solov'ev's antithesis to Marxism has become so central to the entire "Russian philosophic and religious renaissance" that there can be no better name for it than the Russian idea. "What an illusory, crazy, and utopian idea! Wouldn't it lead us away from the reality of our urgent problems?" Such questions, says

Vinogradov, would inevitably arise before our skeptical contemporaries. However, he counters the doubters of the Russian idea with this question: "But how about your [allegedly] sober and wise idea of building a happy social paradise on earth without God, without absolute moral standards rooted in the Ten Commandments. Didn't we drag our miserable country through seventy years [of that paradise] and only managed to take it to the brink of a catastrophe?" It is precisely because of the staggering failure of the allegedly "scientific," and borrowed from the West, Marxist utopia that Soviet people today have been increasingly turning to Russia's pre-Communist spiritual heritage symbolized in a single shorthand phrase, the Russian idea. Its adjective "Russian" is fully justified in view of the fact that the Communist rulers, while undertaking their social experiment under the slogan of "proletarian internationalism," endeavored to destroy and stamp out Russia's national heritage.

The Russian idea unifies in itself several aspects. It is Russian, but opposed not to the West, as Yanov alleges, but only to Marxist "proletarian internationalism" which, as many Soviet scholars now acknowledge, in reality turned into "national nihilism" and Stalinist "Russian-big-brother" chauvinism. It is Christian, but it is opposed not to Muslims, Buddhists, or Jews, but to Soviet state-sponsored atheism, which has made a mockery of freedom of conscience (even for atheists who disagree with Marxism-Leninism). Far from being intolerant, as Yanov alleges, it affirms freedom of conscience as a precondition for solving all other problems. It is a national, but it is not necessarily a nationalist idea, certainly not in the sense of national egotism and xenophobia, which have often accompanied excessively nationalist causes. Finally, unlike the Marxist-Leninist ideology, the Russian idea not only presupposes that there are universal human values but also encourages the Russians to take an active part in their affirmation throughout the world.[6]

RUSSOPHOBIA AND JUDOPHOBIA

As was argued in Chapter 1, one of the major reasons for the spread of judophobia in the USSR was the failure of the West to recognize the legitimacy of the striving of ethnic Russians for their national emancipation from the yoke of Communism. The best antidote to Pamyat-like extremism can be found in the moderate mainstream of the Russite movement, represented by such people as Solzhenitsyn (abroad), Likhachev, Zalygin, Averintsev, and Latynina, to name but a few. Regretfully, John Dunlop's 1983 recommendation[7] that the West should try to send some favorable signals to the moderate Russian nationalists was not followed, and the negative Western attitude to *all* manifestations of Russian nationalism since then has actually hardened.

This conclusion was chiefly based on my personal experience during several research visits at Radio Liberty, including a six-week stint in the fall of 1987. My conclusion was further confirmed in a 1987 open letter, "To Russian Emigration," signed by a group of thirty-one human rights activists in Moscow.[8] The authors complained that Western radio stations broadcasting in Russian have failed in their mission of disseminating a broad range of opinion on the events in the USSR by paying excessive attention to the issue of emigration at the expense of other vital issues. According to the letter, this excessive attention to "the issue of emigration and to the personal problems of certain renowned dissidents" has antagonized the majority of Soviet listeners, who have come to associate "dissidents" not with the people who unselfishly work for the benefit of the country but with those who want merely to emigrate. Moreover, since it is commonly known that the majority of both the the emigres and the "dissidents" are Jews, and that the Jews form less than 1 percent of the Soviet population, the excessive attention to their problems at the expense of others objectively "pours water on the mill of anti-Semitism," says the letter.

The authors did not suggest that the issue of emigration was unimportant. But they asked that it be reduced so that it would not overshadow issues "which concern the majority of the population," such as "the religious renaissance, the restoration and development of national cultures, and the historical traditions of all peoples of the USSR, economic problems, free trade unions and ecology." Although the majority of the signees have Russian surnames, it is noteworthy that the letter was not written from an exclusively ethnic Russian viewpoint. It concluded with a call for a consolidation of "the Russian emigre forces through [formulation of] a positive program of action in the area of the country's true interests." Its criticism of Western broadcasting, the letter said, was "completely friendly" and not meant to offend anyone.

Another group of Soviet dissidents criticized Western broadcasting in Russian in an open letter dated June 20, 1989.[9] Addressed to the U.S. Congress and to the Board of International Broadcasting (which oversees the activities of both the Voice of America and Radio Liberty), this letter, signed by six prominent Russian dissidents of Christian orientation, goes into some detail criticizing Western broadcasts in Russian, particularly those of Radio Liberty.   After thanking the Congress for providing funds for broadcasting to the USSR, the authors point out that the cessation of Soviet jamming of Radio Liberty broadcasting has opened new opportunities for the fulfilment of that station's mission, "to improve mutual understanding among nations."   However, that mission has hardly been fulfilled at all. In fact, since about the second half of 1987 the "old flaws in the policy of Radio Liberty (especially its Russian Language Service) have tended to rapidly become worse."

Among the principal flaws [nedostatki] the authors name not just "ignoring the problems of long-suffering Russian people" (which was the main complaint of the first letter), but also an active dissemination of "russophobia" through a number of Radio Liberty programs. As an example, they singled out a program entitled "The Russian Idea." "When Radio Liberty announced this new program, we anticipated it with great hope. But it turned out to be the opposite of what we hoped for." One segment of the program was devoted to Yanov's "russophobic conceptions," three to those of Andrei Siniavskii, and in the remaining two segments [Harvard University professor] Richard Pipes and Boris Khazanov subjected to a "haughty and incompetent critique" an article by V. Aksiuchits (one of the letter's signees) that appeared in the Christian samizdat journal *Vybor*. As to Solzhenitsyn, "the [principal] contemporary exponent of the Russian idea," Radio Liberty had no place for him at all, says the letter. "One gets the impression that a conspiracy of silence exists not just in the Soviet press, but also in Western radio stations in regard to Solzhenitsyn's ideas, which are the most destructive for Communist ideology."

The letter particularly criticizes Radio Liberty for giving excessive attention to Pamyat. "There are extremists in every country and in every movement. All true Russian patriots condemn [such ultra-radical tendencies as those present in] Pamyat's anti-Semitic wing," says the letter. However, by giving disproportionate attention to this "small group of demagogues," Radio Liberty in effect popularizes it as if they were an "all-Russian political movement." As a result, "the Jews feel intimidated, the Russians feel indignant because they are equated with this small band of fanatics, [and] this [artificially fostered] mutual embitterment could indeed lead to an actual confrontation."

Just as Radio Liberty programs about Pamyat contribute to mutual antagonism between Jews and Russians, so the incessant flow of Radio Liberty programs about "russification" of national minorities produces a similar effect in border-area republics. Instead of helping to promote mutual understanding, Radio Liberty programs have produced the opposite effect. This is chiefly due to the failure of Radio Liberty authors and editors to point out that the Communist "russifiers" have been using, and abusing, the Russian language to propagandize Communist ideology, not the Russian national heritage. The only beneficiaries of such biased programs, the letter suggests, are the Communist rulers, who are only too happy to see public attention diverted from the inherent flaws of the Communist system to quarrels among the peoples, all of whom, including the Russians, have been its victims.

"Our people, en masse, exhibit a strong anti-Communist tendency. Therefore, it is a potential ally to all forces of freedom and democracy," says the letter. "But [the surge of] russophobia, this blind aggression against the Russian people, forces it to seek a rapprochement with the ideological regime. As a result, such an unnatural phenomenon as 'Soviet patriotism' gets a boost." Moreover, "since russophobia is being disseminated under the auspices of Western radio stations, it not only fosters among Russians a hostility toward the West, but also diminishes their receptiveness to universal humanistic values."

The authors are confident that eventually the Russians will free themselves from "the Communist yoke," regardless of what the West does or does not do. They are convinced that only then will the peoples of the USSR be able "to humanely figure out whether to live separately or find some other forms of coexistence." As to ethnic Russians, they will have so many wounds to heal and so many problems to solve that they would not want even to hear about any sort of expansionism, nor would they want to hold onto any people who want to live independently." In conclusion, the authors expressed a hope that the "russophobic" tendencies in Radio Liberty programs (and, to a lesser degree, in Voice of America Russian-language programs) are not representative of U. S. policy, but are rather due to "a peculiar trait of the personnel of these stations: many of them neither love nor respect the country and the peoples to whom they broadcast their programs."

One cannot easily dismiss either of the two letters. The first was signed by thirty-one people, many of whom have been champions of human rights for years. At least three (V. Novodvorskaia, Evgeniia Debrianskaia, and Tsar'kov) are active in the Democratic Union, (*Demokraticheskii Soiuz*), one of the earliest informal groups that has been most consistent in its opposition to the Communist "autocracy" and its advocacy of a Western-style multi-party democracy. The second letter was signed by six long-time dissidents,[10] none of whom has ever been identified with anti-Semitism or xenophobia. In fact, one of the signees, Valerii Senderov, a mathematician and former political prisoner, has been one of the most effective critics of both official and popular Soviet anti-Semitism. A self-proclaimed member of the National Labor Union of the Russian Solidarists (better known under its Russian initials as NTS), the only Russian emigre political organization with membership inside the USSR, Senderov was sentenced, in March 1983, to a seven-year term in the Gulag for his "anti-state" activities on behalf of the "subversive" NTS. Since his release in 1987 as part of Gorbachev's amnesty, he has been a prolific contributor to a number of samizdat publications. His role in the formation of independent public opinion in the USSR is comparable to that of Sergei Grigoriants, the editor of *Glasnost'*, and Lev Timofeev, the editor of *Referendum*.

In July 1988 Senderov wrote an open letter to Aleksandr Iakovlev, reputed to be the "most liberal" member of the Politburo, demanding investigation of official anti-Semitism at Moscow University's Mathematics Department, of which Senderov is a graduate. According to Senderov, student admission is so discriminatory that if a Russian has a 90 percent chance to enroll, a Jew has only 50 percent. Receiving no reply, Senderov accused Soviet authorities of abetting racism.[11] A year later he repeated the charge.[12] Three-quarters Jewish and a Christian (by his own admission), Senderov finds it easy to empathize with both Jews and Russians. He is equally sensitive to bigotry on both sides. Pointing to the tendency of some overzealous Soviet Jews to equate Christianity with anti-Semitism, Senderov accused them of mirror-imaging those Russians who assume that all Jews are russophobes.[13] Senderov has called on both Jews and Russians to respect each other's religious heritage and, at the very least, to give each other the benefit of the doubt.

That Senderov practices what he preaches is evident in his review of Igor' Shafarevich's controversial book, *Rusofobia*, which he has read in samizdat.[14] First of all, Senderov points out the legitimacy of the topic. According to him, russophobia as a social phenomenon has become so widespread both inside the USSR and abroad that it has become "an evil no less dangerous than judophobia." He points out that russophobia had been observed and discussed by a number of earlier authors, most notably Solzhenitsyn, Mikhail Bernshtam (a Soviet emigre scholar who now works at the Hoover Institution, Stanford University), and V. Borisov, one of Solzhenitsyn's co-authors in the collection *From Under the Rubble* and now an editor at *Novyi mir*.[15] Unlike Shafarevich, none of them blamed the spread of russophobia on the Jews in the way that Shafarevich did. Still, even after discovering that Shafarevich's book was primarily focused on Jewish russophobia, says Senderov, he did not exclude *a priori* that some of his arguments might be "of value," especially since he admired Shafarevich's "erudition and his talent as a historian," demonstrated in his previous book, *Socialism as a Phenomenon of World History*. However, after having read Shafarevich's new book, Senderov found it largely counter-productive to its otherwise laudable goal of exposing the evils of russophobia.

The chief reason for that failure Senderov sees in Shafarevich's reducing the complexity of causes and manifestations of russophobia to the hostility of "Jewish nationalists" toward Russia. Without denying the fact that many Jews whom Shafarevich cites (Pipes, Yanov, Khazanov, and a number of Radio Liberty broadcasters) have indeed been contributing to the spread of russophobia, Senderov denies that they have anything to do with Jewish nationalism, or Zionism. He particularly reproaches Shafarevich for taking Yanov as an "outstanding spokesman of Jewish nationalism." According to Senderov, not only is Yanov an "atheist," but he has shown little concern for Jewish religious traditions or for the state of Israel. Moreover, having emigrated, Yanov nonetheless remained "fully a Soviet [propaganda] journalist" whose "methodology" reflects just that. Yanov has "scandalized" himself, says Senderov, because his "russophobic output" completely lacks such essential attributes of scholarship as objectivity and the ability to discriminate (for instance, between various strands of Russian nationalism). By taking Yanov seriously both as a spokesman for Jewish nationalism and as a scholar, Shafarevich doomed his own work.

It is out of place here to discuss all the details of Senderov's critique of Shafarevich's book. Suffice it to say that Senderov condemned Shafarevich's tendency to fling charges of russophobia at any Jew (or non-Jew) who happened to be critical of the Russians for whatever reason. For example, Senderov rebuked Shafarevich for accusing Naum Korzhavin (see the Kozhinov-Sarnov debate) of russophobia on the basis of a single quatrain of his poetry. According to Senderov, Korzhavin is just one of numerous victims of Shafarevich's unwarranted attacks. Senderov concluded his review by expressing sadness at Shafarevich's failure to understand that love of one's own people should not necessarily mean hostility to others.

In another article Senderov praised an open letter to Shafarevich in which *Rusofobia* was subjected to "substantive" criticism.[16] The author (a religious and nationalist Jew, Senderov assumes) was effective in exposing Shafarevich's "judophobic tendency" because he countered it with facts and arguments and because he did so with sadness rather than malevolence. Senderov cited this letter as an example of a sound approach to nationality relations. But he had nothing but scorn for Boris Khazanov's review article, "*Obyknovennyi fashizm*" [Ordinary Fascism]. Khazanov's thesis, suggested in the title, was just as unsubstantiated as Shafarevich's book. "This is not just a flaw [of the article]," says Senderov, "it is its entire method." Like Shafarevich, says Senderov, Khazanov merely exhorts the like-minded who share his russophobia.[17]

Senderov concluded with a general observation on the character of the Russo-Jewish debate in the USSR that ought to be of interest to the West.

The views of both judophobes and russophobes are a mirror image of each other. However, there is a difference. As a rule, judophobes are concerned with finding some sort of 'theoretical' and 'scholarly' basis. Perhaps they vaguely realize that 'to dislike the Kikes' is not 'bon ton.' Russophobes, on the other hand, are usually free from such compunctions. For them, Russia is a bitch, a myth, and a slave. As to the Russian people, they dismiss them as Byzantine or Tartar bastards. Therefore they feel no need for 'The Protocols of the Wizards of Zion' to support such 'high-quality' assumptions [about the Russians].

One would wish that the West, with its long tradition of free speech and civilized debate, had played the role of moderator in this growing and potentially dangerous conflict by steering it toward a frank and open dialogue between the two groups. However, judging by the two open letters from the USSR, so far the United States has apparently failed to play such a role.[18]

SHOULD RUSSIA SECEDE?

When, shortly after his election to the Russian presidency, Boris El'tsin steered the Russian parliament to the proclamation of the sovereignty of the Russian Federation on June 12, 1990, Western politicians and sovietologists were caught by surprise. Accustomed to associating the Russians with expansionism, they could not quite understand why the allegedly dominant majority would want what the minorities wanted, sovereignty in their own land. Had the West paid more attention to the Russian problem, it would have found it much easier to understand such a development. In fact, the need for the Russians to develop their own national statehood in contradistinction from the ideocratic Soviet state has been debated by the Russians at home and abroad for quite some time, as will be shown below.

The first to attract country-wide attention to the issue was Valentin Rasputin, a people's deputy of the USSR, a former member of the now-defunct Presidential Council and leading ruralist writer (see Chapter 2). In his speech before the Spring 1989 session of the Congress of People's Deputies, responding to secessionist tendencies among border-area republics, Rasputin suggested, half in jest, that perhaps Russia herself should secede from the Union in order to get her own house in order. Rasputin's remark attracted the attention of at least one Western scholar. In an article published in *Moscow News* on July 23, 1989, as part of an East-West dialogue, Helene Carrere d'Encausse, a French sovietologist who had predicted the downfall of the Soviet Empire through the growth of separatism among minorities but never paid much attention to the Russians, described Rasputin's remark as indicative of "profound discontent" among ethnic Russians with their role in the Union.[19] She put the remark in the context of the rise of "Russian nationalism," a phenomenon that "should not be underestimated." The Russians are justified in thinking that "they have been paying [too] high a price for [maintaining the present structure of the Union] and that, by helping the poorer nations [of the USSR], they have slowed down their own development," said D'Encausse. She acknowledged as a plausible option Rasputin's suggestion that, "in order to save Russia, it might be necessary to leave the Union." However, citing the activities of Pamyat, she suggested that "national embitterment" among the Russians represents a distinct threat to "a common future" for all peoples of the USSR.

In his reply to D'Encausse, Vitalii Tret'iakov, a *Moscow News* political observer, made light of Rasputin's remark. The remark was a "polemic exaggeration" in order to show the "absurdity" of the centrifugal tendencies among minorities, wrote Tret'iakov. Calling the remark "unfortunate," Tret'iakov suggested that the writer was either facetious ("because such a development is out of the question") or simply did not know what he was talking about. There are reasons to believe, however, that Rasputin was neither facetious nor ignorant of the issue. Even if his remark was a "polemic exaggeration," it was probably aimed not at the "absurdity" of the centrifugal tendencies but at the absurdity of ignoring the interests of ethnic Russians. And if it was facetious, it was so in a sense that overturns the common assumption of the identity of interests between the Communist rulers and their Russian subjects. Its sting was aimed as much at those "centrifugal" nationalists who assume the "Russianness" of the Kremlin as at those centripetal "internationalists" in the Kremlin who assume that, by making the Russian language into a lingua franca of the USSR, they have bought the allegiance of the Russians.

Rasputin probably has nothing against the Soviet Union or the Communist Party that rules it. He might be even a loyal Party member. But he is definitely not a *partiot*, but a *patriot*. That is, his first priority is *Patria*, and his first concern is the well-being of Russia, whose very survival, he feels, is now at stake. Therefore, if he were to be convinced that the cost of holding the Union together is too high for Russia, he would consider it his patriotic duty to let Russia secede. He would certainly not want to use force to prevent secession. As he has said, there will be no order in one's country unless there is an order in one's soul. And there can hardly be order in one's soul unless one is free to stay or go. As a Siberian, Rasputin knows full well that the greatest problem of the Russians is not the lack of land but the way the government treats that land, "as if it were a temporary holding or a concession."

Rasputin's remark was fully consistent with the views of many *Russites*. As a ruralist, Rasputin was no doubt aware of what Solzhenitsyn had to say on the subject. As far back as his 1973 *Letter*, Solzhenitsyn made it clear that "no peripheral nation should be forcibly kept within the bounds of our country" (see Chapter 1). Other dissident Russians have been articulating their opposition to the imperial structure of the Soviet Union at least since Igor' Ogurtsov founded the underground All-Russian Social-Christian Union for the Liberation of the People (better known by its Russian initials as VSKhSON) in February 1964. The VSKhSON program, largely based on Vladimir Solov'ev's and Nikolai Berdiaev's idea that Russia has a special role in uniting Christianity, stipulated "national self-determination" for "those foreign countries in which Soviet forces are temporarily stationed" (presumably, including Central Europe and the Baltic Republics). It even offered help to "initiate their own self-determination." Although the VSKhSON program (in the conditions of the underground it was more a rough draft than a definitive document) left open the fate of non-Christian minorities, it did declare, "All known religions must have the right to preach without hindrance."[20]

Sergei Soldatov's 1969 Program of the Democratic Movement of the Soviet Union, an underground political organization better known by its Russian initials as DDSS, was even more specific in stipulating national self-determination for border-area nations. It envisioned the creation of a confederation, "The Union of Democratic

Republics," but only after a national referendum, under the auspices of the United Nations, determined if a nation wished to secede. As to nations opting to stay with Russia, they were promised full "cultural and economic autonomy."[21]

Anatolii Fedoseev, a leading Soviet electronics expert who defected to France in 1971, in his 1980 book about a political alternative to the Soviet system, goes even further in wishing to assure that no nation be forced into a future Russia.[22] For that purpose he proposed that Moscow first declare *all* union republics independent. Only then would each republic decide, through a national referendum, whether to join the new Russian Federation, whose constitution Fedoseev deliberately modeled on that of Switzerland.

Finally, the NTS Program says that "the population of the present union republics of the USSR will decide themselves if they wish to become part of Russia or prefer to live in separate states. If it is their wish, they will be able to continue their historical paths jointly with Russia on the basis of a confederation."[23]

In fact, as I showed in my 1985 paper, "Images of the Soviet Future," virtually all Russian oppositional groups and individuals, from VSKhSON to NTS, from such "westernists" as Andrei Sakharov and Anatolii Fedoseev to such Russites as Solzhenitsyn and Vladimir Osipov, have been steadfast in their desire to see the Soviet Empire dissolved. The only exception was the dissident Marxist historian Roy Medvedev, who had objected specifically to Solzhenitsyn's allowance of secession of border-area republics.[24]

I do not presume that Rasputin knew about all of the above programs. Circulated in the samizdat and tamizdat underground, they were not widely available to Soviet citizens and, judging by the two open letters we have discussed, Western broadcasters hardly helped Rasputin to be better informed. Rasputin's remark was nonetheless consistent with the sentiments of many Russites. It may have echoed a proposal of Vladimir Balakhonov, who spent fifteen years in the Gulag for advocating such ideas. Now a member of the Democratic Union, Balakhonov published an article on this issue in a 1989 samizdat bulletin.[25] Claiming that he had conceived the idea in 1977, he argued in favor of Russia's voluntary secession from the Union. In 1983, while still in the Gulag, he sent a letter to the Politburo in which he for the first time spelled out his proposal. Balakhonov argued then, as he does now, that "the instinct of self-preservation" dictates that the Russians take this path.

In the summer of 1987, while Gorbachev was boasting, in his book and elsewhere, about "ethnic harmony" in the USSR, Sergei Grigoriants, another dissident of Armenian origins, wrote an article, "The Empire or the Union?", in which he predicted the exacerbation of the nationalities problem.[26] Drawing attention, as Pamyat did, to the growing discontent among ethnic Russians because of (among other things) the "terrible poverty even in comparison with the [low] living standards in national republics," Grigoriants suggested that the Russians were facing the prospect of either being "annihilated" by the surrounding hostile minorities or becoming extinct as a nation. Grigoriants then quoted Balakhonov as saying that "the only salvation for the Russian people would be secession of the Russian Federation from the USSR." Grigoriants made it clear, however, that he preferred another option: "If there will be a democratic government in Russia, we shall stay with her. But if all remains as it is, we shall fight for independence."

I am not suggesting that Rasputin had read either Balakhonov's or Grigoriants' article. What I do suggest is that the idea of Russia's secession should not have surprised Western political observers. It has been widely discussed among the Russians. An increasing number of them now realize that their "imperial instinct" has been ruthlessly exploited by the Communist rulers for goals that are contrary to the most vital Russian national interests. They are as unhappy about the present unitary structure of the Union as are minorities. They believe that the struggle for national self-determination among the minorities not only is morally justified, but might be in the interests of the Russians. Some of the Russites would want to see greater autonomy for minorities in the framework of a federation; others would prefer a confederation. By bringing the option of Russia's secession to the attention of the Soviet public, Rasputin only dramatized the fact that the Communist regime has served the national interests of the Russians no better than those of the Estonians or the Georgians. Rasputin and his Russite associates would not go as far as wishing to split up Russia herself, as Balakhonov suggested. But they would probably agree with Grigoriants that a democratic Russia may yet serve as a core of a commonwealth of free nations.

Rasputin's speech did not pass unnoticed by the non-Russians. On June 14, 1989, a Georgian newspaper carried an interview with Zaza Siradze, a young Georgian musician who had just become a Party member.[27]   Among all events in the country Siradze singled out Rasputin's speech. He felt that although Rasputin spoke as a Russian patriot, his speech boded well for the development of more harmonious relations between all Soviet nationalities. "I know that many didn't like it. However, I greatly respect his feelings as a Russian patriot. Every person should, first of all, be a patriot of his own people." By suggesting that Russia's secession would give the nation greater opportunity for its own development, Rasputin encouraged the non-Russians to think along similar lines.

Unlike Siradze, Poel' Karp, a "liberal" journalist, saw Rasputin's speech primarily as an expression of "Russian great-power chauvinism."[28]   Whereas Siradze interpreted it as a good omen for all non-Russians, Karp read it as a warning to the minorities not to leave the Union "unless they want to perish [without Russia]." Karp made Rasputin's reference to Stolypin the centerpiece of his article. By quoting Stolypin's famous challenge to the revolutionaries, "You are looking forward to great upheavals, but we [the Russians] are looking forward to a great Russia," Rasputin has brought his "chauvinistic" tendency to "its logical [?] conclusion, the throne of the tsars," alleged Karp. As "a convinced republican," Karp condemned Rasputin for his "reckless candor" in admitting his "monarchism." [29]

By equating Rasputin's admiration for Stolypin with "monarchism" and "Russian chauvinism," Karp has, at best, shown his ignorance. This is not necessarily his personal fault but rather the result of the decades of "glasnostlessness," when Marxist-Leninists used their monopoly to warp the minds of Soviet people, Russians and non-Russians alike.[30]   Following Lenin's condemnation of Stolypin's reforms--precisely because Lenin thought they might succeed and thus prevent a revolution--Soviet propaganda has completely distorted this page of Russia's history in order to scare away the very thought that there was, or might have been, an alternative to the revolutionary way of social progress. It is hardly surprising, therefore, that when Solzhenitsyn came across Western sources on Stolypin, he found it necessary to tell the true story of Stolypin's reforms in the first "knot" of *The Red Wheel*.[31]

THE REHABILITATION OF PETR STOLYPIN

That the Gorbachev leadership was worried about the growing attractiveness of Stolypin's reforms as an example of successful *perestroika* was clear from Aleksandr Iakovlev's speech before Soviet propagandists on April 17, 1987. Commonly regarded in the West as one of Gorbachev's closest "liberal" allies, Iakovlev was then Politburo member in charge of ideology. Deploring the "departure of a number of historians and literati from a class struggle approach to evaluating historical events and personalities," Iakovlev condemned the "tendency to beautify the reality of pre-revolutionary Russia." This nationalist tendency has been at times disguised by "pseudopatriotic proclamations," said Iakovlev, alluding to the works of the ruralist writers. "But if one adheres to Leninism," Iakovlev went on, "then it is clear that Lenin's patriotism is that of the noblest son of Russia, whereas Stolypin's is that of a bureaucratic servant of autocracy."[32]

Iakovlev made it clear that Soviet leaders are especially worried about the growing revival of national memory among the Russians. They know full well that the real challenge to the defective system--and to the inept way in which they are trying to restructure it--comes not from the nationalisms of border republics, but from that of Russians. They know that the more a Russian thinks of his country's fate in this century, the more likely he will compare Stolypin the reformer with Lenin the revolutionary, and the comparison will not be in Lenin's favor. They also know that whatever virtues Lenin may have had, patriotism was not one of them. Certainly not if it is defined in terms of the universal ethical standards to which Gorbachev now says his Party has decided to return.

Iakovlev was right that, unless one is a Leninist, one would not recognize Lenin as a patriot. But what about the majority of the Russians, who are not Leninists? What if their conscience does not permit them to regard Lenin as a patriot? As Iakovlev admits, people have become more and more vocal in denouncing "the revolution and the Soviet system for their allegedly destructive policy in respect to national cultures." But while warning against turning to religion as "the protector of cultural values," Iakovlev offered no effective antidote to that "pernicious tendency" except the same old triad: class struggle, socialism, and proletarian internationalism. How Iakovlev attained in the West the reputation of the most "liberal" reformer remains a mystery.

Even while Iakovlev was denouncing him, a re-evaluation of the legacy of Stolypin and his reforms was already underway. No sooner was Stolypin's name invoked, thanks to Rasputin, in the halls of the Congress of the People's Deputies, than readers wanted to know more about him. First, the Russite weekly, *Literaturnaia Rossiia*, obliged. In a long article Igor' D'iakov described Stolypin as a great reformer, a Russian patriot, and a realist who knew how to advance Russia's national interests.[33] D'iakov gave very high marks to Stolypin's 1907 agrarian reforms, including the dissolution of an economically inefficient peasant commune, the strengthening of private, market-oriented farming, and the resettlement of Siberia by homesteading. According to D'iakov, Stolypin's reforms were opposed by both the revolutionary left and the conservative right. Pointing out the growth of Russian agricultural exports in the wake of these reforms, D'iakov suggested that the United States and other exporters who competed with Russia were understandably less than enthusiastic about Stolypin. While accusing Soviet propagandists of deliberately minimizing the success of Stolypin's reforms, D'iakov reproached Western scholars for failing to appreciate their progressive and democratizing thrust.

D'iakov gave even higher marks to Stolypin's "second program" of reforms which he dictated in March 1911 and which was nullified by his assassination in September 1911. Disputing those who have portrayed Stolypin as a narrow-minded Russian chauvinist and monarchist committed to the expansion of an "autocratic Russian empire," D'iakov argued that Stolypin was not "a chauvinist, but a proponent of a stable and dynamic statesmanship aimed at securing peace and prosperity to everyone, regardless of his religion or nationality." He particularly debunked the "myth" of Stolypin as a "hangman." According to D'iakov, Stolypin's "very essence was a challenge to any form of violence--be it violence against the people's natural way of life or against a sober approach to affairs of the state." Making clear that his appraisal of Stolypin was essentially similar to that by Solzhenitsyn contained in the first volume of *The Red Wheel*,[34] D'iakov ended his article by stressing Stolypin's relevance for perestroika, not as a "monarchist," but as a reformer who knew how to make things work.

A month later, on August 19, 1989, a Soviet youth newspaper *Sovetskaia molodezh'*, which has not been identified with Russite causes, published another laudatory article about Stolypin. Entitled "Stolypin: A Word and a Deed," the article, written by V. Ol'gin, makes it clear that the need for re-evaluation of Stolypin's reforms is not only a matter of historical justice but a political necessity.[35] The article contains a number of quotations from Stolypin for which the author gives brief comments. Thus, quoting Stolypin's famous utterance (which Rasputin used in his speech), Ol'gin shows that it was made in the context of Stolypin's opposition to the utopian ideas of revolutionaries and was not meant to deny the rights of national minorities. Like D'iakov, he portrays Stolypin as an unselfish hero and farsighted statesman, who, in his fight against leftist terrorists, sought to strengthen the democratic grassroots of the country by turning impoverished peasants into prosperous farmers. Stolypin's reforms were opposed by both "leftist demagogues" and the entrenched aristocratic bureaucracy, says Ol'gin. Pointing to Stolypin's dedication to the rule of law, Ol'gin credits him with stopping the Jewish pogroms. Like D'iakov, he makes it clear that Stolypin's reforms are a model of success that Soviet reformers can ill afford to ignore. Had Stolypin's reforms been allowed to continue, Ol'gin argues, Russia could have caught up with the United States by 1930. The article ends with a quotation from Seliunin (see Chapter 2) to the effect that the Bolshevik revolution aborted Russia's march toward a prosperous and equitable society.

Finally, on September 8, 1989, *Literaturnaia Rossiia* published a chapter from the book about the reformer, written by his son, Arkadii Stolypin, who now resides in Paris, France. In an editorial preface it was revealed that the newspaper had been flooded with responses to D'iakov's article. Not all readers were happy. One even denounced the author in a letter to the Central Committee of the Party. However, the majority of responses were positive, and the readers wished to know more about Stolypin. Even though the chapter from the book was limited to Stolypin's ideas on agrarian reforms, the newspaper suggested that his ideas on "strengthening statehood, developing self-management, and fighting bureaucracy" are just as relevant for perestroika.[36]

THE AGONY HAS STARTED. WHAT IS AHEAD?

By the summer of 1989 it had become apparent that the death agony of the regime had started. The primary question now is not whether the regime will survive but how long its agony will last. Hence the urgency of the next question: How to make the inevitable exit of the regime the least painful to the peoples it rules? This question concerns Russians first and foremost. Regardless of what one might think of them as a people, it is they who will play, or not play, the decisive role in how events develop. They are by far the largest ethnic group in the country (nearly half of the total population). Unfavorable demographic tendencies notwithstanding, they will remain for the foreseeable future the largest potential democratic constituency. That fact alone thrusts on them the greatest responsibility of all.

Willingly or not, ethnic Russians have been the chief pillars of the regime. It is incumbent upon them to assure that the roof of the "bright building of socialism" they had been urged to build does not collapse on the people inside. While the peoples inhabiting Soviet border areas can hope to escape (through secession) when the roof caves in, there is no such hope for the Russians. The others can secede out; the Russians can only secede in. If the roof, or even the entire building, collapses, it will bury in its ruins both Communists and non-Communists, Russians and non-Russians. Only the Russians--because of their numbers, geographic position, and their role in the structure of the Soviet state--can prevent such a sudden collapse. And they must do so not only for themselves but for all the nationalities involved. As part of the restructuring of the whole building, they must strengthen the existing pillars and crossbeams, as well as create new ones. But while doing so, they must keep the doors and windows of the tottering building wide open to allow the unwilling to escape. It is a matter of honor, as well as of common sense. The risk of catching cold should certainly not deter them from letting others escape.

One thing the Russians have belatedly discovered was that within their multi-national building they alone, among the fifteen union republics, did not have their own separate abode. Other nationalities can at least hide themselves in niches along the outer walls and in makeshift tents scattered across the land. But Russians have nowhere to hide. An increasing number of them now realize that they must, without delay, start building the infrastructure of the future Russian state. Officially, they are in charge of the whole building. But in reality they have no place, no house in it that they could call their own. Nor do they seem to have the memory of how a Russian house should be built. That is why they had seized on perestroika as an opportunity to build their own shelter, even if under a common roof. And they had taken glasnost as an opportunity to restore their national memory.

This explains the emergence, among other informal groups, of the National-Patriotic Front Pamyat (see Appendix 1) and similar groups. By the latest count there are at least a dozen groups contending for the honor of representing the genuine memory (Pamyat) of the Russian past. (In addition, numerous groups bear such suggestive names as "Fatherland" and "Salvation.") It is hard to measure Pamyat's popularity, but by all accounts its anti-Zionist rhetoric has not won it a large following. However, the very proliferation of such groups suggests that they fill an important need in the development of Russian national identity and self-awareness. While all of them are primarily concerned with the preservation of Russian national memory, only a few have engaged in anti-Semitic or anti-Zionist rhetoric, and those who have, did not do well at the voting booths.

Some scholarly efforts to restore Russian memory have been made as well. We have already talked about the return of Russian non-Marxist philosophy. Moreover, the publication of the works of the previously proscribed Russian writers, such as Zamiatin, Platonov, Bulgakov, Pasternak, and now Solzhenitsyn has meant the beginning of a cultural reunification of Russia. These two measures amount to the beginning of the end of the cultural "Berlin Wall" that has for decades separated the Russians inside the USSR from their brothers abroad and ancestors at home.

In January 1989 plans were announced for the worldwide celebration of 1991 as "the year of Russian culture."[37] Among the members of the organizing committee are Likhachev, Averintsev, Rasputin, several hierarchs of the Russian Church, and a number of other prominent personalities, such as Tatiana Zaslavskaia and Sviatoslav Richter, who are not associated with Russite causes. Among the honorary members of the committee are Solzhenitsyn and Iosif Brodsky. The year 1991 was chosen to coincide with the anniversaries of the birth of the writer Mikhail Bulgakov, the poet Osip Mandel'shtam, and the foremost Russian saint, Sergei of Radonezh. The three main goals of the enterprise are (1) to acquaint the world with the Russian axiology, that is, the system of spiritual values, including those of Russian religion, literature, and philosophy; (2) to restore trust between the Russian diaspora and the motherland on the basis of a new national self-awareness; and (3) to create an infrastructure for cultural and economic relations with "all peoples of the world." The announcement made it clear that from now on the tree of Russian culture will be united with both its spiritual roots in pre-revolutionary Russia and with its non-Communist branches in the Russian diaspora.

In March 1989 *Literaturnaia gazeta* announced the formation, at the end of 1988, of a scholarly board for publishing the first Russian [*Russkaia*] Encyclopedia, not to be confused with the Russian language Great Soviet Encyclopedia. The newspaper carried a long interview with the chairman of the board, Oleg Trubachev, a linguist and corresponding member of the Academy of Sciences. Pointing out that the Russians are just about the only people in the USSR who do not have their own national encyclopedia, Trubachev defined the purpose of the new enterprise as providing "a Russian view of the world." Trubachev emphasized that no political distinction would apply to entries on Russian personalities regardless of whether they live at home or abroad. For the first time, Nabokov and Solzhenitsyn will be treated as part of Russian culture, and so will Mandel'shtam and the painter Il'ia Levitan (both of Jewish origin), and the Kirghiz writer Chinghiz Aitmatov, who writes in Russian. In regard to Marc Chagall, who was born in Russia, but is better known abroad, Trubachev left the question open. He emphasized the public (non-governmental) character of the enterprise.[38]

Also in March 1989 *Pravda* carried an interview with Vladislav Teterin, a documentary filmmaker, who announced the formation of a group to sponsor an ambitious project, the "Russian People's House." The project includes creating a Russian realistic theater, a film studio, a concert hall, a workshop for traditional Russian handicrafts, a Russian bath-house, and a Russian tavern. The construction may start in Moscow, but contacts were also made with the provinces, where plans were made for taking over some abandoned estates. Teterin emphasized that the project can be viewed both as an educational program (about "a national way of life") and as a commercial enterprise aimed at the promotion of diligence, sobriety, working skills, and traditional Russian craftsmanship. Leaving aside the government-controlled Russian art workshops, such as the world-renowned Palekh and Fedoskino, this is the first attempt to recreate the rudiments of a genuine Russian House.[39]

While the Russian House project is still in the planning stage, the first All-Russian [*Vserossiiskaia*] Academy of Painting, Sculpture and Architecture will open its doors in Moscow in the fall of 1989. So says Il'ia Glazunov, a champion of the Russian realist school of painting, who was appointed president of the Academy. In a *Pradva* interview Glazunov pointed out that until now the RSFSR, unlike Georgia or Latvia, did not have its own national academy of arts where specifically Russian artistic traditions could be cultivated. Glazunov made it clear that his academy will continue the traditions of the Russian realist school, which, according to him, Soviet proponents of avant-garde are trying to stamp out.[40]

Founded in November 1988, the Association of Russian Artists [*Tovarishchestvo Russkikh Khudozhnikov*] had by the summer of 1989 raised millions of rubles to finance the promotion of Russian national renewal in three spheres: spiritual, cultural, and commercial. The "salvation of the country is in the hands of the people, of each of us," said Boris Tsarev, one of the founders of ARA, in an interview with *Literaturnaia Rossiia*.[41] Describing the situation in the country as critical--"abandoned fields, polluted streams, and cut-down forests"-- Tsarev said that worst of all was the despair and apathy among the Russian people. His organization set the task of awakening the Russians to save, first of all, Russian nature. Therefore, the ARA closely coordinates its activities with various groups of the growing "Green movement." Its activities consist of "cultural-enlightenment" lectures, exhibits, concerts and publication. Financed through self-financed and cooperative ventures, ARA has established a fund for awarding prizes and citations for contributions to "national renewal" among the Russians. With its affiliates in dozens of cities, ARA is represented by "more than twenty" deputies in the Congress, said Tsarev. Concerning relations with other nationalities, he quoted an open letter in which both russophobia and forced russification were condemned.

Simultaneously with the efforts to erect a Russian House, a grassroots initiative was undertaken to revive what one might call a Slavic village. In March a fund was created for the Cyrillic Script and Slavic Cultures [*Fond slavianskoi pis'mennosti i slavianskikh kul'tur*].[42] Its main task is to promote closer contacts and cooperation between the three East Slavic nations which for centuries have formed the Russian tri-unity: the Belorussians, the Russians, and the Ukrainians. Among the more than eighty collective co-sponsors are various academic institutions, non-profit organizations, and other enterprises representing the three republics. The list includes the Soviet Committee of Slavic Scholars, the All-Russian Cultural Fund, the Russian Orthodox Church, and the Church of Old Believers. Not surprisingly, the governing board includes several well-known Russites, such as Rasputin, Yurii Bondarev, Yurii Loshchits, and Vladimir Krupin, as well as a number of Ukrainian and Belorussian nationalists. Academician N. I. Tolstoi was elected chairman of the board.

According to a report in *Literaturnaia Rossiia* (one of the co-sponsors), the idea of the Fund originated from a 1986 initiative in the city of Murmansk to celebrate a festival of Slavic cultures. In 1987 that initiative developed into an All-Russian festival in Vologda, and in 1988 similar festivals in Leningrad and Novgorod attracted participants from the Ukraine and Belorussia. From above, this grass-roots initiative was supported by the Union of Writers of the RSFSR, and by the Council on the Problems of Russian Culture, itself recently created at the Academy of Sciences of the USSR in response to pressure from below.

Literaturnaia Rossiia carried a number of commentaries on the tasks facing the new Slavic Fund. Dmitrii Balashov, a well-known historical novelist, described the creation of the Slavic Fund as "a desperate effort to overcome a crisis" afflicting all three Slavic cultures. He emphasized that this public initiative was being undertaken in view of the absence of state-sponsored efforts. (According to a report in *Literaturnaia Rossiia*, Central TV in Moscow paid no attention to the creation of the Fund.) Yurii Loshchits pointed out the desperate quality of the undertaking by saying that in the past fifty years about 95 percent of "our cultural values" have been destroyed. He suggested that the future of the three Slavic peoples depends on their ability to restore the vital links of their common heritage. Loshchits made it clear that the Slavic Fund is one of several emergency measures taken to stave off the total breakdown of civil order in the USSR. Saying that that possibility was very real, he called for the renewal of the "national self-awareness of all nations" as the last line of defense against the imminent assault of "chaos." The sense of urgency was further emphasized by both Academician Tolstoi, representing the secular culture, and Metropolitan Pitirim, representing the Russian Church. Both suggested that the Fund was an expression of the newly-rediscovered *sobornost'* [communal spirit], which has always been a distinctive trait of "the Slavic family of nations."

Also in March 1989 about two hundred delegates of "patriotic groups" from all parts of the USSR formed the Alliance for the Spiritual Rebirth of the Fatherland [*Soiuz dukhovnogo vozrozhdeniia otechestva*].[43] The purpose of the Alliance is the promotion of unity among patriotic forces of the country "on the basis of spiritual and moral rebirth." Mikhail Antonov, a well-known Russite economist, was elected its chairman. The Alliance's focus on the need for spiritual rebirth was motivated by the realization that the current economic and ecological crisis was a consequence of the loss of faith among the people, said Antonov. He spelled out three principal goals of the Alliance: (1) turning the Soviet economy away from its current quantitative objectives and toward improving the quality of life, including spiritual and physical health, greater longevity and more free time; (2) producing alternative economic programs that would pay greater attention to the preservation of nature; and (3) restoring the cultural and spiritual traditions of Russians as well as of Russia's "small peoples," who are on the brink of extinction.

Carried in the newspaper of the Moscow writers' organization, *Moskovskii literator*, the Alliance's appeal made it clear that its chief concern was not with the loss of faith in Marxism-Leninism. "Our heart is broken at the sight of our present miseries: the banishment of patriotic history from books, cinema and theater; the distortion of the classics of Russian literature (an allusion to Marxist-Leninist influence on Soviet literary criticism. For more, see Chaikovskaia's article in Chapter 2); the slandering of champions of national culture; the ignoring of the peoples' traditions; and the destruction and profanation of historical monuments." Although Antonov mentioned his adherence to socialism, the Alliance's chief priority is clearly not the preservation of socialism, but a restoration and cultivation of Russia's spiritual tradition. Significantly, the first meeting of the Alliance took place in a Russian church.

Antonov further defined the Alliance's place within a broader spectrum of non-formal organizations in an article published in the magazine *Slovo*.[44] He criticized both extreme nationalist and "liberal-democratic" organizations. Noting that there are some people who regard the "dominance of minorities" in the government apparatus as the main cause of our misfortunes, Antonov took exception, saying that such people waste their energy on negation, instead of becoming more creative in their own right. Condemning their excessive patriotic zeal as "egotistical," he emphasized that the Alliance adheres to internationalism because it believes that there are no inferior or superior people on Earth. Although, unlike "liberal-democratic" organizations, the Alliance adheres to the "ideas of socialism," it does so only as long as these ideas serve the real needs of the people, said Antonov. "We resolutely reject all efforts of convergence, or the merging of socialism and capitalism, because such efforts will lead to the loss of our social gains," he explained. "We are not the Democratic Union, nor are we the Popular Front, nor Pamyat. Do not confuse us with them," warned Antonov. The Alliance's program of "spiritual rebirth" aims at a recovery of Russia's spiritual heritage, including its own advanced "philosophy of economic life." "The Japanese know how to make computers that are better than ours, but if you ask them for what or in the name of what they produce, they, like westerners, cannot answer the question," said Antonov.

He made it clear that he believes in neither the command economy system, nor in the way the government is now trying to change it. Without rejecting Marxism-Leninism outright, Antonov nonetheless pointed out its failure to provide a spiritual foundation for economic restructuring. The improvement of the ecological health of the country should be the first priority of the Soviet economy. The ecological situation in the USSR is so bad, Antonov said, that the country is already on the brink of demographic catastrophe because "in recent years almost all new-borns were either sick or deformed, or suffer from some kind of debility." The creation of the Alliance was prompted by the realization that the government does not know what to do. "We are firmly convinced that no theoretician, no political leader will have a future unless he finds support among the patriotic forces of all nationalities, and unless he realizes the priority of the spiritual foundation of life," warned Antonov.

Finally, in July 1989 the formation of an even broader alliance under the name *Edinstvo* [Unity] was announced in the weekly *Literaturnaia Rossiia*, which has become an important forum for Russite views.[45] Calling itself in full the Movement of the Lovers of the Literatures and Arts of Russia, Edinstvo purports to be a sort of umbrella organization for "all the healthy national and intellectual forces of Russia." As such, it issued an invitation to the Association of Russian Artists, the Alliance, the Slavic Fund, and a number of similar groups to join its struggle for the consolidation of a "patriotic commonwealth of fraternal peoples." However, unlike the previously discussed groups which focus on the needs of ethnic Russians (and their East Slavic brethren), Edinstvo's main focus is on the need for unity among all nationalities of the Russian Federation, including the Tartars, Mongols, Kabardinians, etc. If the previous groups aimed at the building of an ethnic Russian [*russkii*] House, that is, a sort of Russian *izba*, the founders of Edinstvo promote the idea that the survival of all national "houses" under the crumbling structure of the Communist regime can be best assured by cooperation within the federated Russian "village."

The reality of today is so alarming, reads Edinstvo's appeal, that either we act collectively to stop the exacerbation of national conflicts, or we will all succumb to the "forces of nationalist ambitions and demagogic anarchy who use the flag of perestroika and glasnost to rock our multi-national boat." While stressing cooperation within the Russian Federation, a special pitch was made for the unity of the three East Slavic peoples. Mentioning neither socialism nor Marxism-Leninism, the Edinstvo founders suggest that unity should be based on "the millennial spiritual legacy" [Christianity is understood] and the best traditions of the Russian nineteenth-century intelligentsia, who were concerned with the well-being of people regardless of their ethnic identity.

There are five principal directions planned for Edinstvo's activities, to be financed on the basis of self-accounting: (1) the creation of the Academy of Literatures of Russia to protect the "cultural distinctiveness" of literatures in all languages of the Federation; (2) the creation of a monthly magazine, a film studio, and a theater to acquaint Russians with the works of Russia's national minorities; (3) the acquisition of a separate television channel for the Russian Federation; (4) the encouragement of contacts with the twenty million Russian-language speakers abroad; (5) the education of the young in the spirit of patriotism and friendship with other peoples, providing them with a "broad humanist world-view." The list of Edinstvo founders includes such Russite authors discussed in this book as Rasputin, Kuniaev, and Shafarevich, as well as a number of writers from Dagestan, Bashkiria, Yakutia, and other minority ethnic regions.

All of the above initiatives and groups reflect a growing alarm at the prospect of the country's falling apart. They express a sense of urgency and suggest the need to introduce extraordinary protective measures. All emphasize that the Russian people ought to take upon themselves a greater share of responsibility than has so far been the case. Although they do not challenge the authority of the Soviet state per se, they do not even pretend to pay lip service to the Marxist-Leninist foundations on which it stands. On the contrary, all of them suggest that the foundation is rotten and ought to be replaced with old-fashioned--that is, national, non-ideological--patriotism. Although all were publicized or at least announced in officially approved Soviet periodicals, none seems to rely on or ask for government support.

But there have been some efforts toward building a new non-Communist Russia which have not received any coverage in official Soviet press at all. One of them is the formation of the Christian Patriotic Alliance [*Khristianskii Patrioticheskii Soiuz*] in December 1988. It was formed on the basis of an informal group, "For the Spiritual and Biological Salvation of the People," which had been founded earlier in 1988. Vladimir Osipov, a long-time Russite dissident who had spent fifteen years in Soviet jails, was elected chairman. The CPA documents which have reached the West make it clear that it sees itself as a political party.[46]

In a preamble to its program, the CPA describes the country's current situation as an "economic, political, and cultural dead-end." "Our peasantry, the root of the nation and the carrier of its time-honored traditions, is destroyed. Our soil is damaged. Food is poisoned with chemicals. Intellectual and physical degeneration grow unimpeded. The destruction of the historical memory of the nation has resulted in the Russians no longer considering themselves a single nation." The CPA blames the situation on the "monopoly of atheism" which has led to the spiritual impoverishment of the Russians and contributed to the "epidemics of alcoholism," narcomania, crime and breakdown of family units.

The CPA sees the solution in the development of the "national-patriotic self-awareness of [all] peoples of Russia." For the Russians, that self-awareness means, first of all, an awareness of their Orthodox Christian traditions. Saying that "Christianity is the source of morality," the CPA advocates the separation of the state from atheism, so that each Russian family can decide whether to educate children in atheism or religion. To attain this goal, the CPA will seek "representation in the government of the country on an equal footing with the Communist Party and other public organizations." Calling for "a wider participation of people" in decision-making through the use of referenda on all important issues, the CPA vows to support all initiatives aimed at "fundamental perestroika."

The CPA favors a three-tier economy: private, cooperative, and state. Proclaiming that "each citizen has the right to own a piece of land," the CPA advocates the development of small-scale, ecologically sound private farming, boosted by voluntary migration from urban areas to villages. It promises to strengthen the family by providing greater financial security for women, enabling them to devote more time to rearing children and to the domestic household. Vowing to strenthen the legal protection of "inalienable individual rights," the CPA proposes a re-introduction of jury trials (abolished by the Bolsheviks).

Concerning the nationalities question, the CPA vows to fight for "true equality of Russians with other peoples of the USSR." To attain this goal, it advocates establishing a separate Russian Academy of Sciences and the transfer of the capital of the USSR to another city while retaining Moscow as the capital of the Russian Federation. The CPA vows to fight the spread of russophobia through a campaign of enlightenment, including teaching Russians to respect the culture of their neighbors. "A true patriot is the one who loves his own national culture but also respects the culture of other nations." In foreign relations, the CPA "strives for cooperation with all nations who have renounced annexations by force and all forms of genocide."

On August 5, 1989, another Christianity-inspired political party was formed, the Christian-Democratic Alliance of Russia [*Khristiansko-Demokraticheskii Soiuz Rossii*].[47] The Coordinating Council of the CDA includes Aleksandr Ogorodnikov, a long-time Christian activist who, like Osipov, has been imprisoned for his dissident activities prior to perestroika, and Rev. Vitalii Lapkovskii from Leningrad. Like the CPA, the CDA openly proclaims itself a political organization, founded on the "ethical and moral foundations of the Gospels given by our Lord, Jesus Christ." Like the CRA, the CDA sets as its main goal "the spiritual rebirth of Russia." Also like the CPA, the CDA advocates the "de-ideologization of the state" (the CPA calls it "separation of the state from atheism"), the rule of law, a three-tier economy, ecological balance, and a harmony between man and nature.

However, unlike the CPA, which has explicitly identified itself with Russian Orthodox Christianity, the CDA advocates the interests of all Christians "regardless of their confession." Moreover, the CDA is more emphatic in its support of a multiparty "parliamentary Russia." (The CPA favors further democratization but stops short of endorsing any particular form of government.) In comparison with the CPA, the CDA is also more specific in its proclamation of the right of national self-determination, including secession. In foreign relations the CDA proclaims its adherence to the principles of the already existing International of Christian Democracy and, in particular, emphasizes the need to cooperate with all "Christian and democratic forces both within [the USSR] and without."

In its "Appeal to the Christians of Russia," the CDA explains the reason for its formation in terms of national emergency: "The regime that was built by the Communists on [the basis of] fear, oppression and exploitation, is on the brink of collapse. What does tomorrow hold for us? Poverty? Destruction of our homes? A multi-national bloodbath? A new dictatorship?" According to the CDA, the "Party-and-State apparatus" is incapable of averting the impending disaster. The new Supreme Soviet is utterly unrepresentative because none of the "non-Communist faiths, neither Christians, nor Muslims, nor Buddhists, nor Jews" are represented there, except for a few token appointees. "We believe that the rebirth of the country is impossible without liberation from the totalitarian Communist ideology and without equal participation in the process of renewal of all layers of the population and of all political parties." The Appeal ends with a call to all Christians to join the forces for the "salvation of our Fatherland."

In my Alaska speech in February 1988 (see Chapter 1), I predicted that the rebirth of Russian nationalism was "but a tiny visible tip of a huge iceberg that for the first time in Soviet history seriously threatens the Communist Party's monopoly on power." Since then the number of Russite groups and their membership has shown momentous growth. Many initiatives of a distinctly Russite orientation have been undertaken to fill the vacuum left by the shrinking authority of the Communist government. Fortunately, the anti-Zionist and judophobic rhetoric has remained the exception rather than the rule among the Russite groups and initiatives. Thanks to their concerted efforts, the existence of the Russian national problem is now openly admitted.

Although none of the above groups has achieved influence comparable to that of the national fronts in a number of the non-Russian republics, there is little doubt that sooner or later their efforts will coalesce into a broad political movement, capable of mounting a real challenge to the Communist Party's monopoly on power.[48] That challenge does not have to be in the form of a single "Russian Party." There might be more than one "Russian Party." There might be one leaning toward a new form of socialism or toward social-democracy akin to that in Western countries. There might be another similar to the Gaullists in France. There might be yet another favoring such conservative schemes as Reaganomics or Thatcherism. There might be attempts to emulate Le Pen's National party. Finally, the Communist Party itself, if it wants to survive, would have to address the Russian national problem. It is futile to try to predict which one of these prospective parties might form the first post-totalitarian Russian government. But, as the available programs indicate, the West has no reason to fear any of them. The West will continue to be considerably more threatened by the current Soviet regime and the attempts to hold it together. This regime has yet to renounce its universalist Communist utopia, in quest for which the national interests of all Soviet peoples, including especially the Russians, have been so ruthlessly trampled. No government in Russia can assure stability in this part of the world unless it earnestly tries to solve or alleviate the Russian national problem.

Notes

1. N. Berdiaev, S. Bulgakov, M. Gershenzon, A. Izgoev, B. Kistiakovskii, P. Struve, and S. Frank, Vekhi: Sbornik statei o russkoi intelligentsii, (Moscow, 1909; reprinted by Posev in 1967).

2. S. Askol'dov, N. Berdiaev, Sergei Bulgakov, S. Frank, P. Struve et al., Iz glubiny: sbornik statei o russkoi revoliutsii (1967 reprint by YMCA Press, Paris).

3. Among his books are Slavery and Freedom (New York, 1944), Dostoevsky: An Interpretation (New York, 1934), The Meaning of Creative Art (New York, 1954), The Russian Revolution (London, 1931), The Origin of Russian Communism (Ann Arbor, 1960), and The Russian Idea.

4. Alexander Yanov, The Russian Challenge and the Year 2000 (New York: Blackwell, 1987). According to Yanov, the "main tenets" of Russian nationalism include "militant anti-westernism" bordering on "the ideology of the Ayatollah Khomeini" and "dogmatism and intolerance." As such, Russian nationalism today possesses an "explosive potential" similar to that of Bolshevism in 1917. In a sweeping generalization, Yanov traces "the ideology of the Russian New Right from its emergence (simultaneously with Marxism) in the 1830s up to the early 1980s, when fascist demonstrations took place in the streets of Moscow." To counter this "threat," Yanov proposes "to return to the Kennedy-Khrushchev political agenda of 1963" (whatever that agenda was). According to the dust jacket, the book "makes a cogent plea that the West respond to the threat posed by the Russian New Right by supporting the emergence of Russia from political and cultural isolation."

5. Renata Gal'tseva, "Nikolai Aleksandrovich Berdiaev," Literaturnaia gazeta, No. 31, August 2, 1989. Her article was part of a series on the "Golden Age" of Russian philosophy. Besides Berdiaev, there is a growing demand for such other Russian religious thinkers as Sergei Bulgakov, Georgii Fedotov, Pavel Florenskii, George Florovskii, Semen Frank, and Vasilii Rozanov. Their work is now being made available for the general Soviet reader for the first time since the revolution. Together with Berdiaev, they were part of the Russian philosophical renaissance that began with Solov'ev and lasted through the first decades of this century.

6. It is another matter that the exponents of the Russian idea tend to define these values in Christian terms. But, as we have seen, Solov'ev's Christianity was rather unorthodox (even though he was a member of the Russian Orthodox church), and he regarded freedom of conscience as a fundamental human right and indispensable precondition for a dialogue between different religions and cultures. It was in the

West that Berdiaev came to be known as the "philosopher of freedom." A Christian inspiration underlying the Russian idea makes it both less nationalistic and more compatible with the West, with which Russia shares the common Judeo-Christian heritage. For more, see Nicolai N. Petro, "Challenge of the 'Russian Idea': Rediscovering the Legacy of Russian Religious Philosophy," Christianity and Russian Culture in Soviet Society (Boulder, CO: Westview Press, 1990).

7. John B. Dunlop, The Faces of Contemporary Russian Nationalism (Princeton, N.J.: Princeton University Press, 1983), pp. 286-290.

8. For the Russian text of the letter of thirty-one see Novoe Russkoe Slovo, November 19, 1987. It was printed there, in full and without a commentary, under the title "V interesakh strany" [In the interests of the country]. The names of the signees were listed, and the place was given (Moscow), but there was no date. I assume it was written shortly before its publication in Novoe Russkoe Slovo.

9. "Pis'mo iz Moskvy," as an open letter, was published in Russkaia mysl', No. 3786, July 28, 1989.

10. The six signees were Viktor Aksiuchits and Gleb Anishchenko, the two editors of Vybor, Father Dmitrii Dudko, a long-time dissident and Russian Orthodox priest, Feliks Svetov, an editor of the samizdat Christian Bulletin, Viktor Trostnikov, a dissident Moscow University physicist, and Valerii Senderov.

11. Valerii Senderov, "Daesh' men'she antisemitizma, ili perestroika vse-taki est,'" Russkaia mysl', No. 3737, August 12, 1988.

12. Valerii Senderov, "Rasisty b'iut iz podpol'ia," Novoe Russkoe Slovo, July 27, 1989.

13. Valerii Senderov, "Khristianstvo i antisemitism: Otkrytoe pis'mo Sergeiu Lezovu" [Open Letter to Sergei Lezov], Russkaia mysl', No. 3750, November 11, 1988. Aron Katsenelinboigen, a Soviet emigre and now professor at the Wharton School of the University of Pensylvania, made similar charges against Russian Christians, particularly implicating Likhachev in anti-Semitism. See his article, "Will Glasnost Bring the Reactionaries to Power," Orbis, Spring 1988, and his exchange with George Gibian that followed in the Summer issue of the same journal.

14. Shafarevich's book, Rusofobia, was later published by a Russian emigre group, Russischer Nationaler Verein, in Munich, West Germany, 1989. An abbreviated rendition of the book's thesis appeared under the same title in Nash sovremennik No. 6, June 1989, pp. 167-192. In my discussion of Senderov's review of Shafarevich's book I relied on its magazine version.

15. See also Mikhail Kheifets, "The Resurgence of Christianity and Russian-Jewish Relations," Christianity and Russian Culture in Soviet Society, Nicolai Petro, Ed. (Boulder, CO: Westview Press, 1990).

16.   Valerii Senderov, "Natsional'nye problemy na stranitsakh 'Strany i mira'," Russkaia mysl', No. 3788, August 11, 1989. See Senderov's polemic with Lezov.

17.   For another competent critique of Shafarevich's book, see Aleksei Shmelev's article, "Po zakonam parodii?", Znamia, June 1990, pp. 213-225.

18.   I do not know whether these letters had any effect on the quality of RL Russian programming. Judging by the Radio Liberty research materials I receive, there was some improvement, especially, during Paul Goble's stint with the radio. However, at least one Russian part-time RL staff writer, Mikhail Nazarov, finding no improvement in RL programming, in 1990 quit his job in protest. He motivated his decision by the lack of "positive" ideas in Russian-language programming. In his article, "O radiogolosakh, emigratsii i Rossii," published in the Soviet monthly Slovo (No.10, 1990), Nazarov disagreed with President Bush who gave RL high marks on April 2, 1990.

19.   Helene Carrere d'Encausse, "Videt' real'nuiu opasnost'," and Vitalii Tret'iakov, "Novaia natsional'naia politika," Moskovskie novosti, No. 30, July 23, 1989. D'Encausse is the author of L'Empire eclate (Paris, 1979), translated into English as Decline of an Empire: The Soviet Republics in Revolt; and Confiscated Power: How Soviet Russia Really Works (New York: Harper, 1980).

20.   VSKhSON's entire program and a commentary are available in English in John B. Dunlop, The New Russian Revolutionaries (Belmont, Mass.: Nordland, 1976), esp. pp. 293 and 287. In Russian see VSKhSON: Programma, sud, v tiur'makh i lageriakh (Paris: YMCA-Press, 1975).

21.   Sergei Soldatov, Zarnitsy vozrozhdeniia (London: Overseas Publication Interchange, Ltd., 1984), p. 353.

22.   Anatoly Fedoseyev, O novoi Rossii: Al'ternativa (London: Overseas Publications Interchange, Ltd., 1980), p. 252.

23.   Programma Natsional'no Trudovogo Soiuza Rossiiskikh solidaristov (Frankfurt/Main: Possev, 1974).

24.   Vladislav Krasnov, "Images of the Soviet Future: The Emigre and Samizdat Debate," in The Soviet Union & the Challenge of the Future, ed. Alexander Shtromas and Morton Kaplan, Vol. 1 (New York: Paragon, 1988).

25.   Vladimir Balakhonov, "Sokhranenie imperii ili samosokhranenie" [Preservation of the empire or self-preservation], Svobodnoe slovo, No. 13. Reprinted in Russkaia mysl', No. 3781, June 23, 1989.

26.   Sergei Grigoriants', "Imperiia ili Soiuz," Russkaia mysl', No. 3689, September 4, 1987.

27. Zaza Siradze, "Nikto ne reshit za nas nashi problemy," Zaria Vostoka, June 14, 1989.

28. Poel' Karp, "Metropoliia ili respublika?", Knizhnoe obozrenie, No. 29, July 21, 1989.

29. Actually, Rasputin used the phrase "a great country," not "Great Russia," but Karp insinuates that he did so in order to disguise his "Great Russian" ambitions. In fact, Stolypin's program envisioned the equality of all nationalities of the Empire.

30. Karp's fundamentally Marxist-Leninist position is apparent in his article "Gde zhe liniia razdela?" [Where Is the Dividing Line], Knizhnoe obozrenie, No. 21, 1989. In a letter to the editor one of the readers pointed out Karp's excesive "piety" toward the "bloodthirsty class struggle" utterances of Marx and Lenin. (See Knizhnoe obozrenie, No. 33, August 1989.) Karp's dogmatic invocation of the authority of Marxism-Leninism is indeed not very different from that of Nina Andreeva.

31. For more on Solzhenitsyn's portrayal of Stolypin, see Vladislav Krasnov, "Solzhenitsyn's New August 1914: A Novel Attempt to Revise History," Aspects of Modern Russian and Czech Literature: Selected papers of the Third World Congress for Soviet and East European Studies, Arnold McMillin, Ed. (Columbus, Ohio: Slavica, 1989), pp. 129-149.

32. Aleksandr N. Iakovlev, "Dostizhenie kachestvenno novogo sostoianiia sovetskogo obshchestva i obshchestvennye nauki," a speech given at a conference of Soviet sociologists on April 17, 1987, Vestnik Akademii Nauk SSSR, No. 6, 1987, esp. p. 68.

33. Igor' D'iakov, "Stolypin," Literaturnaia Rossiia, No. 28, July 14, 1989.

34. See note 26.

35. V. Ol'gin, "Stolypin: Slovo i delo," [Stolypin: Word and Deed] Sovetskaia molodezh', August 19, 1989.

36. See Arkadii Stolypin's chapter in Literaturnaia Rossiia, No. 36, September 8, 1989. It was introduced by Sviatoslav Rybas.

37. "Vsemirnyi god russkoi kul'tury," Novoe Russkoe Slovo (New York), January 31, 1989.

38. "Russkaia entsiklopediia," Literaturnaia gazeta, No. 12, March 22, 1989.

39. "Narodnyi Dom Rossii," an interview with Vladislav Teterin, Pravda, March 18, 1989.

40. "Vserossiiskaia Akademiia," an interview with Il'ia Glazunov, Pravda, February 2, 1989. About the significance of Glazunov's art in the context of Russian national self-

awareness, see Vladislav Krasnov, "Russian National Feeling: An Informal Poll," in Robert Conquest, ed., The Last Empire: ,Nationality and the Soviet Future (Stanford, CA: Hoover Inst. Press, 1986).

41. "Siloi Rossiiskogo bratstva," an interview with Boris Tsarev, co-chairman, Tovarishchestvo russkikh khudozhnikov, Literaturnaia Rossiia, No. 24, June 16, 1989.

42. On the Slavic Fund see Literaturnaia Rossiia, No. 11, March 17, 1989.

43. Moskovskii literator (No. 14, March 24, 1989) carried three items on the Alliance of Spiritual Rebirth of the Fatherland: a report about its formation, a statement by Antonov and the Alliance's appeal.

44. Mikhail Antonov, "Vernut' zabytie istiny," Slovo, No. 7, 1989.

45. "Za edinstvo i sodruzhestvo," Literaturnaia Rossiia, No. 30, July 28, 1989. According to its report of May 18, 1990, this group was registered under the new name Edinenie.

46. See AFP report from Paris, January 6, 1989. A copy of the CPA Program and By-Laws in Russian can be obtained through the CPA representative in the USA, Vera Politis, Ann Arbor, Michigan. The CPA representative in West Germany is Igor' Ogurtsov, the founder of the VSKhSON, who was recently allowed to emigrate. Since early 1990 the CPA changed its name to Khristianskoe vozrozhdenie [Christian Renaissance].

47. About the CDA see Russkaia mysl', No. 3790, August 25, 1989.

48. One such positive sign may be seen in the formation of the Committee of National Concord [Komitet Natsional'noe Soglasie]) in the Fall of 1990. Composed of a number of outstanding Russian writers and public figures, the CNC unites both the Westernizers and the Russites (Viktor Astaf'ev, Dmitrii Likhachev, Igor' Zolotusskii), those living inside of the USSR and emigres (Vladimir Bukovskii, Vladimir Maksimov, Eduard Lozanskii, e.g.), Jews and Russians. In January 1991, the CNC issued a statement in which the use of armed force in Lithuania was condemned. The statement also condemned both anti-Semitism and russophobia. (See Novoe Russkoe Slovo, January 22, 1991). However, according to S. Sokolov's article, "Shpionskie strasti" (Komsomol'skaia pravda, November 11, 1990), the KGB's primary task now is to prevent oppositional groups from forming a united front by spreading compromising rumors about their members. One cannot discount the possibility that the KGB might have infiltrated some oppositional groups. However, the KGB today is not what it used to be. The case of Oleg Kalugin, a former KGB general and a spy, seems to indicate that one can no longer automatically assume that the KGB is solidly behind the current regime. After publicly criticizing the KGB, Kalugin was deprived of all honors by Gorbachev, only to be elected people's deputy in September 1990.

6

Conclusion:

A New Russia and the West

In order for a grain to be reborn, it must fall into the ground and die.

-John 12:24

THE TOWER OF BABEL

I believe what Plato believed: ideas, rather than men, rule the world. Ideas themselves are immaterial, but their consequences are not; the quality of our life and sometimes life itself depend on the kinds of ideas that rule us. Of course, they rule the world through the men and women who create or adopt them. In this respect, ideas are like laws by which all citizens of a country are supposed to abide. In fact, a country's laws are but ideas invested with the power to make people obey them. Once adopted, a country's laws reign supreme over everyone, including those who have written them. Similarly, the ideas that rule the world do so by ruling over people, including those in whose mind they may have originated. As long as there are provisions made for changing laws as times change, blessed is a country that is ruled by law rather than the arbitrariness of men. However, since there is no international law that is enforceable in every country of the world, it is only prudent to conclude that now, as during Plato's time, the world continues to be ruled by ideas to a far greater extent than by laws.

Although they lack the power of laws, ideas can attract and inspire people to action. Like laws, ideas have consequences. Once it finds followers, an idea can create a durable trend or a fleeting fashion. There are all kinds of ideas: profound and shallow, noble and pedestrian, predatory and harmless, beautiful and ugly, eternal and mundane, divine and profane, useful and useless. But as long as there

271

are people who accept them, they all have the "right" to exist. The ideas that rule the world are as good as the people who accept them. That is, Adam Smith's economic theory of the free market is just as applicable to ideas as to industrial goods. One might even say that the invisible hand of supply and demand has been guiding mankind not only to economic prosperity, but also to the heights of intellectual and spiritual achievement. As long as the freedom of the ideational market is assured, we do not have to worry about a pernicious or foolish idea seizing total control of the world. (That is, if we believe that the majority of humans are neither evil nor foolish.)

That freedom, however, like any other freedom, has been under constant assault by enemies of freedom throughout history. It has been under a particularly vicious assault in this century. Alas, it has been poorly defended. So, if the twentieth century turned out to be considerably more tragic than the nineteenth-century futurists projected, it was precisely because the free market of ideas had been allowed to shrink dramatically. The West, where the idea of the free market originated and flourished, has done more (though hardly enough) to assure the freedom of the economic market than to protect the free exchange of ideas. And the greatest reason for this dereliction of duty was the West's reluctance to check the spread of another Western idea, one which managed to establish an intellectual monopoly over one-third of mankind while playing havoc with the rest.

It was the idea according to which a certain Western scholar had finally succeeded in discovering a "scientific" law of social development. According to this "law," the progress of mankind could be achieved only through class struggle and violent world revolution. If only mankind could follow through on that "law," it would soon be rid of exploitation, poverty, hard toil, injustice, wars, and national strife. This was certainly a rationalist, though hardly a rational, idea. It also was an atheist idea. Not only was it atheist in the sense of denying God's existence but it was an actively theomachic, God-fighting idea. It stipulated not only the overthrow of God (or gods and religion in general), but also the enthronement of man, with his "omnipotent science," as the new ruler of the universe. A Russian philosopher described it as the idea of Man-god. As such, it was the exact opposite of the Christian idea of God-man.

It was Karl Marx's idea. It was the Communist idea. It was a totalitarian idea. It proved to be both attractive and destructive. One of the major reasons for its "popularity" was the fact that, when it was launched, an era of unprecedented scientific and technological progress had begun in the West. As more and more nations have been drawn into this progress, the role of secular science-worshiping intellectuals to whom this idea had a special appeal has become much more prominent. Buoyed by this new role, they came to think of themselves as the priesthood of a new god, the god of man-centered technological and material progress.

The Marxist idea appeals especially to the young semi-intellectuals and students because it flatters their growing (but not grown) and allegedly "rational, empirical, and scientific" minds. It encourages their rebellion against parental, governmental, and church authority. In a stable and prosperous society such a rebellion would have been little more than a tempest in a teapot. Therefore, aware of the intellectuals' proverbial inability to act, Marx made a special pitch to the "exploited" proletariat of the capitalist West. When this did not work (because, contrary to Marx's law of progressive impoverishment of the proletariat, it was actually turning into a middle class), Marx's followers re-directed the pitch to the oppressed masses of colonized and less-than-capitalist countries, one of which was Russia.

Thus modified, the idea acquired a new virility. It was particularly successful in preying on the "westernized" intellectuals of non-European developing countries. Stricken with an inferiority complex toward the technologically advanced West, they forsook their "backward" native traditions, customs, and gods (as a result of secular, technology-oriented education) and jumped impatiently on Marxism as a means of modernization and a shortcut for "catching up" with the West. The Marxist idea certainly appeals to those who want to prove their manhood in war, violence, and destruction. For the above reasons, it proved to be a very successful idea. Since 1917 it has spread, like a virus, to developing countries anxious to catch up with the West. It has infected thousands of their intellectuals with the "progressive" idea of revolutionary violence against their native "reactionary," "barbaric," and "Asiatic" regimes, which are allegedly supported by "Western imperialism." It has caused political mass epidemics that have already felled millions of people and dozens of nations.

As a disease of technological civilization, the Marxist idea afflicts, first and foremost, its secular priesthood, the intellectuals. Although hugely capable of destruction, it is, however, just as incapable of creation except for creating governments and tools that destroy. It has certainly created governments capable of destroying capitalism-- and all life on earth. But none of these governments has "caught up" with the West in anything but armaments. On the contrary, most have fallen further behind. These governments are not even capable of feeding their people. Nor will they let people feed themselves. Nor can they create something that is worth buying on the free market because these governments are controlled by an idea which kills all creative ideas--an ideocidal idea. First of all, it kills all native ideas. Ironically, Marxism has proven to be a form of Western cultural imperialism. Although fundamentally hostile to the very underpinnings of Western civilization, it nonetheless advances narrow Western ethnocentrism. It seems to afford the West a dual benefit. While Western Marxists take satisfaction in raising foot soldiers for their cause in non-Western countries, Western capitalists are smiling because they know that as long as these countries remain committed to Marxism, one need not worry about their competition in a free market.

Such an idea could not but have tragic consequences for mankind, first of all, for its own proponents. Arguably, more Communists were killed by Communists than by "capitalists." And the toll keeps on rising. It was a bad idea not because it was not clever. There were hundreds of ideas that were much less intelligent. And yet none has flopped so tragically and so totally. It was bad because it was presumptuous. It presumed not only on God but also on the free market of ideas. It presumed both on the common sense of mankind and on the naturalness of its division into nations. In fact, it presumed on nature itself. And because it was ideocidal it turned out to be both homicidal and genocidal.

The major reason for the Marxist idea being ideocidal was its exclusivity. Once it was declared "scientific," it was only a matter of time before all competing ideas were declared "unscientific" and therefore nonsensical. Thus, the idea became an ideology. And not just like any other political ideology, but the all-embracing, omniscient, omnipotent, and "only true" ideology of "scientific" Communism. It became the religion of secularized mankind--a godless religion worshiping man. It became more fanatic and intolerant than any religion because what a religion only *believes*, Marxism *knows*. Marxism is an expression of the arrogance, fanaticism and intolerance of an atheist mind toward all that is unknown, including God.

It was on the sand of this ideology that the Soviet Union was built. Now the world is witnessing the unraveling of the greatest folly on earth since the Tower of Babel: the frenetic efforts of Soviet "superintendents of perestroika" to straighten out, or reconstruct [*perestroit'*] the wobbly Tower of Socialism (Communism) they have built at enormous cost to the country. As we remember, their biblical predecessors were presumptuous both in economics and politics. In economics they were apparently inspired by the invention of a better mortar. In politics they were driven by the ambition to unite a whole nation in one language and one project.

> And the Lord came down to see the city and the tower, which the sons of men had built. And the Lord said, "Behold, they are one people, and they have all one language; and this is only the beginning of what they will do; and nothing that they propose to do will now be impossible for them. Come, let us go down, and there confuse their language, that they may not understand one another's speech." So the Lord scattered them abroad from there over the face of all the earth, and they left off building the city. (Genesis 11:1-9)

As we see, the Lord's punishment was both stern and swift, but hardly excessive. He merely prevented the completion of the project by scattering the builders abroad. He neither killed anyone nor destroyed what they had built. The punishment befitted the crime.

These latter-day tower builders have followed the biblical archetype in their arrogant and presumptuous desire to surpass God in might and glory. But their predicament is considerably more complicated and tragic. First of all, their offense is much greater. Unlike in the Bible, the modern builders did not build on an empty plain. They first destroyed a "city" that already was there and killed many of its defenders. Their political hubris was greater still. For they wanted to unite, by one language and one project, not a single nation but the whole world. As if in defiance of the Lord of the Bible, those whom He had scattered gathered again. Not only did they try to surpass God in His might and glory, but they denied and blasphemed Him, killing and persecuting His priests and His people. As to technological prowess, they had none. Therefore, they relied on "non-economic coercion" to make people work. Their only technological innovation was that the mortar they used was mixed with the sweat, blood, and tears of their own people.

Another major deviation from the biblical archetype was that, in the final account, they built but their own prison. One might well doubt whether the Lord would want to punish them more than they have already punished themselves. But the jury is still out. And the sand of ideology has not yet been cemented or replaced by a more solid foundation. May the Lord allow them to reconstruct the prison into something else. But if He decides to destroy it altogether, may He do it without destroying its captive laborers. For even those who once complained of being scattered on the face of the earth as a cruel punishment are now praying for it as a blessing.

Of course, the Bible is not the only key to understanding what is going on in the USSR today. A number of Marx's contemporaries, especially those endowed with a poetic gift, foresaw and predicted the inevitable dead-end to which the hubris of man-centered "scientific" progress will drive mankind. Mary Shelley warned in her novel, *Frankenstein: or The Modern Prometheus*, that "supremely frightful would be the effect of any human endeavor to mock the stupendous mechanism of the Creator of the world." Dr. Frankenstein, a Western scientist, did just that when, in a fit of theomachic rebellion against "our dark world," he created a monster who then killed the scientist's bride and best friend. Prophetically, the monster found his refuge "amidst the wilds of Tartary and Russia," where he went on a rampage. But at least Dr. Frankenstein and his friends felt responsible enough to lure the monster back to Europe. Marx's Promethean effort, on the other hand, resulted in Russia being turned into a laboratory for the creation of a new human species, *Homo Sovieticus*, and a new society. The monster that resulted is still at large, and the West does not seem to be in a hurry to eliminate one of its least fortunate products.[1]

In the United States, Herman Melville created his own myth of modern man coping with the ambiguity of Good and Evil. In his novel *Moby Dick*, the white whale is the embodiment of evil, or so it appears to Captain Ahab, who had lost his leg to him. Determined to avenge the whale, Ahab became so obsessed by his belief that he thought that by killing the beast he would free the world from its thralldom to Evil. Not only did he fail in his task, but he lost his own life and sacrificed his crew. This myth suggests that all efforts to fight the perceived evil (of capitalism, imperialism, white domination, etc.) by obsessively violent means are not only futile but counterproductive, in that they contribute to the augmentation of the evil they intended to fight.

Marx's Russian contemporary, Dostoevskii, devoted his life to showing the folly of atheist efforts to achieve good by evil means, even if justified by a rationalist theory. In *Crime and Punishment* he depicted the drama of Raskol'nikov, a poor Russian student, who commits a crime for an allegedly noble cause. He is inspired by a Western "Napoleonic" idea that there are some elite people who need not abide under common standards of humanity as long as they dedicate themselves to a good purpose. He plans to kill an old miserly pawnbroker in order to use her money to further his education, to help his abused sister, and ultimately to become a benefactor of humanity. But his rationally conceived plan fails. Unforeseen circumstances force him to kill not only the pawnbroker but also her sister whom he actually admired. Moreover, he found himself emotionally incapable of using the acquired wealth. Only after falling in love with Sophia, an uneducated and abused but pure-hearted and deeply religious Russian girl, does he bring himself to publicly admitting his crime.

Similarly, the Bolsheviks in Russia had planned to kill off only a few capitalist "pawnbrokers" but wound up killing not only millions of innocent people, but also their own comrades. Just like Raskol'nikov, they proved to be incapable of putting to good use the wealth they had acquired. We may never know whether those Bolsheviks who faced the Stalinist terror machine they helped to create wanted to repent for their crimes. But there are signs that their descendants might follow Raskol'nikov's suit and admit their own guilt. According to Dostoevskii's prophecy, this would not happen unless they are blessed with the love of and for their Sophia, that is, a Russia that has kept its faith and common sense in spite of being abused by its rulers, past and present. Like the biblical grain, that Russia has fallen to the ground and died only to be reborn.

In *The Possessed* Dostoevskii depicted Russian revolutionaries as elitist, nihilist, and selfish individuals who have cut themselves loose from the religion, customs, and traditions of the Russian people. Using the parable of the Gadarene swine, he prophesied that Christ will save Russia from whatever nihilist ideas ("their name is Legion") may possess it by transferring them onto a band of revolutionary "swine" who would then cast themselves into an abyss of self-destruction. Thus healed, the Russian man would then sit "at the feet of Christ, clothed and in his right mind." (St. Luke, 8:35) The first part of this prophecy, the self-destruction of the revolutionaries, was largely fulfilled in Stalin's purges. The second part, the healing of Russia, is underway.

It is impossible to understand what is going on in the USSR right now in political or economic terms alone. For what is going on is a revolt of Soviet intellectuals, especially Russian writers, against the suppression, with the help of the Marxist ideological monopoly, of religious, spiritual, mystical, occult, metaphysical, and generally idealistic ideas and viewpoints. Ironically, it is Marxist "science" that proved to be more like witchcraft, certainly in economics; Marxist "rationalism" that proved to be irrational; Marxist dialectics that ossified into dogmas; Marxist atheism that became the greatest enemy of the freedom of conscience; and Marxist materialism that failed to satisfy even the basic material needs of the people.

Ironically, it is under the banner of Marxist "internationalism" that such aberrant expressions of nationalism as Russian "big brother" chauvinism, judophobia, and russophobia have flourished. And under the same banner the Iron Curtain and Berlin Walls were raised, isolating the country from foreign ideas. It is hardly surprising, therefore, that this revolt against "internationalist" Marxist abstractions is also a revolt for a return to national roots. After having searched in vain for a utopia in Marxist-Leninist skies, Soviet intellectuals seem to have no way to go but to land on the firm ground of reality. And that reality is Russia, with the millennium of its Christianity behind it. Like the legendary city of Kitezh, which was miraculously "saved" from the Mongol destruction by being completely submerged in a lake, a new Russia now appears ready to surface again, with its essential russianness fully intact.

Soviet Communists have always claimed that theirs was a revolution of "world-historical" significance in that it has reversed the entire course of history since "exploitation" started in Biblical times. It is not about the scale of their undertaking that they erred, but about its meaning. The meaning is: not only is the first avowedly atheist and God-fighting state in the world a complete fiasco, but it is at a dead end from which it cannot extricate itself. One major reason for the failure was Marx's, and his followers', arrogant disdain for the unknown that some call God. Another reason was their flight from the reality of the national, linguistic, cultural, and religious divisions of mankind. It was the Marxist obsession with constructing a fool-proof socio-economic structure in complete disregard for the indigenous traditions of each nation that produced the monster known as "utopia in power."

Here is a lesson to mankind. Far from showing the way to a better future, as the founders of Communism promised, they have shown only where *not* to go. And before Soviet Communists can go anywhere, they must first extricate themselves from the monster they created. However, their Marxist disregard for the complexity and unfathomableness of human nature--particularly its aesthetic, religious and irrational dimensions--makes them less than a match for the monster, even if we assume that since Gorbachev they have become revisionist enough to wish to undo it. At least now they are beginning to realize their helplessness. They may not necessarily turn to God for help themselves. But, having acknowledged the impotence of their Marxist "science" to find a solution, they now appear to be ready to allow people to search for help in God, metaphysics, or whatever. Meanwhile, they hope that some sort of *deus ex machina*--perhaps, from the West?--would make their own turning to God and to their own people unnecessary. Now, as this book shows, the people, particularly the Russians, have spoken. It is up to the government to find out, in a free election, if the ancient proverb *vox populi, vox Dei* holds true in the USSR.

FROM A WESTERN PERSPECTIVE

Society is indeed a contract. It is a partnership in all science; a partnership in all art; a partnership in every virtue and every perfection. As the ends of such a partnership cannot be obtained in many generations, it becomes a partnership not only between those who are living, but between those who are living, those who are dead,

and those who are to be born. Each contract of each particular state
is but a clause in the great primeval contract of eternal society.
                                                    -Edmund Burke

It is against the Marxist idea that Western democracies have
failed to do battle. As a result, even though it failed to establish a
monopoly in any of the Western democracies, this Marxist idea has
permeated the Western market of ideas to the extent that it has
rendered it incapable of producing any sort of intellectual antidote or
alternative to Marxism-Leninism. It has also hampered the Western
study of Communism by diverting its attention to trivialities and by
confusing its terminology. Even while intellectuals in Communist
countries have been lately shedding their Marxist delusions at an
increasing speed, the same cannot be said about their Western
conrades. The totalitarian temptation, in Jean-Francois Revel's
phrase, remains strong in the West.

The United States is no exception. As Peter Collier and David
Horowitz (see Chapter 4) have shown, the influence of Marxist ideas is
not limited here to left-wing groups. In various guises and disguises
these ideas have insinuated themselves, through a kind of osmosis, into
the very fabric of American intellectual life, among "the best and the
brightest" of its academic establishment. A common Western
argument is that there is nothing wrong with either Marx or Marxism; if
Communism has led to such things as Stalinist terror and economic
stagnation, this was not due to the the falsity of Marxist ideas
themselves but rather to the "barbaric" ("despotic," "Asiatic," "oriental")
heritage of the Russian (Chinese, Cambodian, Rumanian, Albanian,
Cuban) people, who could not but distort this "progressive" Western
teaching. Once such an argument was accepted, the American
academic establishment was soon flooded with all sorts of Marxists,
para-Marxists, crypto-Marxists and sundry Marxoids, to say nothing of
those who did not even bother to conceal their Communist convictions.

With the influx of such "scholars," the establishment (colleges,
research institutes, media) became a purveyor of various socialist,
totalitarian, and Marxist ideas.[2] Proudly it calls itself liberal. Others
call it liberal in a derogatory sense. (Remember the "L" word of Bush's
presidential campaign?) Still others, more appropriately, call it left-
liberal. But in actual fact it is left-illiberal. For it would not pass the

muster of free and fair discussion of an idea which is perceived, by the intellectual elite, to be reactionary, or anti-Communist. Our current confusion about what is going on in the Communist world is largely due to this predominance of left-illiberal views among our sovietologists and sinologists.

The confusion is by no means limited to those who sympathize with Communism or Marxism. It proved to be contagious even for people whom nobody would suspect of such sympathies. One such person is Professor Richard Pipes of Harvard University. A respectable historian, he has exerted considerable influence on U.S. foreign policy since he was a National Security adviser in the Reagan White House. He has also been one of the chief purveyors of an essentially russophobic conception of Russian history. In accordance with this conception he blames, for instance, the brutality of the Soviet regime chiefly on Russian national character as embodied in Russian peasants.[3] Pipes is an avowed Solzhenitsyn opponent. Not only did he allege that the writer was "anti-Semitic" but ruled out any positive role for Solzhenitsyn in Russia's future.[4] A number of the authors of this selection (Seliunin, Latynina, Senderov, e.g.) have criticized Pipes for his russophobic views, and there is no reason for me to go further.

Another influential russophobe is Zbigniew Brzezinski. While foretelling the death of Communism in his book, *The Grand Failure*, Brzezinski foresees that the most likely successor to Gorbachev's regime will be "some highly nationalistic form of dictatorship, perhaps what I call a 'holy alliance' between the Soviet Army and the Orthodox Church, galvanized by a sense of desperate Great Russian nationalism. . . ."[5]

Henry Kissinger, too, paid tribute to the russophobic tendency to predestine Russia to nothing better than an expansionist and autocratic rule. In a January 22, 1991 article published in *The Washington Post*, he warned against any hopeful "illusions" about Russia's future.[6] "The Utopian image of Gorbachev single-handedly reversing 500 years of Russian history will emerge as a mirage," predicted Kissinger, as if totally forgetting about two things. First, the most vital task facing all Soviet nationalities today is not reversing "500 years of Russian history," but 74 (or 51 for the lucky ones) years of Communism, which proved to be the greatest folly of the twentieth century and from which, as was shown above, the West was by no means immune. Second, if by the "500 years" Kissinger means the heritage of Russian empire, then it is not Gorbachev who is trying "to reverse" it. On the contrary, Gorbachev is trying, not quite "single-handedly," to preserve the empire, albeit in the incongruous shape of a United [Reform?] Communist state.

In that task, Gorbachev indeed bucks the tide of Russian national rebirth. Kissinger is apparently aware of the strength of this tide. He recognizes that, "In the end, Russian nationalism may outweigh liberalism [Gorbachev's?] and provide the motive for cohesion that communism [equated with liberalism?] seems to have lost. . . . The West will be faced with an autocratic state stretching over two continents and possessing 30,000 nuclear weapons." As a true diplomat, Kissinger has even prepared a compliment to Russian nationalists, in advance of their expected victory: "Disillusionment must not drive the West into equating the new Russia with its Stalinist predecesors. Even if the repression [by Communists? Russian nationalists?] succeeds. . . what emerges will be most comparable to the imperial Russia of Czarist times." The compliment is back-handed, of course. That the repression will come, Kissinger takes for granted, and it doesn't seem to matter for him who will repress whom. Russian nationalists should not feel entirely discouraged, however. Since "it proved possible for long periods to deal with [Czarist Russia]," Kissinger expressed the hope that it would be equally possible to deal with "the new Russia."

While I understand that there is and must be room for honest disagreement between scholars on any legitimate issue, including the issue of chauvinism (which does exist among Russians, as it does among other nationalities), I find this russophobic tendency morally reprehensible. Moreover, it is harmful to free inquiry and is a major obstacle to understanding what is going on in the USSR. For the last reason, I offer below my review of an article which typifies this regrettable tendency. Titled "The Challenge of Russian Nationalism to Soviet Stability," the article was written by Professor Hugh Ragsdale (University of Alabama) and published by a leading American magazine in the summer of 1989.[7]

It must be said that Mr. Ragsdale's assessment of the intellectual climate in the USSR largely coincides with the one presented in this study. He notes, for instance, a growing conflict between the Gorbachev leadership which tries to hold onto the Marxist-Leninist ideology (or, at least, its phraseology) and the Russian people who reject it. "Among the broad masses Marxism-Leninism entirely lacks the power to inspire, and among the intelligentsia, it has acquired the power to disgust. It is singularly insipid, soporific, anesthetic, hugely numbing," says Ragsdale convincingly.

Like me, Ragsdale warns against underestimating the degree of discontent with Communism among ethnic Russians. He argues that "though it is hardly demonstrable, it is not implausible that the most frustrated and discontented nationality in the Soviet Union is precisely the one that is in charge, the Russian." He points out that in private conversation "one hears over and over again, from Communists and non-Communists alike, 'The Russians live worse than all the rest.'" Moreover, "many Russians seem to regard the Party as little more than a conspiracy whose function is to exploit whatever is rich and Russian." Pointing out that "the entire Soviet empire, both inside the Soviet Union and outside it--i.e., the fourteen non-Russian republics as well as the countries of the Warsaw Pact--has become a burden and liability for the Russians," Ragsdale suggests that "the discontent among the Russians is the only element of the Soviet domestic crisis which has the capacity to precipitate *sudden* disaster."

Thus, in contrast to the prevalent Western view, he concludes that the main challenge to Soviet stability comes neither from the Baltic republics nor from the Muslims but from the ethnic Russians. Reading this part of his article, one is moved to congratulate him and, in his person, the entire corps of American sovietologists, with finally discovering the discontent of the Russians under Communism. True, the discovery is somewhat belated (seventy-two years, to be exact), but better late than never. At least, at present the discontent among the Russians is recognized as a fact. One would naturally expect Mr. Ragsdale at least to raise this question: How could this discontent among the "master-race" of the Soviet Empire possibly be factored into a more general process of liberation of *all* peoples from the yoke of Communism?

But Mr. Ragsdale has no such concerns. In fact, the whole purpose of his article is exactly the opposite: to urge the adoption of "new political thinking" along the lines of "how to spare and save Soviet power. From whom? Primarily from the Russians." From Russian nationalists, to be exact. To wit, Solzhenitsyn, Valentin Rasputin, Vladimir Soloukhin, Vasilii Belov, Viktor Astaf'ev, the late Vasilii Shukshin and Fedor Abramov, and even Sergei Zalygin and Dmitrii Likhachev who, Ragsdale grudgingly admits, are "liberal nationalists." For "waiting in the wings to supply their favorite remedies should Gorbachev falter is perhaps the world's largest contingent of armchair politicians and myth-mongering intellectuals, people whose incessant cerebral fever is matched only by their total divorce from hands-on experience." That is how Ragsdale describes these new "enemies of the West" collectively.

Compared with this group of "myth-mongering intellectuals," says Ragsdale, "Gorbachev belongs to our world. For the Communists of the Soviet Union have now had seventy years of the experience of reality to temper the illusions of their doctrine." Ragsdale is no Communist dupe. If he prefers Soviet Communists to Russian nationalists, it is not because of any sympathy for the former but for the sake of American national interests as he sees them. Basing his views on "the geopolitical and ecumenical" concepts of Paul Kennedy and William McNeill, he regards both the USA and the USSR as "empires in decline." "Though the military power of both countries remains intact, the economic power of both is eroding, and both are burdened by 'imperial overstretch,'" he quotes Kennedy. Therefore, both the USA and the USSR share "something like a condominium of conservative interests," the primary one of which is "the preservation of international order and world peace." However, the USSR "is more wounded than we are." Therefore, "if the decline of [Soviet] military power relative to ours is a favorable development for the U.S., the deterioration of its whole situation, beyond a certain point, is not."

Hence Ragsdale's recommendation: "We must exert ourselves to sustain and support a certain degree of [Soviet] stability and strength--even if cautiously and not too much." In practical terms, this means that the U.S. should ally itself with the Gorbachev leadership against Russian nationalists who, Ragsdale is sure, endanger "Soviet stability." For, only as long as the pragmatic Communists remain in power, will the Soviet government be able to continue to share with the United States the burden of maintaining "international order and world peace."

"And here is the crucial consideration: *viewed impartially in a global perspective, the role of the Soviet government is a civilizing one*," enunciates Ragsdale. "It maintains, at enormous cost to the Russian people, a semi-civilized order over two parts of the world almost infinitely disorderly. The first is the Balkans and Eastern Europe. The second is the Soviet side of the 'crescent of crisis'--the Caucasus and Central Asia." According to Ragsdale, "The preservation of order in this area of the world is more vital than the progress of human rights-- to us, to the world at large, and probably, perhaps unbeknownst to them, to the peoples who live there." The bottom line of Ragsdale's "new political thinking" is this: "From the viewpoint of American interests, we could scarcely conceive a more advantageous political design for Eastern Europe and Western Asia than an economically unworkable but ethno-politically functional Soviet system."

To put it plainly, Ragsdale's plan calls for a conspiracy between the U.S. government and Soviet leaders against the national aspirations of not just the Russians but also the "East Europeans," the "West Asians," and the unnamed other peoples forcibly drawn into the orbit of Soviet power. Reading his recommendations, one is at a loss to decide whom he offends more. The "West Asians" and "East Europeans," among whom the Russians are urged to continue to keep "a semi-civilized order"? Or the Russians, who are supposed to be stupid enough to accept the honor of playing "a civilizing role" on behalf of the West but "at enormous cost" to themselves? Or the West Europeans, who in the midst of their euphoria over the disintegration of the Iron Curtain are asked to respect the integrity of the Soviet Empire? Or the Americans, who had thought that they protected democracy in the world and now find out that their "empire" was not really different from the Evil One? While we ponder the answer, we must assume that for Ragsdale no offense is too great if the intent is to preserve "international order and world peace."

In all fairness to Ragsdale, he is aware of the ethical vulnerability of his proposals. He concedes that "the idea of assisting a state so recently called--not altogether implausibly, considering the 1930's--an empire of evil, is repugnant to the thinking of almost all of us whatever our place in the currently confused categories of liberal and conservative." This swell of noble feelings notwithstanding,

Ragsdale manages to suppress it with the convenient argument that "our interests are more humane than our sentiments."

There is precious little that is really new in Ragsdale's "new political thinking." Rather, it is an effort to salvage the worst kind of "old thinking" in the face of momentous changes occurring in the USSR and the entire Communist world. It is founded on the same false assumptions about Communism that we have discussed in the introduction. One such assumption is that, no matter how objectionable it might be to us civilized Western folks, Communism is a blessing to "less civilized" peoples, for whom, "perhaps unbeknownst to them," it is a source of stability. Another assumption is that Communism is preferable to any alternative to it, especially a national one. Such assumptions have underlain our policy toward the Soviet Union throughout post-World War II history. They underlay our failed efforts at detente. They were at the heart of Helmut Sonnenfeldt's doctrine, according to which the Soviet presence in "Eastern Europe" was deemed then, just as Ragsdale thinks now, a guarantee of stability.[8]

What is new in Ragsdale is the shift of emphasis in the old argument that Soviet power assures stability in the area it dominates and thus contributes to world peace. Based on that argument, Western politicians seldom set their goal higher than containing Soviet expansion by making a deal with Soviet leaders aimed at dividing the world into spheres of influence. However, in arguing for such a deal in the past, Western scholars emphasized the "popularity" of Communism in the areas it dominates. Feigning ignorance of a widespread discontent among the "captive nations" of the Soviet Empire, they professed no doubt about the loyalty and devotion of their "captors," the Russians, to Communism.

Now glasnost has put an end to both our ignorance (or attempts to feign it) and our false assumptions. Ragsdale got that message straight. But old habits of mind die hard. So he makes an about-face. Now a deal with the Communists has to be made precisely because the opposite is true, that is, Soviet power lacks popular support, especially among the Russians. Therefore, the West should try to "save" it not only for the sake of "world peace," but also--here comes the new emphasis--for the sake of the captive nations who might not know yet that the prison they live in was built for their own protection--against the "myth-mongering" Russian intellectuals.

One might say, then, that Ragsdale's "new thinking" is a logical extension, *ad absurdum*, of the "old thinking." Neither goes beyond Communism. Neither trusts the Russians (nor the other nations chafing under Communism) to produce anything better than "Reform Communism." Both credit Soviet power with "a civilizing role" for certain "lesser breeds." However, if the "old thinking," in its daring moments, aimed at containing Soviet power within its present domain, the "new thinking" aims at retaining it there, even against the will of the peoples it rules. It is as a blunt re-statement of the old Western thinking in the face of the crumbling Communist world that Ragsdale's article deserves our attention.

Whatever "new" there was in the article, it was outdated even before it appeared. If nothing else, the events on Tiananmen Square should have shown the fallacy of Ragsdale's assumption that Communism has irrevocably "grown benign through weakness" and is about to transform itself from a wild, predatory tiger of the past into a nice "reform Communism" kitty-cat of the future. Then the fall of Communist governments in "Eastern Europe" in the autumn of 1989 put a hefty dent in his "design" of keeping "a semi-civilized" Soviet order in this "infinitely disorderly" part of the world.

One might agree with Ragsdale's theory that, without the preservation of stability in "Eastern Europe," the progress of human rights there might become precarious. A problem with this is that Ragsdale finds the main source of stability in an inherently unstable regime. Another problem is that people do not always behave according to a theory, even a good one. It is much easier to accept this theory for those who, like Ragsdale and myself, enjoy peace, human rights and prosperity. But how could we have persuaded the East Germans not to flee to the West and to accept the Berlin Wall as a price for peace? Would we be willing to pay the same price? Should we ask Lithuanians not to declare independence for fear they might jeopardize a Soviet-American summit? Or could we convince the Chinese students not to demonstrate for democracy lest they disrupt the "stability" of Sino-American relations for which American diplomats have so tirelessly worked?

We may heartily endorse Ragsdale's emphasis on stability as a precondition for democratization. But his suggestion to seek it in the maintenance of the Soviet regime is not only cynical but utterly unrealistic. Common sense would tell us that, unless a government has popular support, it cannot guarantee genuine stability either inside or outside of its domain. Ragsdale is aware of the argument that Gorbachev's ultimate goal might be to make the USSR "a more effective antagonist of ours." However, he dismisses it with a cavalier statement that "[that] goal is, except in the form of brute military confrontation, quite beyond his reach." In this case, it is the exception that counts. Whereas Soviet economic competitiveness seems even less imminent now than before perestroika, the "brute military confrontation" remains a strong possibility precisely because Soviet leaders might use force as a last resort in trying to save the system. By committing ourselves to "saving" Soviet power, by endorsing the Soviet "right" to police "Eastern Europe" and "Western Asia," as Ragsdale urges us, we would only increase the Soviet temptation to use force. Thereby we would put world peace and stability at greater risk.

In fact, Ragsdale comes close to admitting that he is not interested in genuine stability at all. After all, his "design for Eastern Europe and Western Asia" stipulates the maintenance of "an economically unworkable but ethno-politically functional Soviet system." Can such a system be a source of genuine stability? Hardly. First, to call the Soviet "ethno-political" system "functional" is to indulge in wishful thinking. Certainly, it does not function well enough to satisfy either the Soviet leaders or their subjects. Second, an "economically unworkable" system can hardly be regarded as truly stable. So, Ragsdale's "design" actually calls for maintaining a permanently uncertain status quo. It would allow the Soviets to barely function ethno-politically and yet prevent them from fully recovering economically for fear that such a recovery might be translated into a greater military threat. But who needs stability on the brink of disaster?

Presenting himself as a pragmatist, Ragsdale wants to save Soviet power precisely because it "has grown benign through weakness." To keep it this way, he suggests assisting it only to the extent that it is powerful enough to suppress national discontent at home and yet powerless to do any mischief abroad. Speaking metaphorically, his "design" amounts to a vision of a dinky Soviet barge which the West will keep barely afloat, allowing it neither to sink nor to sail. There are, however, several problems with this "stable" barge. First, there is a conflict there between its Communist captains, on the one hand, and its mostly Russian crew and non-Russian passengers, on the other. This conflict concerns the barge's future. The captains now realize that their misadventure on the high seas of world revolution and international terrorism can no longer be sustained. They know that the barge is leaky, and that its engine is out of steam. But they hope that the leakage (because the old Marxist-Leninist hull can no longer hold water) can be patched up (with neo-Leninism, "market socialism") and the engine restarted, with Western help. They hope they can make the barge seaworthy without going to a home port.

The crew, on the other hand, knows that unless the barge is towed from rough international waters to a Russian shore and a Russian home port, for a complete overhaul (fundamental *perestroika*, or *perestroika-liberation*) at a Russian dock, it will never be seaworthy again. The non-Russian passengers, too, know of the danger of staying on board this leaky barge. They would rather be delivered to their national shores. Or else they would board life-boats and head home themselves. But the captains, professing their faith in Soviet power, do not let anybody go. Nor do they want to return to the home port, because they know that they are not needed at the docks. And so they continue to fish in international waters for Western help.

Ragsdale offers them neither life-savers nor life-boats but an American anchor to keep the barge afloat. The captains would certainly be tempted to have their captaincy underwritten by the West, as Ragsdale suggests. But is it really in American interests to conspire with Soviet captains against their crew and passengers? Ethics aside, the proposal is impractical for two reasons. First, even with our full support Soviet captains might not be able to prevail over the discontented crew and passengers. In fact, a quiet mutiny has already broken out among the passengers, who, without waiting for orders, are jumping into the life-boats heading for their national shores (Poland, Hungary, East Germany, Czechoslovakia, Bulgaria, Estonia, Latvia, Lithuania, and more to follow). This mutiny was caused exactly by the conditions of life, between floating and sinking, which Ragsdale wants to perpetuate. Should the mutiny spread to the Russian crew, the captains will be overthrown and America embarrassed.[9] Second, even without such a mutiny, the barge will continue to threaten world peace as long as the conflict onboard remains unresolved. And Ragsdale makes no provision for resolving it.

Ragsdale's plan might at first sight look advantageous to America. In fact, it runs counter to the main objective of U. S. foreign policy which is, in Ragsdale's words, "international order," "stability" and "world peace." For keeping an economically unworkable system afloat, letting it neither sink nor sail, will only add to the misery of its captive population. Far from stabilizing the area, it will destabilize it even more until it finally explodes in an uncontrollable paroxysm. Moreover, should the West try to "spare and save" the Soviet regime against the will of its people, the most likely result will be an exacerbation of the already dangerous conflict. Such a policy might indeed precipitate that "*sudden* disaster" which Ragsdale wanted to avert.

While Ragsdale's trust of Soviet Communists does not go as far as letting them sail under their own power, he has only distrust for the "Russian nationalists." Why? Basically, for three reasons. First, because they are "nationalists," which, for him, is bad enough. Second, many of them are religiously inspired, which makes them worse. Third, they are Russians, and that tells it all, since for Ragsdale they are a nation of extremists. (Hence his equation of "Russian nationalists" with "the Russians.") "Rather like religion, nationalism has a bad name in the modern world, and, rather like religion, it more or less deserves it," he quotes an authority who urges preventing nationalism from "tearing apart the whole fabric of modern civilization."

Noticing that the twentieth century has been marked by "a nostalgic revolt against the galloping values of material progress, urbanism, and technological innovation," Ragsdale treats Russian nationalism as part of this global phenomenon which he defines as "romantic, revolutionary conservatism" and "nostalgic nationalism." Among other manifestations he mentions "the Islamic revival in the crescent of crisis," the evangelicals in the USA, the agrarian literature in the American South, the back-to-nature fiction of Michel Tournier in France, the Green movement in Germany, and the Mishima-style nostalgia for the past in Japan. He evinces little sympathy for any of them, insinuating their collective affinity with "proto-Nazi literature."

He has even less sympathy for this phenomenon's Russian manifestation, "evident chiefly in the school of writers most commonly known as neo-Slavophiles or *derevenshchiki* [ruralist writers]." While acknowledging that "nostalgic nationalism has been the most powerful and the most creative movement in the Russian arts," Ragsdale denounces "Russian nationalists" as "armchair politicians, totally divorced from hands-on experience." (It does not occur to him that in a totalitarian system nobody but the rulers can have "hands-on experience.") To him, they are more dangerous than the Communists. One can expect from them nothing but "sudden disaster" (which he fails to explain).

In terms of historical antecedents, he distinguishes between "the liberal and tolerant [nationalism] of Herder and Mazzini and the violent nationalism of Treitschke and Mickiewicz." He is certain, however, that in Russia only the second type can possibly prevail. Finding only two "liberal nationalists" in the USSR, Likhachev and Zalygin, he gives them no chance. It is only "the more virulent nationalists," those who "are viscerally antagonistic to the West, loathe American mass culture, are strongly anti-Semitic, and believe in the influence of a Jewish-Masonic conspiracy in American policy" who will triumph. Hence his conclusion that Americans should "spare and save" Soviet power from these Pamyat-like extremists.

Why such a certainty that only the extremists can triumph in Russia? The answer is simple. It is rooted in the character of the Russian people. They are a nation of "believers," "ideolaters" and "iconodules." They can go only from one extreme to another, from one obsessive 'ism to another. They could be socialists and Christians, democrats and authoritarians, but they cannot be "liberals."[10] Moreover, it is "a culture whose whole folklore and history respond to the idea of the work ethic with a cosmic yawn." In short, they are predestined to be ruled by despots and dictators. They hardly deserve to be ruled by Gorbachev who "belongs to our world." Besides forcing them to work, Gorbachev can make them serve the higher ends of Western civilization. Such as? At this point Ragsdale apparently cannot help "complimenting" the Russians while insulting a few "minor" nations: he grants the Russians the honor of maintaining "a semi-civilized order over parts of the world almost infinitely disorderly," that is policing "Eastern Europeans" and "Western Asians" on behalf of the

West. "To borrow one of Pushkin's favorite ideas," says he, in an effort to convince the Russians to stay put in his scheme of things, "there is a sense in which the Soviet Union is buffering Western civilization from the chaos of Western Asia today as Russia did in the era of the Mongol Empire."[11]

If Ragsdale calls this type of reasoning "new thinking," one wonders what "old thinking" is? It is the same narrow-minded, West-centric, condescending and ultimately chauvinistic view of non-Western peoples that distinguished Marx's thinking about "historical" and "non-historical" nations and about the West's paving the way, through Communist world revolution, for the rest of mankind. Ragsdale might be a bona fide conservative, but he certainly shares with Marx a disdain for non-Western cultures and civilizations. Although he claims that his article was written from an "impartially global perspective," it is both parochial and overbearing. It does a disservice to America and the West.

It is in his estimate of contemporary Russian nationalism that Ragsdale errs most. What he fails to take into account are the particular historical circumstances in which modern Russian nationalism (if one accepts the term as value-free) has arisen. Foremost is the fact that since 1917 Soviet leaders have been guided in their nationalities policy by the Marxist "internationalist" theory that national distinctions and nations will disappear with the demise of capitalism. Since this theory was proven false beyond all reasonable doubt, but since also its falsity could not be admitted for fear that Marxist "science" might then disintegrate, all resources of the totalitarian state were used to make reality conform to the theory, that is, to make the Russians (along with others) disappear as a distinct nation.

The goal was the creation of a Russian-speaking but Marxist-thinking, transnational political entity, the so-called Soviet people. The result was as predictable as the one that issued from Marx's economic "science"--a monstrosity. More precisely, the monstrosity of the Soviet Empire where, as Ragsdale correctly observed, the "imperial" majority feels even more abused than the "colonized" minorities. While Soviet propaganda spared no effort to obliterate the national self-consciousness of the Russians, the terror machine and the Gulag did the job of their physical destruction. The destruction of the non-

Communist Russian intelligentsia, de-Cossackization, de-kulakization and demoralization of the working class and collective farmers have drastically reduced the genetic pool of the Russians, warped their national self-awareness, and undermined their work ethic. (Contrary to Ragsdale, it was under Communism that the Russians have "unlearned how to work," as Soviet newspapers now admit.)

It is against this "ethno-political" monstrosity that Russian nationalists are rebelling. And they know its main source--Marxist ideology. If all previous nationalisms were primarily directed against the perceived encroachment of, or suppression by, other nations, contemporary Russian nationalism is a defensive reaction against practices rooted in an inherently anti-national ideology. Consequently, its goal is liberation not from the dominance of an oppressing nation but from the yoke of a utopian socio-political system that issued from that ideology. Only then will the Russians attain equal opportunities with the other nations which were fortunate enough not to fall under the sway of that ideology. This anti-ideological thrust sharply distinguishes contemporary Russian nationalism from its historical antecedents and contemporary parallels in other countries. For that reason, it may be more appropriately called a neo-nationalism.[12]

It is quite understandable that the Soviet leaders, whose mandate to rule is derived from Marxist ideology, would want to protect their ideological raison d'etre. They know that the main challenge comes from this neo-nationalism of the Russians. They also know that the only chance to defeat it is to divert its energy and passion from its main target, the totalitarian ideology, to targets that are more typical of the "old" nationalisms, namely, other nations. As I have shown in the essay on Pamyat, it was certainly in their interests to have Pamyat's leaders blame the misfortune of the Russians on the Freemasons and Zionists, rather than on the ideology that has oppressed both Jews and Gentiles.

It is also understandable that the apologists of Marxism throughout the world would want to malign and distort the true nature of contemporary Russian nationalism. What is more difficult to understand is that even conservative scholars, such as Ragsdale, would, consciously or not, indulge in the same reasoning. The only explanation I can think of lies in the fact that, on the assumption that pre-revolutionary Russian culture is a thing of the past, American academic programs (and funding establishments) have been paying little attention to the study of that culture as something more than an aesthetic relic, refusing to recognize it as a vital tradition with regenerative power capable of affecting the political future. As a result, ignorance about pre-revolutionary Russian philosophy, religion, and political thought (as well as about those of Russian emigres) abounds. It is on that ignorance that Soviet leaders capitalize in their effort to maintain the monstrosity of the Soviet Empire.

According to Ragsdale, as a nation of extremists, the Russians cannot help becoming obsessed with "the isms." Russian nationalism is but another 'ism that threatens to fill the vacuum left behind by the disintegrating Marxism-Leninism. The error here is not that there is a vacuum that needs to be filled. The error is in the prejudice that the Russians are incapable of filling it with anything but yet another totalitarian ideology. In fact, none of the writers he mentions suggests any such thing. The vacuum will not be filled with any single omniscient 'ism, but rather with a re-. It will be filled with the rebirth of Russia, the renaissance of its culture, ancient customs, traditions, and religion. It will be filled with the restoration of the Russian land and economy as part of the global ecosystem. And it will be filled with the renewal of Russian literature.

It is no accident that virtually all people whom Ragsdale dubs "Russian nationalists" are neither economists nor political "scientists" but men of letters. Echoing Marshall McLuhan's phrasing, one could perhaps say that their medium, Russian literature, is also their main message. They do not oppose Marxism by writing anti-Communist manifestoes. Nor do they counter Marx's *Das Kapital* with pseudo-scientific volumes of their own. (To do so would be to accept the chief methods of Marxist proselytizing: sloganeering and "scientific" browbeating). No, they challenge Marxist *maculature* with Russian *literature*. While Soviet ideological watchdogs have largely succeeded in stamping out Russian philosophical, political, economic, and social thought, they have failed to uproot Russian literature. This failure is not for lack of trying, though. It is because, even for them, Russian literature has too much common sense.

Even in the coldest days of totalitarian winter, Russian writers managed to keep alive the Russian spiritual tradition, buried as it was deeply underground. They protected the grain of the Russian nation from spiritual decay and death. They prepared the soil where it might sprout. Gumilev and Akhmatova, Zamiatin and Bulgakov, Platonov and Pasternak--they all have kept the flame of the Russian nation alive. In the flickering light of that flame, they told the truth about Communism. Then Solzhenitsyn became the torch-bearer. Like his predecessors, he depicted Soviet reality as that of an evil empire. Unlike Western sovietologists, he foresaw and predicted its downfall. And even though the government expelled him abroad, his torch had already been passed to the many *derevenshchiki* who kept the flame lit through the dark years of *zastoi* [stagnation]. And it is this group of writers, including Solzhenitsyn, that Ragsdale accuses of extremism. In actual fact, if they are extremists at all, they are so only in the art of survival--and in their faith in Russia's rebirth.

If there is a single 'ism that is a common denominator for all "Russian nationalists," it is not an 'ism of ideology or speculative thought. It is the 'ism of feeling, the feeling of love for Russia, its history, its landscape, its culture, and its people. This feeling needs no rationalization, as one needs none to love one's mother. This feeling is universally known as patriotism. It is not unknown in Ragsdale's country. As Collier and Horowitz report, it was the loss of that feeling that made the American New Left vulnerable to the totalitarian idea during the Vietnam war. And it was the rediscovery of patriotism that proved their best medicine. "One of the things I'm proudest of in the past eight years [was] the resurgence of national pride that I called 'the new patriotism,'" said President Reagan in his farewell address to the nation. His warning that a decline of "informed patriotism" would spell doom for America was born out of the same concern that Russian nationalists have for Russia.

In fact, Ragsdale himself likes to talk, if not about American patriotism, then about American *national* interests which he defines as transcending "the currently confused categories of liberal or conservative." That is exactly what Russian nationalists want. They want *Patria* to stand above *Partia*. They want Russia's national interests to be defined in a way that transcends ideological and political categories. They want to emancipate Russian patriotism from the shackles of "Soviet patriotism," an adjunct to that same ideology which even Ragsdale finds "soporific." In short, they want the same *national* patriotism which Ragsdale regards as his birth-right.

It was Russian patriotism that saved Russian statehood and preserved the cultural identity of Russian people in the most trying moments of its history: in the struggles against the Mongol yoke, against the Polish invasion during the time of troubles in 1600-1613, and against Napoleon in 1812. It was because of the collapse of Russian patriotism during 1914-1917, mostly due to the Bolshevik defeatist propaganda, that Russia not only lost the war but was plunged into the bestiality of the Revolution and Civil War. Russian patriots were persecuted and killed en masse during the subsequent decades when Stalin was forcing the country into the heaven of an "internationalist utopia" (both economic and ethno-political).

Only during World War II, realizing that Marxism-Leninism could not stop Hitler's armies, did Stalin allow some expressions of Russian patriotism. But by assigning the Russians the "big brother" role among the minorities, he encouraged Russian chauvinism. He made some concessions, most notably, to the Russian Church. And he made many promises, most of which were broken after the victory was won. Along with the Western allies, the Russians were deceived. But if some of them continue even now to identify with the Soviet Empire, they are certainly no more "Stalinists" for that than the many Western liberals who have been aiding and abetting the Soviet regime for years. To the present day, Stalin's successors follow his strategy of coopting Russian patriotism into "Soviet patriotism" to serve the goals of the one-party system, not Russian national interests.

But that strategy no longer works. The Soviet Empire is falling apart not only at its seams but also at the core--where the Russians refuse to identify with it. Neither Marxism-Leninism nor "Soviet patriotism" can hold the empire together. In vain does Ragsdale try to separate the "unworkable" Soviet economy from the allegedly "functional" ethno-political system. The two are but Siamese twins that can neither function together nor be separated. Both issued from the same pseudo-science. That is why Gorbachev's efforts to "reanimate" the Soviet economy, while keeping intact the Soviet Empire, are doomed from the start. Something which is moribund cannot be reanimated. The only exit from this double bind, of an unworkable economy and a (barely) functional "Union," is to dissolve the latter, letting each nation form its own *national* government and organize its own *national* economy within its own *national* territory.

For the Russians this would mean Russia proper, that is, the territory that is left after all national minorities have exercised their right of national self-determination, including secession. That is what the Russian crew on board the Soviet barge is expecting the captains to undertake. It would be a grave mistake, therefore, for the United States to try to "spare and save Soviet power," as Ragsdale advises, by siding with the Gorbachev leadership against the Russians. Such a policy would amount to siding with the captains against the discontented crew and passengers, with perestroika-coercion against perestroika-liberation, with the *partiots* against the *patriots*. Such interference in Soviet domestic affairs would be both imprudent and improvident.

Whether Gorbachev would want such a *deus ex machina* from the West is not clear. It might do more harm than good to him personally. It might further reduce his already narrow base of support among both the conservative Communists (the *partiots*) and the conservative non-Communists (*patriots*). It will not prevent the disintegration of the Soviet Empire. Nor will it stop the evolution of the Soviet system beyond Communism. It might prolong the agony of Soviet power, but it will not forestall its death. It might delay and aggravate the birth of a new Russia, but it will not stop it. Instead of stabilizing the situation, it will destabilize it to a point where it becomes uncontrollable. Instead of winning new friends for the United States, it might create new enemies.

Why should we interfere with the efforts of the crew and the passengers to override their captains and have the barge towed to the Russian shore? Instead of allying itself with the Communist captains to keep the Russian and non-Russian subjects of the Soviet "barge" at bay, America should proclaim its neutrality. That stance would be more consistent with our democratic principles. It would allow us to play a mediating role. We could try to convince the Soviet captains that they cannot indefinitely ignore the demand of their crew and the passengers to get out of international waters and head for a home port. This kind of mediating effort could only be beneficial for a peaceful evolution of the Soviet system. Further, by declaring its neutrality, America will have returned an old favor Russia bestowed on us during our war of independence when Catherine the Great rejected the efforts of the British to enlist Russian support and proclaimed instead the policy of neutrality. That Russian policy was a blessing to America. It certainly helped to make the birth of the American republic less painful. There is no reason why America should look less favorably on the birth of a new Russia.

Although Ragsdale tries to sell his "new thinking" as a conservative policy, actually it is not. It is reactionary. It is reactionary because it wants to freeze change in Communist countries at their "reform Communism" stage, barring their evolution out and beyond Communism. It is reactionary because it stands in the way of the historical forces of change which alone can establish genuine peace and stability in these countries and the world. These are the forces of a national-democratic revolution against Communism. These are the forces the emergence of which the West has failed either to foresee or to recognize in a timely fashion (much less encourage) precisely because the Western study of Communism has been caught, and squashed, between the Scylla of marxophilia and the Charybdis of russophobia of which Ragsdale's article is a prime example.

Ragsdale has every right not to like Russian nationalists. Nobody expects him to love Russians. Certainly, he does not have to believe in their political creativity. But he should not aspire to have veto power over Russian history. His article gives credence to the cynical witticism that has been making the rounds among American professors: As long as Russia stays under Communism, America need not fear another Japan. It is certainly more cynical than Lenin's adage about the rope-selling capitalists. Driven by the profit motive, these suicidal capitalists cannot be suspected of malice toward Russia. The witty professors, on the other hand, make one suspect that they want to keep Russia down. One need not be a Russian nationalist to wonder: Does Ragsdale really care for "world peace" and "international order"? Does he really believe that the Russians can cause "sudden disaster" because they are "armchair politicians"? Or is he afraid that, should the Russians (Chinese, East Germans, etc.) free themselves from the yoke of Marxism, they might become formidable competitors with America in the global free market of goods and ideas? If he is, he must be a peculiar kind of American nationalist, one who not only distrusts other nations but lacks faith in the American people.

WHITHER GORBACHEV?

At that time shall arise Michael, the great prince who stands for the children of thy people. And there shall be a time of trouble, such as never has been since there was a nation till that time. But at that time your people shall be delivered, every one whose name shall be found written in the book.   -Daniel 12

"God marks a rogue."   -Russian proverb

When I entitled my Alaska speech "Beyond Gorbachev" I did not mean to suggest a lack of respect for the man. I am certainly willing to give him the benefit of the doubt. What I wanted to say was that, contrary to those who ascribe to him almost exclusive authorship of, and control over, perestroika, "he does not own it, had little choice whether to start it or not, and that the tide of change sweeping the USSR may well take us into a future beyond Gorbachev." "Beyond Gorbachev" meant that the country's future will not be defined by Gorbachev, especially not by the Western media's hyped-up image of him as a jolly good fellow and "Reform Communist" with a human face. I also predicted that the tide of change Gorbachev released will reach beyond Marxism-Leninism, to which Gorbachev says he is committed. Finally, I foretold the emergence of a new political entity, a new Russia, in place of the USSR.

The events of 1988-89 have fully confirmed my original assessment of the nature and the general trend of change in the USSR and in the Communist world in general. In fact, the tide of change has already reached beyond Communism in parts of the Soviet Empire. It is only a matter of time until it will sweep over its Russian core. For what we are witnessing in Central Europe now is a popular anti-Communist uprising that cannot be contained by either Soviet troops or Soviet borders, nor by Western diplomacy. Peaceful as it has largely been, it is nonetheless a political earthquake, or a series of tremors, causing Communist governments to fall like dominoes. These events represent an enormous tectonic change. They have brought to the surface what has long been asserted by critics of Communism: that along the entire stretch of the Communist world, just barely below its propaganda crust, there runs a deep fault line. The name of that fault line, on which the entire structure of Communism was built, is Marxism-Leninism. And that is where it is cracking.

The message Central Europe has sent to Communist leaders all over the world is loud and clear; the days of Communism, everywhere on earth, are numbered. And that includes the USSR, the matrix of the world Communist movement. Verily, this is the writing on the wall, on the Berlin Wall and all other walls inside which the Communists have imprisoned their countries. Does Gorbachev not see the writing? In all languages of the Communist International, from Russian and Chinese to German and Hungarian, it spells the same: people will not be deceived into accepting "reform Communism" as a substitute for freedom, even if it were accepted by the West. They do not want "Reform Communism;" they want reforms out of and beyond Communism. The sooner Communist rulers get this message, the better chance they will have to play a constructive role in a peaceful and orderly dismantling of the totalitarian system. That is what the quakes in Central Europe mean.

The next such earthquake of popular discontent may strike any Communist country anytime. But nowhere will it have a more devastating effect on world Communism than when it happens in Moscow. It is in preparation for such an emergency that Gorbachev must evolve beyond his present image, which satisfies so many abroad and so few at home. Up until recently he has kept barely half-a-step ahead of the game he has started. However, events in Central Europe put him a full step behind. He now has to play a catch up game. The Soviet people now expect him to deliver changes at home which he was said to have triggered in Central Europe. These expected changes include the *de facto* abolition of the Communist Party's monopoly on power, the elimination of Marxism-Leninism as the state ideology, freedom of conscience, and granting equal opportunities for oppositional parties to compete for the popular vote. Once enacted, such changes would mean the end of the totalitarian system and the beginning of a march beyond Communism.

Introducing such changes would require of Gorbachev much more than a superficial change of color, to which any politician is prone. It would require deep personal soul-searching. It would require a bold decision and a strong will to carry it out. He certainly cannot do it without reconsidering his commitment to Marxism-

Leninism and to the Soviet Empire. For his own political survival, he has to evolve "Beyond Gorbachev." Can he do it? Perhaps, but chances for success are quickly evaporating with the passage of time. Yel'tsin was right. Gorbachev has months, not years, to set things aright.

Compared to other Communist leaders, his is a special case. As General Secretary of the Communist Party, Gorbachev has the dubious distinction of having opened the floodgates for the tide of change. This distinction is certainly dubious from the viewpoint of dogmatic Communists. Blind and deaf, they can neither hear nor see the coming tide. They cannot understand that, as chief guardian of the Communist flame, Gorbachev could not have acted otherwise. He did not create the tide. He tried to cope with it. He tried to carry out the task the Politburo assigned to him: to change the old ways in order to consolidate the Party's hold on the country. But with glasnost, which was thought necessary for economic perestroika, there came a tidal wave of popular discontent.

Now Gorbachev's chief Party task seems to be to try to relieve the pressure of discontent on the retaining walls of Communism by letting the overflow run out onto the ground and around the flame. It is not his fault that the overflow has turned out to be more powerful than any of his former Politburo colleagues anticipated. If anything, it was their fault that they did not try to open the gates sooner. True, he cannot shut the floodgates now. But who can? All one can possibly do is to hang on. And that is what Gorbachev is doing, as best he can. Dangling and with feet wet, he desperately tries to hold onto the gate frame lest he be washed away. This way he can try, if not to divert the flow from the Communist flame, then at least to allow its guardians to escape. They should be grateful to him.

However, besides being the Party boss, Gorbachev got himself elected President. Thereby he no doubt increased his personal power. It is unclear, however, for what purpose. To consolidate the Party's "leading role"? Or to outflank his dogmatic opponents? As the titular head of state, he owes his primary allegiance not to the minority Party but to all Soviet citizens, the Russians and non-Russians, Christians and Muslims, Jews and Buddhists, atheists and agnostics, conservatives and liberals, socialists and non-socialists. It is they who should be uppermost in his mind when he stands at the floodgates of the "revolution from below." After all, even a political flood might be felt as a natural disaster. It can destroy people, regardless of whether one is a Communist or not. Nor does it choose which flame to extinguish.

By assuming the presidency, Gorbachev has put himself in an ambiguous position. Sooner or later, he will have to decide where his priorities are: with the Party or with the country? It appears that Gorbachev has not yet made that decision. He certainly has not yet told the people that his highest priority is the improvement of the economic, political, and spiritual conditions of the country, rather than the preservation of the Party's monopoly on power. Even though he has started his reforms in the name of the Party, it is the Party, its bureaucratic and dogmatic elite, that has failed to keep pace with the rest of the country. Thus, the Party has became the main obstacle for the reforms he initiated.

As General Secretary, he must bear responsibility for this blockage. Had he listened more attentively to his domestic critics-- some of the most patriotic and intelligent of whom are presented in this book--rather than to the flatterers from abroad, he should long ago have concluded, and persuaded his Party, that neither the one-party system nor the Soviet Empire (and that's what Communism practically means) can be saved. But the people of all nationalities and all political persuasions can and must be saved--from the debris of the crumbling system. Only when Gorbachev realizes it, will he hopefully make the right decision.

Under the present calamitous circumstances, protecting and saving the lives and property of citizens should be Gorbachev's foremost duty as the titular head of state. There is no better way for him to discharge this duty than by letting the people save themselves. Let the unwilling members of the Union go their way. Let the Russians, instead of dissipating their energy on maintaining the moribund system, repossess their own orphaned land. Should Gorbachev accept the inevitable, he will find his "crown of the Monomakhs" easier to bear. He may then go down in history as a distinct improvement over his Communist predecessors. Should he fail to accept it, he may tarnish and even nullify his accomplishments and go down the road of the other Soviet dictators.

In terms of our study, the choice Gorbachev is facing is that between the *partiots* (mostly the Party and government bureaucracy) and the *patriots* (the majority of the people, including many rank-and-file Party members). He has been straddling the fence between the two groups for too long. This indecision may have helped him to stay in power, but it has not been helpful for solving the country's problems. It might not yet be too late for Gorbachev to get off the fence and to place himself squarely on the side of the *patriots*. In practical terms this decision would mean taking steps toward a legal and orderly dissolution of the Soviet Empire, speedily withdrawing Soviet troops from Central Europe, letting national minorities secede (if they wish), and consolidating statehood in Russia proper. It would also mean abolishing the Party's political monopoly, removing Marxism-Leninism's ideological monopoly, separating the state from atheism, and establishing freedom of conscience and political persuasion (liberalism, social-democracy, conservatism, socialism, or whatever).

In personal terms, siding with the *patriots* would mean a first step in his evolution "Beyond Gorbachev," that is, shifting from an ideologically-oriented Communist leader to a national Russian leader. To show that he has no personal interests at heart, Gorbachev should at once declare his Presidency interim, contingent upon changes in the constitution. Meanwhile, he should assert his Presidency over his role as General Secretary. After all, as the titular head of state he owes his first allegiance to the country, not the Party. By doing so, by, in effect, putting *Patria* above *Partia* and personal interests, he would signal to the people that in their actions they too should be guided by national, not personal or partisan interests.

As interim President he could do a number of things. First of all, he could clearly and loudly proclaim that from now on his paramount objective is getting the country out of its present dead end, not strengthening the Party's leading role, as he announced in his book. Next, he could allow each of the fifteen union republics to exercise its right of national self-determination (already granted in the current constitution) in respect both to which form of government they prefer and to whether they wish to stay in the Union. Only by taking these two steps can Gorbachev avert, or at least be better prepared to cope with, an approaching political earthquake similar to the one that shook Central Europe.

As President he can take the initiative of forming an interim coalition government, including Communists and non-Communists, which would run the country until a new government is formed in accordance with a new constitution. As General Secretary, he must initiate reforms within the Party and perhaps lead it back to its social-democratic beginnings. He must persuade his colleagues that the days of Party monopoly are over, that the Party has so discredited itself that the only chance for its survival is reforming itself out of its present omniscient Marxist-Leninist mold.

It is to Russia that Gorbachev owes his primary loyalty and debt. Unless he realizes this and acts as one of Russia's sons, he will have no political future. This is not merely a question of changing his image. There has to be a profound personal change that cannot take place without thorough soul-searching. Listening to the voices of glasnost assembled in this book might be a place to start. After all, these are the voices of some of the most loyal, patriotic, and intelligent among his fellow citizens. They represent the new thinking he has said he wants, even though it exceeds the confines of "socialist pluralism" he set for it.

These voices say many things, but their cumulative message is that Communism must go and that a new Russia must be allowed to be born. Neither the one-party system nor the Soviet Empire can be saved. Neither deserves to be saved. On the contrary, both are obstacles to the improvement of peoples' lives. What can and must be saved is Russia, with all the peoples populating it. Russia cannot be saved by any sort of *deus ex machina* from the West. Nor can it be bailed out of its economic difficulties by Western credits and gifts, no matter how generous. At present, it is like a sieve that cannot hold water, whether it comes from foreign or native sources. Russia cannot be saved unless and until it restores the national fabric of its life. Before it can be westernized or japanized or can absorb any other influence from abroad, it must russify itself. It must heal its historical roots and cultivate its as-yet feeble sprouts of spiritual rebirth. It must strengthen its national character through a better work ethic, thrift and enterprise. To be saved, it must be reborn.

Only by re-establishing its own national identity--by restoring itself as a unique civilization that has something of Europe, something of Asia, and much that is entirely its own--can Russia assume its rightful place in the global community. Only after building their own Russian House can the Russians consider joining, as an equal partner, the Common House of Europe or any other international community. Only then can Russia behave as a responsible member of the global village. A new Russia may yet serve as a magnet for a commonwealth of good neighbors but first it must prove to the world and itself that it can live all alone.

It is a tall order for anyone. It might seem an impossible task in the face of the current confusion in the USSR. In reality, one can only expect things to get worse before they have a chance to get better. But the stakes are just as high. Since Gorbachev ascended to power, the country has been plunged into an apocalyptic mood. This sensation is especially eerie in an officially atheist country where people are not accustomed to speaking in religious terms. On the one hand, Gorbachev's rule has meant rejuvenation and hope. On the other, it has brought a decline in living standards and an increase in crime. It has been marked by a series of natural and man-made disasters. Among the latter, the nuclear reactor meltdown at Chernobyl has greatly contributed to the spread of the apocalyptic mood. Both Russian theologians and lay people insist that Chernobyl is but a native version of the star of Wormwood (Artemisia) which, according to the Revelation of St. John, "blazing like a torch," will have fallen from the sky after "the third angel blew his trumpet." The fallout is strikingly similar to that of the nuclear catastrophe: "A third of the waters became wormwood, and many men died of the water, because it was made bitter."

Ironically, because of the suppression of religion, popular superstitions rather than theological speculations predominate in the public mind, where the profane and the sacred are often mixed. One such superstition concerns the blot on Gorbachev's forehead. According to the oft-quoted Russian proverb, "God marks a rogue" [*Bog shel'mu metit*]. Since, contrary to his promises, living standards under Gorbachev have fallen, many Russians ventilate their frustrations by quoting this proverb at Gorbachev's expense. This growth of "anti-rogue" sentiment has been met with consternation in the government-controlled media. The largest Communist youth newspaper, with a circulation in the millions, found it necessary to publish an interview with a Russian cleric in which the atheist readers' questions concerning the spread of the apocalyptic mood were dealt with.[13]

One question was: "Is it true that the Bible says that the name of the last ruler before the end of the world will be Michael?" Realizing that the question alluded to the sinister role of Mikhail (Michael) Gorbachev, the learned priest defended the atheist ruler the best he could. First of all, he denied the connection "which, for some reason, people make" between that "last ruler Michael" and "the marked one" (*mechenyi*), that is, one of the beasts of Anti-Christ expected to appear before the end of the world (Revelation of St. John, Chapter 13). Instead he referred the readers to the prophecy of Daniel (quoted as an epigraph to this chapter) in which "the great prince Michael" saves his people from the worst time of trouble ever. It may have been wishful thinking on the part of the priest. Or maybe it was a thank-you note for Gorbachev's concessions to the Russian Church--or even a thinly veiled effort to nudge him onto the path of the righteous Russian rulers.

In any case, by offering its pages to the priest, the Communist newspaper has unwittingly defined the fundamental choice which Gorbachev has to make. Unless he behaves as the great prince Michael who, at the time of trouble, "stands for the children of thy people" and eventually delivers them, he runs the risk of being remembered, if not as a "red dragon" of Anti-Christ, then as a "marked" rogue.

Notes

1. For a detailed discussion of how Mary Shelley's myth applies to Communism, see Wladislaw Krasnow, "Karl Marx as Frankenstein: Toward a Genealogy of Communism," Modern Age (Winter 1978) Vol. 22, No. 1, pp. 72-82.

2. Consider, for instance, A. Kent MacDougall's admission that during his twenty-four-year career as a reporter for The Wall Street Journal and The Los Angeles Times he "helped popularize radical ideas" as a "usually covert, occasionally openly anti-Establishment reporter." A self-avowed Marxist, he takes credit for his work as a "closet socialist boring unobtrusively from within [the] bourgeois press." Significantly, he is now a tenured journalism professor at one of the best universities in the country.

3. See my debate with Pipes, "Richard Pipes's Foreign Strategy: Anti-Soviet or Anti-Russian?," The Russian Review vol. 38, no. 2, 1979; reprinted in the British Encounter magazine (April 1980), it appeared in Russian translation in Posev no. 1, 1980.

4. For more on Pipes's criticism of Solzhenitsyn, see Vladislav Krasnov, "Solzhenitsyn's New August 1914," in Aspects of Modern Russian and Czech

Literature: Selected Papers of the Third World Congress for Soviet and East European Studies, ed. Arnold McMillan (Slavica Publishers, 1989).

5. From an interview with Z. Brzezinski, Time, Dec. 18, 1989.

6. Henry Kissinger, "No Illusions About the USSR," The Washington Post, January 22, 1991.

7. Hugh Ragsdale, "The Challenge of Russian Nationalism to Soviet Stability," The Virginia Quarterly Review, vol. 65, no. 3, Summer 1989.

8. For a critique of Western policy in Central Europe see my review of Michael Charlton's book, The Eagle and the Small Birds. Crisis in the Soviet Empire: From Yalta to Solidarity (Chicago, Ill.: University of Chicago Press, 1984) in The St. Croix Review vol. XIX, No. 5, October 1986.

9. In fact, the mutiny of the Russian crew already started when Boris El'tsin was elected to the Russian presidency on the eve of the Bush-Gorbachev summit in Washington in May 1990. With the subsequent declaration of sovereignty of the Russian Federation, the mutiny is far from over and may yet cause America a greater embarrassment. See the article on El'tsin in the appendix.

10. For Russia's liberal-democratic tradition, see Sergei Pushkarev, Self-Government and Freedom in Russia (Westview Press, 1988).

11. Apparently, Ragsdale misattributes Aleksandr Blok's famous line about Russians "holding a shield between the two hostile races, the Mongols and Europe," to Pushkin. It comes from Blok's poem "The Scythians" in which Russia's Eurasian distinctiveness is emphasized. The meaning of the poem is rather obscure, but it appears to be far less pro-Western than Ragsdale imagines. Pushkin, by the way, was also appreciative of the distinctiveness of Russian civilization.

12. I do not wish to dispute Ragsdale's linkage of Russian nationalism with the phenomenon of "romantic nationalism." However, modern Russian nationalism has much more in common with the nationalism of the Poles, Hungarians, Estonians, Armenians or Soviet Jews than with anything Ragsdale suggests. Insofar as all these nationalisms issue from the failure of Marxism, they might be regarded as varieties of anti-ideological (anti-Marxist) neo-nationalism. Russian nationalism is different only in the sense that while the others tend to blame the Russians for the imposition of Marxism, the Russians (with the exception of Pamyat) have no such excuse.

   Otherwise, Russian nationalism falls within Ernest Gellner's definition of nationalism as "primarily a political principle, which holds that the political and the national unit should be congruent" (Nations and Nationalism, Ithaca: Cornell University Press, 1983). While usually nationalists want to expand the political unit up to the size of their national unit, the Russian nationalists (of the Solzhenitsyn stripe) want to shrink the Soviet political unit to Russia proper.

As to its antecedents, I see its greatest philosophic affinity with the conservative nationalism of Edmund Burke whose <u>Reflections on the Revolution in France</u> closely anticipates the essence of Solzhenitsyn's critique of the Bolshevik Revolution. Russian nationalists reject the Communist "social contract" not only because it was imposed on Russia by force, but because it represents a break with Russia's traditions.

13. "Apokalipsis?," an interview with Rev. Mikhail Dronov, <u>Komsomol'skaia pravda</u>, July 9, 1989.

Appendix 1:

Pamyat: A Force for Change?*

Since May 1987, when the Russian nationalist group Pamyat sponsored a number of demonstrations in Moscow, it has been roundly condemned in both the Soviet and Western media for its self-declared anti-Zionism and alleged anti-Semitism. This rare unanimity of usually opposing views should warrant a pause for sound skepticism and thoughtful analysis. Strangely enough, while Western reaction to Pamyat has been long on condemnation, it remains short on analysis and on understanding of both Pamyat and its condemnation in the Soviet press.[1]

The purpose of this report is three-fold. First, it will show that, in spite of its superficial consonance with the West, the Soviet condemnation of Pamyat has been prompted by motives that remain little understood in the West. Second, it will attempt to define Pamyat's place within the broader spectrum of the rising national self-awareness of the Russians. Third, it will address the general question of our panel: What is the role of rising Russian nationalism in the process of perestroika? And in particular: Is Pamyat a force for change?

While it is never an enjoyable task to play the role of devil's advocate, on this issue it is essential that someone play that role, for in

* This paper was delivered at the American Association for the Advancement of Slavic Studies national convention in Honolulu, Hawaii, November 19, 1988.

the Dark Ages, accused "heretics" were entitled to have their "advocate." Should we deny that right to Pamyat? It certainly behooves scholars to ask a skeptic's questions, such as: Has Gorbachev renounced Soviet anti-Zionist policy? Has he instructed his "new-thinking liberals" to withdraw the Soviet signature from under the 1975 U.N. Resolution No. 3379 condemning Zionism as a form of racism? Has he pledged to reverse the present tilt in Soviet foreign policy toward the radical Arab states?

The answer to the above questions is "no." So why then do we, in the West, condemn Pamyat's anti-Zionism more, and more vehemently, than we condemn official Soviet anti-Zionism? The usual explanation is because Pamyat's anti-Zionism is much more equatable with anti-Semitism, or judophobia.[2] It is also said that Pamyat's judophobia is more dangerous because it allegedly stems from a deep-seated popular Russian tradition. While there is some truth in such explanations, to a greater extent they are unsatisfactory because they ignore and obscure this paramount fact: in its worst aspects, Pamyat is, first and foremost, not a Russian, but a Soviet phenomenon, a product of Soviet political culture in general and of official Soviet anti-Zionism in particular.

Let me explain why. First of all, it seems most likely that having originated before perestroika,[3] Pamyat could not have developed its "Zionist-Masonic conspiracy" rhetoric without the connivance and even the help of the KGB. This is not meant to suggest that either Dmitrii Vasil'ev or any other Pamyat leader did actually conspire with the KGB. Rather, it is meant to suggest the plausibility, and even probability, that from the very start Pamyat leaders were made to understand that as long as they refrained from blaming the Party for the destruction of Russian national monuments and instead blamed anonymous "Zionists" and "Freemasons," they would be immune from prosecution and would be allowed to use government buildings for their lectures. Such a silent concordat would explain the considerable following Pamyat has in the ranks of the KGB, the armed forces, and the Party.

Apparently, for quite some time Pamyat leaders had no trouble keeping such a concordat with the KGB. However, the situation changed with the advent of glasnost. Now the people wanted to hear the names of the culprits. And when Pamyat began to name such people as Lenin's close associates Trotsky and Bukharin, Stalin's henchmen Kaganovich and Iaroslavskii, as well as Gorbachev's Politburo promotee Aleksandr Iakovlev, it became apparent that Pamyat decoded the sobriquet, "Zionist-Masonic agents," differently from what the original concordat with the KGB implied. In other words, while agreeing to the use of the sobriquet, the KGB reckoned that it would be used in the sense of "agents of Israel and its Western allies." The KGB did not quite expect that it could be used in a sense suggesting that some higher-ups in the Party itself might have been involved in that "conspiracy." Nor did it anticipate that Pamyat's defense of Russian national monuments would escalate to a defense of Russian national values and thus challenge the Marxist-Leninist ideological monopoly.

It is precisely this *implicit* anti-Marxist-Leninist thrust--not its *explicit* anti-Zionism and judophobia--that worried Soviet ideologists most when Pamyat's activities broke out into the open, culminating in a meeting with Boris Yel'tsyn in May 1987. Only then did Soviet ideological watchdogs realize the threat Pamyat posed to Marxism-Leninism, the entrenched bureaucracy and the one-party system itself. Naturally they responded by subjecting Pamyat to an unprecedented propaganda barrage. The intensity and the scope of this hate campaign against the "Russian nationalists" seemed to overshadow whatever unkind words Soviet propagandists had to say about the rise of national sentiment among non-Russian nationalities.

The barrage was started by the most dogmatic wing of the Soviet propaganda apparatus. Elena Losoto accused Pamyat of failing to define patriotism as Lenin did, that is, "socialism as fatherland." She particularly denounced Pamyat for defending the Russian religious tradition. "If one regards the Orthodox [Christian tradition] part of our history [worthy of preservation]," declared Losoto, "this kind of history we have knocked out from under our people's feet and we were right in doing so." She also denounced Pamyat for its interest in the reformer Petr Stolypin who, according to her, "gave the green light to the kulaks and whose name is a symbol of reaction." Pamyat activities are contrary to Marxist-Leninist principles of "class struggle" and "proletarian internationalism," concluded Losoto.

Another attack was mounted by Andrei Cherkizov.[4] Like Losoto, Cherkizov attacked Pamyat from "the positions of Marxism-

Leninism," because, he said, "only this great philosophic teaching is convincing and provable [?] for me." Denouncing Pamyat for its failure to define patriotism in Marxist-Leninist terms, Cherkizov clarified his point by contrasting Pamyat's "false" patriotism with the "genuine Soviet patriotism" of Soviet "internationalist soldiers" who, according to him, performed their "patriotic" duty in Afghanistan.

Remarkably, neither Losoto nor Cherkizov saw any connection between Pamyat's anti-Zionist rhetoric and official Soviet anti-Zionism. On the contrary, both authors criticized Pamyat for giving ammunition to Israel and the West to attack the Soviet Union for "anti-Semitism." "To get to the bottom of the truth," declared Losoto, "Pamyat makes the Zionists happy because it plays into their hands by giving them a reason to shout about anti-Semitism in the USSR."

Cherkizov accused three official Soviet anti-Zionist authors--Yevseev, Begun, and Romanenko--of being frequent guest lecturers at Pamyat gatherings. By singling them out, Cherkizov clearly wanted to create the misleading impression that the rest of Soviet anti-Zionist "scholarship" was both Marxist-Leninist and "scientific." Neither Cherkizov nor Losoto (nor any other Soviet author, to my knowledge) raised the question that perhaps, besides its "Russian" roots, Pamyat's "anti-Semitism" has some other sources, such as the anti-Jewish writings of Marx himself. Nor did they respond to Vasil'ev's allegation that Lenin kept "The Protocols of the Elders of Zion" in his Kremlin library.

During 1987 and later there appeared in the Soviet press dozens of similar articles. With minor variations,[5] all were uniform in condemning Pamyat for its allegedly pre-revolutionary "Black Hundred mentality" and "anti-Semitic hysteria." None suggested even the slightest possibility that a connection with official Soviet anti-Zionism might exist. None found any justification for Pamyat's existence. No Soviet paper offered its pages to Pamyat leaders or tried to interview them.

Ironically, the predominant Western reaction to Pamyat has been to join the chorus of Soviet propagandists. Western newspapers and early analyses uncritically repeated Losoto's and Cherkizov's denunciation of Pamyat for its allegedly pre-revolutionary "Russian" anti-Semitic mentality. At the same time, they largely ignored Soviet sources of Pamyat's rhetoric and conduct.[6]

Yet, to understand the phenomenon of Pamyat, one has to realize that there is more to it than the "Zionist-Masonic conspiracy" rhetoric. In addition to its emphasis on the preservation of Russian national monuments, Pamyat raised a number of other important issues. One such issue is the status of ethnic Russians in the USSR. Contrary to a common view in the West that ethnic Russians are the privileged elite of Soviet society, their actual situation is just as bad as or worse, than that of national minorities, Pamyat alleges. This is clear from the few more or less "official" Pamyat "manifestos" that are available in the West. Let me briefly focus on just two of them: the four-page Appeal of May 21, 1986, and the considerably longer Proclamation of December 8, 1987.[7]

As one could expect, both documents are full of anti-Zionist and anti-Masonic rhetoric. Both blame the misfortunes of the Russian people on the Zionists, the Freemasons, and, implicitly, on the Jews and their friends. "Global imperialism, nurtured by Zionism and its mercenary Freemasonic lackeys, is trying to drag the world into a spiral of a new planet-wide catastrophe," reads the Appeal.[8] Likewise, the Proclamation ominously warns that the "Enemy is the one who regards the problem of Zionism and Freemasonry as an idle invention."[9]

The two documents differ, however, not just in size, but in tone. The Appeal exudes the air of optimism and faith in perestroika. It calls the faithful to unite "around the Central Committee of the Communist Party. . . headed by Mikhail Gorbachev" and to reject "those party members. . . who are trying to adapt themselves to perestroika while discrediting the new political course."[10] The Proclamation, on the other hand, issued after the media campaign against Pamyat, assesses the situation in the country in a somber vein: "The reasonable and healthy forces of our society. . . have been again trampled into mud. This perestroika bluff can no longer be continued."[11] The Proclamation protests against the campaign of defamation and repression against Pamyat members. For lack of a formal Pamyat program, let us now take a closer look at the Proclamation's programmatic statements.

In the field of economics, for instance, it urges the restoration of private land ownership by those who till it. (Although Petr Stolypin's name is not mentioned in "official" Pamyat documents, Vasil'ev seems to want to adapt his approach to Soviet agriculture, whereas Losoto is apparently satisfied with Stalin's collectivized farms.) Pamyat decries the "unnatural" life in communal apartments in huge impersonal buildings crowded in "giant cities" and advocates instead the construction of private family homes.[12]

Declaring itself a force for perestroika and glasnost, Pamyat urges people to exercise control over the Soviet media, "which continue to lie."[13] Pamyat deplores the suppression of heterodoxy (*inakomyslie*) "in violation of the [Soviet] Constitution and the Law."[14] It also advocates the use of referenda to decide vital country-wide issues, and it urges people to create their own Committees for Perestroika.[15]

Pamyat warns of the impending "ecological catastrophe" and accuses the authorities of squandering the country's natural resources through foreign trade. It declares itself to be against both "the ideological and alcoholic poison that destroys the nation."[16] It demands "freedom of conscience" and the separation of "atheist propaganda from the state."[17] Finally, though it does not directly advocate a multi-party system, it insists on an equal partnership between the Party "minority" and the "non-party (*bespartiinoe*) majority.[18]

While being primarily concerned with ethnic Russians, Pamyat leaders profess a desire to act in concert with other peoples of the USSR. They urge "brothers and sisters of all nations" to create their own Pamyat-type groups for preservation of their national cultures in their republics, cities and villages, and to assert their right "to be masters of their own land."[19] They denounce the destruction of "an enormous number of monuments of universal significance that belong to the Russian and other peoples."[20]

In foreign affairs Pamyat seems to take a strictly pacifist line. It deplores the nuclear arms race and denounces all wars, including the "criminal bloodshed in Afghanistan."[21] (This is in contrast to Cherkizov's praise of Soviet "internationalist soldiers"). On the other hand, although it does not condemn capitalism as such, Pamyat denounces "international Zionist capital," "imperialist forces," and their agents inside the country. "They re-animate Trotskyism in order to discredit socialism, to sow chaos and to open the country's gates to Western capital and Western ideology,"[22] says the Proclamation.

Were it not for its wild and vicious "Zionist-Masonic conspiracy" rhetoric, Pamyat could have passed for one of the more radical oppositional groups in the country (even though it eschews the word "opposition"). It has correctly identified a number of very serious problems. Moreover, the solutions it has proposed, such as the reintroduction of private property, the separation of atheist propaganda from the state, and the sharing of Party power with the rest of the population, also seem sound. At any rate, they are not out of line with the demands of avowedly democratic informal groups favoring fundamental systemic change, such as the Democratic Union or Sergei Grigoriants' Glasnost'.[23] And yet Western critics of Pamyat, having almost exclusively focused on the allegedly "Russian" roots of Pamyat's judophobia, have largely ignored the fact that Pamyat's specific proposals challenge the one-party totalitarian system which is the root cause of the Soviet global menace.

Meanwhile, in the fall of 1987 the unanimity of Soviet condemnation of Pamyat began to falter. In October Vadim Kozhinov, a prominent literary critic, disputed Losoto's assertion that her approach to Pamyat was based on Lenin. While reproaching Pamyat's leaders for their "infantilism" and "ignorance," Kozhinov said that positive aspects of the group should not be overlooked.[24]   On November 12, 1987, APN reported that Vasil'ev's Pamyat is but a splinter group of a larger movement that is not "anti-Semitic."[25]   Then Valentin Rasputin, one of the most popular Soviet "villagers," criticized the indiscriminate "bombardment" of Pamyat and reproached the "left-wing" of the Soviet press for denying glasnost to Pamyat and for labeling all Russian patriots as the "Black Hundredists."[26]

One of the most authoritative assessments of Pamyat appeared in a lengthy January 1988 interview [*beseda*] with Gavriil Popov, a "liberal" Soviet historian (now mayor of Moscow). This interview was more sober, more objective, and more balanced than any of the previous articles. While there are reasons to feel apprehensive about Pamyat, said Popov, we should not forget that among its members there are "many honest, sincere patriots."[27] Popov admitted that "there are profound, objective reasons for the emergence of Pamyat," such as "the demographic situation [unfavorable to ethnic Russians], the [miserable economic] state of Nechernozemie [the historical cradle of the Russians], the scale of alcoholism, and much, much more. . ."

Not only "[was] Russian historical memory subjected to a brutal, vicious persecution [*utesnenie*]," Popov acknowledged, but among all peoples of the USSR, "The heaviest blows of the ["administrative"] system fell on the Russians whose past suffered most." But why were ethnic Russians singled out for this especially harsh treatment? Popov offered several reasons.

One reason was that "the Church was against the revolution" (some would put it the other way around), and therefore the revolution had to wipe out Russian "religious memory." The second reason had to do with the strength of the monarchist tradition among the Russian people. Naturally, it had to be wiped out. (Popov failed to notice, however, that the entire body of Russian pre-revolutionary political tradition, both monarchist and non-monarchist, liberal and social-democrat was wiped out.) The third reason was that Stalin, according to Popov, rejected Lenin's idea of an alliance with "the peasant majority." Consequently, the Russian "peasant memory" had to be wiped out as well. (One wonders, then, what was not wiped out?)

Finally, Popov offered a fourth reason: "It was necessary to debase Russian culture and Russia's past in order to turn the Russians into brutes, to free them from their memory, so that they could carry out the role that the administrative system assigned to them." Concluded Popov: "One can understand, if not justify the emotions of Pamyat."[28]

Popov's assessment of Pamyat amounts to an admission that Communist rulers have deprived ethnic Russians of their national memory in order to make them accept slavery for themselves and to make them more "efficient" in carrying out the Party's orders to keep other nations enslaved. It is clear that such an admission could not have been made in the pre-glasnost period. If Pamyat helped it to be made, then it helped to expand the limits of glasnost a bit further. At least on this score, it is hard to deny that Pamyat has been a force for change.

The Gorbachev leadership was finally beginning to recognize the existence of the problem. A new approach to Pamyat had to be used. It was apparently decided to embark on a more cautious divide-and-conquer tactic. That tactic possibly included the authorization of the APN article suggesting that the "anti-Semitic Pamyat" is but a splinter group of a larger, older and fully respectable movement. It also included efforts to isolate the "bad" Pamyat by the expulsion of its sympathizers from the Party. A certain amount of police action was also to be used, but only selectively, and Vasil'ev did in fact receive a KGB warning.[29]

But it was also deemed necessary to make a number of concessions, not directly to Pamyat, but to the sentiments that nourish it. Several such concessions were made to the Russian Orthodox church in conjunction with its millennium. Moreover, the authoritative *Pravda* rebuke to Nina Andreeva took notice of "the growing interest of popular masses in our past." It was carefully worded so as not to antagonize either of the two alternative "towers," which, Andreeva complained, were challenging Marxism-Leninism from opposite directions: the tower of the "pro-Western left liberals" and the tower of "preservationists and traditionalists."[30] *Pravda* made it clear that the main threat to the unity of the country came not from Pamyat, but from the dogmatic Marxists, such as Andreeva (and the Ligachev faction), who quote Marx and Engels to justify their search for a "scapegoat" among certain "counter-revolutionary nations" (Andreeva's code word for the Jews and Israelis).

This cautious approach seems to prevail to date. On August 13, 1988, a group of Leningrad intellectuals, upset over a series of Pamyat-sponsored meetings in Rumiantsev Square, published a letter in *Izvestiia* demanding legal action against this "unregistered" group. But even though *Izvestiia* editors endorsed the letter, no legal action has been taken. As late as September 25, Dekhtiarev, a Leningrad Party leader, was saying that there were no plans to disband Pamyat, though he did not rule out "administrative measures" against its members.[31]

The September 30, 1988 shake-up in the Kremlin resulted in the transfer of Aleksandr Iakovlev from his watchdog ideologist post, in which he had for a while substituted for Ligachev. That transfer might be seen as a concession to Pamyat, which had long demanded Iakovlev's resignation. At any rate, it is a concession to the sentiments Pamyat shares with many nationally-minded Soviet intellectuals, especially those among the "villagers."

It now appears that Soviet leaders have learned how to live with Pamyat. They may have figured out that, as long as it remains unregistered and exists only in limbo, it can be contained. Moreover, it might be potentially useful for the government. It could be used as a sort of lightning rod in two ways. First, it could be used to divert the "lightning" of growing popular discontent with the failure of economic perestroika--from the Party to the "aliens among us." Second, it has been and will be used to divert Western critics from the official Soviet anti-Zionism to a largely mythical threat from "the Russian New Right." But even if the Party had decided to suppress or outlaw Pamyat, it is highly doubtful it would be able to do so without discrediting its own promise of "democratization."

The Pamyat phenomenon is undoubtedly one of the most disturbing symptoms of the general malaise of the system. Above all, it shows the failure of Marxism-Leninism to solve the nationalities problem. Pamyat is but one of several manifestations of the revolt of nationally-minded Russians against the double yoke to which they have been subjected under Communism: the yoke of being enslaved, like any other people in the USSR, and the yoke of being hated and maligned for their involuntary role in keeping others enslaved. Co-opted by the regime to play that role under the conditions of a forcibly-induced amnesia of their own national identity, ethnic Russians are beginning to revolt against their masters. Insofar as this revolt aims at the emancipation from that double yoke, it is justifiable and deserves the sympathy of all freedom-loving people. On the other hand, I am equally convinced that Pamyat's insinuations against the Jews are unfair, misleading, and inflammatory. They have been, and ought to be, condemned.

Moreover, such insinuations are counterproductive to the cause of emancipation that Pamyat advocates. Pamyat's "anti-Zionist" rhetoric seems particularly ugly when compared with the following passage from Aleksandr Solzhenitsyn's essay "Repentance and Self-Limitation in the Life of Nations":

> Our native land, after centuries of misapplying its might. . . after making so many useless acquisitions abroad and causing so much destruction at home. . . is perhaps more than any other country in need of comprehensive inward development. . . Our foreign policy in recent decades might have been deliberately devised in defiance of the true interests of our people. We are ready in our conceit to extend our responsibility to any other country. . . even on the other side of the globe, provided it declares its intent to socialize the means of production and centralize power. All these world tasks, which have been of no use at all to us, have left us tired. We need to get away from the hurly-burly of world rivalries. . . . The healing of our

soul! Nothing now is more important to us after all that we have lived through, after our long complicity in lies and even crimes.

This essay appeared in the 1973 samizdat collection *From Under the Rubble*. Together with a number of his compatriots, Solzhenitsyn then, fifteen years ago, first endeavored to breathe the air of national memory into a country that was just climbing out from under the rubble of cultural destruction.[32] He particularly drew attention to the tragic plight of the Russians. However, unlike Pamyat, Solzhenitsyn did not blame any other people for Russian misfortunes. On the contrary, he called on the Russians to follow the path of repentance and self-limitation.

It is well-known how this Solzhenitsyn endeavor ended. It was ignored, and so was his *Letter to the Soviet Leaders*. Solzhenitsyn was kicked out of the country. And even today, despite growing pressure from the Soviet public, Gorbachev's government has failed to restore Solzhenitsyn's right to live and work in his native land.

The major reason for this failure has to do with the fact that Solzhenitsyn is living proof of the proposition that one can be absolutely opposed to Marxism-Leninism and yet love one's country. In clear violation of their own Constitution, which stipulates freedom of conscience, Soviet leaders reject this proposition. The Kremlin knows that Solzhenitsyn embodies the vitality of Russian national memory. The Kremlin knows that Solzhenitsyn's return to the USSR, either through his writings or in person, would speed up the emancipation of Russian patriotism from cooptation by the regime and accelerate the consolidation of Russian nationalism as the most viable alternative to the regime.

Unlike Pamyat and Popov, to say nothing of the Losotos and Cherkizovs, Solzhenitsyn will not indulge in lies and half-truths about the root cause of the Russian problem. And this is more than the present level of glasnost can allow. It can allow Popov to tell a half-truth when he blames the tragedy of the Russians on the impersonal "administrative system." It can allow Pamyat to lie--albeit only in public lectures, not in print--about the "Zionist-Masonic" scapegoats for that tragedy. But it cannot tolerate a word of truth from the man who has unequivocally called Marxist-Leninist ideology the root cause of the destruction of the national life not just of Russians, but also of

Ukrainians, Estonians, and all other Soviet peoples, including the Jews. He has convincingly shown how Communist rulers have "succeeded in saddling and bridling Russian nationalism" to goals that are contrary to Russia's national interests. And he has also predicted that "a Russian national reawakening and liberation would mark the downfall of Soviet and with it of world communism."[33]

Alas, Solzhenitsyn's efforts to call attention to the plight of the Russians were ignored not just by the Soviet government. They were also largely ignored by Western sovietologists. His later efforts to point out Western misconceptions about Russian nationalism[34] likewise fell on deaf ears. There are but few American scholars who have studied contemporary Russian nationalism, and there are still fewer who have understood it. Among the latter is John Dunlop of the Hoover Institution. In his 1983 book he has called it "folly" "for the West to continue to ignore the concerns of ethnic Russians and the not-so-few Eastern Slavs who identify with them."[35] Dunlop discerned several "faces" of Russian nationalism, including some ugly ones akin to Pamyat. But he also made it clear that its mainstream, which he identified with Solzhenitsyn and other proponents of Russian "national and religious renaissance," is both wholesome and moderate.[36]

And yet Dunlop's suggestion that the West should try "to send a favorable signal to the moderate nationalists," first of all through the use of foreign broadcasting, was not followed. Not only was it not followed, but in many respects the negative Western attitude toward *all* manifestations of Russian nationalism has hardened. Recently Dunlop warned that a failure "to differentiate between an Alexander Solzhenitsyn and a Nina Andreeva. . . could lead to irreversible consequences."[37] The same applies to our failure to differentiate between Nina Andreeva and her mighty sponsors in the Politburo, on the one hand, and the "preservationist and traditionalist" forces like Pamyat, on the other.

So now back to the question of whether Pamyat is a force for change? From what has already been said above, it is clear that the answer has to be in the affirmative. First, Pamyat has already helped the process of change by forcing the Soviet government to recognize that there exist in the USSR not only national minority problems, but the Russian national majority (or plurality) problem. At the very least, as Popov's interview demonstrates, the taboo on the discussion of that problem in the Soviet press has been lifted.

Second, Pamyat's emphasis on the importance of Russian national values implicitly but unmistakably challenges the Marxist-Leninist ideological monopoly. In the long run, it will serve to undermine the stability of the totalitarian regime which largely derives its mandate to rule from that ideology. Third, keeping in mind that Pamyat is just one of several non-formal groups of Russian nationalist orientation,[38] one has to conclude that Pamyat represents a resurgence of Russian national sentiment that has the potential to become a decisive force for fundamental systemic change, that is, change away from the present ideocratic and totalitarian system toward a form of government that is both more responsive to the interests of its own people and more compatible with neighboring nations. Ultimately, this change would lead to the country's transformation from its present abnormal condition caused by the dominance of Marxism-Leninism to a normal country with normal national, and international, interests that are not predicated on a mandatory political ideology as they now are.

The West has yet to realize that there is no better antidote to Pamyat's judophobia than recognizing the legitimacy of the striving of Russians for their national emancipation from the yoke of Communism. As a first step in this direction, the U.S. Congress could rescind or amend its July 17, 1959 resolution, PL 86-90, on the "captive nations," which creates the impression that it is the Russians, not the Communists, who have imposed the yoke on one-third of mankind. To all Russians who refuse to be coopted by the Communist regime, the West gives but a terrible choice: either go back to cooptation by the Communist regime or be called "anti-Semite and chauvinist." The cooptation of Russian patriotism by the regime is bound to end sooner or later. It is high time for the West to recognize the legitimacy of Russian nationalism on an equal footing with minority nationalisms in the USSR. Moreover, as long as we in the West fail to resist the tendency to lump all Russian nationalists together as a bunch of inveterate judophobes and chauvinists, we will be of little help to the forces of moderation in the USSR.

There is no doubt that, by blaming various Soviet problems on the "international Zionist-Masonic conspiracy," Pamyat has cast aspersions on all Jews. Thus, it has done much to discredit Russian nationalism. These aspects of Pamyat activities have been, and should be, condemned. It should not be forgotten, however, that Pamyat has thrived in conditions of government-sponsored double-think, double-talk, spy mania, secrecy, censorship, half-truth glasnost,[39] and, above all, of the Marxist-Leninist ideological monopoly on which the totalitarian Soviet state still rests. Therefore, we should never yield to the temptation of condemning Pamyat's nefarious code-word tactics without condemning, at the same time, the totalitarian Soviet system of which Pamyat is the true offspring.

. . .

Since this report was delivered in November 1988, nothing has happened that would cause me to revise or alter my main argument. Nonetheless, it might be worthwhile to point out a number of later developments and articles that will shed more light on the dynamics of the movement.

In June 1988 there were rumors circulating in Moscow that Pamyat was about to start pogroms against Jews in the suburbs. In fact, no attacks on Jews were reported. In July 1988 dozens of Soviet officials received letters containing the following statement: "The vengeance is coming. We'll get rid of you. Stormtroopers of the patriotic front Pamyat." One of the addressees was Grigorii Baklanov, the Jewish editor of the magazine *Znamia*, in which Popov's relatively mild assessment of Pamyat was published. Unfortunately, this time Baklanov failed to exhibit better judgment. Without waiting for the investigation, he jumped the gun and, in the pages of his magazine, denounced Pamyat for making the threats, a charge Pamyat leaders indignantly denied. Meanwhile, one suspect, a Leningrad resident Arkadii Norinskii, was arrested. On November 18, 1988, a Leningrad court found him guilty and sentenced him to a year and a half of forced labor. Norinskii, a Jew, confessed to writing the letters but did not admit his guilt. However, in a recent interview with *Ogonek* (No.9, March 1989), Norinskii admitted that he had violated both "our ethics and our Constitution." The interviewer, on the other hand, revealed that, before the interview, many of his colleagues and he himself were inclined to regard Norinsky as an *agent provocateur* acting on behalf of Pamyat.

On November 23, 1988, the governing Council of the "National-Patriotic Front Pamyat" (of which Vasil'ev appears to be the chief spokesman) issued in Moscow yet another proclamation in which the leadership of the Leningrad Pamyat was condemned for allowing "chauvinistic and antisemitic" statements to be made during a meeting in Rumiantsev Square on October 22. The Moscow Council alleged that the Leningrad Pamyat leaders succumbed to the pressure of local Party and KGB officials who tried to discredit the "patriotic movement" as a whole by getting it involved with "anti-Semitism."[40]

Among the more significant articles in the Soviet press that appeared after this report was delivered are the following. Lena Zelinskaia, one of the editors of the non-formal magazine *Merkurii*, in an interview with the official magazine *Vek XX i mir* (January 1989), stated: "It is not clear to me who is more aggressive, Pamyat or my good friends, decent and intelligent people, who. . . fight against Pamyat." Zelinskaia defended her decision to devote an entire issue of *Merkurii* to Pamyat because it "was the first group of people who raised the issue of the tragedy of the Russian people." On December 12, 1988, *Sovetskii zhurnalist* published an article, "How Myths Are Created," in which the author, I. Bespalova, disputed Losoto's allegation that the Sverdlovsk group *Otechestvo* (Fatherland) was "a younger brother" of Pamyat. Alla Latynina, writing in the liberal magazine *Novyi mir* (No. 8, 1988), compared the smear campaign against Pamyat with the one against Pasternak thirty years ago, when many a Soviet writer went on record as saying, "I did not read his novel, but I condemn it."

The above developments suggest that Western observers cannot automatically assume aggressiveness and evil designs on the part of Pamyat and nothing but fairness on the part of Pamyat's Soviet antagonists. They confirm our contention that Pamyat's extremist tendencies cannot be effectively dealt with by mere denunciations, no matter how noble and sincere. A more discriminating, more objective, and more sympathetic attitude, if not to Pamyat then to the plight of the Russian people, is urgently needed to help the forces of moderation among Russian nationalists to avert the potentially dangerous explosion of Russian national sentiments.

Notes

1. See, e.g., Walter Laqueur, "Glasnost's Ghosts," an article distributed by USIA on August 10, 1987; Howard Spier, "Soviet Antisemitism Unchained: The Rise of Pamyat," and "Russian Chauvinists and the Thesis of a Jewish World Conspiracy: Three Case Studies," Institute of Jewish Affairs Research Reports Nos. 3 and 6 (July and August), 1987; Vladimir Tolz, "Zhido-Masonskii mif Sovetskoi propagandy i pravda istorii," a program script, broadcast in Russian by Radio Liberty on June 1, 1987; Julia Wishnevsky, "The Emergence of Pamyat and Otechestvo," Radio Liberty 342/87, August 26, 1987; "A Second Pamyat Emerges," Radio Liberty 463/87, November 16, 1987; and "Reactionaries Tighten Their Hold on the Writers' Union," Radio Liberty 148/88, March 28, 1988. See also Aron Katsenelinboigen, "Will Glasnost Bring the Reactionaries to Power?" and George Gibian's critique of it in the Spring and Summer, 1988, issues of Orbis.

2. The word "judophobia" is used in this paper in lieu of "anti-Semitism." The latter seems especially unsuitable in the discussion of Pamyat whose leaders profess sympathy for the Arabs who are Semitic like the Jews.

3. There exist different versions of Pamyat's history. According to Ogonek, No. 21, 1987, it originated in the early 1980s under the wings of the Ministry of Civil Aviation. However, Pamyat's own Proclamation, issued in December 1987, mentions a three-year span of its activities. In any case, it started before perestroika. In English see Wishnevsky's Radio Liberty research articles (note 43). Unfortunately, Wishnevsky often fails to separate fact from opinion. Moreover, she does not discriminate between various ideological strands among Russian nationalists, labeling them all as "reactionaries," "anti-Semites," and "Stalinists."

4. Andrei Cherkizov, "O podlinnykh tsennostiakh i mnimykh vragakh," Sovetskaia kul'tura, June 18, 1987.

5. Some tried to accentuate a distinction between Pamyat's "hysterical" leaders and well-meaning "patriotic" members who have done some "good deeds." Ogonek's Anatolii Golovkov and Aleksei Pavlov (No. 21, 1987), for instance, said that they "could have written a whole article devoted to Pamyat's good deeds" (but they did not). Pavel Gutiontov (Sovetskaia Rossiia, July 17, 1987) mentioned that he could not ignore "the bitter facts" of the destruction of Russian culture, but he failed to describe a single bitter fact. Anatolii Yezhelev (Izvestiia, August 1, 1987) defended a Leningrad cultural preservation group "Spasenie" from Cherkizov's insinuation that it was just as anti-Communist as Pamyat.

6. One notable exception is Franz Kossler's report on Austrian television, which included an interview with Vasil'ev. In his own interview with Moscow News (No. 7, 1988), Kossler pointed out that "the atmosphere of being semi-legal and 'harassed' is an asset for Pamyat, because it gives it some mythical aura and creates a legend around its martyrdom. . . . The criticism should be businesslike, specific and well-reasoned. All too often a caricature is drawn, which is then criminalized." It was prudent advice

to Soviet journalists. But it has hardly been followed by Kossler's Western colleagues, such as Esther Fein of The New York Times. Based on interviews with whomever wanted to pass for a Pamyat member, her latest report (February 27, 1989) suggests that all Pamyat sympathizers are inveterate "conservatives," "anti-Jewish," and "Stalinists," while it says nothing about Pamyat's programmatic documents.

Remarkably, Soviet samizdat publications have shown more objectivity in their treatment of Pamyat than either the Western or the Soviet press. Aleksandr Podrabinek's Ekspress-Khronika ran an interview with Vasil'ev (reprinted in Russkaia mysl' on June 17, 1988), and Sergei Grigoriants' information bulletin, Glasnost', published Gleb Anishchenko's polemic article, "Who Lobotomized the Russian People?", one of the most objective assessments of Pamyat (See English edition, Glasnost, issues 13-15, October 1988, pp. 55-61). The Russian emigre newspapers, Novoe Russkoe Slovo (New York) and Russkaia mysl' (Paris) have been rather negative in their reporting on Pamyat. Yet Vladimir Kozlovskii's series of articles in Novoe Russkoe Slovo (January 1988) is an excellent example of objective and responsible reporting.

7.   The full titles of the two "manifestos" are: (1) "Obrashchenie patrioticheskogo istoriko-literaturnogo ob"edineniia Pamiat' k russkomu narodu, ko vsem narodam nashei velikoi derzhavy, zhelaiushchim sokhranit' otechestvo svoe ot pozhara" (Appeal of the Patriotic Literary-Historical Association Pamyat to the Russian People and to All Peoples of Our Great Country who Wish to Protect Their Fatherland from Conflagration), issued on May 21, 1986 by Pamyat's governing body (Arkhiv Samizdata No. 6079, October 9, 1987); and (2) "Vozzvanie patrioticheskogo ob"edineniia Pamiat' k russkomu narodu, k patriotam vsekh stran i natsii" (Proclamation of the Patriotic Association Pamyat to the Russian People and to Patriots of All Countries and Nations), issued on December 8, 1987 (AS No. 6138, February 1, 1988). Henceforth, they will be referred to respectively as the Appeal and the Proclamation.

8.   "Appeal," p. 1.

9.   "Proclamation," p. 16.

10.   "Appeal," p. 1.

11.   "Proclamation," p. 2.

12.   Ibid. p. 8.

13.   Ibid. p. 9.

14.   Ibid. p. 2.

15.   Ibid. p. 12.

16.   Ibid. p. 3.

17. Ibid. p. 13.

18. Ibid. p. 12.

19. Ibid. p. 7.

20. Ibid. p. 2.

21. Ibid. p. 14.

22. Ibid. p. 2.

23. It is noteworthy that Vladimir Petrov, in a Pravda article entitled "Pamyat' and Others" (February 1, 1988), indirectly linked Pamyat with Sergei Grigoriants' magazine Glasnost'. According to Petrov, both Pamyat and Glasnost' discredit the non-formal movement by undermining our "patriotic, internationalist upbringing and socialist ideals."

24. Vadim Kozhinov, "My meniaemsia?", Nash sovremennik, (October) No. 10, 1987, pp. 160-174.

25. See Wishnevsky's "Second Pamyat" (note 43).

26. Valentin Rasputin, "Zhertvovat' soboiu dlia pravdy: Protiv bespamiatstva," (Speech at the 5th congress of VOOPIK, July 1987), Nash sovremennik, No. 1, 1988, p. 171.

27. G. Kh. Popov and Nikita Adzhubei, "Pamiat' i 'Pamiat'", an interview (beseda) about "problems of historical memory and contemporary nationalities relations," Znamia, No. 1 (January), 1988, pp. 188-203, esp. p. 196.

28. Ibid., p. 193.

29. Argumenty i fakty (No. 23) reported that on May 28, 1988, Dmitrii Vasilev was warned by the KGB to cease and desist from "anti-social activities which might provoke national discord." (See his interview with the Ekspress-Khronika reprinted by Russkaia Mysl', June 17, 1988). In October 1988 the Washington Times reported that Vasilev sued the KGB for "defaming" Pamyat (Novoe Russkoe Slovo, November 2, 1988).

30. "Printsipy perestroiki: revoliutsionnost' myshleniia i deistvii," Pravda, April 5, 1988.

31. Ekspress-Khronika, No. 39, September 25, 1988.

32. Alexander Solzhenitsyn et al., From Under the Rubble (Boston,Toronto: Little, Brown and Co., 1975), pp. 138-140.

33.   Aleksandr Solzhenitsyn, "Misconceptions About Russia Are A Threat To America," Foreign Affairs, April 1980, pp.797-834, esp. 814.

34.   See note 76.

35.   John B. Dunlop, The Faces of Contemporary Russian Nationalism (Princeton, NJ: Princeton Univ. Press, 1984), p. 290.

36.   In his latest article on the subject, "The Contemporary Russian Nationalist Spectrum" (Radio Liberty Research Bulletin, Special issue of December 19, 1988) Dunlop has identified the moderates with the "liberal nationalists," such as Academician Dmitrii Likhachev, the philosopher Sergei Averintsev, a number of the "villagers," and the group of intellectuals around Sergei Zalygin's magazine Novyi mir. Close to them, in his opinion, stands an even larger group of "Centrists," represented by many authors of the magazine Nash sovremennik (Valentin Rasputin, Vadim Kozhinov, e. g.) and the painter Ilia Glazunov.

37.   See Dunlop's letter to the editor, Policy Review, No. 45, Summer 1988, p. 88.

38.   Pamyat is not the only informal group concerned with the preservation of Russian national heritage. Besides Pamyat's affiliates in Leningrad and Novosibirsk (and perhaps in dozens of smaller towns), there are Spasenie [Salvation] and Epitsentr in Leningrad, Otechestvo [Fatherland] in Sverdlovsk and Krasnoyarsk, Soiuz Blagodenstviia (a vaguely monarchist group) and a NTS group in Moscow, a group called Rossiia (formerly Radonezh) in the Moscow oblast'. There are also a number of informal groups and seminars that are primarily concerned with Russia's religious heritage, such as the samizdat magazine Vybor [Choice]. In addition, there are some informal periodicals of Russian nationalist orientation, such as Vladimir Osipov's Zemlia (Earth) in Moscow and Rossiiskie vedomosti (Russian News) in Leningrad. With the exception of Pamyat, none of them has been overtly anti-Zionist or judophobic. Valerii Senderov, an NTS member and a long-time critic of Soviet anti-Semitism, has repudiated Pamyat leaders, but spoke very favorably of the Russian monarchists (Possev, No. 7). On December 17, 1988, a Christian-Democratic Party [Khristianskii Patrioticheskii Soiuz], was founded in Moscow by thirty-two delegates from various cities. One of its founders, Osipov, criticized Pamyat for its judophobia, but insisted on its right to speak out.

39.   Dmitrii Likhachev, who has occasionally been attacked by Pamyat, nevertheless defended its right to exist. Agreeing with Likhachev, Darrell Hammer likewise concluded that "while [Pamyat] has flourished under glasnost', its success is due in part to limitations on glasnost'." (See Hammer's article in a special issue of the Radio Liberty Research Bulletin on December 19, 1988.)

40.   Reported by Ekspress-Khronika, No. 48, November 27; reprinted in Russkaia mysl', December 2, 1988.

Appendix 2:

Why Not Solzhenitsyn?*

Last week's sessions of the Communist Party Central Committee were without doubt a major step in the strategic retreat of Communism. It has become clearer than ever that the Party Mikhail Gorbachev heads is powerless to prevent the country from disintegrating. Gone are the days when Gorbachev could fool the world, if not himself, that his reforms were aimed at strengthening Communism and that he controls the tide of change in the USSR. One wrong step, and down he goes. In his fall he will drag down to its grave the Communist system he was assigned to rescue.

However, there is no reason for gloating. The collapsing Communist system may bury in its ruins millions of innocent people who have already been victimized by it and who have no stake in its preservation. Morever, the uncontrollable collapse might destabilize the entire structure of global peace. No wonder stock markets from Tokyo to New York grew jittery as Gorbachev's ability to stay on top has waned.

Boris El'tsin, a former Moscow Party boss ousted by Gorbachev, was right when he predicted last September that unless something drastic is done, the country may slide within months toward the precipice of ethnic strife, economic chaos, and civil war. But his prediction was self-serving. El'tsin was intimating that he can do better than Gorbachev. As a Central Committee member he was intimating

---

* Appeared in <u>The San Diego Union</u>, February 11, 1990, under the title "Could Solzhenitsyn Lead the New USSR?" It is reprinted here by permission of <u>The San Diego Union</u>.

the same during the popular demonstration last Sunday when people pressed for the abolition of Party monopoly.

No, El'tsin cannot do it, either. This has nothing to do with his personality or political savvy. It has to do with his background. Times are changing, and El'tsin's career in the Party ranks has become his greatest liability. It rules him out as a new national leader. No one who has risen in the Communist hierarchy as high, could have done so without exposing himself to the ravages of moral compromise. As the events in Eastern Europe have shown, people are now looking for a new breed of leaders, such as Solidarity founder Lech Walesa or Czech dissident playwright Vaclav Havel.

As for the Soviet Union, no one is better qualified for the role of a national leader than Alexander Solzhenitsyn, the Nobel Prize winning novelist, who was forcibly exiled in 1974 and now resides in Vermont. After the untimely death of Andrei Sakharov, a nuclear scientist and a fellow dissident Nobel Peace prize winner, none comes even close to the high moral ground Solzhenitsyn so eminently occupies.

Solzhenitsyn's name is virtually synonymous with glasnost'. In 1962 his first novel, *One Day in the Life of Ivan Denisovich*, broke official silence about Soviet slave labor camps. It was neither Gorbachev nor El'tsin, but Solzhenitsyn who demanded glasnost' in the dead of the Brezhnevite winter. "Those who deprive our fatherland of glasnost'," he wrote in an open letter to Soviet writers in 1969, "do not wish to rid us of our social malady." After the KGB discovered the manuscript of *The Gulag Archipelago*, the author was thrown out of the country by the Brezhnevite clique who could not care less about social malady. The first to demand glasnost', Solzhenitsyn is the last to benefit from it. Defying the objections of Vadim Medvedev, the Party ideology chief, Soviet magazines and publishing houses are now rushing his work to print. As a result, his popularity is soaring.

Solzhenitsyn is a truth-teller who has exposed, with unsurpassed art, the incongruity of the Soviet system. He has also shown an exit from its dead end. Before his exile he mailed to Politburo members his *Letter to the Soviet Leaders* (a Harper booklet, 1974), in which he diagnosed the malady and prescribed the cure. Referring to the enormous cost of the Communist experiment to Russia, he pleaded with Soviet leaders: "We need to heal our wounds, cure our national body and national spirit. Let us find the strength, sense and courage to put our own house in order before we busy ourselves with the cares of the entire planet."

Predicting that the "bubble [of Soviet expansion] is bound to burst," he sketched a program of reforms aimed at decentralization of industry, a greater emphasis on a free-market economy, de-collectivization of agriculture, freedom of religion, and democratization in general. As his *Letter* anticipates many of Gorbachev's initiatives, it may in fact be regarded as the primary blueprint for perestroika (he used that word, too).

The most remarkable feature which distinguished Solzhenitsyn's proposal from those of other dissidents, including Sakharov, is its pragmatism. Realizing that dissidents have no levers of power to implement their noble visions, he proposed that Soviet leaders *themselves* undertake a peaceful, gradual, and orderly transformation of the totalitarian Soviet empire to a normal nation-state. To assure a smooth descent from the "icy cliff of totalitarianism," Soviet leaders would need a certain grace period during which they could rule autocratically without having to subject themselves to the test of popular vote (which "you would lose," he warned). He made it clear, however, that unless they start sharing power with the local Soviets and non-Communists, they will have no popular support for reforms.

But isn't this what Gorbachev has been trying to do? At first sight, it would seem so. Glasnost', for instance, has indeed made great strides. It is also true that Gorbachev has used authoritarian methods (by getting himself elected the country's president, for instance) to promote democratization. But in essence, Gorbachev's perestroika is not what Solzhenitsyn had in mind.

There are many differences. Solzhenitsyn demanded the abolition of the Marxist-Leninist ideological monopoly as the main obstacle to reform. Gorbachev says his "new political thinking" was inspired by Marxism-Leninism. Solzhenitsyn demanded pluralism, Gorbachev reduced it to "socialist pluralism." Solzhenitsyn warned of demographic and ecological perils, Gorbachev ignored both. Gorbachev dreams about partnership in the Common European Home, but Solzhenitsyn says, in effect, that unless the Russians build their national house first, they will be looked upon in Europe as either armed marauders or homeless beggars.

The crucial difference is that of purpose. For Gorbachev, the purpose of reforms is to consolidate the Communist system, that is, both the Soviet empire and the Party's monopoly on power. For Solzhenitsyn, what needs to be saved is not the system but the Russian people whose political, economic, and spiritual creativity has been stifled by that system.

An unabashed Russian patriot, Solzhenitsyn made it clear that neither the Russians nor their neighbors can attain a free and prosperous life as long as they are yoked together in the "Union." Affirming the right of national self-determination, he unequivocally stated that "no peripheral nation should be forcibly kept within the bounds of our country." (By contrast, in his 1987 book *Perestroika* Gorbachev boasts of ethnic harmony.)

This difference in purpose is the main reason for the failure of Gorbachev's perestroika. In the age of glasnost' no policy can succeed without a broad popular support, which Gorbachev cannot have as long as he puts the Party above the country. Communism, as it has existed since 1917, cannot and should not be saved. What must be saved is Russia and her neighbors. Such a task cannot be entrusted to the Party which is chiefly responsible for the present crisis.

Therefore, the drastic (call it "revolutionary," if you will) step that Gorbachev must urgently take is this: declaring his Party-sponsored perestroika a failure, he should resign his presidency and concentrate on his job as General Secretary of the Party. He might then nominate for the presidency Solzhenitsyn, the most respected champion of peaceful change in the USSR. In so doing, Gorbachev would honor countless fellow citizens who have fought, and sacrificed their lives, for change. He would invigorate his "revolution from above" with that "from below." If modified and updated, Solzhenitsyn's *Letter* could serve as a basis for a national (multinational) consensus for dismantling both the Soviet empire and the one-Party system and building a new democratic Russia which may yet become a magnet for a commonwealth of free nations.

To do so, it would be necessary to suspend the present Soviet Constitution (its 1977 Brezhnevite version). The cabinet should resign and be replaced by a coalition government, including members of the loyal opposition. Both the President and the cabinet would then serve for an interim period, say, of one year, until an election for a

Constituent Assembly is called and a new Constitution adopted. That would still leave Gorbachev plenty to do. As Secretary General he has a task carved out for him: perestroika of the Party according to the rule "Healer, heal thyself." The Party has to be restructured from its totalitarian model to be able to contend for popular votes. Only while competing with other parties could it become a genuine force for perestroika. Should Gorbachev succeed in this task, he may yet go down in history as a great reformer. But even if he fails, voluntarily relinquishing his post would assure him a place in history as the first Soviet leader to put the country's interests above his personal vanity or partisan loyalties.

As the new president, Solzhenitsyn will have eliminated the main obstacle for perestroika: the mistrust of Soviet leaders by the people. He will certainly be trusted by the majority of Russians (about 50 percent of the Soviet population). After all, he drew attention to the tragic plight of the Russians under Communism long before Pamyat. But he never blamed it on the Jews or any other national group. He has resolutely condemned both russophobia (hatred of the Russians) and judophobia (anti-Semitism), the two phobias that now inflame nationalistic strife in the USSR. There is no better antidote to Pamyat's "Zionist-Masonic conspiracy" rhetoric than Solzhenitsyn's work.

While letting no one doubt his Russian patriotism, Solzhenitsyn stays clear of ideological quarrels dividing the country. "Sectarian feuding today, when we stand at the edge of an abyss, is a disgrace," he wrote to one liberal Soviet author. Both liberal and conservative Soviet journalists now compete in praising Solzhenitsyn, who seems to have a broad appeal across ideological lines, and even has supporters among the Party's rank-and-file. He is also trusted by national minorities. After all, unlike Gorbachev, he has been speaking for their rights, including that of secession, before they had a chance to assert them.

Will the reclusive novelist accept the presidency? He never wavered in his belief that he will return to a free Russia. He would probably prefer to remain a hermit. He would certainly not seek any political role. However, his sense of historical responsibility is such that, if nominated, he might accept. If he does, he would perform in an exemplary fashion. His literary mission almost complete, he would put no less zeal in political service to his country. A man of extraordinary self-discipline, he routinely works fourteen hours a day. And he knows how to make others work. At 72, he need not borrow energy from either Reagan or Gorbachev. He will set an example of unselfish service that is sorely missing in his country.

What are the chances for this happening? One thing is sure: stranger things have happened in the Communist world. Vaclav Havel, whose work was banned in Czechoslovakia, has moved virtually straight from prison to the presidential palace. And Lech Walesa tries to work for Poland's national reconciliation with Gen. Wojciech Jaruzelski, who had him jailed. Should Gorbachev fail to nominate Solzhenitsyn, someone else will--largely to the same effect. At the very least, Gorbachev must, on behalf of the Politburo, apologize to Solzhenitsyn for the failure of his predecessors of the *zastoi* [stagnation] era to acknowledge the receipt of his alarm-bell *Letter*. Full glasnost' cannot be forever denied to its greatest champion.

For too long, the West has been investing in the red-hot chips of Reform Communism, such as China's Deng Xiaoping and Gorbachev. It is about time we pay attention to blue chips, all of which point beyond Communism.

Appendix 3:

From Communism's Red Flag

to Russia's Tricolor*

Boris N. El'tsin's election to the presidency of the Russian Federation in April 1990 set the stage for a constitutional crisis which has drastically compounded the already complicated situation. The crisis is far from over. Its most likely outcome will be disintegration of the Soviet Union and the end of Communism in Russia. This warrants a speedy revision of US current strategy. In view of the forthcoming visit of President George Bush to Moscow, the United States should reconsider its unconditional support for Mikhail Gorbachev's "Reform Communist" government. It should pay more attention to the will of the Russian people to move away and beyond Communism--under El'tsin's leadership.

Ever since Gorbachev brought El'tsin to Moscow to head the Party organization and then, in 1987, under the pressure of dogmatists, removed him from his post, there has been bad blood between the two. The very process of democratization that Gorbachev released not only made El'tsin's political comeback possible, but also turned him into Gorbachev's most formidable opponent.

Who is the stronger? A Soviet President? Or a Russian President? Who should take orders from whom? Such questions would have been unthinkable just a few years ago. In 1985 the Politburo elected Gorbachev General Secretary of the Party. Having later become Chairman of the Defense Council and President of the

* Published in <u>Russian American Review</u>, Spring 1991, a magazine of the Congress of Russian-Americans, Washington, D.C. It is reprinted here by permission.

USSR, Gorbachev has now as much dictatorial power as a Stalin or Brezhnev. He commands not only the nineteen million members of Communist Party, but also the world's largest armed forces and the KGB.

David and Goliath

But if you've bet on Gorbachev, don't hold your breath. All his muscle flexing notwithstanding, "Goliath" Gorbachev may yet succumb to "David" El'tsin. Not for any lack of political skills or personal charms, but because the Goliath represents a lost cause. The "Union" he presides over is about to disintegrate. The party he heads is fast losing its members (including the mayors of Moscow and Leningrad). It has also lost its faith. In short, there is precious little substance in Gorbachev's Soviet and Communist titles.

El'tsin, on the other hand, as a Russian president, can lay his claim on the resurgent national sentiments of ethnic Russians, that is, half of the country's population. According to a Spring 1990 opinion poll, as many as 43% of the Russians favored Russia's "political and economic independence, even if it would mean secession from the USSR." In another poll, 53.4% supported the right of border republics to secede. Millions of non-Russians likewise see El'tsin as their champion in the fight against the moribund Soviet empire.

Meanwhile Gorbachev's mandate for perestroika given him by the Politburo has been invalidated by the very process of democratization he released. Why didn't Gorbachev seek revalidation in a national election? Many suspect he didn't dare to face the test of popular vote. El'tsin, on the other hand, did it twice, both times winning by a wide margin. El'tsin thus appears to be a legitimate son of "mother" perestroika, while "father" Gorbachev has largely delegitimized himself by straying away from it. If Gorbachev sponsors perestroika as a revolution from above, El'tsin sees it as revolution from below.

Gorbachev certainly lags behind changes wrought in the public mind by glasnost. Just as in his 1987 book, he continues to prattle of perestroika as a means to fortify Communism. "I am a Communist. I shall remain a convinced one. For some people, this may be a fantasy, something up in the air somewhere, but for me it is a goal," says he. In an effort to convince the world that he is a *reform* Communist, he concedes that the goal "is a long way off." Nonetheless, "we proceed along the road chosen by the October [Bolshevik] Revolution, filling our socialist system and our society with real content." Such statements may win him a few supporters among party dogmatists, but not among the voters.

The Road to Nowhere

Glasnost has helped people realize that the October road was "chosen" with bullets, not ballots. In the only free election (to the 1918 Constituent Assembly) the Bolsheviks got less than 25 percent of the vote. The Soviet "Union" was formed only after national independence movements everywhere were crushed by the Communists. More and more Soviet people now realize that it was the Communist Party that led the country from the October "choice" to a succession of purges, Gulags, man-made famines, ill-managed wars, and self-inflicted terror. Soviet sources now put the cost of the Communist experiment at between forty and ninety million lives. The "October road" was but a seventy-year-long detour--to a dead end.

Unlike Gorbachev, El'tsin is more sensitive to the change of public mood. Not only did he quit the Party during its 28th congress in Summer 1990, but he declared Communism "a nebulous dream." He hardly speaks of socialism at all. Nor does he invoke the abstract "Soviet people." Instead, he appeals to the national pride of *rossiiane*, that is, not only ethnic Russians (*russkie*), but also those non-Russians who feel they have a stake in Russia's future. He promises not to "fortify" Communism, but to save the country from sliding into an abyss. As a spokesman for the country's "silent majority," the populist El'tsin now champions Russia's "national rebirth."

Russia's Sovereignty

But does El'tsin have a clear-cut economic program? Perhaps not. However, unlike Gorbachev, he realizes that the country's economic problems cannot be solved as long as its various nations, including Russia, feel they are in bondage to the "Union." At his prompting, on June 12, 1990, the Russian parliament proclaimed the sovereignty of the Russian Federation by an astounding 909 votes against 13. The vote is powerful in its symbolism. It suggests that the largest of the republics has joined the ranks of independence-minded national minorities. The "oppressors" (as the Russians are often perceived) have declared their solidarity with the oppressed. By stipulating that Russia's laws may supersede those of the "Union," the legislators gave El'tsin a green light to challenge Gorbachev on a vast array of issues.

The chief obstacle to solving the country's problems is the fact that the Gorbachev government has totally exhausted the credit of trust. People are disgusted with Communist reformers who just a few years ago praised Soviet socialism as the most progressive system in the world and now say just the opposite. Yet, while praising a free market, unregulated prices, unemployment and other features of capitalism, they continue to draw huge salaries and benefits from the socialist state. Mindful of the disgust most people feel toward such Communist reformers, El'tsin asked "all the Russians" to give him *kredit doveria* [credit of trust] for two or three years. According to an end-of-the-year poll by *Sobesednik*, a Soviet mass-circulation weekly, he may have gotten it. Out of the 2070 people polled, 1420 said they trusted El'tsin above all other leaders, while only 115 named Gorbachev. "Who disappointed you most among Soviet leaders in 1990?" asked the poll. 1535 named Gorbachev--but only 127 were disappointed by El'tsin.

El'tsin's Non-Communist Support

El'tsin has the support of a number of deputies of unabashed anti-Communist convictions. One of them is the Rev. Gleb Yakunin, who has for years exposed the co-optation of the official Orthodox Church by the atheist government. Another is Victor Aksyuchits, a young philosopher, publisher, and enterpreneur. Yet another is the Rev. Vyacheslav Polosin, who heads the Russian legislature's committee on religion. The three represent the Russian Christian-Democratic Movement (RCDM), a newly formed political party that openly proclaims "consistent anti-Communism, Christian spirituality, and enlightened patriotism" as its main tenets.

El'tsin is also supported by such former Communists as Marina Salie and Nikolai Travkin. They were members of the "Democratic Russia" bloc that nominated El'tsin.   Now they represent the Democratic Party of Russia (formed last May). The DPR advocates convened a Constitutional Assembly to decide on Russia's form of government.   Just as anti-Communist as the RCDM, the DPR stresses neither Christianity nor patriotism.   Yet the DPR has joined the RCDD in the demand to restore the Russian national banner, the tricolor.   Unlike the red flag of Communism, the tricolor stands for political pluralism and national unity across ideological and ethnic lines.   While the RCDM was clearly inspired by Aleksandr Solzhenitsyn's call for a national and spiritual rebirth, the DPR bases its ideology on Andrei Sakharov's defense of human rights.

Toward a National Government

There are some signs that El'tsin may be able to pave the road for the creation of a truly representative national government which must include bona fide opponents of the totalitarian regime, the long-time supporters of both Sakharov and Solzhenitsyn.   Not only did El'tsin leave the Communist Party, but he has also quit the "Democratic Russia" bloc that nominated him.   He favors a direct election of Russia's future president, who should not be beholden to one party or another.   The recent decision of the Russian legislature to declare Christmas (celebrated by the Orthodox on January 7th) a full state holiday can only add to El'tsin's popularity, certainly among some eighty million Russian Christians.

Vladimir Osipov, a dissident Russian patriot who spent 15 years in Soviet jails, reproached El'tsin for the failure to include dissidents and Gulag victims in his government.   It should not be forgotten, however, that it was Ivan Silaev, El'tsin's prime minister, who invited Solzhenitsyn, the famed author of *The Gulag Archipelago*, to visit the USSR.   The exile's exchange with Silaev led to the publication of his brochure, *How to Revitalize Russia*, in the USSR, where it has sparked a national debate on the country's future.   Invoking Lenin as his model,

Gorbachev hurredly denounced (and misinterpreted) Solzhenitsyn's political ideas as those of "the past Russia, the czarist monarchy." El'tsin, on the other hand, had only praise on his lips. He proudly took credit for making the brochure available for all people's deputies "so they could read it with the utmost attentiveness."

But isn't El'tsin an opportunist, demagogue, and intellectual lightweight, as some American observers claim? Perhaps he is. Be that as it may, he deserves at least as much benefit of the doubt as the West has lavished on Gorbachev. For one thing, El'tsin's democratic credentials are much stronger than those of Gorbachev. While El'tsin twice won at the voting booths by a huge margin, Gorbachev has yet to face the test of a national vote. Moreover, it would be the height of hypocrisy to assert that Gorbachev's "fortify Communism" ideology is more compatible with the spirit of Western democracies than El'tsin's repudiation of it.

Not only is El'tsin the overwhelming choice of the Russian people, but his approach to solving the country's problems is more realistic than that of Gorbachev. As an undisputed leader of the Russian national opposition to "Union" government, he has a better chance to find a formula for a peaceful divorce with those republics which are unhappy with the imposed "matrimony." El'tsin's popular mandate enables him to take greater political risks in a situation when taking risks is a must.

Don't Buck the Tide

Does it mean that the West should switch its support from Gorbachev to El'tsin? I would not advise such a move. Rather, I would like to see the U.S. government take a more even-handed approach. Refraining from taking sides, we should stay benevolently neutral toward both leaders. In order to assure the stability and civil order that are necessary for a peaceful dissolution of the Soviet empire, we could even try to mediate between the two. We could try to persuade Gorbachev that he can yet serve his country by leading his Party out of its monopoly on power. Above all, we should stop pinning all our hopes on one or the other Soviet reformist, no matter how charismatic. Instead, we should begin to put our trust in the good sense of the Russian people, allowing their leaders to rise in a truly indigenous democratic process.

But aren't the Russians an inherently anti-democratic, anti-Western, xenophobic and anti-Semitic people? Are they capable of making a democratic choice?   Aren't they better off with the authoritarian but benevolent rulers, like Gorbachev?   Isn't their preference for El'tsin a sign of political immaturity? There are some influential Western scholars who want us to believe this. To support their distrust of the Russians, they cite Russia's "abominable" historical record. It is out of place here to challenge their arguments, some of which might not be entirely wrong. But there is certainly nothing "inherent" about the alleged Russian faults. To claim otherwise is to indulge in a bigotry of our own. Unless we wish to appear in the eyes of the rising democratic Russia as self-righteous bigots, we must show greater respect for their choice.

It's time we stop supporting "Reform Communism" against the surging tide of Russian history. The only reform that can have broad popular support in Russia is a reform out of and beyond Communism. The Stars and Stripes should stop guarding the red flag of Communism against the march of the renascent national-democratic banners, among which the Russian tricolor is too conspicuous to be ignored. Come to think of it, Russia had never had a serious conflict with the United States--until the red flag was hoisted over her.

About the Author

A native of Perm, the USSR, Vladislav Georgievich Krasnov received his Diploma in History and Anthropology from Moscow University. While working as an editor of Radio Moscow's Foreign Broadcast, he defected to Sweden, where he was granted political asylum. In 1976 he became a U.S. citizen. Holding a Ph.D. from the University of Washington, Seattle, he is director of the Russian Studies program at the Monterey Institute of International Studies, Monterey, California. He has taught at the University of Texas, Austin; Southern Methodist University; and the University of Lund (Sweden). He was a post-doctoral fellow at the University of Chicago and did research at Hokkaido University (Japan). He is the author of *Solzhenitsyn and Dostoevsky* (University of Georgia Press) and *Soviet Defectors*: *The KGB Wanted List* (Hoover Institution Press). His articles have appeared in *The Russian Review*, *The Slavic Review*, *Russian Language Journal*, *Modern Age*, *The Wall Street Journal*, *The New York Times*, *Kontinent* (Paris), *Grani* (Frankfurt am Main), and *Chishiki* (Tokyo). He is a former director of the Center for Contemporary Russian Studies at MIIS.

Index